Techniques and Assumptions
in Jewish Exegesis before 70 CE

by

David Instone Brewer

J.C.B. Mohr (Paul Siebeck) Tübingen

Die Deutsche Bibliothek – CIP-Einheitsaufnahme

Instone Brewer, David:
Techniques and assumptions in Jewish exegesis before 70 CE /
by David Instone Brewer. – Tübingen : Mohr, 1992
  (Texte und Studien zum antiken Judentum ; 30)
  ISBN 3-16-145803-6
NE: GT

© 1992 J.C.B. Mohr (Paul Siebeck), P.O. Box 2040, D-7400 Tübingen.

The book was typeset by Typobauer, Scharnhausen using Times typeface, printed by
Gulde-Druck in Tübingen on acid-free paper from Papierfabrik Gebr. Buhl in Ettlingen
and bound by Heinrich Koch in Tübingen.

ISSN 0721-8753

Preface

This book was originally submitted as a PhD thesis at Cambridge, England. I would like to acknowledge the assistance and encouragement of Dr William Horbury of whose breadth of knowledge I have yet to discover the limits. He is truly "a plastered cistern which loses not a drop" (mAv.2.8). His suggestions have been acknowledged occasionally, but every page has been influenced by his careful and balanced scholarship.

I would also like to thank Barnabus Lindars and Raphael Loewe for their careful reading of the complete text. I have followed Raphael Loewe's advice about translation of Mishnaic Hebrew at many points, but the literal and 'un-English' translation style is my own. This style is intended to facilitate the recognition of rabbinic formulae and to help those who are not very familiar with Hebrew to follow the original text. Martin Hengel and Nicholas De Lange also kindly read large portions of this work and their comments have resulted in much rethinking and enrichment.

I would like to thank the Trustees of the Baptist Union Scholarship Fund and the Tyndale Fellowship for financial assistance.

My wife, Enid, has proof-read the whole work and Sharon Rice corrected the final manuscript. Their help was invaluable and I doubt that I could have finished the task without them.

Contents

Part I:
Exegeses in Scribal Traditions

Part II:
Exegesis in Non-Scribal Traditions

Foreword

G.F. Moore (1927 I:249f.) characterised Jewish exegesis as:
"atomistic exegesis which interprets sentences, clauses, phrases and even single words independently of the context or the historical occasion, ... combines them with other similarly detached utterances and makes use of analogy of expressions, often by purely verbal association".

He added that:
"The interpretation of the Scriptures in the New Testament is of precisely the same kind.".

Sixty years later most scholars still agree with his assessment, and the consequences are profound. R.N. Longenecker (1987:8), having repeated Moore's conclusions, warns that we cannot therefore emulate the NT exegetical methods:
"Let us admit that we cannot possibly reproduce the revelatory stance of pesher interpretation, nor the atomistic manipulations of midrash, nor the circumstantial or *ad hominem* thrust of a particular polemic of that day – nor should we try."

The results of the present study show that the predecessors of the rabbis before 70 CE did not interpret Scripture out of context, did not look for any meaning in Scripture other than the plain sense, and did not change the text to fit their interpretation, though the later rabbis did all these things.

If the conclusions of this work are correct it demands a fresh examination of the New Testament, which may yet provide a model for the modern exegete.

General Introduction

The backbone of this study is a survey of exegeses preserved in rabbinic literature which are likely to have originated before 70 CE. These exegeses have been analysed with regard to their exegetical techniques and assumptions. The conclusions from this survey are compared with the exegesis of contemporary Jews, particularly in Alexandria and Qumran.

The exegetical techniques and assumptions used by the Jews of the late Second Temple Period should help us to understand the exegesis of the Old Testament in the New.

The term "Scribes" will be used in this study to refer to authorities before 70 CE who were regarded by the rabbis as their predecessors. This term is used simply as a short-hand way of referring to a group which has no distinct name and which is very difficult to define. It does not imply that all the exegeses in rabbinic traditions from before 70 CE come from Scribes or that the Scribes of this period are linked with the Scribes or Sopherim of the Great Assembly associated with Ezra, although both may be the case.

Although the Tannaim themselves did not use the term 'Scribe' [סופר] (G.G. Porton 1986:60), it is possible that it was used by the Amoraim to refer to early Tannaim. The phrase "words of the Scribes" is used frequently to refer to anonymous pre-mishnaic rulings (references in Schürer 1973 III:324f.) which can be as late as Beth Hillel (yBer.1,3a), and which were regarded as Oral Law (mSanh.11.3; bEr.21b). It is therefore possible, as S. Safrai (1987c:148–153) and J. Jeremias (1964) conclude, that the rabbis used 'Scribe' and 'Sage' synonymously when referring to the period before 70 CE.

It is also likely that the Scribes were the main exegetes of the Law before 70 CE (E.E. Urbach 1957). The Scribes were a profession rather than a religious party because there were 'Scribes of the Pharisees' (Mk.2.16 cf. Lk.5.30; Act.23.9), Scribes who were Zealots (War.2.17.8f.(433,445)) and presumably Sadducean Scribes, although there were probably very few of the latter. M. Black (1962) suggested on the basis of Mk.7.1ff. that the Scribes represented the majority of the Jerusalem Pharisees, and therefore led the party. Neusner (1973c) has also suggested that the predecessors of the rabbis included the Scribes, in order to explain the origin of the common rabbinic theme that Torah study is equivalent to worship, which is not found in any Pharisaic traditions.

This does not of course suggest that the non-scribal Pharisees were not exegetes, nor that the Scribes always taught halakah based on Scripture. However the Scribes were clearly more important than mere copyists because they are often pictured as leaders of the people (IMacc.7.12; IIMacc.6.18; Ecclus.38.24ff.; War.2.433[17.8]) and they were known as teachers or inter- preters of the Law (Lk.5.17; Act.5.24; War.1.648[33.2] = Ant.17.149[6.2]).

The links between the scribes of the late Second Temple and those of the time of the Great Assembly are more difficult to assess. These scribes or 'Sopherim' are generally attributed with the emendations of the Torah, both those listed (GenR.59.7 etc) and those inferred (M. Fishbane 1985) and even with the beginnings of the Masorah (I. Harris 1888, M.J. Mulder 1988b), while some scholars have regarded them as primarily exegetes (e.g. Lauter- bach 1914–). However they should probably be regarded separately from the later scribes, if only because the early scribes were primarily priests (E.E. Urbach 1975 : 568–71).

However, the use of the term "scribe" in the present study does not imply any conclusions concerning the ancient Sopherim, the NT Scribes or even the rabbinic 'words of the Scribes'. It is used merely as a way of distinguish- ing between the rabbis after 70 CE and those whom they regarded as their predecessors.

Jewish exegesis is usually termed midrash, but this has a variety of defini- tions. The traditional Rabbinic Midrashim are late collections of individual exegeses which are attributed to the Scribes, Tannaim, and Amoraim, but most of which are anonymous. In modern times the term has become used in two senses: to describe a method of exegesis, and to describe the genre of literature which employs this method.

R. Bloch (1957, following L. Zunz 1892) characterised the midrashic method as exegesis of Jewish Scripture which is homiletic (i.e. popular, not academic), attentive to the text, and which 'actualises' Scripture so that it addresses the text to the problems of the present. She identified this not only in the traditional Midrashim but in many types of Jewish literature such as the OT itself, the ancient translations such as the LXX and Targumim, the OT Apocrypha including especially the Apocalyptic literature, the NT and all Rabbinic exegetical haggadic and halakic literature.

A.G. Wright (1966) refined the characterisation of the midrash method in order to define the literary genre of Midrash (see also E.E. Ellis 1969, B.S. Childs 1972, G.G. Porton 1981, A. Goldberg 1985). He pointed out that Bloch's characterisation was so broad that almost all Jewish literature could be described as midrashic. He distinguished between citations or allu- sions which were made for the sake of the text which was referred to and those which were made for the sake of the text being created. Those which were made for the sake of the text being referred to attempted to elucidate the message of that text and could properly be called midrash, but those which used a text merely to provide Scriptural language or imagery for the sake of the text being created were better called the 'Anthological' style (as characterised by A. Robert 1957).

However, as R. Le Déaut (1969) pointed out, these attempts at defining literary genres has not resulted in much greater understanding of the mentality behind them. Bloch succeeded in highlighting the inter-relations between different types of Jewish exegetical literature (which has spurred much fruitful work – G. Vermes 1961), but the genre, even after being refined by Wright, was still too broad and appeared to contain a variety of different genres. Le Déaut suggested that the underlying assumptions represented the real sub-divisions in the literature. M. Kadushin identified the pursuit of such assumptions as the new trend in rabbinic research set by I. Heinemann's *the Methods of the Haggadah* (M. Kadushin 1951) and his own work (1952) set out to clarify how the Rabbis thought rather than what they did with the text.

The present work attempts to compare and contrast the assumptions concerning Scripture behind the exegeses of the Scribes with those of contemporary Jews, by examining the specific hermeneutic techniques employed by them.

Studies of rabbinic exegetical techniques have rarely taken into account the dating of the source materials. Such studies are mainly concerned with the collection and illustration of the Middoth, or "Rules" of exegesis. The very first of these studies can be said to be that attributed to R. Eliezer b.R. Yose the Galilean (mid. 2nd C.), which consists of a list of 32 middoth, including the 7 rules attributed to Hillel (1st C. BCE) and the additional rules in the list of 13 attributed to R. Ishmael (early-mid. 2nd C. CE) The original list of 32 middoth may possibly be Tannaitic (as H.G. Enelow 1933 argues) but the commentary which explains and illustrates them is certainly much later. The total number of middoth recognised in rabbinic sources continued to grow, so that Malbim (R. Meir Loeb ben Yehiel Michael, 1809–1880), in his commentary on the Sifra, was able to make them number 613 to agree with the number of precepts in the Torah (H.L. Strack 1931:93; W.S. Towner 1982:130).

Modern studies include the important ground-work by H.S. Hirschfeld (1840:123ff., 1847:382ff.), W. Bacher's *Die Agadah der Tannaiten* (1884) and *Die Exegetische Terminologie* (1905 cf. also W. Bacher 1902,1904), A. Schwarz's works on Talmudic exegesis (1897,1901, 1909,1913,1916), sections on the middoth in introductions to the Talmud by M. Mielziner (1968, 1st ed. 1894) and by H.L. Strack (1931, 1st ed. 1887), and useful contributions by J.Z. Lauterbach (1904b, 1905, 1906a), L. Jacobs (1971a–b, 1973, 1984) and others (e.g. D. Hoffmann 1903, J. Weingreen 1951, W.S. Towner 1982).

Recently the middoth have been neglected while the wealth of Qumran and targumic material has been explored. These studies have highlighted the wider context in which rabbinic exegesis existed, suggesting that at least some of the middoth were used by Jewish exegetes long before Hillel, and that the Jews learnt them from the Hellenistic world (J.Z. Lauterbach 1910-, D. Daube 1949,1953,1961,1980a, S. Lieberman 1950:47ff., F. Maass 1955, E.E. Halevi 1959,1961, H.A. Fishel 1973, H. Dorrie 1974) or even from the Ancient Near East (F. Maass 1955, J. Koenig 1982:379ff., S. Lieberman 1950:75f., M. Fishbane 1985).

However, by the first century these middoth were thoroughly Judaised and evidence for at least some of them has been found in the Targumim (J.W. Bowker 1969, G.J. Brooke 1985:25ff.), the Qumran texts (G.J. Brooke 1985, W.H. Brownlee 1951, L.H. Silberman 1961), Philo (Z. Frankel 1854:33ff., C. Siegfried 1875 p168ff.), the Septuagint (J. Koenig 1982) and the Old Testament (M. Fishbane 1985, I.L. Seeligman 1953, G.R. Driver 1960, J. Weingreen 1976).

These and many other studies which illustrate the close relationships between the Targumim, Qumran literature, Philo, and later Midrashim (e.g. G. Vermes 1969b, 1975, D. Rokeah 1968), demonstrate that the interest in midrash (i.e. exegesis) is at least as old as the interest in Mishnah (i.e. the collection of halakot), and the work in the Hebrew Bible summarised by M. Fishbane (1985) pushes back the origins of both activities to at least the Exile.

This lays to rest the debate concerning the priority of mishnah or midrash, in which S. Zeitlin and J.Z. Lauterbach represented opposing viewpoints. Zeitlin (e.g. 1953) argued that midrash was a later justification from Scripture of halakot which had been established by custom, while Lauterbach (e.g. 1914–) replied that the Pharisees had introduced midrash as a method for deriving new halakot to supplant the Sadducean traditions. J. Neusner has given support to both sides, arguing both that form-critically the Midrashim must be considered later than the Mishnah (e.g. 1984) but also that large portions of Mishnah are founded on Scripture (e.g. 1975b, 1980a), although some are manifestly not (R.S. Sarason 1980). Ultimately this is a 'chicken and egg' question: exegesis produces new halakot, and new halakot provoke exegesis, and it is meaningless to discuss which one has the priority or to determine the time when either of them emerged.

The origin of the middoth is still a subject of debate. The traditional view that these middoth were introduced to Israel by Hillel has been energetically defended in different ways and to different degrees by A. Kaminka (1926:

Hillel learned them during time spent in Alexandria), I. Sonne (1945, after A. Geiger 1857: Hillel introduced them in order to establish the Oral Torah on Scripture and deflect Sadducean criticism) Daube (1949: Hillel learned them from his teachers Shemaiah and Abtalion who spent time in Alexandria, or from the Sadducees who were open to Hellenistic influence), L. Jacobs (1961: criticising especially Schwarz's comparisons of the first three middoth with Arisotelian logical methods), S. Zeitlin (1961,1963: Hillel gave the names to techniques already present in Scripture), and A. Guttman (1970: 74ff.: Hillel introduced Scriptural exegesis during the leadership vacuum created by Herod's massacre of the Sanhedrin).

However there is little reason to regard the attributions of the lists of 7 middoth to Hillel or the 13 middoth to Ishmael as historical.

Hillel is supposed to have introduced his seven middoth after using them to prove to the Bene Bathyra that Passover over-rides the Sabbath prohibitions. However the tradition recording this dispute with the Bene Bathyra (tPis.4.13) and the list of his seven middoth (tSanh.7.11) are clearly separate traditions, because they are recorded separately in pre-Talmudic sources and because they preserve different versions of his opponents' title ("Bathyra" in tPis, "Pathyra" in tSanh). The Passover dispute is also unsuitable for demonstrating the use of the seven middoth because Hillel uses only two of the seven (Qal vaHomer and Gezerah Shavah) to prove his point, as well as one rule which is not in the list (Heqesh). This dispute was probably chosen because it is the only one in which Hillel used any of the rules attributed to him.

Ishmael's list of middoth poses similar problems because, as M. Chernick (1980) and G. Porton (1976- IV:160ff.) demonstrated, in all the numerous exegeses preserved in Ishmael's name, only six of the 13 rules attributed to him are employed while many others which are not in his list *are* used, including some rules which were espoused by his 'opponent' Aqiva.

It therefore seems likely that these lists of middoth did not originate with Hillel and Ishmael. It would appear that these lists represent either a justification of these middoth by attribution to a former authority, or a gross simplification of the methods and principles of these two famous promoters of biblical exegesis. However this does not mean that these rules were later inventions nor that they were unknown to Hillel or Ishmael.

S.K. Mirsky (1967) suggested that Hillel may not have invented the middoth, but that he systematised them. W.S. Towner (1982) and Brooke (1985:12f.) suggested that these lists represent a growing acceptance and recognition of exegetical techniques by the authorities. Many more techniques were known and used by Jewish exegetes, but only these few were officially sanctioned. These techniques would have been learned from contact with Hellenistic and other influences, and would have been developed by the homiletic preachers of the Synagogue in Palestine and the Diaspora.

This conclusion, that the lists of middoth represent a limited acceptance of a widespread use of many different exegetical techniques, means that it is almost impossible to pinpoint the origin of these techniques, and that the best way to discover which ones were actually used is not by studying the lists of middoth but the exegeses themselves. The purpose of the following survey of Scribal exegesis is therefore not to discover what exegetical methods were known to the Scribes, but which ones were being *used*. This will provide an insight into their underlying exegetical assumptions.

Part I

Exegeses in Scribal Traditions

I.1 Introduction to the Scribal Traditions

The exegeses of the Scribes before 70 CE have been collected, translated, introduced and analysed with regard to the structure of the arguments and the exegetical techniques which have been used.

I.1.1 These exegeses have been collected from Tannaitic sources, i.e. Mishnah, Tosefta, baraitot and Tannaitic Midrashim, including Mekhilta, Sifré, Sifra, and Midrash Tannaim. Occasional references are made to later rabbinic sources but usually only for parallel traditions. For recent discussions of dating etc. see M.D. Herr 1971b–f, G. Stemberger 1975,1982 A. Goldberg 1987a–d, S. Safrai 1987b, especially with regard to Mekhilta (cf. B.D. Chilton 1988 : 133 contra B.Z. Wacholder 1968). Some of this material may have been written before 70 CE (L. Finkelstein 1941a, J. Neusner 1973a denied by B. Gerhardsson 1961, J.M. Baumgarten 1972,1974) but it was certainly all redacted much later, and problems of dating must always be borne in mind.

The cut-off at 70 CE is somewhat arbitrary, but it is a sufficiently significant date to allow most exegeses to be assigned to a time either before it or after it, and it also marks the beginning of a great diversification in the types of exegeses attested to in rabbinic texts. At about this time Yohanan b.Zakkai popularised the use of a metaphor or parable to illustrate a text and to help expound it, with the name of Homer [חמר] exegesis (tBQ.7.1–7; Neusner 1970 : 257ff.) which later became extremely popular as 'Mashal' exegesis.

Contemporaneous with Yohanan were Nahum of Gimzo and Nehunia b.Hakana who are supposed to have taught new exegetical techniques to Ishmael and Akiva (early 2nd C) respectively, and who were the founders of two opposing schools of exegesis (bShebu.26a). Whether or not this is historically accurate, it illustrates the upheaval that the rabbis were experiencing at this time in their exegetical techniques, as well as in their whole manner of life and worship, and although some of these exegetical techniques may have been used before this time, they came into prominence during this period.

The scribal exegeses collected here come from three main types of tradition:

1 The traditions of named authorities
2 The Pharisee-Sadducee traditions
3 The House disputes

The named authorities are individuals to whom exegeses have been attributed, from Simon the Just to Rn.Yohanan b.Zakkai. Most of this material has already been collected by J. Neusner in his monumental work *The Rabbinic Traditions about the Pharisees before 70* (1971) and in his analysis of the Yohanan b.Zakkai material *(Development of a Legend,* 1970). Material which was not covered by Neusner in these works includes the exegeses of Judah b.Bathyra, Ben Hé Hé, Ben Bag Bag and a few other later authorities who may perhaps be dated after 70 CE, but have been included for completeness. However Yohanan b.Zakkai could not be dealt with in this generous manner, because there is a large amount of exegetical material attributed to him, and because most of this material is clearly from after 70 CE. Therefore only his exegeses which contain indications of a pre-70 origin are included.

The Pharisee-Sadducee traditions are those in which either the Sadducees or the Boethusians are named, but traditions which name only the Pharisees have not been included. This is based on E. Rivkin's principle (1969) that traditions naming the Sadducees or Boethusians are likely to concern a situation before 70 CE or shortly afterwards, but that traditions naming only the Pharisees may refer to later 'separatists'. Some non-exegetical traditions have been included in the survey to illustrate the Sadducean use of exegetical argument forms in non-exegetical contexts, but these have been separated from the exegetical traditions in the conclusions. This collection of traditions is based largely on Rivkin, J. Bowker (1973) and Le Moyne (1972).

The House disputes collected here are only those which include exegesis by one or other of the Houses. Disputes which appear to be based on exegesis, but where the exegesis itself has not been preserved, have not been included. It has occasionally been difficult to decide where the dispute ends because later rabbis have taken up the arguments where the Houses finished. In these cases I have erred on the cautious side and retained arguments which may possibly have been added by later rabbis, but they are discounted as 'late' in the conclusions.

I.1.2 Texts and references have been taken from standard editions (see Bibliography, Bib.1). The standard translations have been consulted, but the parallel format has necessitated new translations, so any errors are my own.

Normally only one version of each pericopé is given, although reference is made to parallels or other manuscripts when relevant. The version used is normally the one likely to be the oldest, but sometimes another is substituted because it represents the majority of the parallels or because the exegesis is not present in the earliest version.

The notes are not intended to be commentaries on the manuscripts or the texts, but merely introductions to the debate. Their purpose is to aid the evaluation of arguments used in the text, and to provide some indication of early or late features.

The dating of rabbinic material is still an inexact art, and for every opinion there is a counter-opinion. Although one should avoid labelling anything as 'early' in documents which were written so late (A.D. York 1974, P.S. Alexander 1983) and although some attestations are pseudonymous (L. Jacobs 1971c,1977) the traditions in rabbinic sources are often earlier than even the earliest attestation (B.J. Bamberger 1949, M.J. Bernstein 1983) and the use of form criticism is now starting to confirm the existence of a core of ancient traditions from which a true picture of ancient Judaism can be built (J. Neusner 1971,1973d,1981a, A.J. Saldarini 1986)

I have relied heavily on Neusner, while often differing from his conclusions. Neusner has applied textual and historical criticism to rabbinic material in a systematic way, but because he was attempting to undo several centuries of conservative scholarship, he has often over-stressed late features of the texts. The notes therefore often highlight early features in order to provide a balance.

One principle often employed is that the later rabbis were unlikely to have added exegeses to bolster up Shammaite or Sadducean arguments. As even Neusner said (1971 II:9):

"After ca.100, no normative teachers known to us were Shammaites, so why should either party have done more than preserve either already redacted collections of materials, or stories and sayings reflecting a poor opinion of the Shammaites?... Perhaps Shammaite exegetical rules and sayings were in fact redacted but suppressed, and only bits and pieces in pretty much their original form survived later on."

However, precise dating remains unattainable, and the term "70 CE" in this study must be regarded as signifying the beginning of an era rather than an exact date.

It is also impossible to say that every exegesis surveyed here originates before 70 CE, and it is certain that many pre-70 exegeses exist in anonymous traditions which are not included. However the conclusions will demonstrate that those scribal exegeses collected here are linked by a common set of techniques and assumptions which differ significantly from those which predominate in later rabbinic exegesis (see I.7).

I.1.3 The texts have been analysed with regard to the stages and techniques of their arguments. Very few of these texts have been analysed in this way before, and many of the observations below are accordingly not to be found in the earlier works known to me.

The analysis uses a methodology which is simple and flexible enough to express each argument separately without imposing a foreign structure on the debates. This methodology divides the debates into series of arguments and counter arguments such as:

1a.   A says x
1b.   B says not x
2ai   B says not × because of y

2aii   and because of z
2b   A says × because of w

No attempt is made to change the order in which arguments occur, so that although A makes the first contribution to the first stage in the debate (1b), he does not necessarily make the first contribution to the second stage. Similarly, no attempt is made to make every stage of the debate consist of only one argument by each participant, to make the reply follow immediately after the point which prompted it, or to tidy up the order of the debate in any way.

This methodology appears at first sight to be so self-evident and simple that its absence would not be missed. However, the debates recorded in these texts have been summarised and abbreviated so severely that it is often difficult to distinguish one argument from another, or even sometimes to decide who is stating which argument.

The individual arguments which make up a debate have been classified on two levels: exegetical mode and exegetical technique.

I.1.4 *The mode of exegesis* refers to the way in which the text has been read, and reflects the kind of assumptions which have been made about the text. Four main modes of interpretation have been identified, although the boundary between any two is often hazy. The four modes are: Peshat, Nomological, Ultra-literal and Derash.

I.1.4 PESHAT [פשט] is a term indicating the "plain" meaning of a text, in contrast to the "Derash", דרש, or "hidden" meaning. It may also be seen as the distinction between the primary meaning and any secondary or allegorical meaning which may be found in the text.

R. Loewe (1964) has shown that it is anachronistic to use פשט with reference to Tannaitic or even Amoraic exposition. In rabbinic and Qumran literature it bears the same nuance that it has in the Bible ("to strip", "to flatten" or "to stretch"), although it may also bear the meaning of "authoritative teaching". The term was associated with the 'plain' meaning at a later stage when, in view of the variety of exegesis in rabbinic traditions, it became necessary to distinguish between the 'plain' meaning of the text and the 'hidden' or 'secondary' meaning, lest the former be neglected.

In this analysis I have used the term "Peshat" for want of a better term. The fact that the distinction between Peshat and Derash was first made by the later rabbis does not imply that all previous exposition followed the Peshat reading of Scripture, because the Philonic works and the Targumim abound in expositions of the hidden and secondary meanings of the text. Therefore, when the term "Peshat" is applied to early exegeses it can be regarded as an anticipation of a distinction which would be defined later but which already existed.

However, Peshat covers too broad a spectrum of ways of reading the Scriptures, so two other terms have been coined to help plot the development from Peshat to Derash: Nomological and Ultra-literal.

I.1.4b The NOMOLOGICAL reading of Scripture refers to the reading of Scripture as though it were a legal document, assuming that the biblical text must be read with all the stringency and accuracy of a carefully worded legal contract. This view of Scripture, according to S. Rosenblatt, underlies the majority of interpretations in the Mishnah and Tosefta (1935, 1974).

This Nomological approach is represented most clearly in halakic disputes, when the whole of the Scriptures are regarded as The Law, and every word carries equal weight and value. Because this legal document has been drawn up by the very highest Judge, it is assumed to contain no contradictions or mistakes. This approach to Scripture can be seen behind many of the rules of halakic exegesis which have counterparts in Greek and Roman rules of legal interpretation (Daube 1949) and even in rules used by modern lawyers (see examples in Mielziner 1968: 130ff.).

Much of Scripture does indeed consist of legal documents, and in these texts there is often very little difference between Peshat and Nomological modes of interpretation. However the Nomological treatment of legal texts denies the possibility of error or contradiction and assumes that the text was crafted by a supremely exact legal Mind so that it does not have any superfluous phrases, and so that every pair of identical phrases, wherever they occur, relate to each other.

However, when Nomological principles are applied to non-legal portions of Scripture, the result often appears to contradict the Peshat meaning. For example, when 2Sam.1 records that David waited in Ziklag for two days before going up to Hebron where he was crowned as king, without having to lay siege to the city, we regard it as a matter of history or narrative. However Shammai appears to treat the matter as a legal precedent which shows that one must sue for peace for two days before starting any siege (Sifré Deut.203). Although this Nomological approach appears to find a hidden meaning in the text, Shammai would have regarded this as the plain meaning, because an example quoted in law has the function of a precedent, so that if David is recorded as waiting two days, then everyone subsequently in a similar situation should also wait two days. Therefore a Nomological reading of a text, or an interpretation based on Nomological assumptions, should not necessarily be regarded as a non-Peshat interpretation, because it may not deny the plain sense of that scripture for a reader *at that time*.

I.1.4c The ULTRA-LITERAL mode of interpretation demands the literal understanding of the words used in a text even when it is denied by the context and by the plain meaning of the idioms used. This mode of interpretation ignores the plain sense of the context but it still has the aim of establishing the primary meaning of the text rather than of finding a secondary or hidden meaning. It does this by isolating a phrase and interpreting these few words according to their literal meaning. Due to the ambiguity of many words in unpointed Hebrew, this Ultra-literal mode of interpretation can sometimes produce meanings which are entirely unrelated to the meaning which those same words have in their original context.

One example of this mode is the proof for the existence of both a Written and an Oral Torah from the terms "written" and "to teach" in the phrase "the Law... which I have written to teach them" (Ex.24.12, see I.3.11). The idiomatic meaning of the phrase has been ignored, but the overall context, the giving of the Law at Sinai, has not been ignored.

It is often difficult to decide between a Nomological and an Ultra-literal reading of the text. This is because 'Nomological' and 'Ultra-literal' are classifications which have been imposed from outside, and which would not be recognised by the exegetes themselves. They are merely convenient terms by which the gradation from Peshat to Derash can be described, so it is to be expected that one will merge into the other.

The cut-off point between Nomological and Ultra-literal readings of Scripture has been chosen as the point at which the plain meaning of the language used is no longer an arbiter of the correctness of the interpretation. A Nomological interpretation is still based on the plain meaning of the text, although it interprets that meaning as though it were part of a legal document. The Ultra-literal interpretation however, may ignore the plain meaning in its search for the literal meaning of each word or phrase.

I.1.4d The DERASH mode of interpreting tries to find a hidden meaning, which may completely ignore the plain meaning, or even the literal meaning of the text. Derash, like Peshat, is used anachronistically for want of a better term. In the Tannaitic period it merely conveyed the sense of "interpretation" without referring to any special techniques or hidden meaning (Gertner 1962:5ff.; Yohanan b.Zakkai in mSheq.1.4).

The hidden meaning may be supplementary to the primary meaning, or it may be a secondary meaning which is completely unrelated to the primary meaning.

A supplementary meaning is one which seeks to amplify the primary or plain meaning of the text. An example of Derash interpretation which leads to a supplementary meaning is that used by the Aqivan rules of Extension and Limitation. These rules find supplementary meanings in particles of speech such as אך ('only') or את (the objective article) which are interpreted as implying unspoken additions or exceptions to the law in which they occur.

A secondary meaning is one which is completely unrelated to the primary or plain meaning of the text. An example of Derash interpretation which discovers secondary meanings is that used by allegorists such as Philo who assumed that a text can have more than one level of meaning, such as a literal or legal meaning and also a spiritual or moral meaning. A secondary meaning may not imply that the primary meaning is to be discarded, but it is completely unrelated to, and unaffected by that primary meaning.

Derash was of great importance in rabbinic exegesis, but it is almost entirely missing from scribal exegeses. The scribes rarely used techniques which are based on the assumptions underlying a Derash reading of the text, such as Extensions and Limitations, Gematria, Unusual Form, Correspondence, Exchange of letters and Notariqon, and they never expounded a secondary meaning of the text.

I.1.5 THE EXEGETICAL TECHNIQUES which are used in the debates have been analysed with an attempt to fit them into the categories provided by the lists of middoth attributed to Hillel, Ishmael and Eliezer. Although these lists are likely to post-date the sources being discussed, their terminology has been employed because they have become the established vocabulary in Jewish exegetical studies. However, the middoth named in these lists are generally conspicuous by their absence from scribal exegeses, most of which rely on the Peshat reading of the text and require no exegetical techniques, while many others use techniques which do not occur in any of the lists.

The exegetical techniques have been classified as far as possible according to those in the three lists of middoth. Those which are found in the three lists of middoth are introduced first, followed by those which are not. Most of the latter have been named in other rabbinic or modern works.

I.1.5a QAL vaHOMER [קל וחומר] is the argument from minor to major, which is the most commonly employed of all the middoth. It is also frequently used in non-exegetical debates.

I.1.5b GEZERAH SHAVAH [גזרה שוה] is used in two completely different ways, which I have termed type I and II, which correspond to Mielziner's exegetical Gezerah Shavah and constructional Gezerah Shavah respectively. This also accords approximately with Schwarz's first two evolutionary stages of Gezerah Shavah (1897:61ff.).

GEZERAH SHAVAH I is the definition of an ill-defined phrase or word in one text by its use in another text where its meaning is clearer. It does not attempt to survey all the possible uses of the word or phrase throughout Scripture but it assumes that the meaning of a word in one text is always the same as its meaning in another.

This should not be seen as an attempt to carry out a philological survey on the uses of a phrase or word elsewhere in related literature, which is how some apologists have interpreted it (e.g. Rosenblatt 1935:2f.,28ff., Mielziner 1968:143f.). The Scribes who used Gezerah Shavah I were content to define the meaning of a word or phrase from just one other text, on the assumption that it has exactly the same meaning everywhere it occurs. A possible exception to this is when Beth Hillel tried to broaden the meaning of the "dust" with which one covered blood, to include ash, because ash is referred to as "dust of burning" in Num.19.17 (I.4.25). Beth Shammai replied that "dust" only ever refers to ash when it occurs in the phrase "dust of burning". However, since the phrase "dust of burning" only occurs once, this example can hardly be called a philological survey. Later rabbis did develop a method of philological survey (often indicated by the formula אין...אלא..., ('not...but...' i.e. 'wherever x occurs it means y' – W. Reiss 1978, I.B. Gottlieb 1979) but examples do not occur in scribal traditions.

I.1.5c GEZERAH SHAVAH II is the interpretation of one text in the light of another text to which it is related by a shared word or phrase. The two texts are often concerned with the same subject, but the existence of the same word or phrase in two texts can suggest a relationship between them even if they are concerned with completely unrelated subjects. This can also be seen as a result of Nomological assumptions, because the divine legislator would ensure that all terms were used with complete consistency, so that the use of the same term anywhere in the legal document would relate to its use anywhere else in the same document.

I.1.5d HEQESH [הקש] does not actually occur in the lists of middoth but it is often regarded as one of Hillel's middoth because it is one of those which he employed when he (supposedly) introduced the middoth to Israel by using three of them to determine whether or not Passover over-rides the Sabbath (tPis.4.13). It is very similar to Gezerah Shavah II in that it brings together two texts by means of a common feature and can be expressed with the same formula.

The main difference between Gezerah Shavah and Heqesh is that the former depends on a similarity of words or phrases which occur in the two texts while the latter depends on a similarity of subject matter. These rules can also be used to connect two topics rather than two texts, in which case the difference between them can be generalised under the rule that Gezerah Shavah forms a link by common nouns, while Heqesh forms a link by common predicates (Mielziner 1968 : 152f.).

However these distinctions are minor, and they are not followed consistently. There is little evidence that these were recognised as separate before anyone attempted to list the middoth. Even when Hillel's list of middoth was made, the rule of Heqesh was assumed to illustrate the list although it was not named in it. It is therefore likely that the rule of Heqesh was originally another name for Gezerah Shavah, and there is little to be gained in emphasising differences which later grew up between them.

I.1.5e BINYAN AB [בנין אב] has not been found in any of the scribal material, which may accord with Schwarz's theory that it is a later development of Gezerah Shavah II (1897:65).

BINYAN AB FROM TWO TEXTS (Hillel's fourth middah) is not found in any of the scribal material, but it may originally have been the rule of Contradiction between two texts (see below). J.W. Doeve (1954:68) pointed out that the Sifra reads only 'Two texts' and that Rabed regarded it as a similar rule to Ishmael's 13th (Contradiction resolved by a third text). Schwarz (1913:193ff.) reached a similar conclusion in his discussion of the relationship between these two rules, suggesting that Hillel's 4th rule is the resolution of a contradiction by means of a clause which is outside Scripture, while Ishmael's 13th utilises a clause which is contained in a third text.

I.1.5f. CONTRADICTION [כחש] between two texts is resolved both with and without the use of a third text. When the third text is absent it can be assumed that the exegete is working in ignorance of Ishmael's list, or at least in independence from it. Schwarz (1913:196) found only four examples of a third text in the whole of talmudic literature, but he only accepted instances where the phrase כתוב שלישי ('third text') actually occurs. Several instances have been identified in these scribal exegeses where this phrase does not occur but where a third text does appear to be employed.

I.1.5g EXTENSION [רבוי] and Limitation [מיעוט] refer to unwritten additions or exceptions which are indicated by the use of particles of speech such as כל את גם אף ('all, with/the, also, also') or מן רק אך ('from, except, only'). These additions and exceptions are not necessarily specified anywhere in Scripture, and their presence can be inferred merely by the presence of these particles, even when the particles are necessary to the sense of the text.

The logic behind this appears to be an extension of Nomological assumptions. Every word in Scripture is assumed to carry equal weight, so that these small particles of speech are assumed to have an importance which is not immediately obvious. Therefore if a ruling contains a particle which suggests exclusion, it is assumed to indicate an unwritten exception to the ruling, and if it contains a particle which suggests inclusion then it is assumed to indicate an additional feature or application of that ruling. The particle מן is presumably regarded as a particle of exclusion because it can be used in the sense of 'without', and the definite objective article את is regarded as a particle of inclusion because it is identical to את, 'with'.

Although the logic behind this rule can be traced back to Nomological assumptions, the result is often a Derash interpretation, because the particles of inclusion and exclusion indicate exceptions and additions to the law which are not in the written text. That is, they indicate the presence of hidden meanings which are entirely independent of the plain meaning of the text, although they are likely to be concerned with the same subject matter as the primary meaning of the text.

These exegetical techniques were introduced by Nahum of Gimzo and were developed by Aqiva into a whole new system of interpretation which assumed that scripture does not always "speak in the language of men" (to quote Ishmael, his opponent). Although it seems likely that Ishmael also used these techniques (G. Porton 1976-, M. Chernick 1980), they were probably not used before this time, and are not expected to occur in exegesis which originated before 70 CE.

D. Barthélemy (1963) has suggested that the translation of גם by καιγε in his 1st C Minor Prophet scroll, which does not follow Aquila's practice of translating את by συν, reflects a limited use of Inclusion in the Hillelite-Ishmaelite school. However there is little or no evidence for the use of Inclusion before 70 CE and the καιγε translation by itself, which is not followed consistently, may merely indicate the wish to differentiate between different Hebrew particles, rather than to suggest an extra inclusive force (cf. L.L. Grabbe 1982).

I.1.5h UNUSUAL FORM [יחוד] refers to an unusual spelling or grammatical construction which points to some hidden interpretation. This is also based on Nomological principles but results in Derash interpretations. It is based on the assumption that the divine legislator would not have made elementary mistakes in spelling and grammar, so that anything which might otherwise be regarded as a mistake must indicate a deeper or hidden meaning. A natural development from this is to regard all unusual constructions or unusual word usage as indications of a hidden meaning.

I.1.5i MASHAL [משל] or "comparison" can include anything from a metaphor to a complex parable (D.W. Suter 1981 discusses various definitions), but among the rabbis it usually refers to an illustrative story. It does not occur frequently in scribal exegeses but it became very popular with later rabbis. It is usually used to illustrate a scripture with a non-scriptural story or analogy, but it can also be constructed from a scripture text (e.g. I.4.22).

The following are exegetical rules which do not occur in the three lists of middoth but can be identified in scribal and in later rabbinic traditions.

I.1.5j ORDER refers to an argument based on the order of words or phrases in the text. This argument sometimes contradicts Eliezer's rules 31 and 32, which state that latter and former phrases or events in the Scriptures may be read in reverse.

I.1.5k WORDPLAY includes the various methods from pun to the method later called "Hint" [רמז] or Paronomasia, which were popular in prophetic and dream interpretation in the Ancient Near Eastern literature and the OT.

This is different from Al Tiqré because no emendation is attempted or even proposed for the sake of the exegesis.

I.1.5l NO REDUNDANCY assumes that Scripture contains no superfluous or redundant phrases. It can be expressed as:

שני כתובים הבאים כאחד אין מלמדים (bKidd.43a)

"two texts [using] the same rhetoric teach nothing [new]". It is often introduced with אם כן למה נאמר, 'If so, why is it written . . .'.

I.1.5m PRECEDENT derives a general law from an incident in Scripture, treating it like an example in case law.

I.1.5n REDUCTIO AD ABSURDUM has been identified as an exegetical technique in Tannaitic and Amoraic literature by L. Jacobs (1961 : 38 ff.). Jacobs was not the first to discover this technique in rabbinic literature (see e.g. Mielziner 1968 : 139 – 1st ed. 1894), but he was to first to outline the verbal formulae used and to attempt to list all the occurrences in Tannaitic literature as well as surveying the hundreds of examples from Amoraic literature. He found twelve Tannaitic examples but only one is early enough to be included in this survey (mYad.4.7). However, several other examples of Reductio ad Absurdum have been identified in the scribal material studied here, which Jacobs presumably did not include because they do not use any of the formulae which he identified. However, since these formulae were relatively unfixed in the earlier literature, these differences do not indicate that a different technique is being used but merely that they are early examples.

I.1.5o LOGICAL INCONSISTENCY is such a basic tool of debate that it should perhaps not be identified as a separate exegetical technique. However on some occasions (particularly in the Sadducee-Pharisee debates) it seems to be used quite self-consciously in order to highlight a discrepancy between theory and practice.

I.1.5p PRAGMATISM is a common technique in secular debates, arguing that a particular course should be followed because it is easier or because it results in greater good. However this is an unusual argument in a religious debate concerning God's Law in the Scriptures, which seeks to establish God's will, and not to discover an easy or comfortable solution.

Nevertheless, because the Law does have to be carried out in everyday life, arguments based on Pragmatism do occur, using phrases such as "for the sake of the order of the world" (e.g. mGit.4.2) and "for the sake of peace" (e.g.mGit.5.8). It is likely that the argument was in fact used far more frequently in determining practice, but that a more convincing argument from Scripture was later found to support the conclusion.

I.1.5q PROPHETIC FULFILMENT is a very frequent form of argument in the
NT, apocalyptic and Qumran literature. It occurs in the Passover Haggadah
(in the comments on Deut.26.5 – I owe this reference to R. Loewe), but it is
almost absent from scribal literature.

I.1.5r SYMBOLISM is used frequently in Jewish literature in order to interpret prophecies and to construct allegories, but it is used sparingly in the
scribal exegeses. It differs from Mashal in that Symbolism says that "x is y"
while Mashal says that "x is like y".

I.1.5s ATOMISATION is the division of a text into different phrases which are
interpreted individually. This is similar to the technique of No Redundancy
in that pleonastic phrases are often given individual interpretations, but
Atomisation is used even when there are no apparently superfluous words or
phrases. It frequently depends on an Ultra-literal reading of the text because
the interpretations given to the individual words or phrases may have little or
nothing to do with the context, and because the overall interpretation is
clearly not implied by the context. This is a very common exegetical technique in Jewish literature, especially in the interpretation of prophecy, but it
does not occur in scribal material.

I.1.5t ALLEGORY is difficult to define because it is a term in common
parlance and even in the world of scholarship it has a wide range of meanings. Lauterbach attempted to make a distinction between Alexandrian and
Palestinian allegory (1910–) and R.P.C. Hanson assumed a similar distinction (1959). Lauterbach assumed that Palestinian allegory (used by the
Dorshe Reshumot) was the same as Mashal, and that Alexandrian allegory
(used by the Dorshe Hamurot) followed the Philonic model. However J.
Pépin (1958:221–231) found a continuity in the allegorical form from the
Homeric commentators, via Philo, to the later rabbis and the church fathers,
and he found no difficulty in deciding that Palestinian as well as Alexandrian
allegory was ultimately related to Hellenistic allegory.

Allegory occurs in only one exegesis surveyed (I.2.37 – which is probably
late) but it is found frequently in contemporary Jewish sources. Allegory
differs from Mashal: Mashal provides a picture to illustrate the meaning of
Scripture whereas allegory derives meaning from a picture in Scripture.
Mashal says "This scripture is like the story of...", whereas Allegory says
"This Scriptural story means...".

I.1.5u AMALGAMATION is the construction of a 'text' by joining texts, without any indication that more than one text has been used. This is different
from Chain quotations which are found commonly in Paul (E.E. Ellis 1957),
in Mishnah (Metzger 1968) and in other rabbinic writings. In chain quotations several texts are cited one after another and they are divided by no

more than a simple "and" [ו], but this is sufficient to show that more than one passage is being used. Amalgamation, however, is the merging of more than one text without any indication that they come from different portions of Scripture.

It is unlikely that any of these exegetical modes or techniques were defined or categorised before 70 CE, so the analysis of the exegeses in these terms is anachronistic. However, analysis must always use categorisation and comparison, and in the absence of categories defined by the scribes themselves, categories must be imposed on them. The modes and techniques of exegesis which have been outlined above are as close as one can get to those which the scribes might have recognised, because most of them have been defined or expressed by the rabbis who inherited their traditions.

I.2 Exegeses by Named Authorities

I.2.1. tNaz.4.7:

(Sifré Num.22; yNed.1.1; yNaz.1.5; bNaz.4b; bNed.9b,10a; NumR.10.7)

Simeon the Righteous said:	אמ׳ שמעון הצדיק
I have never eaten	מימיי לא אכלתי
the guilt-offering of a Nazirite	אשם נזיר
except once only.	חוץ מאחד בלבד
The event [involved] one	מעשה באחד
who came to me from the South	שבא אלי מן הדרום
And I saw him, beautiful eyes,	וראיתיו יפה עינים
and good looks	וטוב רואי
and his locks [in] curls.	וקווצותיו תלתלים
I said: My son,	נמתי לו בני
Why do you look to destroy	מה ראית לשחת
this handsome hair?	שער זה נאה
He said to me:	נם לי
I was a shepherd in my city	רועה הייתי בעירי
and I went to fill [my pot]	ובאתי למלאות
from the river water,	מן הנהר מים
and I looked at my reflection	ונסתכלתי בבבואה שלי
and my impulse swelled in me	ופחז יצרי עלי
and sought to remove me	וביקש להעבירני
from the world.	מן העולם
I said to it: Evil-one,	נמתי לו רשע
it is not for you to be jealous	לא היה לך להתגרות
except of a thing which is not yours,	אלא בדבר שאינו שלך
a thing which is designated to become	בדבר שעתיד לעשות

dust, worm and maggot.	עפר רמה ותולעה
It is upon me [i.e. I vow]	הרי עלי
to shave you for [the sake of] heaven.	לגלחך לשמים
I lowered his head	המכתי את ראשו
and kissed it, and said: My son,	ונשקתיו ואמרתי בני
may those like you multiply,	כמותך ירבו
who do the will of God,	עושי רצון מקום
in Israel.	בישראל
By you is fulfilled	עליך נתקיים
this which is said: [Num.6.2]	זה שנ׳
A man or woman	איש או אשה
when he swears a special vow	כי יפליא לנדור נדר
of a Nazirite, to separate himself to YHWH.	נזיר להזיר לה׳

Notes:

This tradition assumes that Simeon did not approve of Nazarite vows, which were often made on the spur of the moment and for false motives. A tradition concerning Simeon b.Shetah (I.2.5) suggests that he considered it his duty to release as many people as possible from fulfilling these vows when they had been made rashly.

On this occasion he finds someone who has made the vow from the purest of motives, in order to demonstrate that he loves God more than himself. This was truly a vow 'for YHWH' and not in any sense to gain reward for himself.

The relevance of the text which Simeon has cited is not immediately obvious, and Neusner (1971 III:39) concluded that it was added later. However it is suggested below that it is an essential part of the argument.

It is difficult to believe that any genuine traditions of Simeon the Just (who lived at least four generations before Hillel) could have survived. However this was evidently regarded as an ancient tradition and it is recorded in the earliest rabbinic sources, so it cannot be simply rejected.

Analysis:

The shepherd is probably quoting Num.6.2 when he says "for [the sake of] heaven", using 'heaven' as a circumlocution for 'YHWH'. Therefore "it is upon me ... for heaven" is equivalent to Num.6.2: "he swears ... to YHWH". This appears to be the understanding in the margin of bNaz.4b, in the commentaries of Rashi ("this literally means that he swore to heaven") and the Tosafot ("in order to say that the initiation of his vow was entirely to Heaven and he was not hesitating in order to change it"). In his commentary on Num.6.2 Rashi quotes the text using a similar circumlocution (לשם שמים).

The vow was not promised in thanks for a good crop or a male child, but was prompted to allay an inner temptation to love himself more than God. This vow was 'for God' without any strings attached. Although this is not the normal understanding of the text, it is grammatically and contextually possible, so it is still Peshat. The incident then demonstrates the true significance of a Nazirite vow as something done 'for the sake of YHWH'.

The word פלא ('special/wonderful') also meant 'miraculous', especially in mishnaic Hebrew (Jastrow ad loc.) but it is used elsewhere in the OT with regard to vows (Lev.22.21; 27.2; Num.15.3,8) and Simeon does not draw particular attention to it.

I.2.2. *mTaan.3.8:*

(yMQ.3.1; yTaan.3.12; bBer.19a; bTaan.23a; LevR.35.8)

Simeon b.Shetah sent to him [saying]:	שלח לו שמעון בן שטח
If you were not Honi	אלמלא חוני אתה
I would ban you with excommunication,	גוזרני עליך נידוי
but what can I do to you	אבל מה אעשה לך
for you importune before God	שאתה מתחטא לפני המקום
and he does your will for you	ועושה לך רצונך
like a son who importunes his father	כבן שהוא מתחטא על אביו
and he does his will for him;	ועושה לו רצונו
and of you the text says: [Prov.23.25]	ועליך הכתוב אומר
Let your father and mother be glad	ישמח אביך ואמך
and let her who bore you rejoice.	ותגל יולדתך

Note:

The text was probably not added later because it carries an undertone of warning while still appearing to praise Honi (see below), as might be expected from Simeon.

Analysis:

The common Symbol of God as Father is used. The text means more than 'God, your Father, is pleased', which would require only ישמח אביך (G. Vermes 1983 : 264 n86). The Jerusalem Talmud struggles to find a reason for citing the rest of the verse by interpreting "mother" as 'nation' or 'hour of birth'.

Perhaps the whole verse is required to form a link with "The *father* of the righteous shall greatly *rejoice*" (v24). Simeon thereby suggested that Honi's righteousness enabled him to importune God. This both warned other 'less righteous' people from following Honi's dangerous example and also appeared to praise Honi. The mode is therefore Peshat, and implies Contextual exegesis.

I.2.3. *Mekh.Ish.Kaspa.3.31–35:*

(tSanh.6.6; ySanh.4.9; 6.3; bHag.16b; bMakk.5b)

Once Simeon ben Shetah executed	כבר הרג שמעין בן שטח
a [single] false witness.	עד זומם
Judah ben Tabai said to him:	אמר לו יהודה בן טבאי
May I [not] see the Consolation	אראה בנחמה
if you have not shed innocent blood,	אם לא שפכת דם נקי
for the Torah says:	ואמרה תורה
Execute *on the word of* [two] *witnesses* [Deut.17.6] [and]	הרוג על פי עדים
Execute on the word of [two] *false witnesses* [Deut.19.18f.]	הרוג על פי זוממים
Just as [there must be] two *witnesses*	מה עדים בשנים
so also [there must be] two *false witnesses.*	אף זוממים בשנים

Notes:

The parallel versions swap the roles of Simeon and Judah, but this does not affect the arguments used.

Analysis:

The formula ...**מה**...**אף** ("Just as... so also...") is used both in Heqesh and Gezerah Shavah, and either of them could be used here. The word linking the texts is **פי**, 'word', so Gezerah Shavah is probably being used because this usually links texts with a noun whereas Heqesh uses a predicate. However, it is likely that there was little or no distinction made between these two rules in the Tannaitic period.

I.2.4. *Mekh.Ish.Kas.3.37–41:*

(tSanh.8.3; ySanh.4.9; bSanh.37b ; bShab.34a)

And once Judah ben Tabai entered	וכבר נכנס יהודה בן טבאי
a ruin and found there	לחורבה ומצא שם
a killed man [still] writhing	הרוג מפרפר
and a sword dripping blood	והסייף מנטף דם
in the hand of the [apparent] killer.	מיד ההורג
Judah ben Tabai said to him:	אמר לו יהודה בן טבאי
May [a curse] come on me if it is not the case	תבא עלי אם לא
that [either] I or you killed him;	אני או אתה הרגנוהו
But what [can] I do	אבל מה אעשה
in the case where Torah says:	שהרי אמרה תורה
By the word of two witnesses	על פי שנים עדים
the matter is established [Deut.19.15]	יקום דבר
But He who knows even inner thoughts,	אבל היודע ובעל המחשבות
He will punish the man [the offender].	הוא יפרע מאותו האיש
He had hardly come from there	לא הספיק לצאת משם
when a serpent bit him and he died.	עד שהכישו נחש ומת

Notes:

The parallels swap Simeon and Judah, as in I.2.3

Analysis:

A Peshat reading of the text introduces a problem of possible injustice. It is not solved by exegesis but by the story itself, which suggests that God will punish those whom courts cannot convict.

I.2.5. *yBer.7.2 (11b):* (yNaz.5.3; GenR.91.3; bBer.48b)

It was taught:	תני
Three hundred Nazirites came up	שלש מאו' נזירין עלו
in the days of R. Simeon b.Shetah.	בימי רבי שמעון בן שטח
One hundred and fifty he found	מאה וחמשים מצא
for them release [from their vows]	להן פתח

and one hundred and fifty he did not find
for them release [from their vows]

ומאה וחמשים לא מצא
להן פתח

He came to King Yannai
He said to him:
There are here three hundred
Nazirites who are liable for
nine hundred offerings,
but you give half from your pocket
and I [will give] half from my pocket.
He sent to him 450.
A mischief maker went and said to him:
He did not give
anything from his pocket.
King Yannai heard and was angry.
Simeon b.Shetah feared and fled.

אתא גבי ינאי מלכ׳
אמר לי׳
אית הכא תלת מאה
נזירין בעיין
תשע מאה קרבנין
אלא יהב את פלגא מן דידך
ואנא פלגא מן דידי
שלח ליה ארבע מאה וחמשין
אזל לישנא ביש׳ ומר ליה
לא יהב
מן דידיה כלו׳
שמע ינאי מלכא וכע׳
דחל שמעון בן שטח וערק

After [some] days
some important men came up
from the Kingdom of Persia
to King Yannai.
When they were settled and eating
they said to him:
We remember that there was here
a particular elderly man
who was saying before us
sayings of wisdom.
Let him teach us something.
They said to him:
Send and bring him.
He sent and gave him [his] word.
And he came and sat himself
between the king and queen.

בתר יומין
סלקון בני נש רברבין
מן מלכותא דפרס
גבי ינאי מלכא
מן דיתבין אכלין
אמרין ליה
נהירין אנן דהוה אית הכא
חד גבר סב
והוה אמר קומין
מילין דחכמה
תני לון עובדא
אמרין ליה
שלח ואייתיתיה
שלח ויהב ליה מילא
ואתא ויתיב ליה
בין מלכא למלכתא

1a

He said to him:
Why did you deceive me?
He said to him:

אמר לי׳
למה אפליית בי
אמר לי׳

1b

I did not deceive you.
You [gave] from your money
and I from my Law.
As it is written: [Qoh.7.12a]
For wisdom is protection
[and] silver is protection.

לא אפליית בך
את מממונך
ואנא מן אורייתי
דכתיב
כי בצל החכמה
בצל הכסף

2a

He said to him:
And why did you flee?

אמר ליה
ולמה ערקת

2bi

He said to him:
I heard that my lord
was angry against me and I wanted
to fulfil this saying: [Is.26.20]
Hide a small moment
till wrath passes.

אמר לי׳
שמעית דמרי
כעס עלי ובעית
מקיימה הדין קרייא
חבי כמעט רגע
ער יעבר זעם

2bii

And he applied to him[self] the text: [Qoh.7.12b]
And the profit of knowledge [is that]
wisdom makes those possessing her live.

וקרא עלוי
ויתרון דעת
החכמה תחיה בעליה

3a

He said to him:
And why did you sit
between the king and queen?

אמר לי׳
ולמה יתבת
בין מלכא למלכתא

3b

He said to him:
In the Book of Ben Sira it is written:
[Ben Sira 11.1]
Raise her up and she will exalt you
and seat you between rulers.
He said: Give him the cup
to make the blessing.
He lifted the cup and said:
We bless the food
which Yannai and his companions ate.
He said to him:
Does your obstinate [resentment]
go this far?
He said to him:
And what should we say?
... the food which we have not eaten?
He said: Give him something so that
he [too] may eat.
They gave to him and he ate.
And he said: We bless
the food which we have eaten.

אמר לי׳
בסיפרא דכן סירא כתיב
סלסליה ותרוממך
ובין נגידים תושיבך
אמר הבו ליה כסא
דליבריך
נסב כסא ומר
נברך על המזון
שאכל ינאי וחביריו
אמר לי׳
עד כדון את בקשיותך
אמר לי׳
ומה נאמר
על המזון שלא אכלנו
אמר הבון ליה דליכול
יהבו ליה ואכל
ומר נברך
על המזון שאכלנו

Notes:
Neusner (1971 I:97f.) regards this whole story as late, including the first paragraph
which is introduced as a baraita (תני) and is in Hebrew. However Neusner's sugges-

tion that this first paragraph was deliberately translated into Hebrew to resemble a baraita, goes beyond the evidence.

The quotation of Ben Sira 11.1 (replaced by Prov.4.8 in bBer) may suggest an early date, but this is not decisive. There are no halakot or traditional haggadot, and Scripture is used for witty answers rather than teaching or exposition.

The text from "He came to Yannai..." shows no early features and is probably a late tradition added onto the baraita. This late tradition probably developed separately, as in bBer. and more exegeses were gradually added.

Analysis:
1ab.
The text is used to show that wisdom is equivalent to money for "shelter/protection". If this illustrates Simeon's protection of himself in the angry king's presence this is a Peshat reading.

However it is also being used to defend Simeon's action with the Nazarites. Half of the sacrifices were made exempt by Simeon's cleverness in finding reasons for exemption, and the other half were paid for by Yannai. Simeon quotes this text to show that Wisdom = Money, so that he has paid the same as Yannai. This is an Ultra-literal reading, because it goes beyond any implications of the text or context.
2ab.
These exegeses were probably added by the influence of 1b. The use of Qoh.7.12a inspired the exegesis of v12b and later the addition of Is.26.20. Both are used in their Peshat sense.
3ab.
The text is read very literally, but this was probably the Peshat sense for the rabbis.

In bBer. Simeon sits between them because he is the queen's brother, and when Yannai says: "See how much honour I pay you" he replies with Prov.4.8: *She* [Wisdom, interpreted in Talmud as Torah] *will lift you up and honour you when you embrace her*. This is also a Peshat reading.

I.2.6. *bSanh.19ab:*

An event which happened	מעשה שהיה
when a slave of King Yannai	דעבדיה דינאי מלכא
killed a man.	קטל נפשא
Simeon b.Shetah said to the Sages:	אמר להו שמעון בן שטח לחכמים
Place your eyes on him	תנו עיניכם בו
and let him be judged.	ונדונּנו
They sent to him:	שלחו ליה
Your slave killed a man.	עבדך קטל נפשא
He delivered him to them.	שדריה להו
1	
They sent to him:	שלחו לי׳
Come here yourself likewise.	תא אנת נמי להכא
And warning is given to its owner	והועד בבעליו
says the Torah, [Ex.21.29]	אמרה תורה
[therefore] the owner of the ox will come	יבא בעל השור

and stand with his ox.   ויעמוד על שורו

He came and sat.   אתא ויתיב

2

Simeon b.Shetah said to him: א״ל שמעון בן שטח

King Yannai,   ינאי המלך

stand on your feet   עמוד על רגליך

and let them testify against you,   ויעידו בך

for you stand not before us   ולא לפנינו אתה עומד

but before Him who spoke   אלא לפני מי שאמר

and the world existed   והיה העולם

you stand,   אתה עומד

for as it is written: [Deut.19.17]   שנאמר

And both men stand   ועמדו שני האנשים

who have dispute between them etc.   אשר להם הריב וגו׳

He [Yannai] said to him: אמר לו

Not according as you speak   לא כשתאמר אתה

but according to what your associates say. אלא כמה שיאמרו חבריך

He [Simeon] looked to his right.   נפנה לימינו

They pressed their faces to the ground.   כבשו פניהם בקרקע

He looked to his left,   נפנה לשמאלו

and they pressed their faces to the ground. וכבשו פניהם בקרקע

Simeon b.Shetah said to them: אמר להן שמעון בן שטח

So you have [other] thoughts?   בעלי מחשבות אתם

The Master of thoughts will come   יבא בעל מחשבות

and punish you.   ויפרע

Immediately Gabriel came   מכם מיד בא גבריאל

and crushed them on the ground   וחבטן בקרקע

and they died.   ומתו

Notes:

The core of this tradition is likely to be early, because a similar event is described in Jos.Ant.14.168–76(9.4) although with some differences: the king is Herod, who is opposed by Sameas (cf. Ant.15.2–4(1.1); 15.368–71(10.4)) and the rabbis are killed by the king (cf. bBer.48b). S. Zeitlin (1917:510f.) conjectured that "Sameas", "Simeon b.Shetah" in this passage, and "Shammai in bQid.43a (I.2.9) may all refer to Shemaiah.

The ruling that the master is liable for his slave's actions is certainly not a later invention, because it appears to agree with the Sadducees against the Pharisees (cf. I.3.4).

The Ex.21 exegesis is integral to the trial tradition, but the Deut.19 exegesis may have been added later, and the reference to Gabriel is probably a later embellishment.

Analysis:

1. The argument is based on the Symbol of a dangerous ox for a servant. This could perhaps be seen as an example of allegory, but the comparison between a man and a dangerous ox is so common in the area of tort that it can be regarded as a Peshat

understanding of a metaphor. The same comparison is assumed by the Sadducees in a similar case (I.3.4), and it forms the basis of rabbinic law of damages (mBQ.1.4,6 etc). A comparison between a man and a non-dangerous ox is also assumed in the NT (ICor.9.9; 1Tim.5.18).

2. This is a Peshat reading of the text.

I.2.7. *Mekh.Ish.Besh.4.58–61:*

1a

Shemaiah says:	שמעיה אומר
By the sufficiency of the faith	כדי היא האמנה
with which their father Abraham	שהאמין בי אברהם אביהם
believed in Me	
I divided the Sea for them,	שאקרע להם את הים
for it says: [Gen.15.6]	שנאמר
And he believed in YHWH.	והאמין ביי

1b

Abtalion says:	אבטליון אומר
By the sufficiency of the faith	כדי היא האמנה
with which they [themselves] believed in Me	שהאמינו בי
I divided the Sea for them,	שאקרע להם את הים
for it says: [Ex.4.31 – cf. Ex.14.31]	שנאמר
And the people believed.	ויאמן העם

Notes:

This is part of a series of opinions concerning the reason for God's favour at the Sea. Others said the reason God acted was because of His own sake (the Sages), Israel's faith (Rabbi), Abraham's sake (R. Eleazar b.Azariah), the Tribes' sake (R. Eliezar b.Judah), or Joseph's sake (Simon of Kitron). Shemaiah and Abtalion are in direct debate with each-other, and not with the other opinions, so although the traditions all have the same form and were therefore redacted late, the Shemaiah and Abtalion traditions probably form the original debate from which the others developed.

Analysis:

1a. Shemaiah argues that Israel gained benefit from Abraham's faith and uses the Peshat reading to show that Abraham had faith.

1b. Abtalion replies that the faith was of Israel itself, which he proves by a Peshat interpretation.

I.2.8. *bPes.70b:*

And Judah b.Durtai separated himself,	יהודה בן דורתאי פירש
he and Durtai his son,	הוא ודורתאי בנו
and they went and stayed in the South.	והלך וישב לו בדרום
He said: If Elijah should come	אמר אם יבוא אליהו
and say before Israel:	ויאמר להם לישראל מפני
Why do you not sacrifice Hagigah	מה לא חגגתם חגיגה בשבת
on Sabbath?	

What would they say to him?	מה הן אומרים לי
I am astonished at the two	תמהני על שני
great ones of the generation,	גדולי הדור
Shemaiah and Abtalion,	שמעיה ואבטליון
who were/are great Sages	שהן חכמים גדולים
and great exegetes	ודרשנין גדולים
and [yet] do not say to Israel	ולא אמרו להן לישראל
that Hagigah overrides the Sabbath.	חגיגה דוחה את השבת
Rab said:	אמר רב
What is the argument of b.Durtai?	מ"ט דבן דורתאי
1i	
As it is written: [Deut.16.2]	דכתיב
You shall sacrifice Pesach to YHWH	וזבחת פסח לה'
your God [from] flocks and herds.	אלהיך צאן ובקר
But is not Pesach only	והלא אין פסח אלא
from lambs and from goats? [Ex.12.5]	מן הכבשים ומן העזים
But *flocks* refers to Pesach	אלא צאן זה פסח
[and] *herd* refers to Hagigah,	בקר זו חגיגה
1ii	
And Scripture says: [Deut.16.2]	ואמר רחמנא
You shall sacrifice Pesach.	וזבחת פסח
R. Ashi said:	א"ר אשי
And shall we argue for separatists?	ואנן טעמא דפרושים

Notes:
Hagigah (pilgrim sacrifices) could be offered on any day of a feast, but should normally be offered on the first day. B. Durtai believed that when the first day was a Sabbath, they should still be offered on that day. He moved away where he would not be obliged to attend the feasts which he felt were being celebrated incorrectly.

The exegesis is unlikely to be Rab's because, as R. Ashi says, they had no wish to support separatists. After the first century פרש ('Pharisee') meant 'separatist' (A. Guttmann 1962, although E. Rivkin 1969 argues that it always had this sense).

Hillel used the same exegesis as 1i to prove a different point (I.2.13), so perhaps they both learned it from Abtalion and Shemaiah. If this was so, then b.Durtai may be saying: I am astonished that Shemaiah and Abtalion do not agree that the Hagigah overrides the Sabbath, because their own exegesis implies the fact.

Analysis:
1i. A contradiction between Deut.16 and Ex.12 is resolved without a third text, by referring "flock" to Pesach and "herd" to Hagigah.

1ii. This is presumably a reference to the context, especially v3: "You shall eat unleavened bread with it [hagigah] seven days", i.e. including a Sabbath.

I.2.9. *bQid.43a:*

Shammai the Elder said	שמאי הזקן אומר

Texte und Studien zum Antiken Judentum

Herausgegeben von
Martin Hengel und Peter Schäfer

30

in the name of Haggai the prophet:	משום חגי הנביא
His principal is liable	שולחיו חייב
as it is said: [2Sam.12.9]	שנא׳
And you slew him	אותו הרגת
with the sword of the sons of Ammon.	בחרב בני עמון

Note:
The debate concerns whether the person who sends someone to do a crime is guilty.
Zeitlin (1917:510f., cf. I.2.6) suggests the attribution was originally to Shemaiah but this is based on circumstantial evidence.

Analysis:
This is a Nomological reading of the text, taking David's crime as an item of case law, setting a Precedent for similar cases.

I.2.10. *Mekh.Sim.p148.29:* (Mekh.Ish.Bah.7 = I.2.39)

Shammai the Elder says:	שמאי הזקן אומר
Remember it [Ex.20.8]	זכרה
before it comes	עד שלא תבוא
and *keep* it [Deut.5.12]	ושמרה
when it comes.	משתבוא

Note:
This occurs in the middle of a discussion concerning the duplication of Ex.20 and Deut.5

Analysis:
The two terms "remember" and "keep" are assumed to have different meanings because of the Nomological principle of No Redundancy. Shammai therefore concludes that "keep" refers to what one does on the Sabbath itself while "remember" refers to what one does on the days leading up to the Sabbath.

I.2.11. *Sifré Deut.203:*
(tShab.13.10,12–13; tErub.3.7 = I.2.12; bShab.19a)

When you besiege a city	כי תצור אל עיר
...	
for many days. [Deut.20.19]	ימים רבים
1	
Days [indicates at least] two	ימים שנים
Many [indicates at least] three	רבים שלשה
From this they say:	מיכן אמרו
One may not besiege a Gentile city	אין צרים על עיר של גוים
less than three days	פחות משלשה ימים
before the Sabbath.	קודם לשבת
...	

2

Another saying: דבר אחר

When you besiege a city.   כי תצור אל עיר

shows that one should appeal for peace מגיד שתובע שלום

two [or] three days   שנים שלשה ימים

before one goes to battle against it. עד שלא נלחם בה

And thus it says: [2Sam.1.1]   וכן הוא אומר

And David stayed in Ziklag   וישב דוד בצקלג

two days.   ימים שנים

3

And one should not besiege a city ואין צרים על עיר

beginning on the Sabbath,   בתחילה בשבת

but three days before the Sabbath. אלא קודם לשבת שלשה ימים

But if it is surrounded   ואם הקיפוה

and the Sabbath ensues,   ואירעה שבת להיות

the Sabbath does not interrupt the war. אין השבת מפסקת מלחמתה

4

This is one of the three sayings זה אחד משלשה דברים

which Shammai the Elder interpreted. שדרש שמיי הזקן

One may not sail a ship   אין מפליגים את הספינה

to the Mediterranean   לים הגדול

except three days before the Sabbath. אלא קודם לשבת שלשה ימים

Notes:
 The other two sayings of Shammai are difficult to identify with certainty, but the fact that 3 is attributed to Shammai in tErub.3.7 (I.2.12) suggests that 2 is also from Shammai.
 The anonymous exegesis (1) is earlier than Shammai's (2) which depends on it (see below).

Analysis:
 1. The plural could mean two, but "many" indicates at least three. This agrees with the usual assumption that a simple plural is two or more (cf. I.4.9).
 2. Shammai is usually strict about the Sabbath and might be expected to say "six days", to give the maximum opportunity for ending the siege before the Sabbath. However instead he gives support to 1 by saying that the first three days are taken up with peace negotiations.
 David was not suing for peace, but waited for two days while a battle raged. It is probably assumed that David went up to Hebron on the third day (2Sam.1.2ff.; 2.1ff.) where he was welcomed and crowned as king even though he had been expecting resistance (compare "Shall I go up?...Go up" in 2Sam.2.1 with the same language in 2Sam.5.19 and 1King.22.6,12,15). David's wait is therefore seen as rewarded with peace.
 David's example becomes a Precedent, based on the Nomological assumption that events in Scripture are records of divine case law.
 It is unlikely that the exegesis was added later, because the ruling mirrors the uncertainty of the text concerning "two or three days".

3. The exegesis for this is preserved elsewhere (I.2.12).

4. The term שׁרד ("interpreted") suggests that this too was supported by exegesis which has been lost.

I.2.12. *tErub.3.7:* (bShab.19a; Sifré Deut.203)

Our Rabbis taught:	ת״ר
One does not besiege a Gentile city	אין צרין על עיר של גוים
less than three days before Sabbath	פחות משלשה ימים קודם לשבת
but if one starts even on Sabbath	ואם התחילו אפי׳ בשבת
one does not break off.	אין מפסיקין
And thus Shammai the Elder used to interpret:	וכך היה שמיי הזקן דורש
Until subdued [Deut.20.20]	עד רדתה
even on Sabbath.	ואפילו בשבת

Notes:

This provides exegetical support for the last of the three rules in Sifré Deut.203 (I.2.11). Some MSS read 'Hillel the Elder', but the more difficult reading is preferable.

Analysis:

The Peshat reading of Deut.20 implies that a siege may continue through a Sabbath.

I.2.13. *yPes.6.1 (33a):* (cf tNeg.1.16)

For three things	על ג׳ דברים
Hillel came from Babylon.	עלה הלל מבבל
1ia	
He is clean [Lev.13.37]	טהור הוא
One might argue: He is free,	יכול יפטר
and he goes to his [place].	וילך לו
1ib	
Scripture teaches: [Lev.13.37]	ת״ל
And the priest shall declare him *clean.*	וטהרו הכהן
1iia	
If the priest declares him clean	אי וטיהרו הכהן
one might argue:	יכול
If the priest says of the unclean:	אם אמר הכהן על טמא
He is cleansed, then he will be clean.	טהור יהא טהור
1iib	
Scripture teaches: [Lev.13.37]	ת״ל
He is clean .	טהו׳ הוא
and the priest will declare him clean.	וטהרו הכהן
For this came Hillel from Babylon.	על זה עלה הלל מבבל

2a

One text says: [Deut.16.2]	כתוב אחד אומר
And you shall sacrifice the Passover	וזבח׳ פסח
to YHWH your God	ליי אלהיך
[from] the flock and the herd.	צאן ובקר
and one text says: [Ex.12.5]	וכת׳ אחד או׳
From the sheep and from the goats	מן הכבשי׳ ומן העזים
you shall take.	תקחו
How is this?	הא כיצד

2b

The flock is for the paschal sacrifice	צאן לפסח
and the flock or herd is for Hagigah.	וצאן ובקר לחגיגה

3a

One text says: [Deut.16.8]	כתוב אח׳ אומ׳
Six days you shall eat unleavened bread,	ששת ימים תאכל מצות
and one text says: [Ex.12.15]	וכתוב אחד אומר
Seven days you shall eat unleavened	שבעת ימים מצות תאכלו
bread.	
How is this?	הא כיצד

3b

Six from the new [corn after Omer]	ששה מן החדש
and seven from the old.	ושבעה מן הישן

Notes:

Schwarz (1913:76) suggested that these exegeses are pre-Hillel, because Hillel came to Judea to discover whether or not they were accepted by the scholars in Jerusalem. This accords with the suggestion at I.2.8 that Judah b.Durtai learned the second exegesis from Shmaiah and Abtalion.

Analysis:

1. The phrases "He is clean" and "The priest will declare him clean" seem to be synonymous. This breaks the Nomological rule of No Redundancy, so Hillel demonstrates that both phrases are necessary.

1i. If it only said "He is clean" he might think that he need not present himself to a priest.

1ii. If it only said "The priest will declare him clean" one might think that the priest's declaration was valid whatever the physical facts of the case (cf. Montefiore & Loewe 1974:153f. for examples of non-sacerdotalism). The Order is therefore important: God heals before the priest pronounces.

The text is not Lev.13.17 (as Neusner suggests, 1971 I:166), where the phrases are almost identical but in reverse order.

2 & 3. Contradictions between two texts are resolved without using a third, on the Nomological assumption that the perfect Law has no contradictions"

I.2.14. *Sifra Taz.Per.9.16 (Weiss 66d-67a):*

The baldness is healed. [Lev.13.37]	נרפא הנתק

Hillel says:	הילל אומר
Not he whose baldness	לא שנתק
balded within baldness	נתק בתוך נתק

Notes:

This Hillelite saying is typically obscure but unlike I.2.19 & 20 it is dependent on the exegesis. The links with I.2.13 (identical text and subject, and the phrase "Because of this matter Hillel came from Babylon" which follows) further suggest that the exegesis is original.

Analysis:

Lev.13.37 teaches that new hair is a sign that leprosy is healed, but Hillel points out that if new baldness starts in the middle of this healed area, then this is a new outbreak and he is unclean again. The exposition is Peshat, and although it deals with a case not specifically mentioned, the principle is present in the context (cf. v7).

I.2.15. *Sifré Deut.113*

(Mid.Tan.Deut.34.2; mShebi.10.3; mGit.4.3; yShebi.10.2; bGit.36a)

[Whatever is yours]	[ואשר יהיה לך]
[which is] with your brother	את אחיך
your hand should release. [Deut.15.3]	תשמט ידך
but not he who delivers his bonds	ולא המוסר שטרותיו
to the court.	לבית דין

Hence it it said:	מיכן אמרו
Hillel ordained the Prosbul,	התקין הלל פרוסבול
for the sake of 'the order of the world'.	מפני תיקון העולם

For he saw the people	שראה את העם
that they refrained from lending	שנמנעו מלהלוות
to each other	זה את זה
and transgressed that	ועברו על מה
which is written in Torah.	שכתוב בתורה
He promptly ordained the Prosbul.	עמד והתקין פרוסבול

Notes:

Hillel recognised that the seventh year debt cancellation restricted loans to the poor, so he allowed loans to be made via the court which were not liable to this law. The origin of the term 'Prosbul' is uncertain but may come from προς βουλη βουλευτων, 'before the assembly of counsellors', or simply προσβολη, 'delivery' (J.M. Greenstone 1905).

Neusner (1971 I:218) suggests that "ordered ... order" is a separate non-exegetical derivation of the Prosbul from a pun, but this was a normal way of referring to a Taqanah (cf. I.4.16).

The attribution of the exegesis is suspect, but if it were later than 70 CE one would expect a Limitation argument based on the superfluous אפס ('except') which follows in Deut.15.4.

Analysis:

Hillel reads the text Nomologically pointing out (as W. Horbury suggested verbally) that strictly speaking it applies only to what is "yours" [לך] and not to that which belongs to the court [לב״ד]. This is used to justify what was originally a Pragmatic argument.

I.2.16. *Sifra Shem.Par.9.5 (Weiss 56a)*:

(cf. yPes.6.1; tNed.6.5; yNed.10.9; bNed.75b)

And anyone touching their corpse is unclean. [Lev.11.36]	ונוגע בנבלתם יטמא

1b

Hillel says:	הילל אומר
Even if they are in the midst of water.	אפילו הם בתוך המים

1ai

For I might say because:	שהייתי אומר הואיל
The earth elevates	והארץ מעלה
the unclean from their uncleanness	את הטמאים מטומאתן
and the Miqveh elevates	והמקוה מעלה
the unclean from their uncleanness	את הטמאי׳ מטומאתן

1aii

Just as the earth protects	מה הארץ מצלת
the clean from uncleanness	את הטהורים מלטמא
so also the Miqveh will protect	אף המקוה יציל
the clean from becoming unclean.	את הטהורים מליטמא

1b

Scripture teaches: [Lev.11.36]	תלמוד לומר
And anyone touching their corpse is unclean	ונוגע בנבלתם יטמא
– even if they are in the midst of water.	אפילו הם בתוך המים

Notes:

The debate concerns a corpse (such as a dead insect) which falls into a Miqveh (a ritual immersion pool). According to TgJon this is the subject of Lev.11.36. Hillel says that the corpse is still defiling even if it is surrounded by water.

The exegesis is probably genuine because the form is similar to I.2.14, and the saying makes no sense without the text.

The anonymous explanation following Hillel's exegesis has been added later in order to supply a possible argument which Hillel can refute, then Hillel's exegesis is repeated so that he does refute it. This is the reason for the strange numbering given to the arguments (1b, 1a, 1b). This anonymous argument is undatable.

The parallel in tNed and Talmudim mention only the Miqveh:

Miqveh proves it,	מקוה יוכיח
for the unclean is elevated by it	שמעלה את הטמאים
from its uncleanness	מטומאהן

but the clean is not protected
from becoming unclean.

ואין מציל את הטהורים
מלטמא

This suggests that the the argument in 1a which Hillel was supposed to refute was originally something like:

For I might say because:
Just as the Miqveh elevates
the unclean from their uncleanness
so also the Miqveh will protect
the clean from becoming unclean.

שהייתי אומר הואיל
מה המקוה מעלה
את הטמאי׳ מטומאתן
אף המקוה יציל
את הטהורים מליטמא

To this was added the comparison with 'earth' in order to add weight to the idea that Miqveh protects the clean.

Analysis:

1ai. It was probably a common belief that the uncleanness of a corpse was removed by the earth and that it rose to the top of the soil. This is implied by the fact that uncleanness is contracted by walking over a grave, but not if boards are laid over the grave with a gap between them (cf. mPar.3.3) or if it is covered with paving stones (mOhol.18.5). It is perhaps also seen in the principle that uncleanness travels only up or down in soil, and never sideways (mOhol.15.7).

This compares well with Miqvaot where one could see dirt floating away on the surface. This may be one reason for rabbinic rules that a Miqvah only cleanses if it is being replenished constantly (mMik.1.4,8), because then the uncleanness flows away with the surface water.

1aii. The comparison between a grave and a Miqvah is now applied to the question in hand. The argument is not made clear, but the form (מה ... אף...) is that of a Heqesh, Gezerah Shavah or Qal vaHomer. This is probably a Qal vaHomer, though some elements are missing, so the tradition may be defective. The argument is probably:

If a grave prevents uncleanness spreading to clean things, then surely a Miqveh, *which is constructed to make things clean,* also prevents uncleanness spreading.
The italics mark a stage in the argument which has been omitted.

A grave stops uncleanness spreading because although graveyard uncleanness spreads vertically, it does not spread horizontally, even if rain washes the soil on to other land (mOhol.17.4). Similarly therefore, water in a Mikvah might be expected to stop uncleanness spreading.

1b. Hillel's exegesis is based on a Peshat reading of the Context: "an immersion pool [מקוה] is clean – but that touching the corpse is unclean", and backed up by the principle that "that which is in its midst [בתוכן] shall be unclean" (v33).

This context is ignored by Neusner (1971 I:213) who assumes that Hillel is quoting v24. However the text there reads . . . הנגע and ונ(ר)גע occurs only in v36.

I.2.17. *tBer.2.21; 6.24:* (yBer.9.5; bBer.63a)
tBer.2.21:
Hillel the Elder said:

הלל הזקן או׳

1

Do not be seen naked,
[and] do not be seen clothed.

אל תראה ערום
אל תראה לבוש

2

Do not be seen standing
and do not be seen sitting.

אל תראה עומד
ואל תראה יושב

3

Do not be seen jesting
and do not be seen weeping.
From the place where it says: [Qoh.3.4f.]
A time to laugh and a time to weep.
A time to embrace
and a time to refrain from embracing.
tBer.6.24:
Hillel the Elder said:

אל תראה צוחק
ואל תראה בוכה
משם שנ'
עת לשחוק ועת לבכות
עת לחבוק
ועת לרחוק מחבק

הלל הזקן או'

4

At the time of gathering dispense
[and] at the time of dispensing gather.

בשעת מכנסין פזר
בשעת מפזרין כנס

5

At the time that you see that the Torah
is precious in all Israel
and everyone rejoices in it,
you be dispensing it.
As it is written: [Prov.11.24]
There are those dispensing
and gaining more.

בשעה שאתה רואה שהתורה
חביבה על כל ישראל
והכל שמחין בה
את תהי מפזר בה
שנ'
יש מפזר
ונוסף עוד

6

At the time that you see that the Torah
is being forgotten in Israel
and no-one is attending to it
you be gathering it.
As it is written: [Ps.119.126]
A time to work for the Lord.

בשעה שאתה רואה שהתורה
משתכחת מישראל
ואין הכל משגיחין עליה
את הוי מכנס בה
שנ'
עת לעשות לה'

Notes:

These two sets of three sayings by Hillel probably belong together, as Neusner suggests (1971 I:228). He summarises their message as: Do as they do, except with regard to Torah. The scholar should not separate himself needlessly from the community by doing opposite to everyone else. However, with regard to Torah, when it is precious, the scholar should be free with it and when it is discarded the scholar should preserve it.

Neusner also suggests that the proof texts were added later, and there is no reason to disagree. The first text is particularly suspect. It does not match the vocabulary of the sayings and the order of the phrases has been altered to fit the traditional order of Hillel's sayings (see analysis below).

The texts of sayings 5 & 6 fit better but these sayings are probably themselves later commentaries on the two halves of saying 4.

The separate authorship of the latter exegeses and the first is perhaps suggested by the fact that Qoh.3.5a ("time to throw stones, time to gather [כנוס] stones") is not used to illustrate sayings 4 to 6.

Analysis:

1. This should probably be understood as "Do not be noticed to be clothed when others are naked (such as in the bath house) or to be naked when others are clothed."

2. Similarly, do not stand when others sit and vice versa.

3. Perhaps Qoh.3 is being understood as 'do all things at the same time as others'. This may not be the original sense of the passage, but is regarded here as its primary meaning, so the interpretation is based on a Peshat reading of the text.

However the text has been made to fit the sayings as closely as possible, so the particular phrases are probably referred to rather than the general tenor of the text. The order of "laugh" and "weep" has been reversed to fit the order of the sayings, and the intervening "mourn", "dance", "throw" and "gather" have been omitted. The "embrace" phrases are probably included to refer to saying 1.

4. This enigmatic saying is probably Hillel's original saying, which was later expounded by means of the two sayings in 5 & 6.

5. This expounds 'when they gather, scatter'. In Proverbs the analogy of scattering seed is applied to liberality in general. The use of this text is therefore not based on Mashal or Symbol but is a Peshat understanding of the proverb.

6. This expounds 'when they scatter, gather'. Ps.119.126 continues: "they have made void thy law", so the Context is probably in mind, and the reading is Peshat.

R. Loewe has suggested to me that this may also be related to the exegesis of עשה in Gen.12.5 as 'recruiting' souls to YHWH by Abraham (e.g. ARNa.12.6; GenR.39.14 etc.).

I.2.18. *tPis.4.13f.*: (yPes.6.1; yShab.19.1; bPes.66ab)

One occasion	פעם אחת
the fourteenth happened	חל ארבעה עשר
to be on a Sabbath	להיות בשבת
They asked Hillel the Elder:	שאלו את הלל הזקן
Does Passover override the Sabbath?	פסח מהו שידחה את השבת
He said to them:	אמ׳ להם
Do we have [only] one Passover	וכי פסח אחד יש לנו
in a year which overrides the Sabbath?	בשנה שדוחה את השבת
We have more than three hundred Passovers	הרבה משלש מאות פסחים יש לנו
in a year and they override the Sabbath.	בשנה ודוחין את השבת
1a	
The whole temple court joined him.	חברו עליו כל העזרה
He said to them:	אמ׳ להם
The Tamid is a collective offering	תמיד קרבן צבור
and Passover is a collective offering.	ופסח קרבן צבור
Just as Tamid is a collective offering	מה תמיד קרבן צבור
and overrides the Sabbath,	ודוחה את השבת

so also Passover is a collective offering	אף פסח קרבן צבור
[and] overrides the Sabbath.	דוחה את השבת

2a

Another thing:	דבר אחר
It is said concerning Tamid:	נאמר בתמיד
Its appointed time, [Num.28.2]	מועדו
and it is said concerning Passover:	ונאמ׳ בפסח
Its appointed time. [Num.9.2]	מועדו
Just as Tamid	מה תמיד
concerning which is said: *Its appointed time*	שנאמ׳ בו מועדו
overrides the Sabbath	דוחה את השבת
so also the paschal sacrifice	אף פסח
concerning which is said: *Its appointed time*	שנ׳ בו מועדו
overrides the Sabbath.	דוחה את השבת

3a

And further [by] Qal vaHomer:	ועוד קל וחומר
And just as Tamid,	ומה תמיד
concerning which one is not liable	שאין הייבין עליו
to be cut off,	כרת
overrides the Sabbath,	דוחה את השבת
[so also] Passover	פסח
concerning which one is liable	שחייבין עליו
to be cut off,	כרת
is it not logical	אינו דין
that it overrides the Sabbath.	שידחה את השבת

And further,	ועוד
I have received from my masters:	מקובלני מרבותי
that Passover overrides the Sabbath.	שפסח דוחה את השבת

And not the first Passover [only]	ולא פסח ראשון
but [also] the second Passover	אלא פסח שני
and not the collective Passover [only]	ולא פסח צבור
but [also] the individual passover.	אלא פסח יחיד

They said to him:	אמרו לו
What will be [done] for the people	מה יהא על העם
who have not brought knives	שלא הביאו סכינין
and Passover offerings to the Sanctuary?	ופסחין למקדש

He said to them:	אמ׳ להם
Let them rest;	הניחו להם
the holy spirit is on them.	רוח הקדש עליהם

If they are not prophets	אם אין נביאין הן
they are sons of prophets.	בני נביאין הן

What did Israel do in that hour?	מה עשו ישראל באותה שעה
He whose Passover was a lamb	מי שפסחו טלה
hid [his knife] in the wool,	טמנו בצמרו
a kid, he tied it between the horns,	גדי קשרו בין קרניו
and they brought knives	והביאו סכינין
and Passover offerings to the Sanctuary,	ופסחים למקדש
and slew the Passover offerings.	ושחטו את פסחיהן

On that day	בו ביום
they appointed Hillel as Nasi	מינו את הלל נשיא
and they used to learn from him	והיה מורה להם
concerning Passover Halakah.	בהלכות פסח

The Talmudim add refutations to Hillel's arguments:

yPes.6.1 (33a):
Y1b

The Heqesh which you said,	היקש שאמרת
it has a refutation:	יש לו תשובה
No. If you say thus concerning Tamid	לא אם אמרת בתמיד שכן
which has a limit,	יש לו קיצבה
will you say [the same] concerning Passover	תאמר בפסח
which does not have a limit?	שאין לו קצבה

Y3b

The Qal vaHomer which you said,	מ"ו שאמרת
it has a refutation:	יש לו תשובה
No. If you say concerning Tamid	לא אם אמרת בתמיד
which is a most holy thing,	שהוא קדשי קדשים
will you say [the same] concerning Passover	תאמר בפסח
which is a lesser holy thing?	שהוא קדשים קלין

Y2b

The Gezerah Shavah which you said:	גזירה שוה שאמרת
No man can propound	שאין אדם דן
a Gezerah Shavah on his own [authority].	גזירה שוה מעצמו

bPes.66a:
2a

It has been said:	אמר מר
It is said: *Its appointed time* [Num.9.2]	נאמר מועדו
concerning Passover	בפסח
and it is said: *Its appointed time* [Num.28.2]	ונאמר מועדו
concerning Tamid.	בתמיד

Just as *Its appointed time*	מה מועדו
being said concerning Tamid	האמור בתמיד
overrides the Sabbath,	דוחתה את השבת
so also *Its appointed time*	אף מועדו
being said concerning Passover	האמור בפסח
overrides the Sabbath.	דוחה שבת

B2b

And Tamid itself,	ותמיד גופיה
whence [do we know that]	מנלן
it overrides Sabbath?	דרחי שבת
Shall we say:	אילימא
Because it is written concerning it:	משום דכתיב ביה
Its appointed time?	במועדו
Passover likewise,	פסח נמי
there is written concerning it:	הא כתיב ביה
Its appointed time.	מועדו
But *Its appointed time*	אלא מועדו
does not have the alleged connotation here;	לא משמע ליה הכא
likewise *Its Appointed time*	נמי מועדו
does not have the alleged connotation [there].	לא משמע ליה
But the verse says: [Num.28.10]	אלא אמר קרא
The burnt offering of every Sabbath	עולת שבת בשבתו
on top of the continual burnt offering,	על עולת התמיד
implying the burnt offering of the Tamid	מכלל [עולה] דתמיד
is offered on the Sabbath.	קרבה בשבת

3a

It has been said:	אמר מר
And further, Qal vaHomer:	ועוד ק"ו
And just as Tamid	ומה תמיד
which is not punishable by cutting-off	שאין עונש כרת
overrides the Sabbath,	דוחה את השבת
Passover,	פסח
which is punishable by cutting-off	שענוש כרת
is it not logical	אינו דין
that it overrides the Sabbath.	שדוחה את השבת

B3b

This can be refuted:	איכא למיפרך
Just as Tamid which is thus:	מה לתמיד שכן
a [daily] constant and a holocaust	תדיר וכליל
[but the paschal sacrifice is neither].	
He said to them a Qal vaHomer first	ק"ו אמר להו ברישא
and they refuted it,	ופרכוה
and then he said to them	והדר אמר להו
a Gezerah Shavah.	גזירה שוה

But since he had received	וכי מאחר דגמר
a Gezerah Shavah,	גזירה שוה
why did he need a Qal vaHomer?	ק"ו למה לי
But he was adopting their own standpoint.	אלא לדידהו קאמר להו
It is well you do not receive	בשלמא גזירה שוה לא גמריתו
a Gezerah Shavah	
for a man cannot argue	דאין אדם דן
a Gezerah Shavah on his own [authority],	גזירה שוה מעצמו
but a Qal vaHomer	אלא ק"ו
which a man can argue on his own [authority]	דאדם דן מעצמו
you should have judged acceptable!	איבעי לכו למידן
They said to him:	אמרו ליה
It is a refuted Qal vaHomer.	קל וחומר פריכא הוא

Related to this tradition is the list of seven middoth (rules of exegesis) attributed to Hillel. These are preserved in three widely varying forms:

tSanh.7.11:	
Seven things	שבעה דברים
Hillel the Elder expounded	דרש הילל הזקן
before the elders of Pathyra:	לפני זקני פתירא
1 Light and Heavy,	קל וחומר
2 and Equal decree	וגזירה שוה
3 and Building a family	ובניין אב
both [from] one text	וכתוב אחד
and two texts,	ושני כתובין
4 and General and Particular,	וכלל ופרט
5 and Particular and General,	ופרט וכלל
6 and As is similar to it	וכיוצא בו
from another place,	ממקום אחר
7 and Something learned from its context.	ודבר הלמד מעניינו
These seven Rules	אילו שבע מידות
Hillel the Elder expounded	דרש הילל הזקן
before the Sons of Pathyra.	לפני בני פתירא

ARNa.37.10	
7 Rules	ז' מדות
Hillel the Elder expounded	דרש הילל הזקן
before the sons of Bathyra.	לפני בני בתירה
These are thus:	אלו הן
1 Light and heavy,	ק"ו
2 and Equal decree,	וגזרה שוה
3 Building a family	בנין אב
from one text,	(מכתוב אחד
4 and Building a family	ובנין אב

from two texts,	(משני כתובים
5 From general and particular	מכלל ופרט
and from particular and general	ומפרט וכלל
6 As is similar to it	כיוצא בו
in another place,	במקום אחר
7 Something learned from its context.	דבר הלמד מעניינו
These seven rules	אלו שבע מדות
Hillel the Elder expounded	שדרש הילל הזקן
before the sons of Bathyra.	לפני בני בתירה

Sifra Introduction (Weiss 3ab):

Hillel the Elder expounded	הלל הזקן דרש
seven Rules	שבע מדות
before the Elders of Bathyra:	לפני זקני בתירה
1 Light and heavy,	קל וחומר
2 Equal decree,	וגזרה שוה
3 and Two texts,	ושני כתובים
4 and General and particular,	וכלל ופרט
6 and As is similar to it	וכיוצא בו
in another place,	במקום אחר
7 and Something learned from its context.	ודבר למד מעניינו
These are the seven Rules	אלו שבע מדות
which Hillel the Elder expounded	שדרש הלל הזקן
before the elders of Bathyra.	לפני זקני בתירה

Notes:

When Passover fell on a Sabbath, only Hillel knew whether paschal sacrifice should be postponed or not. He answers first from exegesis, using Heqesh, Qal vaHomer and Gezerah Shavah, and then from tradition.

Hillel is then asked concerning those who neglected to carry their knives to the Temple on Friday, because they could not carry a burden on the Sabbath. He gives no answer, but the people know what to do: they let the animal carry the knife.

The tradition in Tosephta is unsatisfactory in several respects, which the Talmudim attempt to clear up.

Why does Hillel not answer the problem of the knives? The Talmudim add Hillel's reply: "I have heard this law, but I have forgotten it", and the Amoraim explain that this was caused by pride.

Why does Hillel use Heqesh, which is not in his list of seven middoth, and is therefore not authorised for exegesis? The Babylonian Talmud solves this problem by omitting the Heqesh exegesis.

Why does Hillel use exegetical proofs as well as tradition? Both Talmudim suggest that this is because his proofs were unconvincing, and they add the refutations. The Jerusalem Talmud also appears to suggest that he momentarily forgot this halakah as well, saying after his proofs: "May [evil] come upon me, thus I heard from Shemaiah and Abtalion".

Why does Hillel use fallacious exegeses at all? This question is not directly addressed by the Talmudim, but the separate tradition concerning his seven middoth may suggest that he was using these examples to teach exegesis to the Bene Bathyra.

Dating the tradition of Hillel's dispute with the Bene Bathyra is very difficult. It is certainly older than the list of seven middoth because if this dispute had been written as a story to illustrate the introduction of his list, one would expect clearer parallels. Hillel used only three exegeses in the dispute, only two of which are in the list and only one of which is named in the oldest version (Qal vaHomer, named in Tosefta). Rab's saying immediately following bPes.66b does not help to date the tradition because it does not relate to the story itself.

Dating the list of seven middoth is equally difficult, but it is likely to be old. The list itself is older than the introduction and conclusion, and varies considerably in its three sources, even with regard to the number of middoth. The introduction and conclusion in Tosefta contradict each other ("Elders of Pathyra" and "Sons of Pathyra") so, as Neusner (1971 I:241) suggests, the tradition in Tosefta already indicates more than one level of editing. The change to "Sons" or "Bene" was probably to emphasise the connection between the list and Hillel's dispute with the Bene Bathyra. Further editing occurred in Sifra and ARN where "Pathyra" is changed to the more common "Bathyra".

Hillel's dispute is historically believable. The Bene Bathyra were probably Temple officials, because Judah b.Bathyra I (of the generation just before 70 CE) was in contact with Temple authorities and appears to have been responsible for collecting Temple funds in northern Babylonia (Neusner 1965:43ff.). "Pathyra" may be based on the Syriac word 'table', which came to be used for money changers (Neusner 1971 I:242).

The Bene Bathyra were not Sadducees. Judah b.Bathyra I was certainly not a Sadducee because he argued on behalf of the Water Libation ceremony during Tabernacles which the Sadducees disagreed with (I.2.43), and his most often quoted halakah, that gifts which are not specified for priests or Temple fall to the Temple, is contrary to the teachings of the priests (I.2.41). Joshua and Simeon b.Bathyra of the next generation are quoted with respect by the rabbis and Simeon appears to accept the law of Erub (mSanh.16.3), so they too were not Sadducees.

If they were not Sadducees, why did they not know the halakah concerning Passover on a Sabbath, which occurred on average every seven years? A. Guttmann suggested (1950:464) that the Sadducees had recently allowed the Pharisees to rule in Temple matters and that their halakah in these matters had been neglected. More recently (1970:59) he suggested that the Bene Bathyra were put temporarily in charge of the Temple after Herod had massacred all the other Jewish leaders, which would explain why they were willing to hand over the Nasi'ship to Hillel when he proved himself a competent scholar. Their favour with Herod may be because they founded the fortified village of Bathyra at his request, in return for which they were free of taxation (Ant.17.23–31 [2.1–2]).

The strongest argument against a late date for this tradition is that it does not show Hillel at his best. He is asked concerning two halakot, neither of which he answers well. He answers the first by using exegetical methods, including Heqesh which is not authorised by his own list of middoth, and although these are accepted by his ignorant questioners, they are in fact fallacious. The second question he cannot answer at all so he waits to see what the common people will do. In some later sources Hillel is replaced by R. Josiah (second century – cf. A. Guttmann 1950:462f.), presumably because it was difficult to believe that Hillel could be such a poor exegete.

It is argued below that Hillel's 'poor' showing as an exegete was because the rules of exegesis developed after his time.

Therefore the three exegeses of Hillel will be assumed to date from before 70 CE, though the refutations are certainly much later.

Analysis:

Hillel's exegeses all depend on similarities between Pesach (Passover sacrifice) and Tamid (daily burnt offering). The "300 Pesachs" per year which override the Sabbath include the two daily offerings, the two additional Sabbath offerings and various additional festival offerings. All these sacrifices override the Sabbath, so why not also Pesach?

1a. Heqesh: The Daily sacrifices and the Paschal sacrifices are similar in that they are both sacrifices made by the whole community. Because they are similar in this respect, they are also similar with respect to overriding the Sabbath.

Heqesh produces a link between two things by showing that they can share a predicate which is often ascribed to both things in Scripture, but in this instance the common predicate is the noun "community" [צִיבּוּר] which does not occur in Scripture.

This type of argument is open to abuse because the common predicate may have nothing to do with the proposed link between the two things, so later rabbis ruled that Heqesh could only be used to support received Tradition (Mielziner 1968 : 155). In this case it is difficult, at first, to see what connection there is between the predicate "community" and the question of whether or not it over-rides the Sabbath, and one is tempted to dismiss Hillel's argument as mere sophistry. However Hillel was probably pointing to the fact that a community sacrifice is one which is carried out on behalf of the people, so that the people are actively involved in the sacrifice.

A paschal sacrifice, brought by an individual on behalf of a family group, was killed by that individual, and then the blood was caught by a priest and thrown against the altar. The Daily Sacrifice was carried out wholly by priests, but because it was on behalf of all the people Hillel would argue that the people are just as actively involved as they are in the Paschal sacrifice.

This principle, that the lay people are actively involved in the Daily Sacrifices, is the basis of a dispute with the Sadducees (I.3.14). The Pharisees would not allow Tamid to be paid for by a rich individual, but demanded that the cost should come from the half-shekels given by every Israelite, so that the sacrifice was shared by the whole Israelite community. Hillel's argument linking the Tamid and the Paschal Sacrifice may have won this Pharisee-Sadducee debate, because the Pharisees celebrated this victory during Passover.

Y1b. Only the Palestinian Talmud includes a refutation to this argument. A refutation to Heqesh is constructed by finding a difference between the two things being compared. For this difference to be significant it should be related to the similarity which has been proposed.

The difference concerns the number of sacrifices which can be brought. For the Tamid there was a fixed number laid down in Torah, but the number of Pesachs depended on the number of families meeting for the feast. This difference is related to the concept of a 'collective' sacrifice, because the normal distinction between a 'collective' [צִיבּוּר] and an 'individual' [יְחִיד] sacrifice would have been whether or not the number was limited.

2a. Gezerah Shavah: The term "Its appointed time" [מוֹעֲדוֹ] is used of both the Tamid and Paschal sacrifices, so the precepts dependent on this term in the one text can also be applied to the other text. The Tamid has to be offered 'at its appointed time' irrespective of whether it is a Sabbath, so this also applies to Paschal sacrifices.

Hillel may have regarded the method used here as identical to 1a, because the same formula is used:

Just as ... So also ...... ‎מה... ‎אף.

Neither method is named in Tosefta, and there was probably little or no difference between Gezerah Shavah and Heqesh at the time of Hillel (see I.1.5d)

Gezerah Shavah is particularly open to abuse, because two scriptures can be linked by any common word which may be completely unrelated to the subject of the debate. However both this term and the dispute can be said to be concerned with the correct time at which to offer Pesach.

Y2b. The Jerusalem Talmud gives no refutation except a reminder that one cannot establish a halakah solely on the basis of an innovative Gezerah Shavah. Because this method was open to misuse, it had to be supported by another method or by a received tradition (Mielziner 1968:151). In the Jerusalem Talmud this is the last argument, so that Hillel has produced it in support of his previous two. Those two are refuted, so this argument is invalid.

The Babylonian Talmud does not change the order, and omits the Heqesh exegesis, so this Gezerah Shavah is the first argument. The Amoraim (after B3b) criticise Hillel severely for putting this argument first because it can only be used in support of other arguments or tradition.

However these criticisms in the Talmudim may be unfair because there is no evidence for this restriction in Tannaitic times (A. Guttman 1950:467, but cf. A. Schwartz 1897:191).

B2b. The Babylonian Talmud has a refutation based on yet another restriction which was made on the use of Gezerah Shavah. The word used to link the two texts should be superfluous in at least one and preferably both texts (Mielziner 1968:150f.). The thinking behind this was presumably the nomological assumption that the divine legislator had left a seemingly superflous word in order to be used for Gezerah Shavah.

The refutation argues that if "Its appointed time" is superflous, it is not this phrase which teaches that the Tamid should override the Sabbath. Rather, this is taught several verses later in v10, where "Its appointed time" does not occur.

There is no evidence for this further restriction in Tannaitic times, so it is doubtful whether Hillel would have known that he had made an 'error'.

3a. Qal vaHomer. It is more important to keep the Passover (the neglect of which will cut one off from Israel) than the Daily offering (which carries no such threat). Therefore, if the Daily offering overrides the Sabbath, then the Passover certainly does so.

Y3b. The refutation for Qal vaHomer consists in showing that the greater is the lesser in some respects, and vice versa. Hillel has argued that Pesach is more important than Tamid, so the refutation must show the reverse.

The factor chosen to establish this should ideally be related to the factor which was used in the original comparison, which in this case was the punishment for not keeping the sacrifice.

The Jerusalem Talmud points out that Tamid has greater sanctity than Pesach. This is related to the punishment for not keeping the offering because one might expect a greater punishment for a sacrifice of greater sanctity.

B3b. The Babylonian Talmud points out that Tamid is greater than Pesach in that it is offered continuously (not once a year like Pesach) and is offered completely as a burnt offering (unlike Pesach which is mostly eaten). The latter point is similar to this refutation in the Jerusalem Talmud, because the sanctity of a sacrifice depends on how and where the offering was consumed or eaten. The former point is similar to the Jerusalem Talmud refutation of Heqesh (Y1b).

An unbiased umpire might agree that Hillel's first and third exegeses have been successfully refuted, but his opponents should be disqualified for changing the rules when refuting the second. All three however illustrate the difficulty of establishing halakah purely on the basis of these methods.

I.2.19. *tSukk.4.3:* (bSukk.53a)

Hillel the Elder said: הלל הזקן או׳

1

To the place which my heart loves   למקום שלבי אוהב
to there my feet lead me.   לשם רגליי מוליכות אותי

2

If you will come to my house   אם אתה תבוא לביתי
I will come to your house.   אני אבא לביתיך
If you will not come to my house   אם אתה לא תבוא לביתי
I will not come to your house.   אני לא אבוא לביתיך

3

As it is said: [Ex.20.24[21]]   שנ׳
In every place where   בכל המקום אשר
I cause my name to be remembered   אזכיר את שמי
I will come to you and bless you.   אבא אליך ובירכתיך

Notes:

The Tosefta has placed these sayings in the context of the celebrations of Sukkot in Temple times. Even without this context Neusner (1971 I:235) argues that it is evident that the Temple is the main subject but that this does not necessarily date it before 70CE. However the obscurity of these two sayings suggests an early date.

The scripture may not be integral, and may have been added later. It appears to presuppose that the Temple is not the only subject because it is taken from one of the few scriptures which can be taken to speak of multiple centres of worship.

Therefore the saying may have originated with Hillel, but the scripture was probably added later. The text does not confirm the saying, but gives it a new message; that YHWH will come to every synagogue or home where He is worshipped. This message fits the post-70 situation far better than Hillel's Jerusalem.

There is a possible parallel with Jn.14.1,13f. ("In my Father's House are many dwellings...If a man loves me...we will make our dwelling with him") which may have Hillel's saying in mind.

Analysis:

1. If you love the Temple, you will visit it.
2. If you visit the Temple, God will visit your home.
3. This scripture does not confirm saying 2, because it says that YHWH will come to the place where he is worshipped, wherever that is. This suggests that whoever added this scripture regarded the synagogue or home as the normal place of worship, rather than the Temple where God was expected to be present already.

This is probably a Peshat interpretation, because "in every place" can naturally imply a plurality of places. This understanding seems to be reflected in the comments (ad loc.) by Nachmanides (the Tabernacle and the Temple) and Ibn Ezra (Shiloh and Nob), although Rashi finds an allusion to the pronunciation of the divine name, and so restricts the reference to the Temple.

I.2.20. *ySukk.5.4 (55bc)*: (bSukk.53a; ARNa.12; ARNb.27)

1

Hillel the Elder,	הלל הזקן
when he used to observe them	כד הוה חמי לון
acting boisterously	עברין בפחז
he used to say to them:	הוה אמ' לון
If we are here, who is here?	דאנן הכא מאן הכא
And of our acclamation does He have need?	ולקילוסן הוא צריך

And it is written: [Dan.7.10]	והכתיב
A thousand thousands serve him	אלף אלפין ישמשוניה
and a myriad myriads	וריבו' ריבוון
stand before him.	קדמוהי יקומון

2

When he used to observe them	כד הוה חמי לון
acting correctly	עבדין בכושר
he used to say:	הוה אמר
If we are not here, who is here?	די לא נן הכא מאן הכא
Although there is before him	שאע"פי שיש לפניו
much acclamation	כמה קילוסין
the acclamations are precious,	חביב הוא קילוסין
of Israel much more than all [others].	של ישראל יותר מכל

What is the reason?	מה טעמ'

2i

And pleasant are the songs of Israel [2Sam.23.1]	ונעים זמירות ישראל

2ii

He dwells [in] the praises of Israel. [Ps.22.4(3)]	יושב תהילות ישראל

Notes:

The parallels have a briefer and more obscure version without any scripture texts:
If I am here, everyone is here
and if I am not here, who is here?
The Palestinian Talmud adds a context, explanation and scripture for each half of the saying. These enlargements may represent Hillel's intentions but they cannot be original because they would not have been omitted in other versions.

The context given to the sayings is the coming together for praise. The lively shouts and processions of Sukkot are a particularly suitable context.

The contrary messages of the sayings are interpreted as referring to two different circumstances: when Israel's praise is acceptable, and when it is not. This necessitates the change from the first person singular to plural.

The exegeses have no verbal links with the sayings. This is particularly striking in the second saying where one would expect the use of זמר or הלל instead of קלס in order to match one of the texts. There is therefore no reason to believe that the exegeses are original.

Analysis:

1. The text is understood in its Peshat sense to show that God has many angels praising him continuously.

2i. 2Sam.23.1 is a description of David, and נעים is singular (from נעים, pl. נעימים), so the last phrase quoted here should probably be translated as "the pleasant one [of] the songs of Israel". In the general context, this would refer to David himself, but in the immediate context it could refer to God: "David... the anointed of the God of Jacob and the pleasant-one [of] the songs of Israel". W. Horbury has suggested that this latter reading is being used in this tradition.

However, the translation "pleasant are the songs of Israel" is implied by the exegesis, because it is quoted in order to say something about the nature of Israel's praises rather than about their author or their subject. Even though this reading ignores the context and misreads the Hebrew, it may still be the Peshat reading because it makes good sense of the phrase (which may be corrupt) and it is followed by the LXX (εὐπρεπεις ψαλμοι Ἰσραηλ). It may therefore have been the 'plain reading' for the Jews at that time.

2ii. The first scripture is sufficient to show that Israel's praises are especially beloved, and this second scripture adds little to it. The purpose of the second text is therefore probably to extend the interpretation of the saying further. It is perhaps suggesting that "who is here" includes God, because God is present wherever he is praised. This would create a link with the other Hillel sayings (I.2.19) which follow immediately after this saying in bSukk.53a.

The MT reads: ואתה קדוש יושב תהלות ישראל According to MT punctuation this is understood as: "You are Holy, dwelling [in] the praises of Israel." This was probably influenced by Ps.80.3: "dwelling [ישב] [between] the cherubim"). But according to the LXX it should be understood as:

"You, the praise of Israel, dwell in a sanctuary." The exegesis appears to accept the MT version, probably because it was the traditional understanding.

I.2.21. *yBer.9.5 (14b)*: (bBer.60a cf. mBer.9.3)

Suppose someone was coming on the road,	היה בא בדרך
what does he say?	מהו אומר
I am sure that these are not	בטוח אני שאין אלו
from within my house.	בתוך ביתי
Hillel the Elder says:	הלל הזקן אומר
He will not fear an evil report.	משמועה רעה לא יירא
[Ps.112.7]	

Notes:

The context in Mishnah concerns vain prayers, such as "Let it not be my house" when someone hears [שמע] an outcry in the city.

Neusner (1974: 264f.) traces the evolution of this tradition from a mishnaic saying, the addition of exegesis by Hillel in yBer, and finally a biographical baraita in bBer. ("Hillel returned from a journey…"). However there is no reason to doubt that the exegesis originated with Hillel.

Analysis:
Hillel provides a substitute 'I'm sure it's not' for the forbidden 'May it not'. Wordplay may link שמועה with שמע though they are sufficiently similar for the Peshat reading to provide the link.

I.2.22. *LevR.1.5 (Margulies I:17)*: (ExR.45.5)

And thus Hillel used to say:	וכן היה הלל אומר
My humbling will be my exaltation;	השפלתי היא הגבהתי
my exaltation will be my humbling.	הגבהתי היא השפלתי
What is the proof?	מה טעם
He is raising/exalting himself to sit/reign,	המגביהי לשבת
He is lowering/humbling himself to see.	המשפילי לראות
[Ps.113.5f.]	

Notes:
The saying is typical of the enigmatic style and parallelism of Hillel, but the exegesis has almost certainly been added later. Although the verbal parallels are good, the opposites שפל and גבה occur together frequently (e.g. Prov.16.18f.; Is.2.11; 2.17; 5.15; 10.33; 57.7,9; Ezk.17.24).

Analysis:
Hillel's saying conforms with a common OT message, that the humble will be exalted, but the proud will be brought low. Ps.113 lacks the strict parallelism found in Hillel's saying and in Ezk.17.24 which would be a better proof text.

However it is possible that the Peshat reading of Ps.113 was deliberately chosen because here God is exalting and humbling himself rather than man, and it lacks the pejorative tone of the other passages. Whoever added this exegesis had a high regard for Hillel and wished to compare his actions to God, rather than to a man who is too proud or a man who has been humbled.

I.2.23. *yNed.5.7 (39b)*: (ARNa.14; ARNb.28; bSukk.28a; bBB.134a)

Eighty pair of disciples	שמונים זוג של תלמידים
belonged to Hillel the Elder.	היו לו להלל הזקן
The greatest among them [was]	גדול שבהן
Yonathan b.Uzziel,	יונתן בן עוזיאל
and the least/youngest among them [was]	והקטן שבהן
Rn.Yohanan b.Zakkai.	רבן יוחנן בן זכאי

Once this one [Hillel] fell ill	פעם אחת חלה
and they all came to visit.	ונכנסו כולן לבקרו
Rn.Yohanan b.Zakkai stood	עמד לו רבן יוחנן בן זכאי
in the courtyard.	בחצר

He [Hillel] said to them:	אמר להן
Where is he who is youngest among you?	היכן הוא קטן שבכם
for he is a father of wisdom	שהוא אב לחכמה
and a father of generations	ואב לדורות
and, it is not necessary to say,	אין צריך לומר
the greatest among you.	הגדול שבכם
They said to him:	אמרו לו
Lo, he is in the courtyard.	הרי הוא בחצר
He said to them: Let him come in.	אמר להן יכנס
Immediately when he came in	כיון שנכנס
he [Hillel] said to them: [Prov.8.21]	אמר להן
To cause those loving me to inherit wealth	להנחיל אוהבי יש
and their treasuries to fill.	ואוצרותיהם אמלא

Notes:

By quoting this scripture when Yohanan comes in, Hillel indicates that his youngest disciple is in fact the greatest.

Neusner (1971 I:252) regards this biographical tradition as a Yavnean polemic in favour of Yohanan against Gamaliel. There is nothing to indicate an earlier origin and this conclusion is probably correct.

Analysis:

It is unclear whether the scripture is quoted to show that Yohanan is the wealth without which the treasury is not full (W. Horbury's suggestion) or that Yohanan is one who loves God and therefore inherits a treasury of wealth.

Both alternatives find support in ARNb which records two possible endings to the tradition: "Concerning you [plural] Scripture says..." and "Concerning you [singular] Scripture says...".

However, a later tradition in ARNb and parallels appears to support the latter: "It was said of Rn.Yohanan b.Zakkai that he mastered Scripture, Mishnah, Gemara, halakoth, haggadoth, toseftoth, the minutiae of the Torah, the minutiae of the Scribes, and all the middoth of the Sages. Not a word in the Torah did he not master, fulfilling the text: *To cause those loving me...*" (ARNa.14).

Either way, some obvious Symbolism is used to interpret the text according to the Peshat meaning in its Context. Hence it teaches that those who love Wisdom (=Torah) inherit riches which are greater than gold (v19), i.e. wisdom itself.

I.2.24. *bHag.9b:*

Mishnah:

[If] the festival passes	עבר הרגל
and no offering [has been made]	ולא חג
he is not liable for the debt.	אינו חייב באחריותו
Of this one it is said:	ועל זה נאמר
The crooked cannot be straightened	מעוות לא יוכל לתקון
and that which is lacking cannot	וחסרון לא יוכל
be counted. [Qoh.1.15]	להימנות

Gemarah:

Bar Hé Hé said to Hillel	א"ל בר הי הי להלל
This "be counted"	האי להימנות
ought to be "be filled"	להמלאות מיבעי ליה
but this [refers to]	אלא זה
he whose associates counted him in	שמנוהו חביריו
for a religious act	לדבר מצוה
but he would not [let himself] be counted with them.	והוא לא נמנה עמהן

Notes:

Neusner (1971 I:271) suggests that the form of this tradition expects a reply, so the pericopé must be deficient. However it is unlikely that later editors would have deliberately omitted a reply by Hillel, or that they would have invented a tradition where Hillel fails to respond.

Analysis:

Bar Hé Hé comments on the use of Scripture in this mishnah which states that a neglected festival offering cannot be offered retrospectively.

It is probable that Bar Hé Hé's attention was drawn to this verse because of the parallelism which suggests that the second half means exactly the same as the first. This would violate the rule of No Redundancy which he is very keen to avoid (cf. I.2.25). The two halves are clearly related (as in I.2.25), but they must not refer to exactly the same situation.

Bar Hé Hé pointed out that "be counted" [להימנות] fitted neither the mishnaic interpretation nor the rest of the line, because it was not the opposite of "to be lacking". The word which should have been there was obviously "be filled" [להמלאות], which suited both the interpretation and the rest of the verse.

The easiest solution would therefore be to propose an emended text (substituting לא for ג, as in the margin of Biblica Hebraica Stuttgartensia) and to interpret the first half of the verse with regard to some other Law breaking (as others did – see examples in bHag.9ab). Instead, he attempts to find an interpretation of the verse in accordance with the received text.

He applies it to a situation where a group have "counted" on an absent friend when registering a sacrifice (cf. mPes.8.4) but that person has made other arrangements so he does not attend the meal. They cannot "count" someone who is "lacking/ missing" as one of their number, and they cannot charge him for his portion of the sacrifice.

This application manages to preserve the received text and also gives a separate meaning to the second half of the parallelism.

This halakah did not require scriptural support because it is obvious that someone cannot be held to an arrangement made on his behalf without his consent. Ben Hé Hé's motive is therefore not to find scriptural support for a halakah, but to avoid Redundancy and emendation in the text. This is based on the nomological assumption that there is nothing superfluous in Scripture and that there is only one valid version of the text.

I.2.25. *bHag.9b:*

1a

Bar Hé Hé [said] to Hillel:	בר הי הי להלל
What [means] the text:	מאי דכתיב
And you will return and distinguish	ושבתם וראיתם
between the righteous and the wicked,	בין צדיק לרשע
between him who serves God	בין עובד אלהים
and him who serves him not. [Mal.3.18]	לאשר לא עבדו
The *righteous* is the same as	היינו צדיק היינו עובד אלהים
he who serves God	
The *wicked* is the same as	היינו רשע היינו אשר לא עבדו
he who serves him not.	

1b

[Hillel] said to him:	א״ל
He who serves and *he who serves not*	עבדו ולא עבדו
are both those who are perfectly	תרוייהו צדיקי גמורי נינהו
righteous.	
But one should not compare	ואינו דומה
him repeating his chapter a hundred times	שונה פרקו מאה פעמים
with him repeating his chapter a hundred	לשונה פרקו מאה ואחד
and one times.	

2a

[Bar Hé Hé] said to him:	א״ל
And because of a single time	ומשום חד זימנא
he is called *he who serves him not?*	קרי ליה לא עבדו

2b

[Hillel] said to him: Yes;	א״ל אין
Go and learn from the market	צא ולמד משוק של חמרין
of the ass drivers	
Ten portions for a single zuz	עשרה פרסי בזוזא חר
Eleven portions for two zuz.	עשר פרסי בתרי זוזי

Notes:

This passage is unrelated to the context of the tractate, but it follows soon after a similar tradition of Ben Hé Hé and Hillel (I.2.24) which *is* concerned with Hagigah.

Neusner comments: "Hillel 'solves' [the problem] by ignoring the question, the context, and the sense of the Scripture, claiming that the Scripture speaks entirely of perfectly righteous people, but among them the one who has studied even one more time is superior and will be discerned apart from the wicked. The exegesis is incredible and Ben Hé Hé says so. Hillel's reply is that small distinctions make a great difference. I do not know what to make of this strange pericope." (1971 I:271).

It is suggested below that Hillel does have regard for context and that Ben Hé Hé does not question the exegesis but its implications.

Analysis:

1a. Ben Hé Hé presents the problem that two phrases in the text appear to mean exactly the same thing. There is no difficulty if one reads them as poetic parallelism or prosaic pleonasm but Ben Hé Hé reads the Prophets as though they were legal texts. He therefore applied the rule of No Redundancy and asked how two phrases in Scripture could have the same meaning.

1b. Hillel answers that they mean different things. The first phrase compares the righteous with the wicked, but the second phrase compares the completely righteous with the almost righteous.

Hillel may perhaps be paraphrased as saying that there are those who are righteous as a result of constant obedience and others whose righteousness depends on forgiveness for occasional disobedience.

The next sentence ("He that repeated his chapter . . .") is in Hebrew, while the rest of the debate is in Aramaic, and may have been added later. It is an illustration of disobedience in a school context where Mishnah was learnt by repetition. The illustration may be based on Gematria, because the first letters of the words עבד אלהים לאשר add up to 101 while in the phrase לא עבדו they add up to 100.

2a. Ben Hé Hé expresses surprise that a single disobedience (or, if the Hebrew sentence is genuine, a single repetition) should make such a great difference to God's estimation of that person.

2b. Hillel's answer is difficult to understand, but it is clearly a Mashal of some kind.

A zuz is a coin having the value of about a denarius, which was a common size of denomination. A פרס is one day's allowance for a slave or a half loaf of bread (cf. E. Bickerman 1951). It is unlikely to to be the former because the wage for a day labourer was about a denarius (J. Jeremias 1969: 111), so it is likely to refer to bread which did cost about one twelfth of a denarius for a loaf (J. Jeremias 1969: 122).

In order to understand Hillel's saying in this context it should presumably be read as "10 loaves can be sold for 1 zuz, while 11 loaves can be sold for 2 zuz". This would then mean either that 'things are not always fair' or that (as Neusner suggests) 'a small difference can result in a large difference'. This latter explanation can be understood if one assumes that coins having a smaller value than a zuz were not used much in the market, so that a man may offer 2 zuz for 11 loaves, but he would only offer 1 zuz for anything less than 11 loaves.

It is interesting to compare this tradition with Jesus' parable of the unprofitable servant (Lk.17.7ff.) which can be read as a comment on Hillel's exegesis. Hillel argues that it is possible to be profitable (i.e. completely righteous), although this is likely to be a rare occurrence, whereas Jesus in Luke argues that even the perfect servant is not counted as righteous, although both agree that the servant is accepted nevertheless.

I.2.26. *bErub.27b:* (yPes.9.5; yMS.1.3)

Ben Bag Bag said: [re Deut.14.26]	בן בג בג אומר
For oxen teaches they may buy	בבקר מלמד שלוקחין
an ox together with its hide.	בקר על גב עורו
Or for sheep teaches they may buy	ובצאן מלמד שלוקחין
a sheep together with its fleece.	צאן על גב גיזתה
Or for wine teaches they may buy	וביין מלמד שלוקחין
wine together with its vessel.	יין על גב קנקנו
Or for strong-drink teaches they may buy	ובשכר מלמד שלוקחין
husk-wine after fermentation.	תמד משהחמיץ

Notes:
The Talmud rejects Ben Bag Bag's interpretation at great length, probably because Mishnah stated one could purchase anything except water or salt (mErub.3.1), and Ben Bag Bag's exposition could be used to prove that brine could be purchased along with fish. This conflict with the Mishnah suggests an early date.

Analysis:
The discussion concerns what could be purchased with the Second Tithe money which had to be spent in Jerusalem. The biblical text only allowed for the purchase of food which was eaten in Jerusalem with the Levites, but it became customary to allow the purchase of non-foodstuffs. This is one of many attempts to derive the custom from Scripture.

Ben Bag Bag argues from No Redundancy. The text has already permitted "whatever your soul desires" so the subsequent list appears to be superfluous. The list must therefore itemise things which one would not expect to be permitted to pay for, such as inedible portions of food (hide), products of food (fleece), containers, and preparation costs (fermentation).

R. Loewe suggested to me that this exegesis may originally have been an Ultra-literal reading of –בַ as 'together with', although later Talmudic discussions assume that it is based on the apparent Redundancy of items in the list or of the list as a whole.

I.2.27. *bPes.96a:* (bMen.49b)

But was it not taught: Ben Bag Bag said:	והתניא בן בג בג אומר
From where [is it taught]	מניין
the Tamid requires examining	לתמיד שטעון ביקור
four days before sacrifice?	ד׳ ימים קודם שחיטה
Because it is written:	שנא׳
Take care to offer to me	תשמרו להקריב לי
at its due time. [Num.28.2]	במועדו
And elsewhere it says:	ולהלן הוא אומר
And you shall keep it	והיה לכם למשמרת
till the fourteenth. [Ex.16.12]	עד ארבעה עשר
Just as there it requires examining	מה להלן טעון ביקור
four days before sacrifice	ד׳ ימים קודם שחיטה
also here it requires examining	אף כאן טעון ביקור
four days before sacrifice.	ד׳ ימים קודם שחיטה

Notes:
Tamid is the daily sacrifice. Ben Bag Bag's exegesis contradicts Mishnah, so it is likely to be genuine. Mishnah says that seven days' examination is required and that the first Passover was an exception.

Analysis:
Ben Bag Bag links the Tamid sacrifice with Passover by means of Gezerah Shavah, recorded with a punctiliously correct formula. The word used to link the two passages is שמר, 'to guard/watch/keep' which can be said to be superfluous in both passages, so that the reason for its inclusion is to provide this link.

I.2.28. *bBekh.12a:*
Mishnah:
One cannot redeem
with a calf,
or with a wild animal
or with . . .

מתני׳
אין פודין
לא בעגל
ולא בחיה
ולא. . .

Gemara:
Who is the Mishnah [based on]?
It is Ben Bag Bag.
As it is taught:

גמ׳
מתני׳ מני
בן בג בג היא
דתניא

Ben Bag Bag says:
It is written here: *lamb* [Ex.13.13]
and it is written there: *lamb* [Ex.12.5]
Just as there it excludes
all these named [animals]
also here it excludes
all these named [animals].

בן בג בג אומר
נאמ׳ כאן שה
ונאמר להלן שה
מה להלן פרט
לכל השמות הללו
אף כאן פרט
לכל השמות הללו

Notes:
Unlike his other Gezerah Shavah exegesis (I.2.27), this is not disputed by Amor-aim, and may have been invented by them to support the Mishnah. However the two exegeses have exactly the same form which suggest they had the same author.

Analysis:
The Mishnah lists animals which cannot be used to redeem a firstling, but what is this list based on?
This Gezerah Shavah uses the link word "lamb" which (as in I.2.27) does not have exactly the same form in both texts (Ex.12.5: שה; Ex.13.13: בשה). However the Amoraim do not dispute it, presumably because it does not contradict Mishnah.

I.2.29. *bBB.4a:*
[Herod killed all the rabbis except Baba b.Buta]
He garlanded him
with a crown of hedgehog [bristles]
to put out his eyes.
One day he came and sat before him.

אהדר ליה
כלילא דיילי
נקרינהו לעיניה
יומא חד אתא ויתיב קמיה

1a
He [Herod] said:
See Sir, this wicked slave,
what he has done now!

אמר
חזי מר האי עבדא בישא
מאי קא עביד

1b
He [Baba] said to him:
What shall I do to him?

אמר ליה
מאי אעביד ליה

2a
He [Herod] said to him:
Let the Master curse him.

א״ל
נלטייה מר

2b
He [Baba] said to him:
[It is written]: [Qoh.10.20a]
Even in your thoughts
do not curse the king.

אמר ליה
[כתיב]
גם במדעך
מלך אל תקלל

3a
He [Herod] said to him:
He is not a king.

אמר ליה
האי לאו מלך הוא

3b
He [Baba] said to him:
And [if] that one is only a rich man,
for it is also written: [Qoh.10.20b]
And in the room of your bed
do not curse the rich man.

א״ל
וליהוי עשיר בעלמא
וכתיב
ובחדרי משכבך
אל תקלל עשיר

4a
And [if] he is nothing but a ruler,
for it is written: [Ex.22.27(28)]
And a ruler of your people
do not curse.

ולא יהא אלא נשיא
וכתיב
ונשיא בעמך
לא תאור

4b
He [Herod] said to him:
[This is] one performing acts of *your people*
and he [Herod] is not
acting acts of *your people.*

א״ל
בעושה מעשה עמך
והאי לאו
עושה מעשה עמך

5a
He [Baba] said to him:
I am afraid of him.

א״ל
מסתפינא מיניה

5b
He [Herod] said:
There is no man to go to tell him
because I and you sit [alone].

א״ל
ליכא איניש דאזיל דלימא ליה
דאנא ואת יתיבנא

6a
He [Baba] said to him:
It is written: [Qoh.10.20c]
For a bird of heaven
may carry the voice
and a lord of wings may tell the thing.

א״ל
כתיב
כי עוף השמים
יוליך את הקול
ובעל כנפים יגיד דבר

6b
He said: I am he [Herod].
If I had known

א״ל אנא הוא
אי הואי ידענא

that the rabbis were so circumspect
I would not have cut them off.

דזהרי רבנן כולי האי
לא הוה קטילנא להו

7a

Now, what is the remedy
which that person should make.

השתא מאי תקנתיה
דההוא גברא

A7bi

He [Baba] said to him:
That person has extinguished
the light of the world,
as it is written: [Prov.6.23]
For the commandments are a lamp
and the Torah a light.

א"ל
הוא כבה
אורו של עולם
דכתיב
כי נר מצוה
ותורה אור

A7bii

Go and be occupied
with the light of the world,
as it is written: [Is.2.2]
And all nations shall stream to it /
be enlightened by it.

ילך ויעסוק
באורו של עולם
דכתיב
ונהרו אליו כל הגוים

There are [some] who say as follows:

איכא דאמרי הכי

B7bi

He [Baba] said to him:
That person has blinded
the eyes of the world,
as it is written: [Num.15.24]
And if it is [hidden]
from the eyes of the congregation.

א"ל
הוא סימא
עינו של עולם
דכתיב
והיה אם
מעיני העדה

B7bii

Go and be occupied
with [the desire of] the eyes of the world,
as it is written: [Ezk.24.21]
I will profane my sanctuary
the pride of your strength,
the delight of your eyes.

ילך ויתעסק
בעינו של עולם
דכתיב
הנני מחלל את מקדשי
גאון עוזכם
מחמד עיניכם

8a

He [Herod] said to him:
I am afraid of the [Roman] government.

א"ל
מסתפינא ממלכותא

8b

He [Baba] said to him:
Send a messenger [to Rome]
and let him travel [slowly] for a year,
delay [there] a year,
and take year to return.
Meanwhile

אל
שדר שליחא
וליזיל שתא
וליעכב שתא
ולהדר שתא
אדהכי והכי

you destroy and rebuild [the Temple].   סתרית ובניית
He did so ...   עבד הכי

Notes:
Neusner (1971 I:391) says that this tradition assumes Herod's Temple took a few
years rather than decades to build, and must therefore originate long after the real
events were forgotten. However Herod did dedicate the Temple after only 18 months
(Ant.15.421[11.6]), although it took decades to complete.

The tradition preserves complaints which were made against Herod, that he was a
"slave" (1a), because he and his family were servants of Hyrcanus who gradually stole
the throne (Ant.14.163–71[9.3]), and that he was not of "your people" (4b), but of
Idumean descent (Ant.14.403[15.2] cf. E. Schürer 1973-:234).

However the story is clearly legendary, and although a core may be early, most of
the exegeses are probably late additions. The quotations of Qoh.10.20b & 20c were
probably inspired by the quotation of Qoh.10.20a. If these scriptures and the later
inquiry by Herod are removed one is left with:
Herod put out his eyes. One day he came and sat before him.
Herod: See Sir, what this wicked slave has done now.
Baba: What shall I do to him?
Herod: Let the Master curse him.
Baba: Qoh.10.20 "Even in your thoughts do not curse the king"
Herod: He is not a king.
Baba: Ex.22.17 "And a ruler of your people do not curse"
Herod: He is not of your people.
Baba: I am afraid of him.
Herod: I am Herod. If I had known the rabbis were so circumspect I would not
have cut them off.

This version has more symmetry than the expanded version which has survived,
and appears to criticise those who needlessly provoke the anger of Herod. Perhaps the
story originated after Herod's execution of the rebel Pharisees (Ant.17.41–5[2.4])
from someone like Sameas, who was not afraid to put Herod on trial, but who
regarded him as a divinely appointed ruler (Ant.14.172–6[9.4], 15.3f.[1.1]).

Analysis:
1ab. Herod pretends to sympathise with the blind Baba.

2ab. Qoh.10 is used according to its Peshat meaning. The exegesis is necessary for
Herod's reply, so it could not have been added at a later stage, unless 3a was also
added.

3ab. The reading is again Peshat. Herod's question in 3a appears to have two
replies (3b & 4a). They have the same general form ('even if he were only ...') but they
use different phrases to express it. This may suggest that 3a has been added to
complement the quotation of the same verse in 2b.

However the second answer (4a) serves to swing the debate into Baba's favour. Up
to now Herod has been asking and Baba has been answering, like a teacher and
disciple, but now the reverse occurs.

4ab. The Peshat reading is used. Herod's reply echoes the common sentiment that
he was not a true Jew, so that this text does not apply to him.

5ab, 6ab. Baba appears to be defeated, and it is only his wisdom from Scripture
which saves him. The reading is again Peshat.

7ab. The debate now switches again so that Herod is asking and Baba answering.

However the questioner is not in the role of a teacher with his disciple but a man seeking counsel. Baba answers in riddles which are explained by means of texts which may have been added later. Two versions are recorded.

A7bi. Herod killed the rabbis, thereby extinguishing the light of the Oral Torah, which they carried. Baba's symbolism is explained by a text using the same symbol. The text is already using metaphorical language, so this is a Peshat reading of it, not Mashal.

A7bii. The light with which Herod should occupy himself is the Temple, which is the subject of Is.2.2. This is a Derash interpretation based on Wordplay, reading the Hebrew נהר, 'stream' as though it were the identical Aramaic root 'to shine', though taking note of the general context which concerns the temple.

B7bi. Num.15.24 concerns the sin which the whole people committed in ignorance. Such ignorance was impossible under the watchful eye of the rabbis, but Herod blinded them.

This exegesis interprets Baba's symbolism by means of the idiom נעלם מעין, (cf. Lev.4.13) 'in ignorance', but literally 'hidden from the eyes'. The eyes are understood literally as those of the rabbis who were killed and of Baba. This is a nomological reading, because it reads a phrase in a literal sense which goes beyond the idiomatic meaning, but it does not ignore the context.

B7bii. The "eye" with which Herod should occupy himself is what the whole world longed to see – the Temple. The Peshat meaning of Ezk.24 was that the Temple was the pride and joy of Israel, but a little hyperbole with regard to its beauty is perhaps understandable in the light of the saying: "He who has not seen the Temple of Herod has never seen a beautiful building" (bBB4a).

I.2.30. *Mekh.Sim.p147.22–148.3:*

1a

Agrippas the Elder asked	שאל אגריפס סבא
Rn.Gamaliel:	את רבן גמליאל
He cannot be jealous	אין מתקנא
unless there are other [gods],	אלא באחרים
as it is said: [Deut.4.39]	שנ׳
Know today	וידעת היום
and lay it on your heart	והשבות אל לבביך
that YHWH, He is God.	כי ה׳ הוא האלהים

1b

He [Gamaliel] said to him:	אמר לו
He is not jealous	אין מתקנא
of anyone greater than himself	לא בגדול ממנו
or anyone like himself	ולא בכיוצא בו
but anyone inferior to himself.	אלא בקטן ממנו
And thus it said:	וכן הוא אומר
For two evils my people did:	כי שתים רעות עשה עמי
They forsook me,	אותי עזבו
the fount of living waters	מקור מים חיים
[Jer.2.13]. If [when]	אלו
they forsook me,	עזבו אותי

the fount of living waters	מקור מים חיים
they were offering insult	עלובין היו
then how much more when	על אחת כמה וכמה
they dig for themselves wells	לחצוב להם בארות
broken wells,	בארות נשברים
which cannot [hold] water.	אשר לא יכילו המים

Notes:

This tradition is historically improbable, because although Gamaliel I is also recorded with Agrippa in bPes.88b, this is clearly a later glorification of Gamaliel. M.D. Herr (1972a:131f.) suggests, on the basis of some late texts, that Gamaliel I spoke with "Agrippa the General" (which he interprets as 'a General in Agrippa's army'). This Agrippa also asked Gamaliel how many Torahs were given to Israel (I.2.32 – "Agenitos the Hegemon" but he is "Agrippa the Hegemon" when the same story is told concerning Yohanan b.Zakkai in I.2.45). There has clearly been some confusion between this tradition and the traditions about Yohanan's discussions with Antoninus the Hegemon, although Herr suggests that the two traditions are completely separate and that both are historically believable.

Neusner (1971 I:342) suggests that this is Gamaliel II, who had several discussions with Gentile rulers, though he could not have met Agrippa the Elder. This would date the tradition after 70 CE.

As in I.2.32,45, Agrippa knows scripture surprisingly well for a Gentile. However this dispute is not related to any Pharisee-Sadducee or Hillelite-Shammaite differences, and as the question throws doubt on the unity of God revealed in Scripture, it suits a speaker from outside Judaism.

According to D. Hoffmann's text (1905:105) Agrippas' question has no exegesis and only consists of:

[Surely] He is not jealous   אין מתקנא

The exegesis may therefore have been added later to explain the basis of Agrippa's question.

The jealousy of God was vigorously debated in the second century and probably in the first century (A. Marmonstein 1929:162f.; A.H.B. Logan 1978), but this debate cannot be dated before 70 CE.

Analysis:

1a. Agrippa points out that if God is jealous, there must be other gods. The verse he quotes occurs at the end of a long exposition of the 2nd commandment (Deut.4.13–40), which includes a description of the punishment He will mete out when his jealousy is provoked (v24–28). Agrippa is not quoting the verse which proves his point, but is pointing to the Context of the whole passage, in its Peshat sense.

1b. Gamaliel answers that God's jealousy does not imply rivals because God is not jealous of superiors or of equals but only of inferiors, as expressed metaphorically by Jeremiah. Gamaliel is not using Mashal because the metaphor has already been applied by Jeremiah to Israel's rejection of God. He is therefore giving a Peshat interpretation.

I.2.31. *Sifré Deut.61:*

And you will break down their altars ...   ונתצתם את מזבחותם

[but] you shall not do thus
to YHWH your God. [Deut.12.3f.]

לא תעשון כן
לה׳ אלהיכם

Rn.Gamaliel says:
And could it enter your mind
that Israel would destroy
their [own] altars?
God forbid!
But you shall not do
according to their deeds,
for your evil deeds would result in
the Sanctuary of our Fathers
being destroyed.

רבן גמליאל אומר
וכי תעלה על דעתך
שישראל נותצים
למזבחותיהם
חם ושלום
אלא שלא תעשו
כמעשיהם
ויגרמו מעשיכם הרעים
למקדש אבותיכם
שיחרב

Notes:
Neusner (1971 I:343) points out that this fits in well with Yohanan b.Zakkai's
exegesis of the same scripture (I.2.44 – which he dates at 40 CE) and that it presupposes that the temple is not yet destroyed, but he still finds the evidence for an early
date inconclusive.

It is suggested at I.2.44 that Yohanan's exegesis is inexplicable unless it is based on
another exegesis such as this one. Since these two exegeses are never recorded together, it is unlikely that this was constructed by later authorities to accompany Yohanan's exegesis. Therefore these exegeses are related and are both pre-70 CE.

Analysis:
Gamaliel finds the Peshat interpretation difficult because it is unnecessary to tell
Jews not to destroy their own Temple. This was of course necessary before the full
acceptance of YHWH worship in Israel, but Gamaliel would assume that Israel had
always worshipped YHWH.

Gamaliel's difficulty is not a lack of historic perspective. Many laws were read in
the light of history, and some were regarded as appropriate only for a limited time
(e.g. certain Passover regulations were only for Egypt – mPes.9.5), and the Taqanot
such as Hillel's Prozbul (I.2.15) show that economic and social realities could result in
changes in the Law. However, his historic perspective would not go so far as to
accommodate the idea of Israel's gradual acceptance of YHWH worship.

He therefore reads כן ("you shall not do *thus*") with reference to heathen practices
which would *cause* the destruction of the Temple. He has either used the Peshat
assumption that כן refers back to the Context of the previous verse (cf. Rashi ad loc.)
or he has used Gezerah Shavah to locate the meaning in the next use of כן in v.31 (as
W. Horbury has suggested to me).

I.2.32. *Sifré Deut.351:*
[*They shall teach your commands to Jacob
and your Torah to Israel.* [Deut.33.10]
Teaching that two Torahs
were given to Israel,

יורו משפטיך ליעקב]
ותורתך לישראל
מלמד ששתי תורות
ניתנו לישראל

| one by mouth | אחת בפה |
| and one in writing. | ואחת בכתב |

1a

Agenitos the Hegemon asked	שאל אגניטוס הגמון
Rn.Gamaliel:	את רבן גמליאל
He said to him:	אמר לו
How many Torahs	כמה תורות
were given to Israel?	ניתנו לישראל

1b

He said to him: Two,	אמר לו שתים
one by mouth	אחת בפה
and one in writing.	ואחת בכתב

Notes:
The exegesis is not attributed to Gamaliel, but was added later to introduce the story. The same tradition is attributed to Yohanan b.Zakkai (I.2.45) where it may have originated as a Sadducean question put into the mouth of a gentile. A similar tradition is attributed to Shammai (bShab.31a) but this does not involve exegesis and it forms part of a biographical reference so it is probably late (cf. J. Neusner 1974, B.L. Visotzky 1983).

There is much overlap between the traditions of Yohanan b.Zakkai and Gamaliel I (cf. I.2.31 & I.2.44). This may have been due to close connections between the two during their lives, or to rivalries between their disciples who both claimed the same traditions for their masters.

Although, as in I.2.45, this exegesis may be early, it will not be counted in the results because one of these traditions is clearly a duplicate of the other.

Analysis:
1a. Although it is not impossible to invent circumstances in which a gentile ruler may have asked this question, it is likely that it originated, as the introduction implies, as a trick question based on Deut.33.10. As at I.2.45, it is perhaps best to assume that it originated to counter Sadducean arguments against the Oral Law.

1b. The answer too implies the exegesis in the introduction. Perhaps this was a common exegesis which therefore did not need repeating.

The exegesis is based on a Nomological reading which assumes that the two terms משפטים and תורה relate to two different law codes, the Oral and the Written Torah respectively.

I.2.33. *bAZ.20a:* (yAZ.1.9)

It happened to Rn.Simeon b.Gamaliel	מעשה ברשב"ג
that he was on the foot of	שהיה על גבי
the step of the Temple Mount	מעלה בהר הבית
and he saw a female gentile	וראה עוברת כוכבים
who was especially beautiful.	אחת נאה ביותר
He said: [Ps.104.24]	אמר
How manifold are your works YHWH.	מה רבו מעשיך ה'

Notes:
Some MSS read כותית ("Samaritan") for עוברת כוכבים ("star worshipper"),
but Goldschmidt's גויה ("female gentile") is probably the pre-censored reading.
In yAZ a similar story is told concerning Gamaliel I, without the quotation.

Analysis:
The reading is Peshat and probably repesents a reference to the whole Psalm, which
praises God for the variety and wonder in all of his creation.

I.2.34. *Sifré Num.42 (Horovitz 46 : 3f.):*

R. Hananiah Prefect of the Priests	ר׳ חנניה סגן הכהנים
says: *And give you peace* [Num.6.26]	אומר וישם לך שלום
- on your house.	בביתך
R. Nathan says:	ר׳ נתן אומר
This peace [refers to]	זה שלום
the kingdom of the house of David	מלכות בית דוד
as it is said: [Is.9.6]	שנ׳
Of the increase of government	למרבה המשרה
and of peace there is no end.	ולשלום אין קץ

Notes:
Neusner assumes that Hananiah/Hanina is from temple times because he is associated with Gamaliel I (mSheq.6.6). "Peace" is a recurring theme of Hananiah (I.2.35;
mAb.3.2).

Analysis:
Hananiah's interpretation, that the Aaronic blessing is conferred not only on the
listener but also on his "house", is based on a Peshat reading. This could have meant
the listener's household or, as suggested by R. Nathan (2nd C), the House of David.
Hananiah's exegesis may originally have been linked, by the common homilectical
method of Gezerah Shavah (II), to Ps.122.5f., which is the only OT passage where
"peace" and "House of David" are juxtaposed. Here the psalmist prays for the peace
of Jerusalem where the House of the Lord is, and where "the thrones of justice were
established, the thrones of the House of David".

I.2.35. *Sifré Num.42 (Horovitz 47 : 10–13):*

R. Hananiah, Prefect of the Priests	ר׳ חנניה סגן הכהנים
says: Great is peace	אומר גדול השלום
which is of equal importance with	ששקול כנגד
all the works of the Beginning [ie. Creation],	כל מעשה בראשית
as it is said: [Is.45.7]	שנא׳
Who is forming light	יוצר אור
and creating darkness,	ובורא חשך
making peace.	עושה שלום
M. Friedmann 1864:11b:	

...

as it is said: [Am.4.13; Is.45.7]   שנא'
For behold,   כי הנה
he who is forming mountains   יוצר הרים
and creating wind,   ובורא רוח
making peace and creating evil.   עושה שלום ובורא רע

Notes:
Horovitz's version has better manuscript support. The 'text' in Friedmann's version is an Amalgamation, i.e. texts which are merged without any indication that more than one text is employed. Amalgamation occurs frequently in the NT and especially in Paul but it is rare in rabbinic traditions. If this is genuine, it is the only example before 70 CE.

Analysis:
Hananiah is either saying that this list contains things of comparable greatness, or that Peace is countered against all of Creation which is evil. In the latter interpretation, Hananiah would presumably say that 'Just as the mountains withstand the wind, Peace withstands Evil'. However the Jews did not regard creation as intrinsically evil, so the former understanding is probably in Hananiah's mind. Either way the exegesis is Peshat.

Dr.W. Horbury has suggested to me that Hananiah may have had in mind the first blessing before the morning Shema which quotes Is.45.7, replacing "and creates evil" with "and creates all things" [הכל] (Singer 1962:38). The liturgy is difficult to date, but J. Heinemann (1975:17f.) notes that this blessing is very early.

I.2.36. *ARNa.20:*
R. Hananiah, chief of priests, said: רבי הנניה סגן הכהנים אומר
Whoever lays the words of Torah   כל הנותן דברי תורה
upon his heart   על לבו
they [heaven] release him from   מבטלין ממנו
thoughts of ruination   הרהורין הרבה
thoughts of hunger   הרהורי רעב
thoughts of madness   הרהורי שטות
thoughts of unchastity   הרהורי זנות
thoughts of the evil inclination   הרהורי יצר הרע
and thoughts of the evil woman   והרהורי אשה רעה
thoughts of vain things   הרהורי דברים בטלים
thoughts of the yoke of flesh and blood.   הרהורי עול בשר ודם
For thus is written in the Book of Psalms   שכן כתוב בספר תהלים
by the hand of David, King of Israel: על ידי דוד מלך ישראל
[Ps.19.9(8)]
The precepts of YHWH are upright   פקודי ה' ישרים
rejoicing the heart   משמחי לב
the commands of YHWH are pure   מצות ה' ברה
enlightening the eyes.   מאירת עינים

And whoever does not lay	וכל שאינו נותן
the words of Torah upon his heart	דברי תורה על לבו
they [heaven] will lay upon him	נותנין לו
thoughts of ruination	הרהורין הרבה
thoughts of hunger	הרהורי רעב
thoughts of madness	הרהורי שטות
thoughts of unchastity	הרהורי זנות
thoughts of the evil inclination	הרהורי יצר הרע
and thoughts of the evil woman	והרהורי אשה רעה
thoughts of vain things	הרהורי דברים בטלים
thoughts of the yoke of flesh and blood.	הרהורי עול בשר ודם
For thus is written in Deuteronomy	שכך כתוב במשנה תורה
by the hand of Moses our Master:	על ידי משה רבינו
[Deut.28.46–48]	
And they will be on you	והיו בך לאות
for a sign and a wonder for ever,	ולמופת ובזרעך עד עולם
because you did not serve	תחת אשר לא עבדת
YHWH your God	את ה' אלהיך
with joyfulness and gladness of heart	בשמחה ובטוב לב
for the abundance of all things.	מרוב כל
So you shall serve your enemies	ועבדת את אויבך
whom YHWH will send upon you	אשר ישלחנו ה' בך
in hunger and in thirst,	ברעב ובצמא
in nakedness and in lack of all things.	ובעירום ובחוסר כל

Notes:

The attribution of this homily is questionable. ARNa.20 appears to be expounding mAb.3.2–11a (ARNa.19 = mAb.3.1 and ARNa.21 = mAb.3.11b-) and although this section of mAb starts with a saying of Hananiah, it also contains a saying of R. Nehuniah b.Ha-Kanah which is similar to this exegesis (mAb.3.5). However this exegesis does concur with his theme of Peace in mAb.3.2 and with his membership of the peace faction in besieged Jerusalem (J. Neusner 1971 I:405).

Analysis:

This is not an exegetical argument, but a homily based on the Proem form. Here the preacher expounds a *seder* (pentateuchal reading) and its accompanying *haftorah* from the Prophets via a third text which is linked to them by Gezerah Shavah II before finally returning to the *seder* (J. Mann 1940-, J. Bowker 1967b). The link words in this case are שמח ('rejoice') and לב ('heart'). The haftorah is not cited (as in many of Mann's examples) and has to be inferred. Perhaps it was Is.65.12–14 which is linked to the sermon by רעב ('hunger'), הרע ('evil') and חרב ('sword' – as found in the Soncino text instead of הרבה, 'ruination') as well containing שמח and לב.

I.2.37. *ARNa.20:*

He used to say:	הוא היה אומר
Do not look on me for I am black,	אל תראוני שאני שחרחודת

tanned by the sun. [Cant.1.6]	ששזפתני השמש
These are the councillors of Judah	אלו בולאות שביהודה
who removed the yoke of the Holy One	שפרקו עולו של הקדוש
(Blessed be He) from over them	ברוך הוא מעליהם
and enthroned over them	והמליכו עליהם
a king of flesh and blood.	מלך בשר ודם

Notes:

The original context of Cant.1.6 refers to the unbecoming tan of Solomon's lover, but here it is applied to the dark deeds of rulers.

"He" is presumably Hananiah, author of the previous tradition (I.2.36), although the anti-monarchy stance does not agree with opinions expressed in his other exegeses.

A. Büchler (1928:63ff.) suggested the context may be the performance of temple rites by the half-Jew Agrippa I (mSot.7.8), which many regarded as a reason for Jerusalem's destruction (bSot.41b). The incident occurred in 41 CE (D. Hoffmann 1977:31f.; E. Schürer 1973- I:447) which is early for Hananiah, but the exegesis may have been inspired by the destruction itself.

Analysis:

If the attribution is correct, this is the first example of rabbinic allegory. R. Kasher (1988:564) pointed out that Canticles was still used as a love song in the Temple period (mTaan.4.8) before Aqiva forbade this practice (tSanh.12.10).

The exegesis presumably depends on the context, especially "my vineyard I have not kept", which could be applied especially to rulers of Jerusalem, YHWH's vineyard (Is.5).

I.2.38. *Sifré Deut.294*:

Eleazar b.Hananiah	אלעזר בן חנניה
b.Hezekiah b.Garon says:	בן חזקיה בן גרון אומר
Here it says: [Ezk.46.11]	הרי הוא אומר
An ephah for a bullock	איפה לפר
and an ephah for a ram	ואיפה לאיל
and an ephah for a lamb [MT: lambs].	ואיפה לכבש
And is therefore the measure of	וכי מדת
bullocks and rams and lambs	פרים ואילים וכבשים
the same?	אחת היא
And elsewhere already it was said: [Num.29.3f.]	והלא כבר נאמר
Three tenths for a bullock	שלשה עשרונים לפר
and two tenths for a ram	ושני עשרונים לאיל
and one tenth for a lamb.	ועשרון אחד לכבש
But the point is to indicate	אלא מלמד
that the large ephah and small ephah	שאיפה גדולה ואיפה קטנה
are [both] called an ephah.	קרויה איפה

Note:
Perhaps this was one of the many contradictions between Ezekiel and the Pentateuch which Eleazar's father was famous for resolving (bShab.13b).

Analysis:
A contradiction is resolved without using a third text. This nomological interpretation assumes that Ezekiel would not have contradicted the Pentateuch. Therefore, instead of concluding that Ezekiel has simplified the ceremonial laws, or that 'Ephah' changed its meaning, it is assumed to be a general term which can refer to more than one measurement.

I.2.39. *Mekh.Ish.Bah.7.66:* (Mek.Sim.p148 = I.2.10)

Eleazer b.Hananiah	אלעזר בן הנניה
b.Hezekiah b.Garon says:	בן חזקיה בן גרון אומר
Remember the Sabbath day	זכור את יום השבת
to keep it holy. [Ex.20.8]	לקדשו
Remember it from the first of the week	תהא זוכרו מאחד בשבת
so if there is assigned to you	שאם נתמנה לך
a pleasant thing	חפץ יפה
prepare it for the sake of the Sabbath.	תהא מתקנו לשם שבת

Notes:
Eleazar was a Shammaite, and this exegesis amalgamates Shammai's practice (I.4.20) with an extension of one of his exegeses (I.2.10).

Analysis:
Although this is a very literal understanding of "remember", it is not Ultra-literal because the context is not being ignored. The interpretation is based on the Nomological assumption that Scripture is a legal document in which every word has been carefully chosen in order to convey exactly the correct meaning. Therefore, instead of regarding this as another way of saying 'be sure to keep the Sabbath', Eleazar reads the "remember" literally so that it means 'do not forget the Sabbath, even during the week'.

I.2.40. *bQid.10b-11a:* (Sifré Num.117; yKet.5.4)

Come and hear:	תא שמע
Yohanan b.Bag bag already sent:	וכבר שלח יוחנן בן בג בג
To R. Judah b.Bathyra at Nisisbis:	אצל רבי יהודה בן בתירה לנציבין
I heard about you that you say:	שמעתי עליך שאתה אומר
An Israelite woman betrothed [to a priest]	ארוסה בת ישראל
may eat Terumah.	אוכלת בתרומה

He sent to him:	שלח לו
And you, do you not say thus?	ואתה אי אתה אומר כן
I am certain of you that you	מוחזקני בך שאתה
are expert in the secret-chambers of Torah	בקי בחדרי תורה
to interpret with Qal vaHomer.	לדרוש בקל וחומר

Do you not know:	אי אתה יודע
If a Canaanite slave-girl	ומה שפחה כנענית
who cannot by [virtue of] her coition	שאין ביאתה
eat Terumah [yet by virtue of	מאכילתה בתרומה
her purchase] money eats Terumah,	כספה מאכילתה בתרומה
[then] this one who by her coition	זו שביאתה
eats Terumah	מאכילתה בתרומה
surely [also by virtue of	אינו דין
her betrothal] money eats Terumah.	שכספה מאכילתה בתרומה
But what can I do	אבל מה אעשה
because the Sages ruled:	שהרי אמרו חכמים
An Israelite betrothed woman may not	אין ארוסה בת ישראל
eat Terumah	אוכלת בתרומה
till the marriage is solemnised.	עד שתכנס לחופה

Notes:
Neusner concludes that there were two men called Judah b.Bathyra at Nisibis in Babylon (Neusner 1984:49). This one is the earlier because he is conversing with Ben Bag Bag. This tradition is likely to be old because it preserves an argument contrary to the ruling of the Sages.

Analysis:
The discussion concerns whether an Israelite betrothed to a priest (an Arusah) can eat the Heave Offerings (Terumah) which only the priests and their families could eat.

Judah argues by Qal vaHomer without using Scripture. He points out that a female slave is counted as a member of a priest's family so she can eat of the holy food. If the slave can eat the holy food, then surely the betrothed girl (who is more important than a slave) can eat from it. He proves the betrothed girl is similar to, and yet also more important than the slave girl, by pointing out that both girls come into relationship with the priest by means of money, but the betrothed girl will also later come into a marriage relationship with him.

I.2.41. *mArak.8.6:*
(tArak.4.32; bArak.28b-29a; bSanh.88a; Sifré Num.117)

Something dedicated to priests	חרמי כהנים
cannot be redeemed	אין להם פדיון
but must be given to the priests,	אלא נותנים לכהנים
just like priestly dues.	כתרומה

1a

R. Judah b.Bathyra says:	רבי יהודה בן בתירא אומר
Unspecified dedications [go]	סתם חרמים
to the repair of the Temple,	לבדק הבית
as it is said: [Lev.27.28]	שנאמר
Every dedicated thing is most holy;	כל חרם קדש קדשים
it is for YHWH.	הוא לה'

1b

But the Sages say:	וחכמים אומרים
Unspecified dedications [go]	סתם חרמים
to the priests,	לכהנים
as it is said: [Lev.27.21]	שנאמר
[. . . holy to the Lord,]	
like a dedicated field;	כשדה החרם
it will be for the priest, his possession.	לכהן תהיה אחוזתו

2a

If so, why is it said:	אם כן למה נאמר
Every dedicated thing is most holy;	כל חרם קדש קדשים
it is for YHWH.	הוא לה׳

2b

[To show that] it applies	שהוא חל
to the most holy things	על קדשי קדשים
and to the lesser holy things.	ועל קדשים קלים

Notes:

Judah's exegesis is probably old because it is specifically refuted by the Sages, and the opinion of the Sages may be pre-Yavnean because it sides with the priests. However, this debate still continued in the time of Rab when Galileans held Judah's position and Judeans agreed with the Sages (mNed.2.4). The arguments 2a and 2b may have been added later, but they too support the Priests so they are likely to be early, although possibly later than b.Bathyra because no reply from him is recorded.

Analysis:

The question concerns whether gifts should be given towards the priests' emoluments or to the Temple fabric funds when the destination is not specified by the giver.

1a. Judah argues from a Peshat reading that all gifts are "to the Lord", which he understands as 'to the Temple' rather than 'to the priests'.

1b. The Sages argue by Gezerah Shavah that "to YHWH" means "to the priest".

2a. However, this means that "to YHWH" in v.28 is Redundant.

2b. The Sages reply that the superfluous "to YHWH" indicates that the "most holy" things (for the Altar, cf. mArak.8.7) go to the priest, as well as the "holy" things of v.21.

I.2.42. *bZeb.63a:* (mMen.1.2)

Ben Bathyra says:	בן בתירא אומר
From where [do we know]	מנין
that if he grasps with the left hand	שאם קמץ בשמאל
he should return it	שיחזיר
and then grasp in the right hand?	ויקמוץ בימין
Scripture says: *Thence* [Lev.2.2]	ת״ל משם
– from the place where he grasped already.	ממקום שקמץ כבר

Notes:

The talmudic discussion concerns the Handful of meal-offering. Mishnah says that it can be taken from any part of the Temple Court, but R. Jeremiah interprets "thence" in Lev.2.2 to mean that it must come from the place where the layman stands giving his offering. Ben Bathyra's exegesis is used to show that "thence" has a different meaning and thereby to support the Mishnah.

Ben Bathyra's argument is clearer in mMen where the exegesis is omitted. The question is: What if the priest accidentally takes the Handful of the Meal offering with his left hand? Ben Bathyra answers that he must replace it and take it with his right hand.

Analysis:

It is not certain whether b.Bathyra is arguing from No Redundancy or Unusual Word.

The word משם is superfluous in the context ("he [the layman] shall bring it ... to the priests, and he [the priest] shall take from it [משם] his handful") so b.Bathyra may have used No Redundancy. However משם is also being used in the unusual sense of "from it" rather than "from there", so b.Bathyra may be using the rule of Unusual Word, as he uses in I.2.43.

With either rule the presence of משם needs to be explained. B. Bathyra said that it indicates that when the Handful is accidentally taken with the left hand, then the Priest must put it back and take it again "thence". This explanation takes full note of the context, so even if Unusual Word is used (which is a Derash method), this should perhaps be regarded as a Nomological reading.

I.2.43. *bShab.103b*:

It was taught:	דתניא
R. Judah b.Bathyra said:	רבי יהודה בן בתירה אומר
It is said: [Num.29.19,31,33]	נאמר
concerning the second [day] *"and their drink offerings"*,	בשני ונסכיהם
concerning the sixth *"and its drink offering"*,	בששי ונסכיה
concerning the seventh *"by their ordinance"*.	בשביעי כמשפטם
Here [is] *Mem, Yod, Mem* [i.e.] Water.	הרי מ״ם יו״ד מ״ם מים
From here [comes] a hint	מכאן רמז
concerning the Water Libation	לניסוך מים
from Torah.	מן התור׳

Notes:

Judah was concerned to prove that Water Libation, (a ceremony during the Feast of Tabernacles) could be found in Scripture. The Pharisees supported this popular custom, but the Sadducees did not.

This baraita is introduced during a discussion concerning the number of letters which may be written on a Sabbath. Although no words can be written, one can write up to two letters which do not make a word or an abbreviation for a word or a phrase. There is then a discussion of how closed and open letters can make up abbreviations, and whether a closed letter such as ם can be used as an open letter (ie מ) in an abbreviation. Judah's baraita is quoted to prove that it can.

Analysis:

Judah pointed out that three words in Num.29 appear to have a superfluous letter. These letters spelled מים, 'Water', which hints at the Water Libation ceremony.

v19: From the context one expects the singular "and its drink offering" [ונסכה].

v31: The normal spelling is ונסכה.

v33: One expects to read "according to the ordinance" [כמשפט] (cf. v18,21,24,27,30,37).

Judah uses Eliezer's rule no.16 concerning Unusual words or forms of words which indicate a secondary or hidden meaning. His reference to רמז may indicate that he is using rule 28 but this is usually called מעל and refers mainly to paronomasia. However he was probably ignorant of Eliezer's list.

He uses a Derash mode of interpretation, looking for a secondary meaning which is independent of the plain meaning. However he does not ignore the context, because Num.29 concerns ceremonies during Tabernacles and each word used concerns drink offerings.

I.2.44. *Mid.Tann.p.58:* (ARNb.31)

You shall utterly destroy ...[Deut.12.2]	... אבד תאבדון
Thence Rn.Yohanan b.Zakkai used to say:	מיכן היה ר' יוחנן בן זכאי אומר
Do not hasten to tear down	אל תבהל לסתור
altars of Gentiles	במות גוים
lest you have to rebuild them with your hands.	שלא תבנה בידך
Do not tear down [altars] of mortar	שלא תסתור של לבינים
lest they say to you:	ויאמרו לך
Make [them] of stone, of stone,	עשם של אבנים של אבנים
and they will say to you:	ויאמרו לך
Make [them] of wood.	עשם של עץ

Notes:

Neusner (1962:105f.) linked this tradition with the Jewish destruction of a brick altar in Jamnia. Caligula (37–41 CE) ordered the Jews to pay recompense by erecting his statue in the Temple. Fortunately he died before this command could be enforced (Schürer 1973–:394–397).

Neusner's views about dating changed dramatically when he wrote his *History of the Jews in Babylon* (1965), and by the time he wrote *Development of a Legend* (1970) he had abandoned his early assumption that the actual words of the rabbis had been preserved (1970:5), but he still believed that this tradition may date to c.40 CE (1971 I:343).

The the text is not quoted in the exegesis, and it is omitted in ARNb. However it is argued below that the argument relies on Gamaliel's exegesis of this same text (I.2.31).

Analysis:

Deut.12.2 tells Israel to destroy all pagan altars but Yohanan warns them not to do so. The lack of an alternative interpretation means that Yohanan is counselling the disobedience of Torah

This should probably be read in conjunction with Gamaliel's exegesis (I.2.31) which demonstrates why one should not, in the present situation, destroy foreign altars. This exegesis may have been well known in Yohanan's time. One of these traditions may be wrongly attributed, so that both originated with Gamaliel or both with Yohanan.

I.2.45. *Mid.Tann.p215:*

[They shall teach your commands to Jacob and your Law to Israel [Deut.33.10]	[יורו משפטיך ליעקב ותורתך ליש'
Agrippas the Hegemon asked this to Rn.Yohanan b.Zakkai.	זו שאל אגריפס ההגמון את רבן יוחנן בן זכאי

1

He [Agrippas] said to him:	אמ' לו
How many Laws	כמה תורות
were given to you from Heaven?	ניתן לכם מן השמים

1b

He [Yohanan] said to him:	אמ' לו
Two: one by mouth	שתים אחת בפה
and one in writing.	ואחת בכתב

2a

He [Agrippas] said to him: Really?	אמ' לו וכי
It is said: *And Your Laws to Israel.*	נאמ' ותורתיך לישראל

2b

He [Yohanan] said to him:	אמ' לו
Nevertheless, Two,	אע''פ כן שתים
for it is said: *And your Law to Israel.*	שנ' ותורת(ך) לישראל

Notes:

The same tradition is recorded of Gamaliel I (I.2.32) with whom Yohanan shares other traditions (cf. I.2.31). Both have other disputes with Agrippa or similarly named gentile leaders (cf. I.2.30,32,49,50,51). A similar tradition is attributed to Shammai (bShab.31a) but it has no exegesis and it forms part of a biographical tradition so it is probably late (cf. J. Neusner 1974, B.L. Visotzky 1983).

Yohanan's disputant knows Scripture too well for a Gentile, and it is likely that his argument originated in Sadducean circles.

Analysis:

Neusner's translation (1970:37) of 2ab reads: He replied: And is it said: *And your Torahs to Israel?* He replied: Even so, two, as it is said: *And Torahs to Israel.*

This makes little sense, because Agrippas supplies Yohanan with his proof text, and Yohanan merely agrees, as if Agrippas is testing Yohanan's orthodoxy. My translation is based on Jastrow re כי and אף על פי.

1ab. It should probably be assumed that Yohanan quotes Deut.33.10 in his reply though it is not repeated here.

2a. Agrippas' scepticism is based on the singular "Your" (omitted in 2b), arguing that a single lawgiver would publish a single law. This argument was implied in 1a where he asks how many Laws were given by "God" (changed to "heaven").

2b. Yohanan says that nevertheless the verse refers to two law codes.

Both exegeses are based on the Nomological assumption that the two different terms משפטים and תורה refer to two separate law codes, the Oral Torah and Written Torah.

I.2.46. *mSot.9.9:*

1

When adulterers increased	משרבו המנאפים
the Bitter Waters ceased.	פסקו המים המרים

2

And R. Yohanan b.Zakkai	ורבי יוחנן בן זכאי
caused them to cease	הפסיקן
for it is said: [Hos.4.14]	שנאמר
I will not punish	לא אפקוד
your daughters when they fornicate	על בנותיכם כי תזנינה
nor your brides when they commit adultery.	ועל כלותיכם כי תנאפנה

Notes:

A suspected adulteress was forced to drink the Bitter Waters, a mixture of water from the Laver, dust from the Sanctuary floor, and ink from a curse which took effect if she lied. The rite could not continue after the Temple was destroyed, but this tradition suggests that it ceased for other reasons before this.

However the reason given, that there were too many adulterers, may have been part of a theodicy to explain the destruction of the Temple (R. Goldenberg 1982). It is unlikely that the High Priest would cancel a Temple rite on the authority of a Pharisee, so this exegesis probably originated after 70 CE, and the phrase "After the Temple was destroyed..." which often accompanied Yohanan's rulings (e.g. mSukk.3.12; mRH.4.1–4; mMen.5.10), was omitted to give the impression that this predated the Temple's destruction.

Analysis:

1. The anonymous introduction gives a pragmatic reason, that too many suspected adulterers were being accused. The Pharisees' underlying dislike of physical punishment, such as the *lex talionis* and capital punishment (cf. I.3.10,11; I.2.3,4) may also be behind this decision.

2. Yohanan gives an exegesis in support of this reason from Hosea's prophecy of the punishment for Israel's moral laxity. He may also have had in mind v18: "their drink is removed".

It is possible that Yohanan regarded this prophecy as concerning the events of his time rather than pre-Exile Israel, in which case this would be a Peshat reading understood as Fulfilment of prophecy.

However Yohanan probably did recognise that this prophecy was originally written concerning another time, and was re-applying it to his own time on the principle that prophecy can be applied to more than one situation. If this is so, this may be the first example of Multiple interpretations in rabbinic traditions (see I.7.2).

I.2.47. *bYom.39b:* (ARNa.4; ARNb.7)

Our Rabbis taught:	ת"ר
Forty years before	ארבעים שנה קודם
the destruction of the House [of YHWH]	חורבן הבית

the sacrificial lot [for YHWH] was not	לא היה גורל עולה
in the right [hand at Atonement]	בימין
and the crimson strap was not	ולא היה לשון של זהורית
whitened [on the scapegoat]	מלבין
and the western lamp was still	ולא היה נר מערבי
burning [in the morning]	דולק
and the doors of the temple used to	והיו דלתות ההיכל
open by themselves till	נפתחות מאליהן עד
Rn.Yohanan b.Zakkai rebuked them.	שגער בהן רבן יוחנן בן זכאי
He said to it: Temple, Temple.	אמר לו היכל היכל
Why do you give the alarm yourself.	מפני מה אתה מבעית עצמך
I know that in the end	יודע אני בך שסופך
you are destined to be destroyed	עתיד ליחרב
as already Zechariah b.Ido	וכבר נתנבא עליך זכריה בן עדוא
prophesied about you: [Zech.11.1]	
Open your doors Lebanon	פתח לבנון דלתיך
and fire will devour your cedars.	ותאכל אש בארזיך

Notes:

The traditions concerning the lot, the red-strap and the western light are probably separate from the tradition of the doors. They are listed here as omens which started to go wrong when Simon the Just died. The "lot" is the lot marked "For the Lord" in the Day of Atonement ceremony by which the goat was chosen for sacrifice, while the other lot ("For Azazel") chose the scapegoat (mYom.4.1). The "Red-Strap" was a red thread which was tied round the neck of the two goats (mYom.4.2) and a piece of which was also tied to the door of the sanctuary (mYom.6.8). The "Western Light" is the western-most lamp in the Lampstand of the sanctuary which was always the first to be filled.

According to the tradition, in the days before Simon the Just died, the lot 'for the Lord' always occurred in the right hand (a good omen), the scarlet thread always turned white when the scapegoat was killed and the lamps continued burning throughout the night. After his death these things happened occasionally, but during the last 40 years of the Temple these good omens never happened. The tradition concerning the doors should be considered separately from these omens which probably came from the separate 'Simon the Just' traditions.

The phrase "forty years before the destruction of the Temple" may mean nothing more than 'when everything started to go wrong', because various bad omens are collected here and this same phrase describes the date when the Sanhedrin lost the right to try capital cases (bShab.15a; bSanh.41a). If this date is taken seriously, the reference to Yohanan here is anachronistic, because he did not join the Sanhedrin till after the power to try capital cases had been removed (bSanh.41a). Perhaps there was some confusion with Yohanan b.Gudgada who was a Temple door-keeper (bArak.11b) or with Hananiah the prefect of the priests, to whom this tradition is attributed in ARNb.7.

Josephus (War 6.294[5.3]) provides some early corroboration of the tradition that the Temple doors opened by themselves and that it was considered to be an omen concerning the future of the Temple. It is unlikely that Josephus acted as a source for the rabbis, particularly as he records other omens which would fit well here. Josephus dates the sign shortly before the destruction, when Yohanan was in the city. He notes that the event was interpreted as a good omen by some ("as if God was opening the gate of happiness") and a bad omen by others.

The use of 'Lebanon' to mean 'the Temple', suggests that the exegesis may be early (see below) although this metaphor continued to be employed for many centuries.

Whether this exegesis should be dated before or after the destruction is difficult to decide. However Josephus' evidence suggests that the omen was widely known, and that its interpretation was in dispute. Therefore this exegesis probably originated before the destruction in support of those who interpreted it as a bad omen, rather than after, when their interpretation needed no such support.

Analysis:
Yohanan regards the omen as a forewarning of prophetic fulfillment. G. Vermes (1961 : 26ff.) showed that "Lebanon" is frequently interpreted symbolically, especially as the Temple or related objects such as the Altar, but also as Jerusalem, the King, the Rich, the Nations etc. About half of the occurrences of "Lebanon" are substituted by such interpretations in the targumim. The interpretation of "Lebanon" as "the Temple" or "Jerusalem" is also found at Qumran (IQpHab.12.1–6) and in Tannaitic midrashim, and can be dated back to the 2nd C BCE (Ecclus.1.8–9,12; 24.10–13).

Prior to Yohanan, Zech.11.1 (and Is.10.34 – see I.2.48) were interpreted as Lebanon = Nations, but subsequent Jewish and Christian exegetes followed Yohanan (G. Vermes 1961 : 33f.; H.F.D. Sparks 1959 : 278). However this alternative symbolism was so common that Yohanan probably regarded the interpretation as Peshat.

I.2.48. *bGit.56ab:* (ARNa.4; ARNb.6; LamR.1.5)
1a

If you were not a king	את דאי לאו מלכא
Jerusalem would not be delivered	את לא מימסרא ירושלים
into your hand. As it is written: [Is.10.34]	בידך דכתיב
And Lebanon will fall by a mighty one.	והלבנון באדיר יפול

1ai

And none [is called] *mighty* except a king.	ואין אדיר אלא מלך
As it is written: [Jer.30.21]	דכתי'
The mighty one will be from him etc.	והיה אדירו ממנו וגו'

1aii

And none [is called] *Lebanon*	ואין לבנון
except the Sanctuary.	אלא ביהמ"ק
As it is said: [Deut.3.25]	שנאמר
This good mountain even Lebanon.	ההר הטוב הזה והלבנון

Notes:
The explanations (1ai & 1aii) do not occur in the parallels, and have probably been added later. However they are necessary for understanding Yohanan's words and may correctly record the traditional exegesis of Is.10.34.

This occurs during the story about Yohanan's escape from besieged Jerusalem. There are no early accounts of this tradition, and Neusner regards the exegesis to be integral to the whole, and no older than the full narrative.

One indication that this exegesis may have originated with Yohanan is the Symbol of Lebanon = Temple which Yohanan uses elsewhere (I.2.47), and which dates from the second century BCE (G. Vermes 1961 : 26ff.).

Analysis:

1. Yohanan sees the Fulfilment of Is.10.34 in Vespasian. This prophecy is meaningless without the supplementary exegeses which he probably considered too obvious to require explanation.

1ai. The Talmud explains that "mighty one" [אדיר] always refers to a king, and proves it by Gezerah Shavah (I). Although "king" does not occur in the text, "mighty one" is paralleled with "ruler" [משל] which is normally used of kings. However the Talmud is probably following the traditional interpretation in the Targum which translates "mighty one" as "king", and "ruler" as "Messiah".

In fact אדיר is also used for people of noble birth who do not rule a kingdom (Neh.3.5;10.29; 2Chron.23.20; Nah.3.18 etc.). Vespasian was a self-made man, and perhaps Yohannan felt that he had to become emperor before he could be called 'noble'. If this is so, it is a good thing that Vespasian did not question his exegesis more closely.

1aii. To show that Lebanon = Jerusalem, the Talmud uses the most common proof text for this purpose (Deut.3.25 – Vermes 1961 : 36). The context is Moses' prayer that he be allowed to pass over the Jordan to see "this good hill country and Lebanon". The text is understood slightly differently here ('this good Mountain, even Lebanon'), but this would be the Peshat meaning in Yohanan's time, because it was self-evident that Moses must have wanted to see the Temple mount rather than Lebanon.

I.2.49. *ySanh.1.2 (19b) :*

1a

Angetos the Hegemon asked	אנגטוס הגמון שאל
R. Yohanan b.Zakkai [about the text:]	לרבי יוחנן בן זכאי
The ox shall be stoned	השור יסקל
and also its master shall die. [Ex.21.29]	וגם בעליו יומת

1b

He said:	אמר ליה
The partner of a bandit	שותף ליסטים
[is treated] like the bandit.	כליסטים

2a

And when he had left	וכשיצא
his disciples said to him:	אמרו לו תלמידיו
Rabbi, this one you repulsed with a reed	רבי לזה דחיתה בקנה
[but] for us, what is the reply?	לנו מה את משיב

2b

He said to them, It is written:	אמר להן כתיב
The ox shall be stoned	השור יסקל
and also its master shall die. [Ex.21.29]	וגם בעליו יומת
As the death of the master	כמיתת הבעלים
thus is the death of the ox.	כן מיתת השור

There is a correspondence between the	הקיש מיתת בעלים
death of the master and the death of the ox.	למיתת השור
Just as the capital charge	מה מית׳
of master is investigated and examined	בעלים בדרישה וחקירה
by [the court of] 23 [judges],	בעשרים ושלשה
so the capital charge	אף מיתת
of the ox is investigated and examined	השור בדרישה וחקירה
by [the court of] 23 [judges].	בעשרי׳ ושלשה

Notes:

This tradition and the two following concern discussions between Yohanan and Angentos/Antoninus/Antigonus the Hegemon. These are almost impossible to date, but M.D. Herr (1971a:128ff.) has suggested that they originated at about 70 CE. He assumes that this Hegemon is a real person, and tentatively identifies him with Marcus Antoninus Julianus, a procurator of Judea, which explains his interest in legal and census procedures among the Jews. The meeting may have occurred while Yohanan stayed in Vespasian's camp outside besieged Jerusalem.

These conclusions far out-weigh the evidence they rely on, and even if these traditions are based on actual meetings, the discussions are very unlikely to have been preserved. Moreover the character of the Hegemon is inconsistent, because he is satisfied with a weak answer in the first debate, and yet holds tenaciously to his argument when he is given a weak answer in the third debate.

However the overall weakness of Yohanan's arguments are an indication that these traditions may be based on genuine debates in which Yohanan was caught off-guard and was thinking on his feet. Neusner (1970:139) even wonders if these accounts are anti-Yohanine, intending to show that Yohanan is incompetent, but he concludes that the editor probably didn't realise how weak these arguments are.

A Gentile leader named Antoninus occurs frequently in the Talmud especially in discussions with Rabbi (L. Ginzberg 1901b), and this may have prompted the naming of an anonymous Hegemon in these traditions.

A fourth debate of Yohanan with an unnamed gentile, concerning the rite of the Red Heifer (Num.R.19.8) will not be discussed because there are no indications for an early date.

This present debate and the fourth debate have the same form:

1. The gentile asks a question, is answered and goes away
2. The disciples demand and receive a better answer.

This is the form in some of Yohanan's Sadducee disputes (cf. I.3.2).

Neusner (1970:138) suggests that in these debates the gentile is palmed off with something which does not answer the question, and that the disciples are given the real answer. However the two answers are given to different types of people with different requirements, and both go away satisfied.

In NumR.19.8 the debate concerns the relevance of the rite of the Red Heifer, which Yohanan explains to the gentile in terms of exorcism procedures for an unclean spirit, and to his disciples in terms of the fear of Heaven. The first answer was acceptable to the gentile but not to the disciples, and the second was acceptable to the disciples but would have meant little to the gentile.

In this present debate the first answer is acceptable to the Roman, who is interested in justice being done, but whose judicial procedure were not so strict when it came to animals. The disciples however were the future rabbis who later produced numerous regulations concerning murder trials, all of which were designed to help acquit the accused (cf. mSanh.4–6). They may also have considered that if an ox is condemned without trial, then this might later be applied to a man, because an ox was commonly regarded as equivalent to a man in sone respects, especially in the area of tort (cf. I.2.6; I.3.4).

Analysis:

1a. If an ox killed a person, the ox was killed, but if the owner had been warned that the ox was dangerous then the owner was also killed. The Hegemon apparently asks why the ox should be regarded as guilty in the latter case. He could of course be asking concerning the death of the man (cf. Bacher 1884 I:40f.) but in 2b Yohanan defends the capital charge passed on the ox, not on the man.

1b. Yohanan says that the ox (or the man) is an accomplice to murder. This answer is difficult to understand because the Hegemon's precise question has not been preserved.

Perhaps his question proposed that an ox cannot be judged guilty any more than an imbecile, who was generally considered innocent when he broke the law. Although the earliest relevant halakot are attributed to Judah haNasi (mMeg.2.4; mPar.5.4) this principle lies at the basis of several tractates (e.g. mHag.1.1; mBQ.4.4; mShebu.6.4) so when, for example, an imbecile was judged even partially guilty for theft it was noted that this was "for the interests of peace" (mGit.5.8) rather than for justice.

However Yohanan does not mention imbeciles and we must assume that the Hegemon did not ask this question. If he had, his quote would have been merely: *The ox will be stoned.* The further quotation about the master would have been superfluous.

The question which Yohanan appears to answer is: Why is the ox killed when it is admitted that the real culprit is the man. Yohanan agrees that the man is the main culprit, but that the ox is an accomplice.

2a. Roman justice is satisfied, but Jewish justice is not. Yohanan's disciples assume that the man will have a proper trial before being punished, but what about the ox? This question is not recorded for us, but is implied by Yohanan's answer.

2b. Yohanan argues by Heqesh, finding a common factor between the owner and the ox which is not based on Scripture but on logic. He connects the two by "death" [מיתת] which is used of the owner in Scripture but not of the ox, though logically the ox will suffer death when it is stoned.

Having shown a link between the two punishments, he says they are also linked by their trial. Just as the man is executed after a proper trial, so also the ox had its own trial before 23 judges (see J.J. Finkelstein 1981).

I.2.50. *ySanh.1.4 (19c); NumR.3.14:* (bBekh.5a; NumR.4.9)
NumR.3.14 (Mirkin IX:66f.):

At the word of YHWH, by their families	על פי ה׳ למשפחתם
all males from age a month and upward.	כל זכר מבן חדש ומעלה
were 22,000. [Num.3.39]	שנים ועשרים אלף
1a	
You find that the tribe of Levi is	את מוצא שבט לוי היו
counted-in-detail as 22,300	בפרט עשרים ושנים אלף ושלש מאות
for there were four families:	מפני שהיו ארבע משפחות

Gershon, Kohath, Merari and Moses. | גרשון וקהת ומררי ומשה
And [if] you call | ואת קורא
each family by itself | כל משפחה ומשפחה בפני עצמה
and count them: | ומחשב אותה

to Gershon	7,500 [Num.3.22]	לגרשון שבעת אלפים וחמש מאות
and to Kohath	8,600 [Num.3.28]	ולקהת שמונת אלפים ושש מאות
to Merari	6,200 [Num.3.34]	למררי ששת אלפים ומאתים
then they total	22,300	והם עולים עשרים ושנים אלף ושלש מאות

And yet when the Levites are | וכיון שהוא כולל את הלוים
counted-in-general
they make 22,000. | תוא עושה אותם עשרים ושנים אלף
What about the 300? | השלש מאות היכן

1b

The answer is that those which are males | אלא אותם שהזכיר
are counted in detail to make-known | בפרט להודיע
how many are in each family. | כמה היו בכל משפחה ומשפחה

2a

And those which are counted-generally | ואלו שנכללו
are 22,000 | עשרים ושנים אלף
but 300 are omitted from them; | וחסר מהן שלש מאות
why? | למה עשה כן

2b

The answer is that it is in order to | אלא מפני שמנאן להקישן
give comparison
to the firstborn of Israel to be redeemed. | לפדות בכורי ישראל
And the 300 deducted from them | ופחת מהן שלש מאות
are the firstborn which are Levites | שהיו בכורות שהיו בלוים
for firstborn cannot redeem firstborn. | שאין בכור פודה בכור

Therefore counting-by-families they are | לכך היו המשפחות
22,300 | עשרים ושנים אלף ושלש מאות
and counting-generally 22,000, | ובכלל עשרים ושנים אלף
to redeem by them | לפדות בהן
the firstborn of Israel. | בכורי ישראל

ySanh.1.4 (19c):

2a

Antoninus the Hegemon | אנטונונוס הגמון
asked Rn.Yohanan b.Zakkai: | שאל את רבן יוח' בן זכאי
In general [counting] | בכלל
they are deficient | חסירין
but in detailed [counting] | ובפרט
they are excessive. | יתורין

2b
He said to him: אמ' ליה
These three hundred excessive ones   אותן שלש מאות יתירין
are the firstborn of the priesthood   בכורי כהונה היו
3b
and the holy [coin] cannot release   ואין קודש מוציא קודש
the holy [tribe].

Notes:
The detailed totals of Levitical families disagrees with the overall total by 300. NumR.3 assumes that there is no real discrepancy so it asks first for the significance of the detailed total and then of the smaller overall total.

The Hegemon is less polite, and demands a reason for the discrepancy. In NumR.4.9 (where he is called "Agenitos") he implies that Moses' motive was embezzlement. The Levites were the payment to YHWH for the 22,273 firstborn of Israel whom He had not killed in Egypt. By lowering the total number of Levites to 22,000, Moses ensured that 273 firstborn would have to be redeemed at 5 shekels each, payable to Aaron his brother.

The account in ySanh.1 is obscure without the parallels and may be the result of over-ambitious summarising. It is therefore surprising to find in ySanh.1 a reference to a new argument which is not present in any parallel (3b, implying 3a – see below). It is possible that "the holy cannot release the holy" (3b) is actually a corruption of "the firstborn cannot redeem the firstborn" at the end of 2b, but there are no verbal links between the two phrases other than their similar form.

Therefore it is likely that Yohanan is referring to a well-known tradition which did not need repeating, but that his questioner did not understand the "holy" status of the Levites so the further explanation in 3b had to be added.

The tradition is also attributed to Gamaliel according to Rashi (marginal note א at bBekh.5a).

Dating this tradition is very difficult. Like I.2.49 this meeting is historically possible but improbable. However the summary nature of the original question and answer suggest that the disputant was merely repeating a common objection, and the presence of 3b suggests that he was unfamiliar with a common OT concept. It therefore becomes more possible that this tradition represents a real encounter with an intelligent gentile who is interested in government matters such as justice and censuses.

Analysis:
1a. The problem is set out in great detail, ending with the question about the significance of the 300.

Although the question has outlined an apparent contradiction, this contradiction is not addressed till 2b. The answer to 1a assumes that the question has raised the problem of No Redundancy: why is the detailed numbering included?

1b. The 300 are significant to the families they belong to. This answer may sound unsatisfactory to modern ears, but when a large family was accounted as great wealth and family or tribal pride depended on its size, this answer made perfect sense.

2a. But why are the 300 omitted from the overall total? This is a question of Contradiction. The 22,000 cannot be a rounded figure because it is used as the basis for calculating the redemption money payable to Aaron.

2b. The 300 are the firstborn of the Levites, which were themselves spared by

YHWH when He killed all the firstborn in Egypt (Num.3.13) they cannot therefore redeem other firstborn.

This solves a contradiction between two texts (Num.3.39 and Num.3.22ff.) by using a third (Num.3.13), in accordance with Ishmael's rule 13.

3a. This question is missing, but must be inferred from the answer which is given. The Hegemon presumably asked: "If the 300 Levites were firstborn, why were they not required to pay five Shekels each?".

3b. Yohanan has to point out that the Levites were already all dedicated to YHWH and could not be redeemed.

The Hegemon does not question the fact that 300 firstborn among 22,300 males means that each firstborn has 73 younger brothers aged one month or older. Presumably a "firstborn" was the head of a family group rather than a nuclear family. This is confirmed by the census of the rest of Israel where 603,550 males above 20 years include 22,273 firstborn (Num.1.46; 3.43). If this number of males is adjusted to include those between one month and 20 years, it totals about 2,000,000 (assuming a stable demography and death at an average age of 65), which means one firstborn to every 90 males.

I.2.51. *ySanh.1.4 (19d)*: (bBer.5a)

1a

Antigonus the Hegemon asked	שאל אנטיגנס הגמון
Rn.Yohanan b.Zakkai:	לרבן יוחנן בן זכאי
Moses your teacher	משה רבכם
was either a thief	או גנב היה
or he was not expert at counting,	או לא היה בקי בחשבון
as it is written: [Ex.38.26]	דכתיב
A Beqa per head.	בקע לגולגול׳
If you make a Centenarius	אין תעביד קינטרא
100 Litras	מאה ליטרי
then he stole one sixth,	וחד מן אישתא גנב
and if you make it 60 Litras	ואין תעבדיניה שיתין ליטרין
he stole half.	פלגא גנב

1b

[Yohanan] said to him:	א״ל
Moses our teacher	משה רבן
was a faithful treasurer	גיזבר נאמן
and an expert counter.	ובקי בחשבון היה

2a

[Yohanan] said to him:	א״ל
And it is written: [Ex.38.29]	והכתיב
And the bronze of the wave-offering	ונחושת התנופה
[was] 20 [MT: 70] Kikkar [and 2400 Shekels].	עשרים ככר
And take note	והיידא לון
they convert to 96 Litras	סלקין תשעין ושית ליטרין
but it is made into a remainder.	ואיתעביד ליה פרוטרוט

2bi

[Antigonus] said to him:	א״ל
The reason is that it cannot	משום דלא
be converted to a Centenarius,	סליק קינטירא

2bii

And if you insist	ואין תימר
that it converts to a Centenarius	דסליק קינטירא
[then Moses] stole a half.	פלג׳ גנב

3a

[Yohanan] said to him:	א״ל
And it is written: [Ex.38.28]	והכתיב
And the 1775 [Shekels]	ואת האלף ושבע המאות וחמשה ושבעי׳
And take note	והייד׳ לון
they convert to 71 Litras	סלקין שבעים וחד ליטרין
but you made it into a remainder.	ואת עביד ליה פרוטרוט

3bi

[Antigonus] said to him:	אל
The reason is that it cannot	משו׳ דלא
be converted to a Centenarius.	סליק קינטירא

3bii

[And if you insist that it converts to a Centenarius	
then Moses] stole half.	פלגא גנב

4a

[Yohanan] said to him:	א״ל
And it is written: [Ezk.45.12]	והכתיב
And the Shekel [is] 20 Gerahs	והשקל עשרי׳ גרה
[and] 20 Shekels	עשרים שקלים
[plus] 25 Shekels	חמשה ועשרים שקלים
[plus] 25 [MT: 15] Shekels	עשרים וחמשה שקלים
shall be a Minah to you.	המנה יהיה לכם
A Kikkar of the Holy One	ככרו של הקדוש
(blessed be He)	ברוך הוא
is to be double.	כפול היה

4b

[Antigonus] said to him:	אמר ליה
[Moses] is a faithful treasurer	גיזבר נאמן ובקי בחשבון היה
and an expert counter.	

Notes:
Greek, Hebrew and Latin coinage is used interchangeably here:
     ταλαντον = centenarium = כבר (Kikkar)
= 60λιτρα   = libra   = מנה (Minah)
= 25στατηρ or τετραδραχμον = שקל (Shekel)
    These equivalences and exchange rates were commonly accepted and are agreed by both sides in the debate.

The dispute concerns the poll-tax of a Beqa or Half Shekel from each of the 603,550 Israelites, which totalled 100 Kikkar and 1775 shekels (Ex.38.25f.). This presumably represents 301,755 Shekels (i.e. 603,550/2), which suggests that each Kikkar was exchanged for 3000 Shekels rather than the normal 1500.

The text of this debate has suffered greatly. The texts differ from the MT (cf. 2a, 4a), though they do not support the argument, especially in 4a where it ruins the calculations. The portion of text quoted is not always the most useful, especially at 2a (where the vital words have been omitted), and the unusual ithpael איתעביד at 2a has been changed in the parallel 3a to את עביד which does not suit the argument. These changes suggest that the debate was misunderstood from an early date, which strengthens the likelihood that it originates with Yohanan.

The confusion within the debate, where both Yohanan and the Hegemon misunderstand each other, also suggests that this originated as a real debate rather than to explain the difficult text.

Analysis:

1a. The Hegemon accuses Moses of either misappropriation or miscalculation because he used an exchange rate of 3000 shekels per kikkar, which is equivalent to 120 litras per centenarium.

The normal exchange is 60 litras, in which case Moses kept half for himself. Even if one is charitable and assumes that Moses thought a centenarium represented 100 litras, he was still out by one sixth.

1b. Yohanan disagrees.

2a. Yohanan wants to show that the sacred kikkar was twice the normal kikkar, so that 120 litras is the correct exchange rate.

2a. He points to the offering of bronze, which did not involve Moses in exchanging Shekels. This is similarly divided into kikkars and remaining Shekels, and indicates that the kikkar used in this text is greater than 2400 shekels or 96 litras.

2b. The Hegemon is not quite sure what Yohanan's argument is. Yohanan calls the 2400 shekels פרוטרוט, which indicates a 'remainder' or an 'exact number', so the Hegemon answers according to both meanings.

2bi. If Yohanan is arguing that the 96 litras was a "remainder", in order to prove that a different exchange rate was being used, then the Hegemon answers that an exchange rate of 100 litras explains it, but still leaves Moses in the wrong.

2bii. And if Yohanan is arguing that the sum could have been exchanged further but was left unchanged in order to be a more 'exact number', then Moses must have accepted the 60 litra exchange rate and therefore he stole half the money when he used the 120 litra exchange rate.

3a. Yohanan does not realise that the Hegemon has misunderstood, and doesn't appear to have listened to his reply.

He continues to emphasise the similarity between the remainder from the bronze and the 1775 shekels remaining from Moses' exchange. He demonstrates that the same abnormal exchange rate has been used, because the remainder is greater than 60 litras.

3bi & ii. The Hegemon thinks that this is the same argument as 2a, and gives the same reply in an abbreviated form.

4a. Yohanan finally gets to the point, quoting Ezk.45 to prove that the sacred kikkar is twice the normal weight, so Moses was quite right to use an exchange rate of 3000 shekels per kikkar.

Exegeses in Scribal Traditions

His overall argument is based on a Nomological resolution of Contradiction of two texts (Ex.38. 25f. & 29) by means of a third (Ezek.45.12).

4b. The Hegemon's reply is probably invented. In the previous two debates he merely walks away once he is satisfied with an answer.

However Yohanan does not appear to have proved that the sacred measurements were exactly twice the secular. If a sacred mina is 60 shekels (20 + 25 + 15) instead of the normal 25, then a kikkar is 3600 shekels. Moses was now at least erring on the generous side, but he was still not a very good accountant.

Perhaps Yohanan used a tradition which concluded that Ezekiel's minah was 50 shekels. Ezk.45.12 is clearly corrupt, and it is possible to extract this conclusion from it by heroic manipulations (such as Boeckh's novel punctuation of a LXX variant, in Keil & Delitzsch).

A more likely explanation is that the Gerah was regarded as equal to the Ma'ah [מעה] (Lauterbach 1906b:485; bBekh.50a) 24 of which made a shekel. Therefore 60 of Ezekiel's shekels (of 20 Gerah/Ma'ah each) were identical to 50 normal shekels.

I.3 Exegeses by Pharisees and Sadducees

Some of the following passages do not contain exegeses of biblical texts but are included because they illustrate the use of exegetical techniques in Sadducee-Pharisee debates.

1.3.1. *ARNa.5:* (ARNb.10)

Antigonus of Socho	אנטיגנוס איש סוכו
received teaching from Simeon the Just.	קבל משמעון הצדיק

He used to say:	הוא היה אומר
Be not like servants	אל תהיו כעבדים
who obey their master	המשמשים את הרב
for the sake of receiving a portion,	על מנת לקבל פרס
but be like servants	אלא היו כעבדים
who obey their master	המשמשים את הרב
not for sake of receiving a portion.	שלא על מנת לקבל פרס
But let the fear of heaven be on you,	ויהי מורא שמים עליכם
so that your reward will be double	כדי שיהיה שכרכם כפול
in the world to come.	לעתיד לבא

1a

Antigonus of Socho	אנטיגנוס איש סוכו
had two disciples	היו לו שני תלמידים
who repeated his words,	שהיו שונין בדבריו
and they repeated to [their] disciples	והיו שונין לתלמידים
and [these] disciples to [their] disciples.	ותלמידים לתלמידים
They decided to scrutinise them	עמדו ודקדקו אחריהן
and said: Why did our predecessors	ואמרו מה ראו אבותינו
say this thing?	לומר דבר זה

Is it possible	אפשר
for a labourer to do toil all day	שיעשה פועל מלאכה כל היום
and not to receive wages at evening?	ולא יטול שכרו ערבית
But indeed,	אלא אלו
had our predecessors known	היו יודעין אבותינו
that there is another world	שיש עולם אחר
and there is a resurrection of the dead	ויש תחיית המתים
they would not have spoken thus.	לא היו אומרים כך
They rose and separated from Torah	עמדו ופירשו מן התורה
and they split into two sects,	ונפרצו מהם שתי פרצות
the Sadducees and the Boethusians -	צדוקים וביתוסין
Sadducees from the name Zadok	צדוקים על שום צדוק
Boethusians from the name Boethius.	ביתוסי על שום ביתוס

2a

And they used vessels	והיו משתמשין
all of silver and all of gold	בכלי כסף וכלי זהב
all their days,	כל ימיהם

2b

not because they were ostentatious	שלא היתה דעתן גסה עליהם
but the Sadducees say:	אלא צדוקים אומרים
The Pharisees have a tradition	מסורת הוא ביד פרושים
that they subject themselves [to austerity]	שהן מצערין עצמן
in this world,	בעוה"ז
but in the world to come	ובעוה"ב
they will not have anything.	אין להם כלום

Notes:

The Mishnah does not contain the words "so that your reward may be double in the world to come", and these were presumably added in order to show that his disciples' interpretation was incorrect. Isaac bar Shelomoh suggested that the words "but let the fear of heaven be upon you" (which *are* in the Mishnah) have been similarly added (C. Taylor 1877:27).

H. W. Basser (1984) suggests that פירשו מן התורה should be translated "they explained [the tradition directly] from the Torah", referring to the Saducean rejection of oral tradition.

E. Bickerman (1951) has convincingly located Antigonus' saying into the time of Antiochus Epiphanes, where the slave without "portion" (i.e. the regular food maintenance due to every slave) was Israel, who continued to serve God even though He had appeared to neglect them. He also suggested that Antigonus was interpolated into the Pharisaic Chain of tradition in order to counter the Saducean claim to his authority.

Although this story about his disciples may be a later invention, their argument from the words of Antigonus is likely to be genuine, because the rabbis would not have fabricated ways of mis-reading them.

It is most surprising to find the tradition end with an unanswered gibe by the Sadducees ridiculing the Pharisaic belief in an after-life. This suggests that there has been less interference with this tradition than one might expect for a debate concerning such a central tenet of rabbinic theology.

Analysis:

1a. The Sadducees saw Antigonus as speaking about workers who will receive no reward, and concluded that he did not believe in heavenly rewards. This was an Ultra-literal interpretation of Antigonus' saying which presumably meant that one should work with the fear of heaven as one's sole motive.

1b. No reply is given because the real meaning of Antigonus' saying was plain enough for the readers of the Mishnah. However, by the time the ARN version was written, there was a need to put Antigonus' position beyond dispute by adding the words "so that your reward may be doubled in the age to come", even though this addition rendered the argument of the schismatic disciples unintelligible. The necessity for this addition probably arose with the widespread acceptance of Ultra-literal arguments, so that his disciples' argument was no longer self-evidently false.

2a. The Sadducees were charged with living luxuriously.

2b. They reply that this was not because they were ostentatious but they wanted to demonstrate their theological position that there is no after-life. They ridicule the Pharisees who think their abstemious life in this world will be rewarded.

H. W. Basser (1984: 551f.) reads the end of this tradition completely differently. The charge concerning luxurious living is made against Zadok and Boethius whom the rabbis wished to defend, arguing that only their misguided disciples rejected the resurrection. It is admitted that they lived in luxury, but this was permitted to them because they were not corrupted by it. He sees an indirect allusion in the phrase "not because they had greedy minds" to the Targum Pseudo-Jonathan on Deut.17.17:

"He shall not increase gold and silver unto himself that his heart not be lifted up so much that he rebel against the God of the heavens"

This phrase therefore indicated that luxury was allowed so long as it did not corrupt the heart. The final comment by the Sadducees demonstrates that they did not recognise or understand this allusion.

This interesting interpretation is spoiled by lack of evidence. The charge of luxurious living does seem to apply to Sadducees in general, and it is hardly surprising that the Sadducees did not recognise the allusion to this interpretation when Basser himself appears to be the first ever to do so.

I.3.2. *mYad.4.6:*

1a

The Sadducees say:	אומרים צדוקים
We complain against you Pharisees,	קובלין אנו עליכם פרושים
for you say:	שאתם אומרים
Holy books	כתבי הקודש
confer uncleannes to hands	מטמאין את הידים
[but] books of Hamiram	ספרי המירם
do not confer uncleannes to hands.	אינם מטמאין את הידים

1b

R. Yohanan b.Zakkai said:	אמר רבי יוחנן בן זכאי
And have we	וכי אין לנו
only this against the Pharisees?	על הפרושים אלא זו בלבד
Behold they say:	הרי הם אומרים

The bones of an ass are pure	עצמות חמור טהורים
but the bones of Yohanan	ועצמות יוחנן
the High Priest confer uncleanness.	כהן גדול טמאים

2a

He said to him:	אמרו לו
As is our love for them so	לפי חבתן היא
[the bones] confer uncleanness,	טומאתן
to deter a man from making	שלא יעשה אדם
the bones of his father and mother	עצמות אביו ואמו
into spoons.	תרוודות

2b

He said to them:	אמר להם
Just so with holy books.	אף כתבי הקדש
As is our love for them, so	לפי חבתן היא
they confer uncleanness,	טומאתן
[but] the books of Hamiram	ספרי המירם
which are not beloved	שאינן חביבין
do not confer uncleanness to hands.	אין מטמאין את הידים

Notes:

"Hamiram" has been explained as 'heretic', 'Homer' or as other authors. Its exact meaning is unimportant for the argument.

E. Rivkin (1969:233) suggests that the real motive behind this halakah was to impede the Priest's access to the written Torah, because the second-degree uncleanness caused by handling them would prevent priests from serving but would not restrict the activities of Pharisees.

The form of this dispute is a variation on the common 'complaint' form which normally consists of:

1. "The Sadducees [or equivalent] say: We cry out against you O Pharisees for you..."

2. "The Pharisees [or equivalent] say: We cry out against you O Sadducees for you..."

3. The reply, which may start "No..." and may involve a counter-complaint whose connection with the first complaint is often obscure because it is intended as a clever or witty answer.

Yohanan's reply here follows the pattern of answering a complaint with a seemingly unrelated counter-complaint, but it does not use the usual phrases, and the fact that Yohanan speaks of the Pharisees in the third person also suggests a later date, when the 'Pharisees' as a group have all but disappeared. This pericopé is also complicated by the way the second 'complaint' (as well as the first) is made about the Pharisees and yet the Sadducees answer it. All this suggests that this tradition has been developed by Yohanan or a disciple from an original tradition which would have been something like the following:

The Sadducees say: We cry out against you, O Pharisees, for you say: The holy books confer uncleanness to hands [and] the writings of Hamiram do not confer uncleanness to hands.

The Pharisees say: We cry out against you O Sadducees, for you say: The bones of an ass are clean, and the bones of the High Priest confer uncleanness.

When the explanations were added to this tradition, it was also necessary to point out that the second 'complaint' applied equally to the Pharisees as to the Sadducees, and that the principle behind it was the same as the principle behind the 'uncleanness' of Scripture.

However the original argument is likely to be early, especially if Yohanan the High Priest is Jonathan who was High Priest in 37 AD (J. Jeremias 1969: 157,197 cf. Act.4.6 where most MSS read Ιωαννης).

Analysis:

1a. The Sadducees complain against the Pharisees who declare a holy book unclean and a secular book clean. The complaint appears to be that the Pharisees are being logically inconsistent.

1b. Yohanan points out that the Pharisees are similarly inconsistent with regard to bones.

However, this 'inconsistency' is thoroughly Scriptural, because although the corpse of an animal who died naturally conveys uncleanness, an animal which is killed does not (Lev.17.13–15), but a human corpse conveys uncleanness whether the person died naturally or is killed (Num.19.16). It may also have been based on the fact that 'bones' are specifically referred to with regard to defilement from a human corpse (Num.19.16) but not with regard to an animal.

The Sadducees, who also followed Scripture, would therefore be equally guilty of this 'inconsistency'. J.M. Baumgarten (1980: 161f.) suggests that the distinction between animal and human bones was not shared by the Sadducees but 2Kings 16.20 demonstrates that it was a very ancient tradition.

2a. The Sadducees give two explanations for this seeming inconsistency:

i. Uncleanness is always in proportion to one's regard for the object.

ii. An argument of Reductio ad Absurdum: if a human corpse would ever be free of conveying uncleanness, then it would be allowable for people to make utensils from their bones, and even make spoons from their own parents.

2b. Yohanan then shows that by defending their own seeming inconsistency, the Sadducees have explained the inconsistency with which they had charged the Pharisees.

In the above passage he shows how their first argument supports the Pharisees' position concerning the uncleanness of Scripture, and in tYad (below) he shows how their second argument also supports this position.

tYad.2.19:

Rn.Yohanan b.Zakkai said to them:	אמר להן רבן יוחנן בן זכאי
Likewise for Sacred Scriptures,	כתבי קודש
as is our love [for them]	חיבתן
so they confer uncleanness,	טומאתן
to deter one from using them	שלא יעשה אותן
as mats for cattle.	שטיחין לבהמה

Notes:

The context is not given in the Tosefta, but it is clearly a continuation of the discussion of mYad.4.6 (above). Neusner (1970: 61) remarks that this is an example where the Tosefta acts merely to supply material omitted by the Mishnah.

Analysis:
Yohanan uses the same Reductio ad Absurdum argument which the Sadducees used concerning bones: If Scripture did not convey uncleanness, then it would be allowable for people to re-use the Torah scrolls, and even to use them for soaking up cattle excrement.

I.3.3. *mYad.4.7*:

1a

The Sadducees say:	אומרים צדוקין
We protest against you O Pharisees	קובלין אנו עליכם פרושים
For you declare clean the unbroken flow.	שאתם מטהרים את הנצוק

1b

The Pharisees say:	אומרים הפרושים
We protest against you O Sadducees	קובלין אנו עליכם צדוקים
For you declare clean the channel of water	שאתם מטהרים את אמת המים
which comes from a graveyard.	הבאה מבית הקברית

Notes:
J.M. Baumgarten (1980) notes that Qumran sectarians agreed with this Sadducean opinion (4QMishnah). This suggests an early date for the dispute.

Analysis:
1a. The Pharisees said that when fluids are poured, uncleanness is not transferred from the receiving vessel to the source vessel, even if there is an unbroken stream (mMakk.5.9). The Sadducees appear to teach that uncleanness is transferred, although we have no other evidence for this.

This would cause few problems for the Sadducees, because liquids in the temple court were free from uncleanness, but it would cause overwhelming problems for Pharisees who attempted to live in purity outside the Temple. Anyone selling wine or water could inadvertently make his stock unclean whenever he poured wine into an unclean vessel. Therefore it would not be safe to buy liquids in the market.

1b. The Pharisees make a counter-complaint which appears to have little to do with the complaint of the Sadducees.

The link between the two complaints is probably based on the implied Sadducean teaching that a receiving vessel can be defiled by uncleanness travelling backwards up an unbroken stream. The Pharisees point out the logical inconsistency of the Sadducees because they did not apply this principle to the unbroken stream from a cemetery.

The apparent lack of connection between the two complaints has prompted S. Zeitlin (1936:271f.) to read ניצוק as "[seed onto which water is] poured" rather than "unbroken stream", saying that the argument centred around the defilement of seed attached to the ground. The Pharisees, unlike the Sadducees, made a distinction between seed which was attached to the ground and that which was not attached (i.e. harvested), saying that only the latter is defiled by water poured on it (tMaksh.1.1). The Pharisees therefore point out that the Sadducees do in fact make this distinction between attached and non-attached when they follow the biblical precept that water (which is attached to the ground) does not carry corpse-uncleanness, unlike other objects which are not attached to the ground (Lev.11.36). Others have proposed equally ingenious theories (L. Finkelstein 1962:811ff.) but these are unnecessary because a link can be demonstrated between the two complaints in their traditional interpretation, as supported by the Qumran evidence.

I.3.4. *mYad.4.7:*

1a

The Sadducees say:	אומרים צדוקין
We protest against you O Pharisees	קובלין אנו עליכם פרושים
for you say:	שאתם אומרים
My ox or my ass	שורי וחמורי
which has caused damage is liable	שהזיקו חייבין
but my male or female slave	ועבדי ואמתי
which has caused damage is exempt.	שהזיקו פטורין
Why is it that for my ox or my ass	מה אם שורי וחמורי
for which I am not liable	שאיני חייב
for commandments concerning them,	בהם מצות
I am liable for damages,	הרי אני חייב בנזקן
[but] my male or female slave	עבדי ואמתי
for whom I am liable	שאני חייב
for commandments concerning them,	בהן מצות
is it not logical	אינו דין
that I am liable for damages?	שאהא חייב בנזקן

1b

[The Pharisees] said to them: No,	אמרו להם לא
if you say [this]	אם אמרתם
concerning my ox or my ass	בשורי וחמורי
which have no understanding	שאין בהם דעת
will you say [this]	תאמרו
concerning my male and female slave	בעבדי ובאמתי
which have understanding?	שיש בהם דעת
For if I anger them	שאם אקניטם
they will go and burn	ילך וידליק
the grain-stack of another	גדישו של אחר
and I will be liable for compensation.	ואהא חייב לשלם

Notes:

The debate concerns the position of the Pharisees (and subsequent rabbis) that the owner of an ox is culpable for damage which it causes (mBQ.1.1 etc.) but that a master is not culpable for damage caused by his slave (mBQ.8.5).

Similar discussions occur in I.2.6,9 where both Simeon and Shammai seem to side with the Sadducees. However these disputes concern slaves who cause damage at their masters' command, in which case the master *is* responsible.

It is significant that both the Sadducees and Pharisees assume that a slave can be compared with an ox, though they disagree as to how far this comparison extends. Neither side advances any arguments in support of this comparison, probably because it was widely accepted. It also found in bSanh.19ab and in the NT (1Co.9.9; 1Tim.5.18).

S. Belkin (1940:91) has suggested that the Sadducean position is due to their acceptance of the Roman and Greek principle that slaves are the property of their master in the same way as an ox.

Analysis:

1a. The Sadducees argue from Qal vaHomer that if an ox is responsible for causing damage, then surely a slave is responsible. A master is liable for any harm he causes his slave (Ex.21.20ff.) while there are no similar commands concerning his ox. Therefore, if the master is more responsible towards a slave than for an ox, and if the master is responsible for the actions of an ox, then surely he is responsible for the actions of his slave.

1b. The Pharisees answer with a Qal vaHomer refutation by finding a difference between an ox and a slave which is relevant to the dispute. The difference is that a slave understands the consequences of his action, whereas an ox does not.

They illustrate this with a practical situation, which is an argument from pragmatism, or a mild Reductio ad Absurdum. They point out that if a master was responsible for any damage which his slave might cause, then the master would always be at the mercy of his slave who could ruin his master by maliciously causing damage.

I.3.5. *mYad.4.8:*

1a

A Galilean Sadducee said:	אמר צדוקי גלילי
I protest against you O Pharisees:	קובל אני עליכם פרושים
For you write	שאתם כותבין
the ruler's name alongside Moses	את המושל עם משה
in a divorce contract.	בגט

The Pharisees say:	אומרים פרושים
We protest against you	קובלין אנו עליך
O Galilean Sadducee:	צדוקי גלילי
For you write	שאתם כותבים
the ruler with the Name in [one] page.	את המושל אם השם בדף
And not only [this] but	ולא עוד אלא
you write	שאתם כותבין
the ruler above	את המושל מלמעלן
and the Name below.	ואת השם מלמטן
As it is written:	שנאמר
And Pharaoh said:	ויאמר פרעה
Who is YHWH that I listen to his voice	מי ה' אשר אשמע בקולו
to release Israel? [Ex.5.2]	לשלח את ישראל

1b

But when smitten what does he say?
YHWH is righteous. [Ex.9.27]

וכשלקה מהו אומר
ה' הצדיק

Notes:

E. Rivkin (1969:211) translates "Sadok of Galilee" following the MSS which read
צדוקי and Josephus who names Sadok and Judas of Galilee as founders of the
Fourth Philosophy (Ant.18.3–10). This does not have the appearance of a Sadducean
dispute but one could imagine a Zealot being concerned about this supposed affront
to Moses.

The Pharisees are speaking on behalf of orthodoxy, so it is likely that this is an
early use of 'prushim'. After c70 CE 'prushim' had the sense of 'extremist' (A.
Gutmann 1962) or 'separatist/heretics' (Rivkin 1969).

Analysis:

1a. The Galilean complains that it is irreverent to place the name of Moses on the
same document as the name of a Gentile ruler.

1b. The Pharisees argue by Reductio ad Absurdum that if they are guilty of
irreverence, then Scripture is more guilty, because there the name of a ruler appears
alongside the name of God, and even above it.

The second citation from Ex.9.27 is unnecessary to the argument. Blackman (ad
loc.) suggests that it was added because this was the last mishnah of the tractate, and
the editors wanted it to end on a happy note.

I.3.6. bBB 115b-116a: (tYad.2.20; yBB.8.1; Meg.Taan.p334)

It was taught:
On 24th of Tebeth
we returned to our law.

דתניא
בארבעה ועשרים בטבת
תבנא לדיננא

1b

For the Sadducees say:
The daughter inherits
with the daughter of the [deceased] son.

שהיו צדוקין אומרין
תירש הבת
עם בת הבן

2a

Rn. Yohanan b.Zakkai joined them
[in debate] He said to them: Fools.
From where do you [learn] this?

נטפל להן רבן יוחנן בן זכאי
אמר להם שוטים
מנין זה לכם

2b

And no-one could find a word
except one old man
who was babbling in opposition
and said:
And if the daughter of his son
who comes from the strength of his son
inherits from him
his daughter who comes from his strength

ולא היה אדם שהחזירו דבר
חוץ מזקן אחד
שהיה מפטפט כנגדו
ואומר
ומה בת בנו
הבאה מכח בנו
תירשנו
בתו הבאה מכחו

is it not logical that
[she inherits from him].

3a

He quoted to him this verse:
[Gen.36.20]

קרא עליו את המקרא הזה

לא כל שכן

*These [are] the sons of Seir the Horite
living in the land,
Lotan, Shobal, Zibeon and Anah.*
and it is written: [v24]

אלה בני שעיר החורי
יושבי הארץ
לוטן ושובל וצבעון וענה
וכתיב

*These [are] the sons of Zibeon,
Aiah and Anah.*
But this teaches
Zibeon had intercourse with his mother
and begat Anah.

אלה בני צבעון
ואיה וענה
אלא מלמד
שבא צבעון על אמו
והוליד ענה

...

3b

He said to him: Rabbi,
you dismiss me with this?

אמר ליה רבי
בכך אתה פוטרני

4a

He said to him: Fool.
You cannot equate our perfect Torah
with your insignificant mumbling!

אמר לו שוטה
ולא תהא תורה שלמה שלנו
כשיחה בטלה שלכם

Why [does inheritance go]
to the daughter of the [deceased] son?
Because in that case her claim is stronger
than that of the brothers.
[But] you must admit that
the claim of [the man's own] daughter
is less strong
than that of the brothers.
And they were defeated, and that day
was declared a festival.

מה
לבת בנו
שכן יפה כחה
במקום האחין
תאמר
בבתו
שהורע כחה
במקום אחין
ונצחום ואותו היום
עשאוהו יום טוב

tYad.2.20:

2b

The Boethusians say:
We complain against you Pharisees:
[For you say] if the daughter of my son,
who comes from the strength of my son,
who comes from my strength,
inherits [from] me, [then]
the daughter who comes from my strength

אומרין ביתותיים
קובלני עליכם פרושים
מה את בת בני
הבא מכח בני
שבא מכחי
הרי יורשתני
בתי הבאה מכחי

is it not logical that   אינו דין
she inherit from me.   שתרשני

4a

The Pharisees say: No.   אומרין פרושין לא
If you speak concerning   אם אמרתם
the daughter of the son   בבת הבן
she shares with the brothers   שכן חולקין עם האחין
[but if] you speak concerning the daughter   תאמרו בבת
she does not share with the brothers.   שאין חולקת עם האחין

Notes:

The debate concerns the laws of inheritance in the situation where the only living children are female, but a deceased son has a living daughter. The Pharisees argued that this granddaughter represents her father, and therefore inherits his portion.

A. Geiger (1857) suggested that the origin of this debate lay in the Pharisees' defence of Herod's inheritance of the Hasmonean throne through Miriamme (his grandmother and the granddaughter of Hyrcanus II). However, as A. Schwarz (1912: 58) and others have pointed out, it is more likely that the Pharisees were simply defending the literal meaning of Num.27.8. In this case it is likely that the dispute was caused by Sadducean practices which were not in line with this scripture, such as treating male and female heirs with equality, as in Roman law. Although there is no evidence that the Sadducees took this point of view, V. Aptowitzer (1928: 286ff.) finds some confirmation in the similar view of R. Yudan the Patriarch in yBB.8.4.

It is difficult to discover the original cause of this dispute, but if (as seems likely) the Pharisees were arguing against the practices of the Sadducees, then this dispute originated before 70 CE when the Sadducees still had legislative power.

The Megillat Taanit (see I.3.11) dates the holiday as the 24th of Ab, and has two explanations for the holiday, the other one being the re-establishment of Jewish law under the Hasmoneans. This alternative explanation seems more reasonable (S. Zeitlin 1922) so Le Moyne (1972: 301) concluded that this passage is completely unhistorical. However A. Schwarz (1912: 55) argued that this was an ancient tradition which was adapted for the Megillat Taanit by later editors.

Neusner (1970: 204f.) points out that this follows the normal form for disputes between R. Yohanan b.Zakkai and Sadducees. This form usually includes:
"Rn.Yohanan b.Zakkai said: How do you know..."
"No one could reply except an (old) man who babbled..."
Yohanan introduces an obscure verse
The Sadducee questions its relevance
"He said to him: Fool! You cannot equate our perfect Torah..."
Yohanan gives a more straight-forward proof (which Neusner calls "the real proof")

Neusner argues that this form is likely to date from at least the second century because the Sadducees are portrayed as a few old men (1970: 106). However "old" is only used in two disputes, and only in the Babylonian Talmud versions.

The similar form does suggest later editing, but it is likely that the arguments originated at a time when the issues were still being discussed. This issue and that of the meal offering (I.3.13) suggest a date before 70 CE.

This form is found in three of the four disputes between Yohanan and Sadducees: here, I.3.12 and I.3.13, (cf. Meg.Taan.p342f. re. Simeon b.Shetah), but not I.3.2 which has the earlier 'complaint' form from which this form probably developed. This earlier form (see. I.3.2–5) consists of a complaint against the Pharisees and a seemingly unrelated counter-complaint or a rebuttal. In both forms the obscure reply appears to avoid the question but actually implies the answer.

The 'complaint' form of the present dispute is preserved in tYad.2.20, which consists of the arguments in 2b (which assumes 1a and 1b) and 4a. Yohanan's exegesis in 3a is also likely to be early because no explanation has been appended, and it was misunderstood from an early date (see below).

Analysis:

1a. The Pharisees' position is not stated and must be inferred. In the situation where an estate is divided between the family of a dead son and a daughter, the Pharisees evidently awarded the son's inheritance to his surviving family.

1b. The Sadducees use Reductio ad Absurdum to show that this means that if the dead son's family consists solely of one daughter, then her grandfather's estate passes to her instead of to his own daughter. This argument is missing, and all that remains is their conclusion: obviously in this case the two must be at least be treated equally.

2a. Yohanan challenges them for a Scriptural argument.

2b. They fail to find one, but use Qal vaHomer. If the granddaughter, who is twice removed, inherits, surely the daughter, who is once removed, also inherits.

3a. Yohanan, of course, has a scriptural argument. He uses the resolution of two contradictory texts by means of a third (which he deliberately omits).

One text says that Anah was a "son of Seir" but another says that Anah was a son of Zibeon and therefore a grandson of Seir. Yohanan b.Zakkai first suggests an improbable solution: that Zibeon had a child by his own mother.

The real solution (which Yohanan wants his hearer to discover for himself) is that Anah is an example of a granddaughter who is counted alongside the sons in terms of inheritance. This can be deduced from the third text (v2 or v14) where Anah is the "daughter of Zibeon". Therefore, when Anah is listed alongside her uncles, it must be assumed that her father has died so that she received her father's inheritance of the land. This honorary position among her uncles also appears to have conferred on her an honorary maleness, because the masculine particle is used of her in v24. Unfortunately Yohanan was probably too clever because he appears to have been misunderstood even by his immediate successors. This confusion is seen in bBB, which is interrupted by a discussion between Rabbah and another about whether Gen.36 could refer to two Anahs.

The Dorshe Hamurot (see II.3) also misunderstood Yohanan, and took up the suggestion that Anah was illegitimate, saying that it was fitting for the bastard Anah to find "mules" (v.24) which are also of illegitimate birth (bPes.54a; yBer.8.8). This same idea was developed by later haggadists (GenR.82.14). It should be noted that even Lauterbach (1910-:513) who regarded the Dorshe Hamurot as pre-70 CE recognised that their exegesis was dependent on Yohanan's.

This misunderstanding of Yohanan's argument was probably due largely to the traditional way of harmonising the male and female 'Anah' in Gen.36 by reading "son" for "daughter" in v2,14 (as in the LXX and Syriac – see Z. Frankel 1851:12). Rashi has a similar solution, also regarding Anah as male, but instead of altering the text he reads "Aholibamah the daughter of Anah [and] the daughter of Zibeon", from which he concludes that Aholibamah was the product of the illicit union of Zibeon and his daughter-in-law, the wife of Anah. This extra evidence of incest prompts Rashi to comment that "they were all of illegitimate birth"!

Rashbam (R. Samuel b.Meir) comments that Yohanan is arguing from an analogy between the sons/grandsons and daughters/granddaughters. Le Moyne (1972:303)

assumes that this is a correct understanding of Yohanan and suggests that the weakness of his argument is evidence that this passage is not based on any early sources.

A. Schwarz (1912) reviewed the comments of the traditional rabbinic commentators, and notes that R. Tam does point out that the argument falls into place once Anah is regarded as female, but Schwarz appears to miss the point and produces yet another ingenious interpretation of Yohanan. He suggests that Yohanan was using Gen.36 to prove the Sadducean ruling that the daughter inherits *with* the granddaughter, because Anah was at the same time a daughter and granddaughter, but that he then turned the argument around by saying that this was emulated by the Sadducees because they too were a family of bastards.

The simpler proposal made above, that Yohanan regards Anah as female, which has been ignored by many modern scholars, was proposed by the Tosafist Rabbenu Tam (Jacob ben Meir, grandson of Rashi) and by the 17th C. Joel Sirkis (both recorded at bBB115b under מלמד and הב"ח respectively).

3b. The Sadducee regards this exegesis as irrelevant.

4a. Yohanan's explanation is not given. Instead the form is completed with material related to the tradition in tYad.2.20, where the Qal vaHomer of 2b is answered with a Qal vaHomer refutation. It argues that the two women cannot be compared because the granddaughter in this case may have brothers, but the daughter may not (because that brother would inherit and the case would not arise).

The argument of 4a is similar. The inheritance rights of the granddaughter are strengthened by the presence of brothers (because then the absurd position of 1b does not arise) but the daughter's rights lapse if she has brothers.

I.3.7. *tYad.2.20*:

1a.

The Morning Bathers say:	אומרים טובלי שחרין
We complain against you Pharisees,	קובלני עליכם פרושים
for you mention the Name	שאתם מזכירים את השם
in the morning before bathing.	

1b.

The Pharisees reply:
We complain against you Morning Bathers
for you mention the Name

| from a body | מן הגוף |
| which has uncleanness in it. | שיש בו טומאה |

Notes:

L. Finkelstein (1969a) adds the words in italics from the Vienna MS (which is not available to me). He suggests that this concerns the use of the Name outside the Temple (because no-one was allowed inside the temple before immersing), and therefore dates before the 4th C BCE when the tetragrammaton ceased to be articulated outside the Temple. The words probably disappeared by homoeoteleuton.

Analysis:

1a. The Name should not be spoken before bathing, presumably because sleep defiles.

1b. The Pharisees reply with a Reductio ad Absurdum, taking their opponents'

position to its logical and absurd conclusion: if a natural process like sleep defiles, then so does digestion, so you have to wash inside as well as outside, which is impossible.

I.3.8 *tKipp.1.8; Sifra AM. Per.3.11; bYom.19b:*
tKipp.1.8: (bYom.53a)

And why did they force [the High Priest]	ולמה צרכו
to swear [to obey the Elders]?	להשביעו
For once it happened	שכבר היה מעשה
with one Boethusian	בביתסי אחד
that he caused incense to rise	שהקטיר
while he was outside [the Holy of Holies]	עד שהוא בחוץ
and the cloud of incense went out	ויצאה ענן הקטרת
and shook the whole Temple.	והרתיע את כל הבית

1a

For the Boethusians used to say:	שהיו ביתסין או׳
He shall raise incense when he is outside,	יקטיר עד שהוא בחוץ
as it is said: [Lev.16.13b]	שנ׳
And the cloud will cover [the mercy seat].	וכסה ענן

1b

The Sages said to them:	אמרו להם חכמים
And is it not already said: [Lev.16.13a]	והלא כבר נאמ׳
And he will put the incense	ונתן את הקטרת
on the fire before YHWH.	על האש לפני ה׳
This [means] anyone raising incense	הא כל המקטיר
must only raise it inside.	אין מקטיר אלא בפנים

2a

If so, why is it said:	אם כן למה נאמ׳
And the cloud will cover the mercy seat?	וכסה ענן הקטרת

2b

[It is] teaching that he puts on it	מלמד שנותן בהן
a smoke-raising agent.	מעלה עשן
If he did not put on it	הא אם לא נתן בה
a smoke-raising agent	מעלה עשן
he is liable to death.	חייב מיתה

Sifra AM. Per.3.11 (Weiss 81a): (yYom.1.5, 39ab)

[Then] he shall bring it within the veil	והביא אל מבית לפרוכת
and put the incense	ונתן את הקטורת
on the fire before YHWH. [Lev.16.12f.]	על האש לפני ה׳
[Teaching] that one should not	שלא
arrange [the incense] outside	יתקן מבחוץ
and bring it inside.	ויכניס מבפנים

1ai

For behold the Sadducees say:	שהרי הצדוקים אומרים
One should arrange it outside	יתקן מבחוץ
and bring it inside.	ויכניס מבפנים
If one does so before flesh and blood	אם לפני בשר ודם עושים כן
much more before God.	קל וחומר לפני המקום

1aii

And it says: [Lev.16.2]	ואומר
For I will appear in the cloud	כי בענן אראה
upon the mercy seat.	על הכפורת

1b

The Sages said to them:	אמרו להם חכמים
And has it not already said: [Lev.16.13a]	והלא כבר נאמר
And he shall put the incense	ונתן את הקטורת
on the fire before YHWH.	על האש לפני ה׳
He shall not put [the incense on the fire]	אינו נותן
except [after he is] inside.	אלא בפנים

2a

If so, why is it said:	אם כן למה נאמר
For I will appear in the cloud	כי בענן אראה
upon the mercy seat?	על הכפורת

2b

[It is] teaching that he shall put on it	מלמד שהוה נותן בה
a smoke-raising agent.	מעלה עשן

    bYom.19b: (yYom.1.5, 39a)

Our Rabbis taught:	ת״ר
It happened concerning one Sadducee	מעשה בצדוקי אחד
that he arranged [incense] outside	שהתקין מבחוץ
and [then] brought it in.	והכניס
When he was coming out	ביציאתו
he was very greatly pleased.	היה שמח שמחה גדולה

His father met him	פגע בו אביו
[and] he said to him: My son,	אמר לו בני
although we follow the Sadducees	אף על פי שצדוקין אנו
we fear the Pharisees.	מתיראין אנו מן הפרושים

He said to him: All my days	אמר לו כל ימי
I was perplexed	הייתי מצטער
by this text: [Lev.16.2]	על המקרא הזה
For I appear in the cloud	כי בענן אראה
upon the mercy seat.	על הכפורת

. . .

Notes:
On the Day of Atonement the High Priest offered incense in the Holy of Holies, but should the incense be lit inside or outside?

The Pharisees insisted that it should be lit inside. Lauterbach (1927) noted that the Pharisees did not argue their case very convincingly and suggested that their original reason was not Scriptural but theological. They wished to refute the common superstition that God lived in the Holy of Holies. The Sadducees, like Philo (Spec.I.72), believed that the cloud of incense would hide the deadly vision of God so they made sure that a cloud was produced before entering. However the Pharisees' argument *is* exegetical and they too probably believed that the cloud was needed to hide God because they ruled that a special smoking agent should be added.

The Sadducees said that the incense should be lit outside, probably because (as Finkelstein suggests, 1962:657) it was exceedingly dangerous to light the incense in the pitch darkness of the Holy of Holies, wearing flowing and inflammable robes.

Whether or not their positions started with Scripture, they are established by exegesis, and the relative weakness of the Sages' arguments suggests that this debate is genuine.

The first two text traditions represented by tKipp. and Sifra are very similar, but neither is wholly dependent on the other. Although M. Kadushin (1952:249) rightly criticises the harmonisation of these traditions by conservative scholars, both preserve some of the original arguments. It is argued below that the Sadducees' text was Lev.16.13b (as in tKipp.) but the Qal vaHomer (only in Sifra) is likely to be genuine because later Rabbis would not invent extra Sadducean arguments, especially when no answer is given.

The third tradition concerns a High Priest who followed Sadducean teaching and was punished by God. This quotes Lev.16.2 but only in the Babylonian Talmud, where it is probably dependent on Sifra.

Analysis:
1ai. The Qal vaHomer argument found in Sifra is based on Mashal, comparing this incense with the offering of incense to a pagan king. One would not imagine preparing incense in a man's presence, therefore much more one prepares oneself for God before going into His presence. This argument is not refuted.

1aii. According to Sifra the text is Lev.16.2, but this would make nonsense of 1b where the Sages quote v13a as something which was "already said". The original text is therefore v13a, as in tKipp.

The Sadducees argue from a Peshat reading that the cloud is needed to "cover". This is best understood in terms of the superstition that God is present in the Holy of Holies, and that one cannot see God and live. This is confirmed by the use of v2 in 2a.

Kadushin (1952:249) rejects this, arguing that it conflicts with 1ai because incense is not offered in order to hide a king's face. However this reasoning takes the Sadducees' illustration too literally.

1b. The Sages respond with a Peshat reading which states that the incense is lit "before YHWH". They too assume that God is especially present in the Holy of Holies.

They also stress the Order of the texts, which shows that the priest is in the presence of YHWH before the covering takes place. This is contrary to Eliezer's rule 31 that order can be ignored.

2a. The Sadducees respond that if "cover" does not imply that the cloud is needed to hide God, then it is Redundant.

The original reply may have quoted v2 (as in Sifra and yYom. and according to the resultant text of G. Larsson 1980:4). Neither version quotes "that he die not" but this occurs in both verses and is referred to in 2b, so it is probably the basis of the Sadducees' argument.

They are therefore concluding from a Peshat reading that the mortal effect of looking on God is obviated by the cloud.

2b. The Sages' argument is not clear, but should probably be understood as in the Talmudim. They explain the death threat as a result of missing an ingredient out of the incense (a capital offence, Ex.30.38). This special "smoke ascender" made smoke "to fill the House" (Is.6.4). This is a possible Peshat understanding of the text.

I.3.9. *tHag.3.35:* (yHag.3.8)

It happened	מעשה
that they immersed the Menorah	והטבילו את המנורה
on the Good Day.	ביום טוב
And the Sadducees were saying:	והיו צדוקין אומ׳
Come and see the Pharisees	בואו וראו פרושין
who are immersing the light of the moon.	שמטבילין מאור הלבנה

Notes:
The Lamp should never have touched uncleanness which required immersion, but the Pharisees felt that the Sadducean priests were not careful enough in cleanliness laws.

This Sadducean taunt has no reply, so it is very unlikely to be a later invention. This suggests that the Pharisees did have a limited influence over Temple ceremonies.

The literal translation 'Good Day' (the first or last day of a feast) in place of the usual 'Festival Day' is adopted to distinguish it from the other feast days.

Analysis:
The Sadducees argue by Reductio ad Absurdum, saying that if you are going to immerse everything 'just in case' then you might as well immerse the moon.

There may also be Wordplay based on לבן, 'white', but this is ignored by yHag which reads גלגל חמה, "circle of the sun".

I.3.10. *mMakk.1.6:* (Sifré Deut.190)

False witnesses are not executed	אין העדים זוממין נהרגין
till the sentence has been pronounced.	עד שיגמר הדין

1a

For the Sadducees said:	שהרי הצדוקין אומרים
[They cannot be executed] till [the accused] has been executed,	עד שיהרג
for it is said: *Life for life.*	שנאמר נפש תחת נפש

[Deut.19.21]

1b

The Sages said to them:	אמרו להם חכמים
And is it not earlier said:	והלא כבר נאמר
And you shall do to him	ועשיתם לו
as he planned to do to his brother.	כאשר זמם לעשות לאחיו

[Deut.19.19]

And this [is possible whilst] his brother
[still] lives.

2ai

And if so, why is it said:
Life for life

והרי אחיו קיים

ואם כן למה נאמר
נפש תחת נפש

2aii

[Because] one might say:
As soon as one accepted their witness
[and it is found false] one should execute them.

יכול
משעה שקבלו עדותן
יהרגו

2b

The text teaches: *Life for life*.
This [shows that] they are not executed
till the sentence has been pronounced.

תלמוד לומר נפש תחת נפש
הא אינן נהרגין
עד שיגמר הדין

Notes:

The Sadducees imposed the death penalty on false witnesses who actually caused
the death of an innocent man, while the Pharisees imposed it on those who intended
to do so but failed, although they normally replaced the death penalty with monetary
compensation.

There are two early examples of this carried out in practice. The first is the story of
Susanna, where the accusers are discovered to be false after the death sentence had
already been passed but not yet carried out. Their falsehood is discovered when they
are cross-examined independently by a young man in whom "God raised up the holy
spirit" (Sus.1.45). Daube (1961:250) suggests that this story was fabricated by the
early Pharisees in order to give an inspired origin to their innovative practice of
examining witnesses independently – a practice which is mentioned in late references
(e.g. mSanh.5.4) but which might date back to Simeon b.Shetah (mAb.1.9 – though it
is not specifically referred to here). It is equally possible that the story was constructed
as a foundation for the innovation of giving the death penalty to false witnesses who
had not actually caused the death of the accused. The startling turning point in the
story, the re-examination of the elders after the sentence had been given, may serve to
emphasise that false witnesses are not killed until the death sentence has been pronounced.

The second early example involves Judah b.Tabbai who put to death a false witness
"in order to uproot from the heart of the Boethusians [their false opinion]"
(tSanh.6.6). However this phrase appears to be a gloss, because it is not present in
parallel accounts and it is extraneous to the main theme.

Analysis

1a. The Sadducees would not kill a false witness unless his testimony had caused
the death of an innocent man, arguing from the Peshat meaning of "Life for life".

1b. The Sages argued that "thought to do" indicated that it had not actually
happened yet.

2ai. The Sadducees argue that if the accused has not yet been killed, then "life for
life" has no meaning.

2aii. They also argue from Reductio ad Absurdum that if the false witness is not to
be killed after the innocent has died, then presumably he should be killed as soon as
his evidence has been found false, which would be in the middle of the trial.

2b. The Sages answer both points by interpreting "life for life" as a reference to the judgement of death rather than to the carrying out of the sentence. This means that the false witness is punished before the innocent man is killed, but after the judgement has been given. This is perhaps an Ultra-literal interpretation because it goes against the plain meaning of the text. However, the Sages would probably have understood the phrase "life for life" as a technical legal term having the specialist meaning of a "life sentence" (cf. A. Schalit 1965: 167f.) which did not necessarily mean punishment by death but which may mean the payment of damages. They would therefore have regarded this interpretation as Peshat.

It is difficult to understand why the Sages took this position. Their argument from Scripture is not particularly strong, and they appear to be forced into a compromise by the Sadducees. However this debate makes perfect sense if one assumes that they are assuming a principle which is not actually mentioned in this debate: their replacement of physical punishment by a payment of damages. When the debate is analysed in terms of this principle, the position of the Sages becomes more understandable:

1a. The Sadducees say that false witnesses are put to death only when they have caused the death of an innocent man.

1b. The Sages imposed the death penalty so rarely that this ruling would remove all sanctions against false witnesses. Therefore they wished to punish false witnesses even if the innocent had not been killed. No doubt they would have found reason to substitute a lesser penalty than death for the false witness.

2a. The Sadducees point out the absurdity of the Sages' position, and suggest that they are ignoring the text "life for life".

2b. The Sages interpret "life for life" as referring to the death-judgement – which is the judgement made on capital cases, but which (according to the Sages) did not necessarily mean that a death sentence was imposed on the criminal.

I.3.11. *Meg.Taan. p331:*

On the 14th of Tamuz	בארבעה בתמוז
the Book of Decrees lapsed.	עדא ספר גזרתא

Scholion:

1a

Because there was	מפני שהיה
written and established by the Sadducees	כתוב ומונח לצדוקים
a Book of Decrees [concerning]	ספר גזרות
those to be stoned and those to be burned	אלו שנסקלין ואלו שנשרפין
those to be beheaded and those to be strangled.	אלו שנהרגין ואלו שנחנקין

1bi

And when they judged	וכשהיו יושבין
and a man asked [concerning it]	ואדם שואל
they would show him in the Book.	ומראין לו בספר
He said to them: From where [is it proved]	אומר להם מנין
that this one is liable to stoning,	שזה חיב סקילה
and this one liable to burning,	וזה חיב שרפה
and this one liable to beheading	וזה חיב הרגה
and this one liable to strangulation?	וזה חיב חניקה

They did not know	לא היו יודעין
how to bring evidence from the Torah.	להביא ראיה מן התורה
1bii	
The Sages said to them:	אמרו להם חכמים
Is it not written: [Deut.17.11]	הלא כתוב
According to the word of Torah	על פי התורה
which they will teach you etc,	אשר יורוך וגו׳
teaching that one should not	מלמד שאין כותבין הלכות בספר
write halakot in a book.	

Another interpretation	דבר אחר
of the Book of Decrees:	ספר גזרתא
2a	
Because the Boethusians said:	שהיו ביתוסין אומרים
An eye for an eye [and]	עין תחת עין
a tooth for a tooth. [Lev.24.20]	שן תחת שן
If a man broke the tooth of his neighbour	הפיל אדם שן חברו
he should break his tooth	יפיל את שנו
[and if] he blinded the eye of his neighbour	סמא עין חברו
he should blind his eye	יסמא את עינו
to be the same as the other.	יהו שוים כאחד
3a	
And they shall spread the sheet	ופרשו השמלה
before the elders of the city. [Deut.22.17]	לפני זקני העיר
Things [should be done] as they are written.	דברים ככתבן
And she shall spit in his face. [Deut.25.9]	וירקה בפניו
proves that she [really] spits in his face.	שתהא רוקקת בפניו
4b	
The Sages said to them:	אמרו להם חכמים
And is it not written: [Ex.24.12]	והלא כתוב
The law and the commandments	התורה והמצוה
which I have written to teach them,	אשר כתבתי להורותם
[i.e.] *the Law, which I have written*	התורה אשר כתבתי
and *the commandments, to teach them* [orally]	והמצוה להורותם
And it is written: [Deut.31.19]	וכתיב
And now write for yourselves	ועתה כתבו לכם
this song	את השירה הזאת
and teach it to the sons of Israel	ולמדה את בני ישראל
[and] *put it in their mouths.*	שימה בפיהם
And teach it to the sons of Israel	ולמדה את בני ישראל
– this is Scripture	זה מקרא
Put [them] in their mouths.	שימה בפיהם
– these are halakot.	אלו הלכות

Notes:
The Megillat Taanit is a list of holidays, with short notes about their significance, and the Scholion is a commentary on it. The Megillah is likely to date from Tannaitic times, and Zeitlin (1922: 72–78) concluded that it was completed at about 70 CE because the last event recorded in it occurred in 66 CE and because events close to this time are given very scant explanations, as if the readers were very familiar with them. The Scholion however is much later, and almost certainly Amoraic, but it contains early material, much of which occurs as baraitot in the Talmudim. Zeitlin's analysis of the historical events behind the Megillat Taanit concludes that the Scholion is least accurate when it is commenting on early events, and he suggests that when the editors did not know the reason for a date they tended to attach it to a victory of the Pharisees over the Sadducees.

It is therefore likely that the holiday of the 14th of Tamuz had nothing to do with the disputes recorded in the accompanying Scholion, but that does not mean that these disputes did not occur, or that this is not a faithful record of the arguments used.

The only detail which the Megillat Taanit furnishes concerning the 14th Tamuz is that the Book of Decrees was annulled. We do not know of this book from elsewhere, and while it is probable that the Sadducees kept such a document, we have no evidence that they did so, although Lauterbach (1913: 35) sees some confirmation in the reference to "two judges of the Decrees" at mKet.13.1. Zeitlin (1922: 83) suggests that this removal of the Book of Decrees is more likely to refer to the concessions granted to the Jews by Demetrius (1Mac.10.29ff.), but he is able to produce little evidence in favour of this idea.

Although the Scholion is late, and its interpretation of the Megillat Taanit is suspect, the exegesis attributed to the Boethusians is likely to be genuine, because it furnishes a strong argument in favour of their position. The argument of the Sages concerning Deut.17 is also likely to be based on early material because, as Lauterbach pointed out (1913: 40ff.; 1914-:208ff.), this was probably the key text in the battle between the Sadducees and Pharisees for the control of the judiciary, and M. Fishbane (1988: 362f.) points out that 11QTemp 56.34 argues against the Pharisaic position in an exegesis of this same text. However the exegeses of the Sages in 4b are unlikely to be early because they do not answer the individual arguments of the Boethusians.

Analysis:
1a. The Boethusians consulted a written record concerning the type of capital punishment required for different crimes.

1bi. The Sages asked for the Scriptural proofs for the different decisions, although when the Sadducees were unable to give any they do not offer any themselves.

1bii. The Sages pointed out that the written law witnesses to an Oral Law: "the mouth/word of the Law" [פי התורה] is seen as a reference to the Oral Law [תורה שבעל פה].

This text is probably being used Nomologically, because although it appears to ignore the context (which concerns the verbal declaration of the Law by a judge) the context of this verse was the source of rabbinic claims to legal authority. In v9 the "judge" as well as the "Levite" decides the law, so a lay expert in the Law could make rulings as well as a priest or Levite. However, if this context is not in mind the reading is Ultra-literal.

2a. The Boethusians applied the Peshat reading of Lev.24 literally.

2b. The Pharisees' position is not given, but presumably they disagreed with this literal interpretation. They probably awarded monetary compensation like later rabbis (see mBQ.8.1 etc.), although it is difficult to determine when the practice started. This passage suggests that the practice was a point of contention between the Pharisees and Sadducees, so that it is likely to predate 70 CE. Belkin (1940: 97f.) wonders whether "blow for blow" may already have had an idiomatic reference to compensation because it appears to have this meaning in Assyrian law codes, in which case the Pharisees may be supporting the Peshat meaning of the phrase.

3a. The Boethusians also demanded that other practices written in the Law should be carried out literally, such as displaying the garment/sheet in a case of suspected non-virginity and spitting in the face when levirate responsibilities are rejected.

3b. The Pharisees' position is again not given, but presumably they did not demand that such practices be carried out. Elsewhere (Mekh.Ish.Nez.6.45;13.17; bKet.46a; Sifré Deut. 237) R. Ishmael supports their position by משל (metaphor/allegory), reading ופרשו השמלה as "make matters as plain as a clean sheet" i.e. "clarify the circumstances" rather than "spread the garment", although R. Bóid (1988: 631f.) has suggested that this may be regarded as a perfectly possible Peshat translation.

4b. The Sages answer the unspoken Boethusian contention that the Oral Law is invalid. The Sages Atomize two texts to show that the Oral Law is attested to even in the written law. This is an Ultra-literal reading of Scripture because the idiomatic meaning of the phrases in their context is ignored.

Ex.24.12 implies a written and oral stage in the law, but they are both the same law. The text is Atomized so that "the law" is related to "written" (i.e. the Written Law) and "the commandments" is related to "instruct" (which refers to the Oral Law, cf. bBer.5a).

Deut.31.19 also implies an oral and written stage, but here the written and oral law are found in two phrases which both apparently refer to the oral stage. This may be based on No Redundancy because "teach" and "put in their mouth" were synonymous in scribal schools. Therefore one refers to Scripture and the other to Oral Law.

The Ultra-literal disregard for the meaning of these atomized phrases in their context is especially obvious with regards to the phrase "put in their mouths" which refers to the singular "song" in the context but is made to refer to the plural "Halakot" in the interpretation.

I.3.12. *bMen.65ab:* (Meg.Taan.p325; bTaan.17b)

1b

For the Boethusians used to say:	שהיו בייתוסין אומרים
Feast of Weeks is after Sabbath.	עצרת אחר השבת

2a

Rn.Yohanan b.Zakkai was joined with them [in debate],	ניטפל להם רבן יוחנן בן זכאי
and he said to them: Fools!	ואמר להם שוטים
From where do you [prove this]?	מנין לכם

2b

And not one man was answering him	ולא היה אדם אחד שהיה משיבו
except one old man	חוץ מזקן אחד
who was babbling in opposition	שהיה מפטפט כנגדו
and said:	ואמר
Moses our teacher	משה רבינו

was a lover of Israel	אוהב ישראל היה
and he knew that the Feast of Weeks	ויודע שעצרת
[was only] one day	יום אחד
[so] he forthwith ordained	הוא עמד ותקנה
[it to be] after the Sabbath,	אחר שבת
so that Israel might enjoy themselves	כדי שיהו ישראל מתענגין
two days.	שני ימים

3a

He quoted to them this text: [Deut.1.2]	קרא עליו מקרא זה
[It is] eleven days [journey]	אחד עשר יום
from Horeb [by] way of Mt Seir.	מחרב דרך הר שעיר
But if Moses our teacher	ואם משה רבינו
was a lover of Israel,	אוהב ישראל היה
why did he detain them	למה איחרן
in the wilderness 40 years?	במדבר ארבעים שנה

3b

He said to him: Rabbi,	אמר לו רבי
You dismiss me with this?	בכך אתה פוטרני

4a

He said to him: Fool!	אמר לו שוטה
Is not our perfect Torah	ולא תהא תורה שלמה שלנו
[better] than your insignificant mumbling?	כשיחה בטילה שלכם
One text says: [Lev.23.16]	כתוב אחד אומר
You shall count 50 days	תספרו חמשים יום
and one text says: [Lev.23.15]	וכתוב אחד אומר
They shall be 7 complete weeks.	שבע שבתות תמימות תהיינה
How [can this be]?	הא כיצד
Now [one speaks] concerning a Good Day	כאן ביום טוב
which falls on a Sabbath,	שחל להיות בשבת
and [one speaks] concerning a Good Day	כאן ביו"ט
which falls on a non-Sabbath day.	שחל להיות באמצע שבת

Notes:

The Feast of Weeks occurred seven weeks after the cutting of the Omer (the first sheaf of harvest) on "the day after the Sabbath" of Passover week (Lev.23.11,15). This was interpreted differently by Sadducees and Pharisees.

The Sadducees interpreted this "day after the Sabbath" as the first Sunday in Passover so that "The Feast of Weeks falls on the day after the Sabbath". This was opposed by the Pharisaic Houses (mHag.2.4).

The Pharisees interpreted "Sabbath" as a "Good Day" (a first or last day of a festival) so they counted from the first day of Passover. This is presumably because in Lev.23, which calls Good Days "holy convocations", they have similar regulations and the terms are used almost synonymously (cf v3, 31f.). Their position is recorded negatively in mMen.10.4: "The Boethusians used to say: The Omer may not be reaped at the close of a Good Day".

Both of these interpretations are Peshat, but there may have been other arguments to back them up which have now been lost. The Sadducean interpretation is the more literal, though the Pharisees take more account of the context.

The context does not quite agree with the Pharisees, because one would expect the "Sabbath" by which the Omer is dated to be the last-mentioned "holy convocation", which is the last Good Day of Passover (v8). This produces a third possible interpretation represented by the Peshitta and Jubilees and followed by the modern Falashas (L. Finkelstein 1923:41).

Finkelstein (1962:642–4) finds practical and theological reasons for these two positions. The Pharisees wanted every Feast to be on a fixed calendar date in order to fit in with their perceptions of celebrating historical events at different feasts. The Feast of Weeks was a celebration of the giving of the Law. The Sadducees had a more pragmatic reason for their interpretation. They wanted to have this one-day feast on a Sunday, when the priests running the temple changed from one Order to another. This meant that both the incoming and outgoing Orders could share in the sacrifices brought during the feast without having to find extra lodgings in Jerusalem.

The practice of delaying the Feast of Weeks by one day if it fell on a Sabbath (implied by 4a and the Hillelite ruling in mHag.2.4) probably dates back to Temple times. This is seen from the strange detail in mHag.2.4 that when this occurred the High Priest was not permitted to wear his ceremonial vestments, so that the people would know that Weeks was not being celebrated in accordance with the Sadducean ruling.

The Megillat Taanit celebrates "the re-establishment of [the correct dating] of Weeks" during Passover. If this document is pre-70 CE (as Zeitlin 1922 concludes), it helps to date this debate. However the debate may have been expanded later. It is one of a group of Sadducee-Yohanan debates (cf. I.3.6).

Analysis:

1b. The Sadducee position is stated in opposition to the unstated Pharisee position.

2ab. Yohanan is obviously asking for an exegetical reason, but they can only provide a pragmatic one, which is very similar to that proposed by Finkelstein above.

Le Moyne (1972:185) notes that it has a close parallel in the sentiments of Philo, who regarded the Festivals as times when the people could be temporarily "released from their cares...to enjoy a brief breathing space amid scenes of genial cheerfulness" (Spec.1.69).

3ab. Yohanan replies (as usual in this form) with an obscure verse which Sadducees regard as irrelevant. The explanation ("If Moses was a lover of Israel...") was probably added later. If the explanation is correct (as seems likely), then Yohanan is arguing from the Peshat meaning of the text.

4a. Yohanan finds a Contradiction and solves it without using a third text.

One text counts the days from the Omer till the Feast of Weeks as 50 days but another says 49 days (seven weeks). He reconciles these texts by saying that the second applies when Passover is on a week day, and the first when Passover is on a Sabbath. This means that if Weeks should fall on a Sabbath, it is postponed by one day (the Hillelite view in mHag.2.4).

I.3.13. *Meg.Taan.p338:*

1b

For the Sadducees used to say:	שהיו הצדוקין אומרין
They eat the cereal offering [which accompanies] a flesh sacrifice.	אוכלין מנחת בהמה

2a

Rn. Yohanan b.Zakkai said to them:
From where do you [prove this]?

אמר להם רבן יוחנן בן זכאי
מנין לכם

2b

And they did not know how to bring
proof from the Torah,
except one [man]
who was babbling in opposition
and saying:

ולא היו יודעין להביא
ראיה מן התורה
אלא אחד
שהיה מפטפט כנגדו
ואומר

2bi

Because Moses was a lover of Aaron
he said: Let him not eat meat alone
but let him eat fine-flour and meat.

מפני שהיה משה אוהב את אהרן
אמר אל יאכל בשר לבדו
אלא יאכל סלת ובשר

2bii

Like a man who was saying
to his associate:
Here for you is meat,
here for you is soft [food].

כאדם שהוא אומר
לחברו
הילך בשר
הילך רכיך

3a

Rn.Yohanan b.Zakkai quoted to him:
And they came to Elim
and there were 12 springs of water
and 70 date-palms. [Ex.15.27]

קרא לו רבן יוחנן בן זכאי
ויבאו אילמה
ושם שתים עשרה עינות מים
ושבעים תמרים

3b

He said to him:
What have these two to do with each other?

אמר לו
מה ענין זה אצל זה

4a

He said to him: Fool!
Is not our perfect Torah
[better] than your insignificant mumbling?
and was it not already said: [Lev.23.18]
They are a burnt-offering to YHWH,
and the meal-offerings,
and the drink-offerings,
for a sweet aroma of fire to YHWH.

אמר לו שוטה
ולא תהא תורה שלמה שלנו
כשיחה בטלה שלך
והלא כבר נאמר
יהיה עולה ליי
ומנחתם
ונסכיהם
לריח ניחח אשה לה'

Notes:
Cereal offerings were presented either on their own or with a drink offering accompanying a sacrifice. Of those presented on their own, a handful was burnt and the rest was eaten by the priests, except those offered by a priest which were burned completely (Lev.6.14–23(7–16)). However Scripture is not clear whether this applied to cereal offerings accompanying sacrifices.

"Animal" [בהמה] usually refers to cattle but also to smaller animals, and it is probably being used generally here. The Sadducees are therefore arguing that the cereals accompanying sacrifices should be governed by the same rules as cereal offerings presented on their own – i.e. eaten by the priests.

Although it is difficult to imagine that the Pharisees forced the priests to give up this significant privilege (as Megillat Taanit suggests) the debate itself is likely to be genuine. The Pharisaic position is not based on any theological considerations and there is no reason to invent the opposite view. The dispute is never referred to again, and the Pharisaic position is simply stated in mMen.6.1f.

As noted above (I.3.11), the Scholion to the Megillat Taanit is particularly untrustworthy when it attributes holidays to a victory over the Sadducees. However this tradition has probably been borrowed from an earlier source which included the two traditions with identical forms (I.3.6, I.3.12), which are preserved as Baraitot in the Talmud as well as in Megillat Taanit.

Analysis:

1b. The Sadducean position is stated.

2a Yohanan asks for Scriptural proof.

2bi. A pragmatic reason is given using similar language to I.3.12.

2bii. A Mashal which is not based on Scripture illustrates that God, like a good host, provides a varied diet.

3ab. Yohanan's seemingly meaningless reply in this form is sometimes explained (cf. I.3.12) and sometimes not (cf.I.3.6). Here it is not, and the explanation can only be guessed at. The explanation should probably follow the language used in I.3.12, so that it would start: "But if Moses was a lover of Aaron/Israel why...".

Le Moyne (1972:290) suggests that the text speaks allegorically of abundant wisdom, which Yohanan applies ironically to the Sadducees. However he does not state why he (or they) should understand the text this way.

Opinion appears to have been divided about whether the springs and palms of Elim were sufficient for Israel. Josephus (Ant.3.3(1.9)) says there was so little water that the palms were parched, but Philo (Mos.I.34) says that there was abundant water and vegetation.

However Yohanan presumably wants the Sadducees to search the Context because immediately after this episode they murmured and God gave them quails and manna. Josephus even implies that this occurred at Elim itself. The 'correspondence' which the Sadducee could not see is now clear: they are acting like the murmurers, demanding meat and cereal (מנחה cf.'manna').

Yohanan's argument is therefore probably: If Moses was a lover of Aaron/Israel why did he take them to Elim, where there was but little food or drink. Moses had faith that God would soon give them all meat and cereal, while Israel did not, and murmured.

4a. Yohanan shows from a Peshat reading that cereal and wine accompanying a burnt offering is burnt with the meat.

This still does not settle the problem of cereal accompanying peace or thanksgiving offerings, concerning which Scripture is particularly ambiguous (cf. Lev.7.11–18). However the Sadducees lumped them all together so Yohanan's argument is sufficient. If this debate had been an invention to clear up ambiguities discovered by later rabbis, this exegesis would have failed to answer the problem.

Yohanan's reply contains evidence of a Sadducean exegesis which has been omitted. The phrase "was it not already said" implies that a previous phrase had been quoted to which this is the reply (cf. I.3.8).

This Sadducean exegesis was probably based on a Peshat reading of v20: "The priest shall wave them [אתם] besides [על] the bread of firstfruit a wave offering before YHWH, besides [על] the two lambs; they are holy to YHWH for the priest".

"Them" cannot refer to the "two lambs" (v19) or the two firstfruit loaves (v17) because they are specified in addition, and it cannot refer to the singular "goat" (v19), and not even to the "seven lambs . . .and one bullock" (v18) because they are a burnt offering which cannot be waved as food for the priest. It must therefore refer to the "food offerings and drink offerings" of the burnt offerings (v18).

Yohanan would perhaps have read the Peshat with slightly different punctuation, putting an Athnah (a semi-colon) before the second "besides" instead of after "lambs" (like some modern translations, but unlike the MT and LXX) so that "them" refers to the two lambs.

I.3.14. *bMen.65a:* (Meg.Taan.p323)

From the first of the month Nisan	מריש ירחא דניסן
to the eighth	ועד תמניא
the Daily Sacrifice was established.	ביה איתוקם תמידא
No mourning.	דלא למספד

1a

For it was that:	שהיו
The Sadducees say:	צדוקים אומרים
An individual may donate	יהיד מתנדב
and bring Tamid.	ומביא תמיד

What is the interpretation?	מאי דרוש
One lamb you [singular] shall prepare	את הכבש האחד תעשה
in the morning	בבקר
the second lamb	ואת הכבש השני
you [singular] should prepare	תעשה
between the evenings. [Num.28.4]	בין הערבים

1b

What did they reply?	מאי אהדרו
My offering, my food, my fire . . .	את קרבני להמי לאשי
you (plural) shall observe. [Num.28.2]	תשמרו
All are to come	שיהיו כולן באין
from the sacred treasuries.	מתרומת הלשכה

Notes:

The dispute concerns whether or not the Daily Sacrifices should be financed from the half-shekel contributed by every Jew, or whether a rich individual can pay the cost himself. It appears that the Sadducees were happy to let an individual cover the costs, but the Pharisees were not.

The Sadducees' motive was presumably pragmatic but they present an exegetical argument. It is unlikely that later rabbis would have furnished them with this argument, and the reply depends on it, so both exegeses are probably genuine.

Meg.Taan. assumes that the dispute concerning the Daily Offering took place between these dates, and that this victory was the reason for the holiday.

S. Zeitlin (1922:72ff.) argued that the real origin of this holiday was the commencement of the Daily Sacrifice after the dedication of the second Temple on the 23rd of Adar (LXX Ezra 6.15; 3Ezra 7.5 – the "3rd of Adar" in the MT of Ezra 6.15 is a textual corruption). This consecration would have taken 7 days (Ex.29), so the Daily

Sacrifices would commence on 1st of Nisan. Zeitlin finds confirmation of this in
bMen.45a where R. Yose explains Ezekiel's command to sacrifice a bull on 1st of
Nisan (Ezek.45.18) as a commemoration of the dedication of the Temple.

A simpler explanation may be that the Daily Offering is linked with these dates in
Lev.8–9 (see discussion in Lichtenstein 1932:290–2).

Analysis:

1a. The Sadducees interpret the singular literally. This is a Nomological interpretation, not Ultra-literal, because it does not deny the meaning of the context.

1b. The Pharisees reply that the plural is also used, so the singular must be a
collective which, in the context, refers to Israel. This is based on a Peshat reading.

I.3.15. *bShab.108a:* (bYom.39a; Sof.1.2)

1

Our Rabbis taught:	ת"ר
Tefillin may be written	כותבין תפילין
on the back of skin	על גבי עור
of a clean domestic animal	בהמה טהורה
or on the back of skin	ועל גבי עור
of a clean wild animal,	חיה טהורה
and on the back of skin	ועל גבי עור
of their *Nebelot* or *Terefot*,	נבלות וטרפות שלהן
and they may be entwined with their hair	ונכרכות בשערן
and they may be sewn with their tendons.	ונתפרות בגידן

2

And [this is] a halakah	והלכה
of Moses from Sinai,	למשה מסיני
that Tefillin	שהתפילין
may be entwined with their hair	נכרכות בשערן
and may be sewn with their tendons.	ונתפרות בגידן

3

But they are not written,	אבל אין כותבין
not on the back of skin	לא על גבי עור
of an unclean domestic animal	בהמה טמאה
nor on the back of skin	ולא על גבי עור
of an unclean wild animal	חיה טמאה
and it is not necessary to say	ואינו צריך לומר
on the back of skin	על גבי עור
of their *Nebelah* or *Terefah*	נבלה וטרפה שלהן
and they are not entwined with their hair	ואין נכרכין בשערן
and they are not sewn with their tendons.	ואין נתפרות בגידן

4a

And a certain Boethusian asked this question	וזו שאילה שאל ביתוסי אחד
of R. Joshua the grits seller:	את ר' יהושע הגרסי מניין
Tefillin may not be written	שאין כותבין תפילין

on the skin of an unclean domestic animal,   עַל עוֹר בהמה טמאה
as it is written: [Ex.13.9]   דכתיב
So that the Law of YHWH will be   למען תהיה תורת ה'
in your mouth,   בפיך
meaning: מדבר
that which is permitted in your mouth.   המותר בפיך
But if so,   אלא מעתה
on the back of skin   על גבי עור
of *Nebelah* and *Terefah*   נבלות וטרפות
let them not be written.   אל יכתבו

4b

He [Joshua] said to him: א"ל
I will make a Mashal for you: אמשול לך משל
With what can one compare the matter: למה"ד
Two men who were made liable   לשני בני אדם שנתחייבו
to execution by the state,   הריגה למלכות
one executed by the king   אחד הרגו מלך
and one executed by the executioner.   ואחד הרגו איספקליטור
Which of them is more prestigious?   איזה מהן משובח
Surely you must say   הוי אומר
this one who is executed by the king.   זה שהרגו מלך

5a

[The Boethusian said:] But if so,   אלא
they should [be allowed to] eat   מעתה יאכלו
[Nebelot and *Terefot]*

5b

He [Joshua] said to him: אמר ליה
The Torah says: [Deut.14.21]   התורה אמרה
You shall not eat any Nebelah   לא תאכלו כל נבלה
And you say: They should eat [it].   ואת אמרת יאכלו

6

He [the Boethusian] said to him: Excellent!   א"ל קאלוס

Notes:
   Tefillin (tiny prayer scrolls worn in obedience to Ex.13.9; Deut.6.8) must be written on the hide of clean animals, like all Scripture. Nebelot (animals which died naturally) or Terefot (animals killed by other animals) of clean species could not be eaten, but the Pharisees said that their hides could be used for Scripture.
   The debate concerns all Scripture, and not just Tefillin (cf. Sof.1.2). The Pharisees believed that Scripture made the hands unclean (cf. I.3.2) so the handling of scrolls made from Nebelot or Terefot caused no further uncleanness than the handling of any Scripture scrolls. However the Sadducees could not accept that Scripture was defiling (cf.I.3.2) presumably because this made Temple service almost impossible at times. Nebelot and Terefot were defiling, so the Sadducees did not want them to be used for Scripture scrolls.

The debate, as it is preserved here, is clearly late, but it is likely that it preserves a genuine Sadducean/Boethusian argument.

The reference to Joshua HaGarsi, a pupil of Aqiva in the late second century, suggests that the term "Boethusian" is being used in a general sense of "heretic" (L. Ginzberg 1902:285). The debate also appears too contrived to be genuine. The Boethusian (who is a Sadducee in bYom, and anonymous in Sof.) appears to act merely as a literary device, changing an exegesis into a debate. He asks the question (4a), makes the obvious response (5a) and then congratulates Joshua on his excellent argument.

However, if the Boethusian has transformed the exegesis of "in your mouth" (Ex.13.9) into a debate by proposing the wrong meaning, then the whole aim of the story is the correct meaning, but none is proposed. Another element missing from this debate is a sufficient reply to the Boethusian's exegesis, because although the Mashal is clever and might be considered to support the practice of using Nebelot, it does not address the exegetical problem posed by the Boethusian.

Therefore it is likely that Joshua HaGarsi has added a reply to an original Boethusian/Sadducean exegesis. The fact that his insufficient reply is accepted with such enthusiasm by his opponent suggests that he was not debating with a live Boethusian but with a tradition. It is unlikely that the rabbis would have invented this exegetical problem to which they found no reply, so the argument of the "Boethusian" probably originated before 70 CE when the Sadducees had more influence.

Analysis:

1,3. The Sadducean debate influenced the formation of this baraita which concerns skins suitable for Scripture scrolls. It uses Tefillin as a central example, presumably because this is the point at which the Sadducees debated the issue.

2. The rabbis found an ancient tradition in support of the use of the hair and tendons, but there is no mention of Nebelot and Terefot.

4a. The Sadducean argument is based on a literal Peshat reading of Ex.13.9: "It will be to you for a sign on your hand and a memorial between your eyes, so that the Law of YHWH may be in your mouth". The Pharisees accepted a literal understanding of "on your hand" and "between your eyes" by wearing the Tefillin on their wrist and forehead. A possible literal understanding of "in/on your mouth" would be to kiss them.

The Sadducees argue that if one is enjoined to put Tefillin "in/on your mouth" this implies that they are made from animals clean enough to be eaten, which excludes Nebelot or Terefot.

4b. Joshua makes a Mashal which is not based on Scripture. He suggests that an animal killed for food is like one killed by a mere executioner, but an animal which dies by itself (the Nebelah) is killed by God. It is not clear whether the Terefot are also considered to have been killed by God.

In the Mashal, the animal killed by the King is greater, so the Nebelot are greater than animals killed for food.

5a. The obvious retort is that this means that Nebelot are even cleaner than animals killed for food, and should be permitted as food.

5b. However there is a clear injunction against eating Nebelot, so they must be superior in some other respect. Presumably they are considered as greater because they are reserved for the construction of Scripture scrolls.

6. The "Boethusian" is satisfied, despite the fact that no alternative exegesis of Ex.13.9 has been proposed.

I.3.16. *bPes.57a:* (bKer.28b)

Our Rabbis taught: ...	תנו רבנן
And again, The Temple court cries:	ועוד צוותה העזרה
Lift up your heads O gates [Ps.24.7]	שאו שערים ראשיכם
and let Ishmael b.Phiabi enter,	ויכנם ישמעאל בן פיאבי
disciple of Phineas,	תלמידו של פנהס
and minister as High Priest.	וישמש בכהונה גדולה
And again, The Temple court cries:	ועוד צוותה העזרה
Lift up your heads O gates [Ps.24.7]	שאו שערים ראשיכם
and let Yohanan b.Narbai enter,	ויכנם יוחנן בן נרבאי
disciple of Pinkai,	תלמידו של פנקאי
and fill his stomach	וימלא כריסו
with the holy things of God.	מקרשי שמים

Notes:

This baraita has four "cries", only the last two of which involve Scripture citation. It follows a song against the Sadducees ('Woe is me because of the Boethusians...') and is given as further evidence of their corruption. Ishmael b.Phiabi (High Priest from 59 CE – Jos.Ant.20.179) is called "Rabbi" and eulogised in mSot.9.15, but here he is counted among the hated Sadducees, so this tradition is earlier than his 'Rabbini-zation'.

Analysis

This taunt song uses the Peshat meaning of the scripture in a sarcastic way. The Psalm welcomes the "King of Glory" into the Temple and this taunt song criticises the high-handed manners of some of the priests.

I.4 Exegeses by Beth Hillel and Beth Shammai

I.4.1. Mekh.Ish.Pis.17.209–216: (yErub.10.1)

From time to time [Ex.13.10]	מימים ימימה
shows that one needs	מגיד שאדם צריך
to examine tefillin	לבדוק את התפילין
after twelve months.	אחת לשנים עשר חדש

1a

It is said in one passage:	נאמר כאן
from time to time [Ex.13.10]	מימים ימימה
and it is said in another passage:	ונאמר להלן
[his right of] redemption shall be for	ימים תהיה גאולתו
[a year of] days. [Lev.25.29]	
Just as *days/time* there means	מה ימים האמור להלן
not less than twelve months	אין פחות משנים עשר חדש
also *days/time* here means	אף ימים האמור כאן

not less than twelve months	אין פחות משנים עשר חדש
– the words of Beth Hillel	דברי בית הלל

1b

Beth Shammai say:	בית שמאי אומרים
He need not ever examine tefillin.	אינו צריך לבודקן עולמית

Shammai the Elder said:	שמאי הזקן אומר
These [are the] tefillin	אלו תפילין
of my mother's father.	של אבי אימא

Notes:

Neusner(1971 II:6f.) points out that this dispute does not have the normal form of a House Dispute, which is a simple statement by Beth Shammai and then by Beth Hillel, both using very similar phrases which usually differ by only one or two words, and which do not involve exegesis. In this pericopé Beth Hillel comes first and uses an exegetical argument.

However none of the disputes surveyed here are 'normal' by this definition because they all involve exegesis, but this need not imply that they are late. The 'normal' form does not guarantee authenticity. On the contrary, the form is a mnemonic device imposed on the debates by later tannaim, so the only wording of 'normal' debates which can be traced back to the Houses is the conclusion. An exegetical debate which does not have this normal form may be more likely to contain the original arguments of the Houses, especially if the argument of Beth Shammai is as good as or better than that of Beth Hillel, because it is unlikely that a later authority would supply a convincing exegesis in support of the defeated House of Shammai.

This pericopé, however, probably *has* been reworked by Hillelites. Either the argument of Beth Hillel has been added later or the answer from Beth Shammai has been omitted, because it is certain that Beth Shammai would not have left this argument unanswered.

The parallel in yErub.10.1 is the same debate but between Rab and Simeon b.Gamaliel respectively, and without any exegesis. The saying "These are from my mother's father" is attributed to Hillel in yErub.

Analysis:

1a. Beth Hillel argue from Gezerah Shavah (I) using the link word "days" [ימים]. The ambiguous use of this word in Ex.13 is expounded via its unambiguous use in Lev.25 where it means a year. Neusner (1971 II:6) reads this argument as a Heqesh, but he does not say why. Heqesh and Gezerah Shavah use the same formulae, but Heqesh tends to link texts by means of a common predicate or a common factor which is not expressly stated in Scripture, while Gezerah Shavah uses link words which occur in both passages and which are usually nouns (cf. Mielziner 1968 : 145ff.).

Underlying this argument is the assumption that Ex.13.10 refers to the wearing of tefillin (which are supposedly referred to in v9) as well as to the Passover (the main subject of the chapter). This could have been deduced by the rule of Context but no such argument is given in support of the assumption.

1b. There is no counter-argument from Beth Shammai. The saying of Shammai the Elder may have been supplied to fill this gap, but its meaning is not clear. It was ambiguous enough to be used in support of the position of both Beth Shammai (as here) and of Beth Hillel (as in yErub.10).

I.4.2. *Mekh.Ish.Nez.15.49–55, mBM.3.12:*
(tBM.3.12; yBM.3.9; bBM.43a-44a; yShebi.8.1; bQid.42b; Sifra Vay.13.13b)
A: *Mekh.Ish.Nez.15.49–55:*

A1a

Whether he has not put his hand	אם לא שלח ידו
to his neighbour's goods [Ex.22.7(8)]	במלאכת רעהו
– for his private use.	לצרכו

A1b

You interpret [it] 'For his private use'	אתה אומר לצרכו
Perhaps it is not [the correct interpretation]	או אינו
but [it means] '[Both] for his private use	אלא לצרכו
and not for his private use'.	ושלא לצרכו
The text teaches: [Ex.22.8(9)]	ת״ל
For every matter/word of trespass	על כל דבר פשע

A2a

For Beth Shammai consider guilty	שבית שמאי מחייבין
one intending [in his] heart	על מחשבת הלב
to put his hand	בשליחות יד
for it is said: [Ex.22.8(9)]	שנאמר
For every matter/word of trespass	על כל דבר פשע

A2b

And Beth Hillel consider [him] guilty	ובית הלל אין מחייבין
only from the moment	אלא משעה
when he puts forth the hand.	ששלח בה יד

A3a

Therefore [when] it is said: [Ex.22.7(8)]	לכך נאמר
Whether he has not put his hand	אם לא שלח ידו
to his neighbour's goods	במלאכת רעהו
[it means] for his private use	לצרכו

B: *mBM.3.12:*

If he put his hand to entrusted things.	השולח יד בפקדון

B1a

Beth Shammai say:	בית שמאי אומרים
He must make up any loss and forfeit any gain.	ילקה בחסר וביתר

B1b

And Beth Hillel say:	ובית הלל אומרים
[He must repay the value]	
according to the time of his sequestering it.	כשעת הוצאה

...

If he intended to put [his] hand	החושב לשלח יד בפקדון
to entrusted things.	

B2a

Beth Shammai say: Guilty.	בית שמאי אומרים חייב

B2bi

And Beth Hillel say: Not guilty	ובית הלל אומרים אינו חייב
till he puts [his] hand to it.	עד שישלח בו יד
As it is said:	שנאמר
Whether he has not put his hand	אם לא שלח ידו
to his neighbour's goods. [Ex.22.7(8)]	במלאכת רעהו

B3a

In what way [is he guilty]?	כיצד
Suppose he tilted the cask	הטה את החבית
and took from it a quarter-log [of wine]	ונטל הימנה רביעית
and [later the cask] was broken?	ונשברה
He need not pay except for	אינו משלם אלא רביעית
a quarter-log.	
If he lifted and carried from it	הגביהה ונטל המנה רביעית
a quarter-log	
and [later the cask] was broken	ונשברה
he shall pay the value of the whole.	משלם דמי כולה

Notes:

The parallel passages do not record the exegesis of Beth Shammai, but this does not cast doubt on the authenticity of Beth Shammai's argument, because it is more likely that later rabbis would have omitted an argument by Beth Shammai than that they should have bolstered up the position of Beth Shammai with an argument of equal weight to Beth Hillel's.

Neusner (1971 II:8) finds no connection in the Mekhilta between the discussion about 'private use' (A1ab) and the House dispute concerning Intention (A2ab) except for the use of the same scripture. The apparent use of an Aqivan Extension argument (in A2a) also suggests late development. However it will be shown that these discussions are related by the House debate in mBM and that the original argument did not involve Extension.

Analysis:

The Mekhilta records two debates which are paralleled in mBM.

A1ab is an anonymous debate which provides exegetical arguments for the House debate in B1ab. It concerns the use of goods deposited with an individual. This matter was of great concern in a society where it constituted an important form of banking. It is discussed by Philo (Spec.4.34) and Josephus (Ant.4.285–7) and occurs in a summary of the decalogue in Mk.10.19 (ἀποστερεω – cf. Josephus).

A2ab is a House debate which is probably identical to B2ab. The Mekhilta uses it to settle the first debate. It concerns the principle of Intention, which S. Zeitlin (1919) regards as the unspoken principle behind many House disputes.

A1a. The text deals with the situation of one who loses goods which are entrusted with him. If they are stolen he is not guilty, but if he has stolen them himself, by making use of them, he is punished.

The situation became more complicated when the person invests the thing entrusted to him and tries to make a profit, so that although he intends to give it back he is also treating it as his own property in the meantime. This is the problem dealt with in B1ab. Beth Shammai said that whether the investment gains or loses, he must be the loser, so that he must repay either the sum entrusted to him or the sum which it has become as a result of investment, whichever is the greater. Beth Hillel said that he must repay the value that the goods had when he first made use of them, so that he keeps whatever profit or loss he made.

The term 'his private use' [צרכו] is literally 'his need/want/lack', which probably refers to what he consumes and cannot pay back, which one might call his 'shortfall'. His שלא לצרכו (literally 'non-need/want/lack') is therefore either what he has invested and is able to return to the owner or it is his profit (which is the most likely meaning in this debate). The common translations "private use" and "non-private use" are therefore completely misleading and make little sense in this context, and they are better replaced by "lack" (i.e. shortfall) and "non-lack" (i.e. profit) respectively.

Therefore A1a says that a person is liable only for the amount which he has lost, which is the opinion of Hillel in B1b.

A1b. Another interpretation is suggested anonymously. Perhaps the person is liable not only for the shortfall but also for the profit he has made.

Scripture is cited according to its Peshat reading, emphasising that "every" trespass is punished, not only in those cases where the person makes a loss.

This is the opinion of Beth Shammai in B1a, that he forfeits any profit but also has to make up any loss.

The argument in A1b is then countered by referring to another debate concerning this same scripture.

A2a. The principle of Intention is proved from Ex.22.8(9). The argument is based on the words "for every case/word" [כל דבר], but it is unclear how the text is used to prove the point.

Neusner (1971 II:8) suggests that the Aqivan rule of Extension is being used, based on כל. "Every case" is thereby understood as 'every case, including those where the intention has not yet resulted in action'.

J.Z. Lauterbach (1933–) translates כל דבר as "every thought", so that the idea of Intention is the result of a Peshat reading of the text. However, although דבר bears a wide range of meanings ('word/thing/object/happening', it does not usually suggest a 'thought' (with notable exceptions, e.g. Deut.15.9; Ps.41.8(9); 101.3).

H. Danby (1933) and P. Blackman (1964) translate חושב in mBM.3.12 as "express/declare his intention" rather than the simple "intend" which one might expect. Danby's reason is found in the footnote where he emphasises דבר as a "word", suggesting that Shammai read it literally as "every spoken-word of trespass".

If (as Danby and Blackman suggest) Beth Shammai understood דבר in the text as a spoken intention, then the argument is based on an understanding of כל דבר as 'every word'. Although this is not the most straight-forward understanding of דבר in this context, it is still a Peshat reading of the text because it is a possible meaning of the word and it does not deny the context.

However this interpretation of 'intention' as a spoken intention is not possible in the Mekhilta where 'intention' is defined as 'of the heart' [הלב].

The following analysis will show that הלב was probably added by the editors of the Mekhilta, because mBM suggests it would have made no sense in the original context of Beth Shammai's argument. This leads to the conclusion that Beth Shammai used a Peshat reading of דבר as "word of intention".

A2b. Beth Hillel appear to present a Peshat reading of "stretching the hand" to show that a trespass is not committed till the deed is actually done, so that the mere intention is not a trespass.

This reply supplies us with a good reason why the word הלב should have been added. If Beth Hillel are replying by means of this Peshat argument, then their argument is weaker than that of Beth Shammai, but if they are using the rule of Limitation to reply to an argument from Extension, then they have defeated Beth Shammai. Later authorities would have assumed that Beth Hillel used the stronger argument, and one way of making this clear is to add the word הלב.

If Beth Shammai used an Extended interpretation of כל דבר as "every spoken [intention of trespass]", then Beth Hillel's Peshat argument that the actual trespass involves "putting the hand" is very weak. The Shammaites could simply reply that "putting the hand" was a trespass because it was a result of intention. Similarly if Beth Shammai have based their interpretation on the General statement "every case of trespass", then the citation of the Specific phrase "put his hand" carries no weight because it occurs before the General. By the rule of Specific-General (Ishmael's no.5), a Specific followed by a General is understood merely as an example of the General, and therefore does not limit the scope of the General statement. Either way, the argument of Beth Hillel is not conclusive, and Beth Shammai wins the debate.

However, if Beth Shammai have based their interpretation on the word כל in order to argue by the rule of Extension, then Beth Hillel's reference to the preceding specific example of "putting the hand" would be using the rule of Limitation. This brings the argument under the Aqivan rule of Limitation-Extension, which is a reverse of Ishmael's rule of Specific-General so that the specific example is seen as a Limitation on the following Extension (Mielziner 1968 : 183). Therefore the general phrase "every case of trespass" would only include instances which are similar to the specific example of "putting the hand". This means that Beth Hillel have successfully shown that "every trespass" refers only to "putting the hand" and similar actions, and that it does not therefore refer to statements of intent which do not involve any such action.

The editors of the Mekhilta would have expected Beth Hillel to win this debate so they probably added the word הלב to prevent subsequent scholars from 'misunderstanding' Beth Shammai's argument as a Peshat interpretation of דבר as "word [of intent]" (cf. Deut.15.9).

This debate (A2a–b) is identical to that in B2a–b, although Beth Shammai's argument is missing.

B3a provides an example case for this debate. The problem of Intention would not occur often in respect of the law of entrusted goods, because there is usually no practical difference between the case where entrusted goods were not used and the case where someone intended to use entrusted goods but did not actually do so. However, in the case of the broken cask the principle of Intention does make a difference. The importance of this example is that the argument attributed to Beth Shammai in the Mekhilta makes perfect sense in this context, but only if the word הלב is omitted.

The dispute concerns someone who uses some wine out of a cask which has been deposited with him, and then subsequently the cask is broken: is he liable for the whole cask or just for the amount he took? Both Houses would have assumed that the man would not be liable for the broken cask if he had not taken any wine. Beth Hillel say that he is only liable for the wine which he actually used, arguing "he put his hand to it", but they add that if he actually placed the cask among his own property then he is liable for the whole cask if it breaks, because he has 'put his hand' to the whole cask.

The position of Beth Shammai is missing, but it can be inferred from Beth Hillel's reply. They evidently said that he was liable for the whole cask from the time he took some of the wine, whether or not he moved the cask. This position is not based on 'intention of the heart' but on intention as revealed by action. This is a pragmatic approach, because intention 'of the heart' could not be proved in a court whereas intention expressed in word or action could be.

The word הלב is therefore out of place in Beth Shammai's argument, and their original argument appears to have been based on a Peshat interpretation of דבר as "a spoken word [of intent]". It was noted above that this is not really the 'plain' meaning of the text but that it does not actually deny the context.

This is corroborated by the traditional interpretation of Ex.22.7(8). In the MT the man comes "to God", but the LXX adds that the defendants must "swear that he assuredly has not done wickedly", as also in Josephus (Ant.4.285–7) and Philo (Spec.4.34). This may be based on the interpretation of אלהים as "judges" (F. Brown 1959 : 43) and is influenced by v10(11): "An oath of YHWH shall be between them".

This practice of a sworn statement provides evidence that the interpretation of דבר as a 'spoken word' would have been regarded as the 'plain' meaning.

A3a. The debate in A1a–b has used a House dispute based on the same text (A2a–b = B2a–b) in order to prove that the phrase "every case of trespass" does not refer to cases of 'non-private use' – i.e. 'non-lack' or 'profit'.

This amalgamation of the two debates, which both originated in the Houses, cannot be dated. However it is presumably post-Aqivan because it assumes that Beth Hillel won the second debate, which is only possible if Beth Shammai argued from Extension.

In summary, the argument at A1b from "every case" appears to be Peshat, arguing that both the person who makes a profit and the person who makes a loss from the use of goods entrusted to him are equally guilty of trespass. However, while Beth Hillel did not exonerate the person who made a profit, they did allow him to keep the profit without any penalty, so it would gradually be assumed that there was no trespass involved in making use of entrusted goods, unless one was not able to repay the value of those goods when they were claimed.

Once the private use of entrusted goods was no longer considered to be a trespass, the Shammaite Peshat argument from "every case of trespass" (A1b = B1a) would have made no sense, so it would have been read as an argument from Extension, arguing that the phrase "every case of trespass" included cases where a profit is made from entrusted goods".

It was likewise assumed that Beth Shammai used Extension in the second House debate concerning this text (A2ab = B2ab), and the later addition of לב firmly established this interpretation. However one example which was discussed by the Houses (B3a) demonstrates that the Shammaites originally argued from a Peshat reading.

I.4.3. *Mekh.Sim.p12.4–5*

Between the evenings [Ex.12.6]	בין הערבים
Meaning what?	הכאי זה צד
From the sixth hour [noon] and onward.	משש שעות ולמעלה
For Beth Shammai say:	שבית שמאי או'
Not in the evening	אין בערב
but from the turning of the day.	אלא משפנה יום

Notes:
Neusner (1971 II:9) concludes that this was an authentic Shammaite exegesis which survived because it agreed with the predominant view (cf. mPes.5.3; Mekh.Ish.-Pis.5.118–120).

Analysis:

There is no obvious exegetical methodology behind this exegesis. The phrase 'turning of the day' is not biblical, although similar phrases do occur (לפנות ערב, 'turning of evening' in Gen.24.63, Deut.23.11; לפנות בקר, 'turning of morning' in Ex.14.27, Judg.19.26, Ps.46.5(6)). Beth Shammai are probably just stating their understanding of the term "between the evenings".

Although the term occurs frequently, concerning both the Paschal sacrifice (Ex.12.6; Lev.23.5; Num.9.3,5,11) and the evening sacrifice (Ex.29.39,41; 30.8; Num.28.4,8), it was not clear what it meant. Originally it probably meant "in the evening" (cf. Ex.16.12f.) but Rabbi rejects this interpretation (Mekh.Ish. Pis.5.118–120). The LXX translated "towards evening"(προς ἑσπεραν).

According to Josephus, the evening sacrifice was offered at 3 pm. (Ant.14.4.3), and the Pascal sacrifice was offered between 3 pm. and 5 pm. (Wars 6.9.3). However, the evening sacrifice had to be completed before the Paschal sacrifice (mPes.5.3) so the evening sacrifice was started an hour earlier, or even two hours earlier if the Passover was a Friday, with the result that the 'evening' sacrifice could be started shortly after noon (A. Edersheim 1926:116). This agrees with Beth Shammai.

Therefore this is an argument from Pragmatism, because Beth Shammai appears to have determined the interpretation from the necessities of practice. It is also significant that they appear to have abandoned the literal meaning of the text although it is not certain what this would have been.

I.4.4. *Mekh.Sim.p149.15–21*
(mShab.1.4–11; tShab.1.20–21; yShab.1.5; bShab.18b)

1a

Beth Shammai say:	שבית שמאי אומ׳
Six days you shall labour	ששת ימים תעבד
and you shall do all your work [Ex.20.9]	ועשית כל מלאכתך
so your work should be finished	שתהא מלאכתך גמורה
before the eve of Sabbath.	מערב שבת

1b

And Beth Hillel say:	ובית הלל אומרין
Six days you labour	ששת ימים תעבד
you do all six [days]	עושה אתה כל ששה
and the remainder of *your work*	ושאר מלאכתך
is performed by itself	היא נעשית מאיליה
on the Sabbath.	בשבת

Notes:

The exegesis occurs in Tosefta but not in Mishnah. The last comment ("and the remainder...") is missing in Tosefta but it is integral to the argument and probably original.

Analysis:

1a. Beth Shammai presents a Peshat interpretation.

1b. Beth Hillel glosses the text so that the second line has a different meaning, probably on the basis of No Redundancy. The particle כל is not exploited for Extension.

I.4.5. *Sifra Taz.Per.3.1–2 (Weiss 59ab):*
(mKer.1.6; mEd.4.10; tKer.1.9; bKer.7b–8a; bPes.3a)

1

For a son [Lev.12.6]
– to make liable for every son.
For a daughter [Lev.12.6]
– to make liable for every daughter.

לבן
לחייב על כל בן ובן
לבת
לחייב על כל בת ובת

1a

But since it says:
Or for a daughter [Lev.12.6]
this includes one miscarrying
on the 81st evening,
that she is liable for the offering.
According to the words of Beth Hillel.

וכשהוא אומר
או לבת
להביא את המפלת
אור לשמונים ואחד
שתהא חייבת בקרבן
כדברי בית הלל

1b

For Beth Shammai
exempt [her] from the offering.

שבית שמאי
פוטרים מן הקרבן

2a

Beth Hillel said to Beth Shammai:
Surely you acknowledge with us
concerning one who sees [blood]
[on] the 81st evening
that she is unclean.

אמרו להם בית הלל לבית שמאי
אי אתם מודים לנו
ברואה
אור לשמונים ואחד
שהיא טמאה

2b

Beth Shammai said to them:
Surely you acknowledge
concerning one miscarrying on the 81st
that she is liable for the offering.

אמרו להם בית שמאי
אי אתם מודים
במפלת לשמונים ואחד
שהיא חייבת בקרבן

3a

And Beth Hillel said to them:
What distinguishes
the 81st evening
from the 81st day?
If it is equal to it in uncleanness
is it not equal to it in offering?

אמרו להם בית הלל
מה שנה
אור לשמונים ואחד
מיום שמונים ואחד
אם שוה לו לטומאה
לא ישוה לו לקרבן

3b

Beth Shammai said to them: No!
If you say [so] concerning one miscarrying
[on] the 81st day
which thus comes out at a time
which is fitting
to bring her offering,
[mKer.1.6 includes:
[you will say [so] concerning one miscarrying

אמרו להם בית שמאי לא
אם אמרתם במפלת
יום שמונים ואחד
שכן יצא לשעה
שהיא ראויה
להביא בה קרבן
[תאמרו בהמפלת

[[on] the 81st evening | אור לשמנים ואחד]
[which does not come out at a time | שלא יצאה בשעה]
[which is fitting | שהיא ראויה]
[to bring her offering. | להביא בה קרבן]

4a

Beth Hillel said to them: And behold!	אמרו להם בית הלל והרי
The one miscarrying on the 81st day	המפלת יום שמונים ואחד
[which] begins to be on the Sabbath	שחל להיות בשבת
proves [the matter]	תוכיח
for it does not come out at a time	שלא יצא לשעה
which is fitting	שהיא ראויה
for her offering	בה קרבן
and she is [still] liable for the offering.	וחייבת בקרבן

4b

Beth Shammai said to them: No!	אמרו להם בית שמאי לא
If you say [so] concerning one miscarrying	אם אמרתם במפלת
on the 81st day	יום שמונים ואחד
[which] begins to be on the Sabbath	שחל להיות בשבת
which although it is not suitable	שאף על פי שאינו ראוי
for an individual's offering	לקרבן יחיד
it is fitting for a community offering,	ראוי לקרבן צבור
will you say [so] concerning one miscarrying	תאמרו במפלת
on the 81st evening,	אור שמונים ואחד
for behold, nights are not fitting,	שהרי הלילות אין ראוים
neither for an individual's offering	לא לקרבן יחיד
nor for a community offering.	ולא לקרבן צבור

5b

She who sees blood	הרואה דם
does not prove [the matter]	אינה מוכחת
for the one miscarrying within	שהמפלת תוך
the completion [of her uncleanness]	מלאת
her blood is clean	דמיה טהורים
and she is exempt from the offering.	ופטורה מן הקרבן

6a

Beth Hillel said to them:	אמרו להם בית הלל
But since it says:	וכשהוא אומר
Or for a daughter. [Lev.12.6]	או לבת
this includes one miscarrying	להביא את המפלת
on the 81st evening,	אור לשמונים ואחד
that she is liable for the offering.	שתהא חייבת בקרבן

Notes:

A woman is unclean after childbirth, 40 days for a son and 80 days for a daughter, after which she brings an offering. A miscarriage occurring during this interval is covered by this offering, but if it occurs after this interval it requires an extra offering. This interval strictly ends on the evening of the last day, but what if a miscarriage occurs before the offering is brought during the next day? Beth Hillel said that an extra offering was needed, but Beth Shammai said that the one offering was sufficient.

In practice, this situation could only arise during the longer interval for a daughter, because a miscarriage before 41 days was not regarded as a foetus (mNidd.3.7), so the disputed period was between the 81st evening and the 81st day.

This is likely to be a genuine dispute, because Beth Hillel uncharacteristically have the sterner ruling and a less convincing argument, and because the normal Shammai-Hillel order is reversed. The Shammaites presumably felt that the offering itself produced the cleansing and therefore included any miscarriage preceding it, while the Hillelites, like later rabbis, felt that God cleansed while the offering itself was power-less but was made in obedience to the Law (cf. C.G. Montefiore & H. Loewe 1974:152f.).

The practical situation which called for a decision in this matter may never have arisen. A miscarriage occurring as a result of the second ovulation after giving birth would be only 4–6 weeks old by the 81st day, and even if it were recognised as anything other than a heavy bleed, it would not be counted as a foetus. Therefore any miscarriage occurring on the 81st evening would have to be conceived from the first ovulation after giving birth, when fertility is suppressed by high progesterone levels, especially when breast feeding. Conception during the first ovulation is even less likely after the birth of a girl because the husband was not allowed to sleep with his wife during her initial two weeks of uncleanness (Lev.12.5). Even if conception did occur during this first ovulation, the miscarriage would have to occur during the few hours of night after the 80th day.

Therefore it is likely that this debate was never sharpened by the practical necessity for a decision, which may be why equally balanced arguments on both sides have been preserved, because the subject could be valued as a purely theoretical discussion.

The exegetical argument is only in Sifra, probably because Mishnah and Tosefta omitted the exegesis, as they usually do. Neusner (1971 II:22) suggests that it was added later because Aqivan Extension is used, but it is argued below that the original exegesis was No Redundancy.

Analysis:
Neusner (1971 II:19) points out that mKer and Sifra both miss out vital elements of the debate and this is not entirely clarified by merging the two sources as Neusner does because 5a is still missing. It is suggested below that the Shammaites may have deliberately changed course after a poor argument at 4b, so that 5a never existed.

The debate as it stands in Sifra continues the exegesis of Lev.12.6 at "for a son or a daughter".

1 The question being answered is: Why are both 'son' and 'daughter' needed? Sifra explains this apparent Redundancy with an Extension argument: They show that *every* son and daughter is included

1a Next "or" needs exegesis, so Sifra quotes a debate in which Beth Hillel appears to use Extension to apply it to the miscarriage on the 81st evening.

However Beth Hillel's exegesis appears to be based on the whole phrase או לבת "or for a daughter", because although this involves only one extra word, every word is relevant in the terse and abbreviated style of these debates.

It is likely that Beth Hillel's original exegesis was based on the apparent Redundancy of או לבת after לבן. They read בן as "child" and argue that בת is specifically mentioned to include a miscarriage which occurs during this questionable period at the end of uncleanness for a girl.

1b. Beth Shammai exempted such a woman from this second offering. The reasons are not given.

The two positions are now presented as theoretical differences which are not differences in practice.

2a. According to Beth Hillel the woman became clean at the end of the 80th day, because the cleansing was performed by God, not by sacrifice, so a miscarriage on the 81st makes her unclean again. Beth Shammai also believed that such a miscarriage made her unclean but believed that this was removed, with the original uncleanness, by virtue of the offering.

2b. Beth Shammai regard the offering as all-important, while Beth Hillel seem to devalue it by saying that cleansing occurs before it, at the end of the 80th day. But Beth Hillel regard the offering as necessary, to obey the Law.

3a. Beth Hillel point out that the Shammaites were treating two identical situations differently. Shammaites admitted that the 81st evening miscarriage caused uncleanness (2a) but they did not demand an offering for it, unlike an exactly similar miscarriage on the 81st day occurring after the 80 day offering.

3b. Beth Shammai argued that the situations were different in that an offering could not be brought during the night. 4a implies that Beth Shammai felt that only miscarriages during the night, and not during the 81st day, were included in the 80 day offering. Therefore they argue here that the woman *could* bring an offering first thing in the morning, so she must not be allowed to benefit from any further delay by being excused the offering for a miscarriage later that day.

4a. Beth Hillel show that this argument breaks down when the 81st day is a Sabbath, when the offering could not be brought. If she had a miscarriage on that day, she would still be liable for two sacrifices, even though she could not have prevented the delay.

4b. Beth Shammai argue that the two situations, of night-time and Sabbath, are not comparable with regard to the prevention of offerings. At night no offerings are permitted, while on Sabbath community offerings (such as Daily offerings) are permitted.

At this point the Shammaites appear to be walking backwards into a corner, because they have implied that night-time and Sabbath *can* be compared with regard to individual offerings, such as uncleanness offerings. However they are saved from complete defeat because the argument changes direction.

5a. This part of the debate by Beth Hillel is missing, and has to be inferred from the answer which is given by Beth Shammai. Perhaps it was: "And behold, she who sees blood on the 81st day will prove the matter, for she comes under the law of blood outside her days of impurity (Lev.15.25ff.) – she remains unclean for 7 days and then offers a sacrifice (Lev.15.25ff.)".

However it is likely that 5a did not exist, and that in 5b Beth Shammai change the direction of the debate by referring back to 2a: "one who sees [blood on] the 81st evening".

5b. Beth Shammai says that in this situation blood is equivalent to a miscarriage, so her blood is cleansed by the 81st day sacrifice and she needs no extra sacrifice.

6a. The exegesis of 1a is restated without any new details. This seems to have been done in order to give Beth Hillel the last word so that they appear to win the debate.

I.4.6. *Sifra Qed.Par.3.7 (Weiss 90ab):*
(mEd.4.5; mPeah.7.6; yPeah.7.5; bQid.54b; mMS.5.3,6f.; yMS.5.2,3;
mTer.3.9; tTer.2.13).

1

All its fruit will be [holy] [Lev.19.24]	יהיה כל פריו
– to include the grape-gleanings	להביא את הפרט
and the defective-clusters.	ואת העוללות
According to the words of Beth Hillel.	כדברי בית הילל

1a

Beth Shammai say:	בית שמיי אומר
The grape-gleanings are his	יש לו פרט
and the defective-clusters are his	ויש לו עוללות
and the poor	והעניים
redeem [them] for themselves.	פודים לעצמם

1b

And Beth Hillel say:	ובית הילל אומרים
It is all for the winepress.	כולו לגת

Notes:

This dispute involves two sets of laws: 1. The produce of new fruit trees, including vines, were not to be eaten for three years, and the fourth year it was eaten in Jerusalem like a Second Tithe or redeemed (Lev.19.23f.). 2. Gleanings, including defective grape clusters, were to be left for the poor to gather themselves (Lev.19.9f.).

Does the law of gleanings apply to the fourth year harvest? Beth Shammai said it did, and the poor redeemed the gleanings but Beth Hillel said that the owner retained and could redeem the whole.

Neusner (1971 II:59ff.) has a completely different explanation for this debate. He links it with the debate which precedes it in most of the parallel passages, concerning the rules of the added fifth and of burning with regard to the fourth year fruit. He suggests that these two debates were originally a single complex debate concerning the application of the rules of the Second Tithe to the fourth year fruit. Beth Shammai said that some Second Tithe rules did apply to the fourth year fruit and some did not, while Beth Hillel said that all the rules of the Second Tithe applied to the fourth year fruit. This complex debate was simplified and remembered in the form of two debates: in the first Beth Shammai say that certain Second Tithe rules do not apply to the fourth year fruit (i.e. the rules of no added fifth and of burning), and Beth Hillel reply "They do apply"; in the second debate Beth Shammai say that other Second Tithe rules do apply to the fourth year fruit (i.e. the rules of grape gleanings and defective clusters), and Beth Hillel reply that "All Second Tithe rules apply".

This interpretation is neat and believable, except for the fact that Beth Hillel do not reply the second time that "All Second Tithe rules apply" but say that "All goes to the winepress", which implies that the whole harvest, including the gleanings, goes to the owner (who has the winepress) and not to the poor. This reply does not answer the question, "Which Second Tithe rules apply to the fourth year fruit?", but it does answer the question "Do the gleanings and defective clusters go to the poor?".

The Mishnah and Tosefta characteristically omit the exegesis, and the Talmudim follow them. Neusner (1971 II:24f.) suggests that the exegesis is a later Aqivan addition, because it uses the method of Extension. It is argued below that Beth Hillel's original argument came from a Peshat reading, and that their ruling is dependent on this exegesis.

Analysis:

1. Sifra presents Beth Hillel's exegesis as though it were an Aqivan Extension argument based on the particle כל. However, as Neusner points out, Sifra often uses כדברי ('according to the words of') to indicate a paraphrase of a ruling. In this case they appear to have paraphrased the exegesis behind 1b.

1a. Beth Shammai applies the law of gleanings to the law of the fourth year harvest. This follows the Peshat reading of both laws.

1b. Beth Hillel claim that the law of gleanings does not apply to the fourth year harvest. All the grapes, including defective clusters, should go into the owner's wine-press to make wine for redemption or consumption in Jerusalem.

Unlike the Shammaite ruling, some justification is required, because a law is being neglected. Beth Hillel are clearly appealing to Lev.19.24 which speaks about כל, "all/ the whole" of the harvest as one unit. Their ruling is therefore based on a Peshat, albeit rather pedantic, reading of the text.

I.4.7. *Sifra Em.Per.15.5 (Weiss 102c):*

1a

Beth Shammai say:	בית שמאי אומר
One may think that	יכול
one may offer Hagigah	יחוג אדם
on the Good day.	ביום טוב
Scripture teaches: *Only* [Lev.23.39]	תלמוד לומר אך
– during the intervening days	במועד
you may offer Hagigah,	אתה חוגג
and you may not offer Hagigah	ואין אתה חוגג
on the Good day.	ביום טוב

1b

Beth Hillel say:	בית הילל אומר
One may think that	יכול
one may offer Hagigah	יחוג אדם
on the Sabbath.	בשבת
Scripture teaches: *Only* [Lev.23.39]	תלמוד לומר אך
– during the Good day	ביום טוב
you may offer Hagigah	אתה חוגג
and you may not offer Hagigah	ואין אתה חוגג
on the Sabbath.	בשבת

Notes:

The Good day of a feast (the Holy Convocation of Lev.23.7 etc.) occurred on the 1st and 8th feast day, and was almost equivalent to a Sabbath. The small differences between what was allowed on a Good day and a Sabbath were the subject of endless debate (see tractate Betzah).

Here Beth Shammai argue that Hagigah (personal festival offerings) could not be brought on a Good day nor a Sabbath, while Beth Hillel argue they could be brought on a Good day but not on a Sabbath.

Neusner (1971 I:25f.) suggests that these exegeses cannot be genuine because they use an Aqivan Limitation argument based on the particle אך. It is argued below that the original arguments are based on a Peshat reading.

The most natural origin of this debate is before 70 CE because it would have had little relevance after the cessation of sacrifices (although this would by no means prevent the rabbis from continuing to discuss it). It is also related to a very early debate (I.2.8) concerning the offering of Hagigah on the Sabbath.

Analysis:

1a. Beth Shammai appear to regard the beginning of v39 as a continuation of the previous sentence: "all your offerings which you will give to YHWH except [אך] on the 15th". The 15th was a Good day, so they concluded that Hagigah were not permitted on Good days.

1b. Beth Hillel point out that the restriction could equally apply to a Sabbath rather than a Good day, because v39 is one of the few places where a Good day is called a "Sabbath" rather than a "Holy Convocation".

Although both Houses read אך with a restrictive force, the interpretation is probably Peshat rather than an Aqivan Limitation argument, whether אך is read as the beginning of a new sentence or the continuation of the previous sentence.

If אך is read as the start of a new sentence, it must be read with the unusual sense of "also/especially". By the rule of Unusual form (Eliezer's rule no.16), this might indicate that a special restrictive force was present. M. Fishbane (1988:371) points out that such restrictions are found at Qumran without any Aqivan particles.

Equally, if אך is read as a continuation of the previous verse (as suggested at 1a), it has the normal sense of "except" which introduces a restrictive sense to the Peshat reading.

I.4.8 *Sifra Behar Per.1.5 (Weiss 106ab):*
(mShebi.4.2; yShebi.4.2,4;9.6; mEd.5.1)
1

And the Sabbath of the land will be	והיתה שבת הארץ
[food] to you. [Lev.25.6]	לכם
From [the product of] the Sabbath of the land	מן השבות בארץ
you may eat,	אתה אוכל
and you may not eat	ואין אתה אוכל
from what is guarded.	מן השמור
From here they said:	מיכן אמרו
A field which is specially prepared.	שדה שנטייבה
2a	
Beth Shammai say:	בית שמיי אומרים
They do not eat	אין אוכלים
its produce in the Seventh year.	פירותיה בשביעית
2b	
And Beth Hillel say:	ובית הלל אומרים
They eat.	אוכלים

3a

Beth Shammai say:	בית שמיי אומרים
They do not eat	אין אוכלים
the produce of the seventh year	פירות שביעית
by favour/ from prepared [soil].	בטובה

3b

And Beth Hillel say:	ובית הילל אומרים
By favour	בטובה
and which is not by favour/ from prepared [soil].	ושלא בטובה

R. Judah says:	רבי יהודה אומר
The rulings are reversed.	הילוף הדברים

Notes:

The phrase "From here they said:" introduces the debate quoted from mShebi.4.2. The exegesis is not present in the parallels but it supports the Shammaite position and is therefore likely to be original, although L. Finkelstein (in Neusner 1971 II:29f.) wonders if it originated with R. Eliezer.

Neusner (1971 II:28) suggests that R. Judah reversed the rulings so that the exegesis supports Beth Hillel, even though this results in Hillelites being stricter than Shammaites.

The last pair of rulings are reversed in mEd. following R. Judah, but the Hillelite ruling is changed to "except by permission" [אלא בטובה].

Analysis:

Fields could not be cultivated during the seventh year or prepared for the next, and their produce was available to anyone. But irreligious Jews did prepare their land and some even guarded them, so should one eat the produce of their fields?

1. The exegesis answers, with a rather literal Peshat reading, that the fields observing the Sabbath rest will provide sufficient food.

This exegesis is the origin of two debates. Neither have precise verbal links with the exegesis, but both are inspired by the exegesis, because שמר can mean both "to keep/ prepare" a field (e.g. Gen.2.15) and "to keep/guard" a field (e.g. Gen.3.24).

2a. The prepared field is not observing the Sabbath rest, so the Shammaites say one should not eat from it. This overrides the general law that one can eat from any field during the Seventh year, and therefore requires some kind of exegesis to support it.

3a. Similarly, produce from a guarded field, from which it is impossible to eat without permission of the owner, should also be left.

2b & 3b. The Hillelite position may simply be the more lenient on the poor people, or it may be more radical in encouraging people to take food from irreligious Jews.

The original purpose of the Shammaite exegesis may have been to prevent the zealous from coming into conflict with the irreligious. The fact that some fields had to be guarded suggests that there were some Jews who were prepared to take food from such a field by force.

R. Tarphon followed the Shammaite position rigorously, so when he wanted some fruit from his own orchard, (which was being guarded by agents of the community for future use), he was careful not to ask permission, and was consequently caught by the guards and beaten (tShebi.4.2; yShebi.35b; L. Finkelstein in Neusner 1971 I:30).

I.4.9. *Sifré Deut.234:*

(Sifré Num.115; cf. bMen41b; bBekh.39b; bYeb.5b)

And they shall make a Fringe. [Num.15.38]	ועשו להם ציצית
I hear: [i.e. It seems to say:]	שומע אני
One may make it from one thread	יעשה חוט אחד
by itself.	בפני עצמו
Scripture teaches: *Tassels* [Deut.22.12]	תלמוד לומר גדילים
With how many [threads] are tassels made?	כמה גדילים נעשים

1a

Not less than three threads,	אין פחות משלשה חוטים
according to the words of Beth Hillel.	כדברי בית הלל

1b

Beth Shammai say:	בית שמיי אומרים
From four threads of blue	מארבעה חוטים של תכלת
and four threads of white;	וארבעה חוטים של לבן
of four [threads of] four fingers.	של ארבע ארבע אצבעות
And the halakah is according to the	והלכה כדברי בית שמיי
words of Beth Shammai.	

Notes:

The anonymous exegetical introduction (1) was probably added later. However it seems to correctly represent the original question answered in this House debate, because it is necessary for understanding the debate, and the rulings of both Houses are understandable as exegeses of the texts introduced. Beth Hillel precedes Beth Shammai (contrary to normal) because the Shammaite ruling prevailed, and perhaps also because the Hillelite position is logically antecedent.

Sifré Num. reverses these decisions (though Friedman re-reverses them) but still says that the law follows Shammai, so the motive is not to make Hillel win.

The Talmud divides the debate into two: "How many" and "How long", while Sifré amalgamates both replies. Neusner (1971 II:31ff.) plausibly suggests the original was "Fringe: Beth Hillel says Three. Beth Shammai says Four" which was applied to both questions. The question "How many" was probably original, because it arises out of the exegesis, and the question "How long" would then develop from the reply.

Analysis:

Two contradictory texts are found concerning Fringes, one using a singular term and one a plural. These are traditionally resolved by wrapping one thread round others to unite them.

The question then arises: How many threads in a tassel? Neusner (1971 II:30) misses the point here by translating: "From how many tassels".

1a. Beth Hillel is either interpreting the plural *Tassels* as three or adding the smallest plural of two *Tassels* to the single *Fringe*. The latter is probably correct because although the Dual form of nouns is more frequent in mishnaic Hebrew than in the OT (M.H. Segal 1927:133), the plural is always understood as 'two or more' (cf. I.2.3–4, I.2.11, I.4.10, I.4.15, contra Neusner 1971 II:32).

This is based on a Nomological reading which assumes that these apparent contradictions in two separate passages of law represent separate portions of a single precept.

1b. The Shammaite answer "four" can be derived in two ways. One possible explanation is the anonymous exegesis in bYeb.5b where a tassel is assumed to be made up of more than one thread: *"Tassel* implies two threads, *Tassels* implies four threads."

Sifré Num.115 explains: "Three of wool and the fourth of blue", suggesting that they have remembered the blue thread also mentioned in Num.15.38 and added it to Beth Hillel's answer.

This latter explanation is preferable because it is attributed to Beth Shammai and it helps to explain why Beth Hillel was defeated. Both use the Nomological approach found in 1a.

I.4.10. *Sifré Deut.166:*

And the first fleece of your flock	וראשית גז צאנך
you shall give to him. [Deut.18.4]	תתן לו
How many sheep shall he have	כמה צאן יהיה לו
in order to be liable	ויהא חייב
for the first of the fleece?	בראשית הגז

1a

Beth Shammai say:	בית שמי אומרים
Two ewes, for it is said: [Is.7.21]	שתי רחילות שנאמר
And it will be in that day	והיה ביום ההוא
a man will keep alive	יחיה איש
a heifer of the herd	עגלת בקר
and two sheep.	ושתי צאן

1b

And Beth Hillel say:	ובית הלל אומרים
Five, for it is said: [1Sam.25.18]	חמש שנאמר
And five sheep prepared.	וחמש צאן עשויות

1c

R. Aqiva says:	רבי עקיבה אומר
First fleece – two	ראשית גז שתים
Your flock – four	צאנך ארבע
You shall give to him – lo, five.	תתן לו הרי חמש

Notes:
Neusner (1971 II:36f.) argues that the exegeses use Aqivan methods, and were therefore added later. However these exegeses can be understood in non-Aqivan terms.

It would appear to be a simple job for later rabbis to find a text to verify these rulings, because "sheep" is very common and frequently occurs with a number. However, in only three texts is this number less than a thousand: in the texts cited here, and in Gen.21.28 where the number is seven. It is therefore either very fortuitous that the Houses picked numbers which could be verified in this way, or (as seems more likely) the Houses based their rulings on exegesis.

Analysis:
The debate concerns the first fleece of a flock which is for the Lord (Deut.18.4). How many sheep must there be in a flock before this command applies?

1a. Beth Shammai are characteristically strict, ruling that even if there are only two sheep and even if they are only ewes, which are worth less than rams, they still come under this command.

This may be based on a Peshat interpretation of the plural "sheep" in Deut.18.4 to mean 'at least two' (cf.I. 4.9). Gezerah Shavah (I) is used to show that the collective term "sheep" can be used of only two animals. The feminine "ewes" may have been influenced by "heifer".

1b. Beth Hillel are less strict, probably recognising that this command affects the poor man with a small flock more than the rich man.

This exegesis is also based on Gezerah Shavah (I) but this time using 1Sam.25 to define the number of "sheep" as five.

1c. Aqiva reads the text in a Derash mode, parsing the verse and counting up the sheep as he goes. He interprets the singular noun and adjective as one each, the plural implied by "flock" as another two, and the singular verb as one more, making five.

I.4.11 *Sifré Deut.269:* (mGit.9.10; yGit.9.11; bGit.90a; ySot.1.1)

And if it happens that she does not find	והיה אם לא תמצא
favour in his eyes. [Deut.24.1]	חן בעיניו
1a	
From this Beth Shammai say:	מיכן היו בית שמיי אומרים
A man may not divorce his wife	לא יגרש אדם את אשתו
except if he finds	אלא אם כן מצא
unchastity in her,	בה ערוה
for it is said: [Deut.24.1]	שנאמר
Because he found in her	כי מצא בה
a matter of unchastity	ערות דבר
1b	
And Beth Hillel say:	ובית הלל אומרים
Even if she spoiled his broth,	אפילו הקדיחה תבשילו
for it is said: [Any] *matter.*	שנאמר דבר
2b	
Beth Hillel said to Beth Shammai:	אמרו בית הלל לבית שמיי
Since it said: *Matter*	אם נאמר דבר
why did it [also] say: *Unchastity*	למה נאמר ערות
and since it said: *Unchastity*	ואם נאמר ערות
why did it [also] say: *Matter?*	למה נאמר דבר
2bi	
Because if it said: *Matter*	שאם נאמר דבר
and it did not [also] say: *Unchastity*	ולא נאמר ערות
I would say:	הייתי אומר
She who is discharged because of a *Matter*	היוצאה מפני דבר

may be permitted to remarry
but she who is discharged because of
Unchastity
may not be permitted to remarry.

תהא מותרת להנשא
והיוצאה מפני ערוה

לא תהא מותרת להנשא

And be not astonished:
If she is forbidden
from him who was permitted to her
(should she) not be forbidden
from him who was forbidden to her?
Scripture teaches: [Deut.24.1f.]
Unchastity . . .
and she leaves his house and goes
and becomes the wife of another.

ואל תתמה
אם נאסרה
מן המותר לה
לא תהא אסורה
מן האסור לה
תלמוד לומר
ערות
ויצאה מביתו והלכה
והיתה לאיש אחר

2biii

And if it said: *Unchastity*
and it did not [also] say: *Matter*
I would say:
She may go because of *Unchastity*
[but] she may not go because of a *Matter*.
Scripture teaches: [Deut.24.1f.]
A Matter . . . and she leaves his house.

ואם נאמר ערות
ולא נאמר דבר
הייתי אומר
מפני ערוה תצא
מפני דבר לא תצא
תלמוד לומר
דבר ויצאה מביתו

2c

R. Aqiva says:
Even if he finds
one who is prettier than her.
As it is said: [Deut.24.1]
And if it happens that she does not find
favour in his eyes.

רבי עקיבה אומר
אפילו מצא
אחרת נאה הימנה
שנאמר
והיה אם לא תמצא
חן בעיניו

Notes:

Neusner concludes that the Shammaite ruling has been preserved faithfully, but
that the Hillelites have suppressed the Shammaite exegesis (which is nevertheless
obvious) and that they have added a full rebuttal of the Shammaite position without
allowing a reply.

Analysis:

1a. Beth Shammai interpret according to the Peshat reading that "some matter of
unchastity" means "unchastity".

1bi. Beth Hillel interpret "matter" as "any matter" apart from unchastity. This is
based on No Redundancy.

2a. Beth Shammai's reply is not given, but presumably they would have said: If
"Matter" means 'any matter', then "Unchastity" is redundant. This has been incorpo-
rated into 2b.

2b. Beth Hillel argue that both "Matter" and "Unchastity" are necessary to prevent misunderstanding.

It is now demonstrated how misunderstanding could result if one omits either "Unchastity" (2bi) or "Matter" (2bii). These may have been added later.

2bi. If "Unchastity" is omitted one might argue that she who is divorced for unchastity should not be allowed to remarry, unlike other divorcees.

The way in which this might be argued is then outlined as a Qal vaHomer. If she cannot marry her previous husband (Deut.24.4) with whom sexual relations had been allowed, then surely she cannot marry someone with whom sexual relations had not been allowed (such as her lover).

2bii. If "Matter" is omitted then one might argue (as Beth Shammai did) that one can only be divorced for Unchastity.

2c. Aqiva takes the argument of Beth Hillel to its logical conclusion, that one can divorce a wife on the grounds of any "matter", including, as the text says, "favour in his eyes".

I.4.12. *mBer.1.3:*
(Sifré Deut.34; tBer.1.4; bBer.11a; yBer.1.6; yShebi.4.2; ySanh.11.4)

1a

Beth Shammai say:	בית שמאי אומרים
At evening every man should recline	בערב כל אדם יטו
to recite [the Shema]	ויקראו
and at morning they should stand,	ובבקר יעמדו
for it is said: [Deut.6.7b]	שנאמר
and when you lie down and when you rise.	ובשכבך ובקומך

1b

Beth Hillel say:	ובית הלל אומרים
Every man should recite	כל אדם קורא
according to his way	כדרכו
for it is said: [Deut.6.7a]	שנאמר
when you walk in the way.	ובלכתך בדרך

2a

If this is so, why is it said:	אם כן למה נאמר
when you lie down and when you rise?	ובשכבך ובקומך

2b

[This refers to]	
the time when men lie down	בשעה שבני אדם שוכבים
and the time when men stand.	ובשעה שבני אדם עומדים

Notes:
This debate is discussed by R. Ishmael and R. Eliezer b.Azariah in the parallels, which gives an early *terminus ante quem*. Ishmael takes the side of the Shammaites.

Analysis:
1a. Beth Shammai use an Ultra-literal interpretation which ignores the sense of the context.

1b. Beth Hillel do not argue against Beth Shammai's method. They use an equally Ultra-literal interpretation of "in the way" [בדרך] to prove that you remain in the "way/manner" you find yourself at the time (P. Blackman 1964) or that you follow your own way/custom (Danby).

It is possible that this is a Pun, but the word in the text and in the interpretation are exactly the same, so it is more likely to be an Ultra-literal interpretation.

The further debate may be later than the Houses. The Babylonian Talmud records further arguments for both sides presented as late as R. Papa and R. Abba b.Zabda.

2a. Someone replies on behalf of Beth Shammai that the Hillelite exegesis makes the phrase "lie down and rise up" Redundant.

2b. Someone replies on behalf of Beth Hillel that this phrase specifies the *time* for recitation. This reply is unlikely to come from the same source as 1a because it uses an idiomatic rather than Ultra-literal meaning. Perhaps it comes from R. Ishmael, who is attributed with the principle that "Scripture speaks in the language of men".

I.4.13. *tTer.3.16:*

He who heaves grapes for the market	התורם ענבים לשוק
and going to make	ועתיד לעשותן
[the remainder into] raisins	צימוקים
figs, and is going to make	תאנים ועתיד לעשותן
[the remainder into] dried figs	גרוגרות
pomegranates, and is going to make	רמונים ועתיד לעשותן
[the remainder into] dried pomegranates	פרד
has heaved [his offering] and does not need	תרומה ואין צריך
to heave a second [offering].	לתרום שניה

R. Eliezer says:	ר׳ אליעזר או׳
1a	
Beth Shammai say:	בית שמיי או׳
He needs not heave a second [offering].	אין צריך לתרום שנייה
1b	
And Beth Hillel say:	ובית הלל או׳
He needs to heave a second [offering].	צריך לתרום שנייה
2a	
Beth Hillel said to Beth Shammai:	אמרו בית הלל לבית שמיי
Behold it is says: [Num.18.27]	הרי הוא או׳
And as fullness of the winepress.	וכמלאה מן היקב
This is not heaved	לא תרם זה
from the winepress.	מן היקב
2b	
Beth Shammai said to them:	אמרו להם בית שמיי
Behold it is says: [Lev.27.30]	הרי הוא או׳
And all the tithe etc.	וכל מעשר וגו׳
If you are saying:	אם אומ׳ אתה
He needs to heave a second [offering],	צריך לתרום שנייה
Even thus he will not have fulfilled	אף זה לא קיים
Holy to YHWH.	קדש לה׳

Notes:

Heave offerings must be presented in the form in which they are finally consumed, so eating grapes were offered as grapes, and raisin grapes as raisins (mTer.1.5,9–10). But if grapes which have been heaved as eating grapes are later made into raisins, should a second offering of raisins be heaved?

Neusner (1971 II:89) notes that the debate is already in this easily memorised form by the time of R. Eliezer, which suggests that House debates were being preserved in this way by the time of early Yavneh.

The exegeses may not have been part of Eliezer's tradition, but the Shammaite exegesis appears to win the debate, so they are also likely to be early.

Analysis:

1a. Beth Shammai rule that although a mistake was made with the original Heave offering, it was nevertheless valid.

1b. Beth Hillel rule that a new Heave offering is needed.

2a. Beth Hillel justify themselves by citing the text which was probably the proof text for the rule that Heave offerings should be presented in the form in which they are finally consumed.

Num.18.27 tells the Levites that they too have to present Heave offerings out of the Heave offerings which they receive from Israel, and that these will be accepted by God as though it were their own harvest, "as grain from the threshing floor and as fullness from the winepress". This description, which could be applied equally to the Heave offerings of Israel, implied that Heave offerings were made up not only of the food (such as grain), but also from what is produced from that food when it is processed (such as wine).

This rather indirect proof text is the best which could be found. The only other references to processed food as Heave offerings are Num.18.30 (which is virtually identical), and some references to the cake made from the first corn (e. g. Num.15.20f.) which could have been regarded as a special case. There is a mention of "wine" and "oil" in the context of Heave offerings in Num.18.12, but they are not linked so clearly to "Heave offerings" as they are in v27.

Therefore it is likely that Num.18.27 is the proof text for the whole practice of giving Heave offerings from the finished product of food processing. The argument is based on a Peshat reading of the text.

2b. Beth Shammai point out that according to the Peshat reading of Lev.27.30, the Heave offering has already been accepted as "Holy to the Lord", so that it cannot subsequently be declared unfit to be a Heave offering.

This appears to be an argument of Reductio ad Absurdum. If a Heave offering is subsequently demanded, then the previous Heave offering was not holy, so the priests have eaten unsanctified food in the Temple. This extremely serious situation was unpreventable and retroactively made all subsequent sacrifices by those priests invalid.

The Hillelites have merely established the status quo without adding any fresh arguments, and they do not reply to the Shammaites who appear to win the debate, though Mishnah does not of course follow them.

I.4.14. *mHag.1.1:*

(Sifré Deut.143; bHag.4a; yHag.1.1; Mekh.Sim.p218.28–29)

All are liable to appear [at Jerusalem]   הכל חייבין בראיה

except the deaf, insane, or child   חוץ מחרש שוטה וקטן

or sexless, or hermaphrodite	וטומטום ואנדרוגינוס
or women	ונשים
or bondmen which have not been freed,	ועבדים שאינם משוחררים
the lame or the blind	החיגר והסומא
or the sick or the aged	והחולה והזקן
or he who is not able to ascend	ומי שאינו יכול לעלות
on his feet.	ברגליו

1a

Who is [considered] a child?	איזהו קטן
Anyone who is not able	כל שאינו יכול
to ride on his father's shoulder	לרכוב על כתפיו של אביו
to ascend from Jerusalem	ולעלות מירושלים
to the Temple Mount.	להר הבית
– the words of Beth Shammai.	דברי בית שמאי

1b

And Beth Hillel say:	ובית הלל אומרים
Anyone who is not able	כל שאינו יכול
to hold his father's hand	לאחוז בידו של אביו
to ascend from Jerusalem	לעלות מירושלים
to the Temple Mount,	להר הבית
as it is said: *Three times.*	שנאמר שלש רגלים
[Ex.23.14]	

Notes:

The debate concerns who is liable to go up to Jerusalem for the feasts. The command does not apply to those who cannot enter the temple, those who cannot walk, and children. But how are 'children' defined? Both Houses define children in terms of their ability to ascend the Temple mount with different degrees of assistance.

The Mekhilta refers only to Beth Hillel and omits the exegesis. This debate must predate the final form of the halakah which precedes it, because the phrase "on his feet" is dependent on the exegesis of Beth Hillel, and because it excludes the position of Beth Shammai. The unusual phrase "on his feet" in this halakah led later rabbis to comment that this excludes people with a wooden leg! (bHag.3a,4a).

Analysis:

1a. Beth Shammai state a position, but no reasoning is given. This position presupposes the existence of a commandment or ruling that all those who are able "to ascend" are liable to do so. This may perhaps be derived from Ps.122.3f. ("Jerusalem ... where the tribes ascend") but a more likely source is an earlier version of the preceding halakah to which the words "on his feet" were added later.

1b. Beth Hillel presuppose the same earlier version of the halakah but add the words "on his feet", which is a Wordplay on "times" [רגלים] referring to the three pilgrimages (Ex.23.14). It is possible that רגלים was read as "pilgrimage", implying a journey on foot, because of a relationship to "foot" [רגל], but this plural occurs only elsewhere at Num.22.28,32f. where it also means "times" (as recognised by Rashi). The meaning "on foot" is therefore derived by Wordplay.

I.4.15. *t Yeb.8.4:* (mYeb.6.6; yYeb.6.6; bYeb.61b-62a)

No man may abstain [from the command to]	לא יבטל אדם
increase and multiply, [cf. Gen.1.28]	מפריה ורביה
unless he has	אלא אם כן יש לו
sons/children.	בנים

...

R. Nathan says:	ר' נתן אומ'

1a

Beth Shammai say:	בית שמיי אומ'
Two children,	שני בנים
like the sons of Moses,	כבניו של משה
as is said: [IChron.23.15]	שנ'
And *the children of Moses:*	ובני משה
Gershom and Eliezer.	גרשם ואליעזר

1b

Beth Hillel say:	בית הלל אומ'
Male and female,	זכר ונקבה
as is said: [Gen.5.2]	שנ'
Male and female he created them.	זכר ונקבה בראם

R. Jonathan says:	ר' יונתן או'
Beth Shammai say:	בית שמיי או'
Male and female.	זכר ונקבה
And Beth Hillel say:	ובית הלל אומ'
Male or female.	זכר או נקבה

Notes:

The debate concerns the number of children which a man must have before he stops marital relations. There is some confusion as to which House said what. Apart from the two versions above, Mishnah omits Beth Shammai's exegesis and changes their ruling to "Two males", while according to R. Nathan in bYeb.62a:

"Beth Shammai said Two males and two females, and Beth Hillel said A male and a female".

The different rulings are:

	Beth Shammai	Beth Hillel
tYeb: Nathan	2 children	male & female
tYeb: Jonathan	male & female	male or female
mYeb:	2 males	male & female
yYeb:	2 males	male & female
bYeb: Nathan	2 males & 2 females	male & female

It is possible that this confusion arose out of a three-stage debate concerning the previous ruling that "No man may abstain ... unless he has children [בנים]".

1) Beth Shammai ruled that the minimum number of children was two because בנים is plural.

2) Beth Hillel ruled that at least one had to be male, so the minimum requirement was one male and one female.

3) Beth Shammai ruled that the minimum of two children both had to be male because בנים can mean "sons".

The Hillelite ruling is verbally dependent on their exegesis and not on the halakah "No man may abstain...". Although the Shammaite ruling can be derived from this halakah, it is unlikely that later rabbis would have provided such a strong confirmation of their views. Therefore both exegeses are probably genuine.

Analysis:

1a. Moses' case proves that the minimum is two children, which bYeb explains were the only children he had before he separated from his wife. It is not clear whether Beth Shammai are using this to prove that "children" indicates 'two' or that it indicates 'two males', but both are probably in mind.

The reply "Two children" is probably based on שני בניה in Ex.18.2f. which may have been the main text behind this exegesis (as suggested by W. Horbury). IChron.23.15 may be quoted because this clearly stated that they were Moses' children, which is not clear in Ex.18.2f.

1b. Beth Hillel cite the only example higher than Moses – God himself. The almost identical text in Gen.1.27 would fit better with the original ruling, but Beth Hillel have in mind the context of Gen.5.2f. which suggests the concept of God as father of Adam: "made him in the likeness of God... and Adam fathered a son in his own likeness".

Both exegeses are based on the Nomological principle that incidents recorded in Scripture are part of God's Case Law, so that these examples are treated as though they were legal Precedents.

I.4.16. *mGit.4.5*:

(mEd.1.13; yGit.4.5; bGit.40b-41b; bArak.26b; bBB.13a; bHag.2a; bPes.88ab)

1a

He who is half a slave	מי שחציו עבד
and half a freeman	וחציו בן חורין
works for his master one day	עובד את רבו יום אחד
and for himself one day	ואת עצמו יום אחד
– the words of Beth Hillel.	דברי בית הלל

1b

Beth Shammai say to [Beth Hillel]:	אמרו לו בית שמאי
You have solved the situation for the master	תקנתם את רבו
but you have not solved it himself.	ואת עצמו לא תקנתם
It is impossible for him [to marry] a slave woman	לישא שפחה אי אפשר
for he is already half a freeman [and] it is impossible for him [to marry] a free-woman	שכבר חציו בן חורין בת חורין אי אפשר
for he is already a half slave.	שכבר חציו עבד
Will he refrain [from union]?	יבטל
And was not the world created	והלא לא נברא העולם
only for reproduction and increase,	אלא לפריה ורביה

as it is said: שנאמר

He did not create it empty   לא תוהו בראה

He formed it to be inhabited. [Is.45.18]   לשבת יצרה

But for the sake of the order of the   אלא מפני תקון העולם

world,

they should compel the master   כופין את רבו

and he makes him a freeman,   ועושה אותו בן חורין

and he [the slave] writes a bond   וכותב שטר

for half his worth.   על חצי דמיו

And Beth Hillel retracted to teach   וחזרו בית הלל להורות

according to the word of Beth Shammai.   כדברי בית שמאי

Notes:

Neusner (1971 II:228ff.) points out that this debate does not follow the normal House debate form, and that it is not really a debate at all. He concludes that the Houses are both dealing with separate problems. Beth Hillel solve the problem of a half-slave by means of a Taqanah, which is a ruling concerning a situation not dealt with in the Torah, and which lapses when that situation ceases to exist (Guttmann 1970:7ff.). The Shammaites did not accept the validity of Taqanot, so they solved the problem by showing that the actual status of half-slave is an impossibility.

This debate is preserved in a large number of places, and the fact that Shammai appears to win the debate rules out the possibility that it is a later invention, although, as Neusner suggests, some elements, such as the explanation "Will he refrain [from union]?" (which is absent from some MSS) and the exegeses, may have been added later. However the exegeses occur in the earliest versions of the debate and they add weight to the Shammaite argument.

Analysis:

The debate concerns a person who is half-slave and half-free. Neusner thinks this may be a purely theoretical entity. Traditionally he is regarded as a slave who was owned by more than one person and who was released by one of them (cf. P. Blackman 1964), which J. Jeremias (1969:335 n97) suggested may come about if the slave is inherited by two people.

1a. Beth Hillel decide that such a person should work for his part-owner one day, and for himself the next. This is not derived from Scripture, which says nothing about this situation, but is a Taqanah, like Hillel's Prozbul.

1b. Beth Shammai do not accept the validity of Taqanot and yet neither can they find anything in Scripture about someone who is a half-slave. They therefore decided that the status of half-slave is itself unscriptural and therefore unlawful.

They prove this by arguing a half-slave cannot marry, because a slave and a free person cannot marry (which I. Abrahams, in Soncino's Hebrew-English Talmud, suggests is derived from Tg.Onk. of Deut.23.18). This contradicts the principle that everyone has the duty to procreate.

The duty of procreation is derived either from a Peshat reading of Is.45.18 (because God's will is man's duty), or a Precedent set by the example of God himself (cf.

I.4.15). W. Horbury suggested that the proof text may in fact be Gen.1.1f. or Gen.1.28 (to which the Targum alludes: "formed it to multiply the sons of men on it"). Isaiah would then be quoted as the first commentary on the Torah, to prove that this interpretation is correct.

Beth Shammai therefore rule that when a slave with more than one master is given freedom by one of them, then the others must sell the slave his freedom. This is not a temporary Taqanah because it is derived from a permanent principle of Scripture, but is also an example of pragmatism, as seen by the phrase "for the order of the world".

This argument appears to be based on the logical inconsistency between the Hillelite practice and the principle that all men should procreate. However, this principle of the duty of procreation was regarded as so fundamental (cf I.4.15) that it is likely that this argument would have been seen as being Reductio ad Absurdum, because it was unthinkable that a law should prevent someone from fulfilling this duty.

Beth Hillel agreed with Beth Shammai, but, as Neusner points out, this is not necessarily a defeat for Hillel. If the status of half-slave ceases to exist, then their Taqanah is no longer required, but it is not rejected.

I.4.17. *tSanh.13.3:* (bRH.16b-17a; ARNa.41)

1ai

Beth Shammai say:	בית שמאי אומ׳
[There are] three classes:	שלש כיתות
one for life eternally	הן אחת לחיי עולם
and one for shame	ואחת לחרפות
[and] for abomination eternally.	לדיראון עולם
These are completely evil.	אילו רשעים גמורים
The evenly balanced of them go down	שקולין שבהן יורדין
to Gehenna and squeal	לגיהנם ומצטפצפין
and rise again and are healed.	ועולין הימנה ומתרפאין

1aii

As it is said: [Zech.13.9]	שנ׳
And I will bring the third [part]	והבאתי את השלישית
through fire	באש
and refine them like silver is refined	וצרפתים כצרף את הכסף
and test them like gold is tested.	ובחנתים כבחון את הזהב
They will call on my name	הוא יקרא בשמי
and I will be God to them.	ואני אהיה לו לאל

1aiii

And concerning them Hannah said: [ISam.2.6]	ועליהן אמרה חנה
YHWH is killing and making alive,	י״י ממית ומחיה
bringing down to Sheol and he brings up.	מוריד שאול ויעל

1b

And Beth Hillel say:	ובית הילל אומ׳
[He who is] great [in] mercy	רב חסד
inclines towards mercy.	מטה כלפי חסד
And concerning them David says: [Ps.116.1]	ועליהן אמ׳ דוד
I love YHWH because he hears	אהבתי כי ישמע י״י

And concerning them is said   ועליהן נאמרה
the whole section.   כל הפרשה

Notes:

The judgement of the completely good or evil was clear, but what would happen to the intermediate class? The Shammaites believed in a kind of purgatory while the Hillelites trusted that God's mercy would keep them from hell.

Neusner (1971 II:238f.) suggests that the original debate took the following form, and the rest was added later:

The intermediates:

Beth Shammai say: They go down [and come up again].

Beth Hillel say: They do not go down [at all].

However, even if the Shammaite texts were added later, it is clear that the Shammaite ruling, and possibly the whole debate, depends on Zech.13.9 which speaks of the "third" group. The other Shammaite text is also persuasive and unanswered so that it is unlikely to have been added by Hillelites.

The Talmud adds another text for the resurrection (Dan.12.2) and ARN gives Beth Hillel different texts (Ps.43.4; Neh.13.12).

Analysis:

1ai. This first argument is based on logic: if the completely evil are punished eternally, then the less evil must be punished for a shorter time. It is perhaps surprising that this has not been expressed as a Qal vaHomer.

1aii. This exegesis interprets "fire" as a Symbol for Hell. This appears to ignore the original meaning of the context, which probably prophesied a time of persecution which only one third of Israel would survive. However the context is eschatological and takes the form of a parable, so it is not easy to determine what the Peshat meaning would be for any particular set of readers. The Shammaite interpretation may have been their 'plain' reading of this passage. The argument is therefore likely to be Fulfillment of prophecy based on the Peshat reading.

1aiii. This text is ideally suited to Beth Shammai's argument, because it describes each group in turn: the evil who die, the good who live, and the third group who descend to Sheol and are then raised. They would not have regarded the parallels as synonyms (cf. I.2.25) so this is a Peshat reading.

1b. Beth Hillel use the principle of God's mercy to argue that in cases of doubt He counts people as righteous. Ps.116.1 appears to be unrelated to this reply but an anonymous editor has noted that they refer to the whole Psalm and the Talmud adds that they refer in particular to v6: "I hung low [in Gehenna] but he saved me".

They presumably regarded this Psalm as though it were written by someone who had actually died and then been saved from Sheol by God's mercy. This would have been, for them, its Peshat meaning, because although being 'near to Sheol' is a poetic equivalent of being 'in great trouble', the scribes did not read the Psalms as poetry (cf. I.6.2.2).

I.4.18. *Mid.Tann.p138f.:* (bShab.25b; bMen.40a)   לא תלבש שעטנז
You may not wear [wool and linen] mingled
[Deut.22.11]

You shall make [woollen] tassels for yourself.
[Deut.22.12]

גדלים תע' לך

From here they said:
Linen [garments] must have [woolen] fringes.

מיכן אמ'
סדין בציצית

1a

Beth Shammai: They are exempt [from fringes].

בית שמאי פוטרין

1b

and Beth Hillel: They are liable.

ובית הלל מחייבין

2a

Beth Hillel said to Beth Shammai:
Will a negative commandment override
a positive commandment?

אמ' בית הלל לבית שמאי
תדחה מצוה בלא תעשה
למצות עשה

2b

Beth Shammai said to them:
We find concerning all
the commandments which are in Torah
that a positive commandment takes precedence
over a negative commandment
except here
the negative commandment takes precedence
over the positive commandment.

אמ' להם בית שמאי
מצינו בכל
המצות שבתורה
שקדמה מצות עשה
למצוה בלא תעשה
אבל כאן
תקדום מצות לא תעשה
למצות עשה

Notes:
Should woollen tassels be put on linen garments? Their presence breaks the negative commandment "do not mix" but their absence breaks the positive commandment "make tassels".

The exegesis is not present in bMen. but it is probably genuine because later rabbis are unlikely to give Shammaites such a strong argument.

Analysis:
1ab. The Houses state their positions.

2a. Beth Hillel state the general rule that positive commands overrule negative.

2b. Beth Shammai agree with this general rule but point out that in this case Scripture has indicated which command should take preference by recording the negative commandment immediately before the positive one.

This is based on a Nomological reading, assuming that the Order of phrases is significant (contrary to Eliezer's rule 31).

I.4.19. *bBer.53a:* (tBer.5.30)
Our Rabbis taught:

ת"ר

[When] they used to sit
in Beth haMidrash
and light was brought in before them:

היו יושבין
בבית המדרש
והביאו אור לפניהם

1a

Beth Shammai say: ב״ש אומרים

each individual   כל אחד ואחד

makes the blessing for himself.   מברך לעצמו

1b

And Beth Hillel say: ובית הלל אומרים

One makes the blessing for all,   אחד מברך לכולן

2a

because it is written: [Prov.14.28]   משום שנאמר

In the multitude of people   ברוב עם

is the glory of the king.   הדרת מלך

Granted, regarding Beth Hillel   בשלמא ב״ה

who explain the reason,   מפרשי טעמא

but Beth Shammai -   אלא ב״ש

what [is their] reason?   מאי טעמא

2b

Probably because   קסברי מפני

Beth haMidrash is interrupted.   בטול בית המדרש

Our Rabbis similarly taught: תנ״ה

Those of Beth Rn.Gamaliel   של בית רבן גמליאל

did not use to say: לא היו אומרים

[Good] health! [when someone sneezed]   מרפא

in Beth haMidrash, because   בבית המדרש מפני

Study would be interrupted.   בטול בית המדרש

Notes:

The debate concerns the Blessing for light in the House of Study at the conclusion of the Sabbath.

The rulings are reversed in tBer.5.30 and Neusner (1971 II:52f.) finds no obvious reason for this. The reason may lie in the pre-70 predominance of Beth Shammai (cf. Neusner 1971 II:3f.) and the subsequent reversal of fortunes of the Houses. Each House had its own blessing (mBer.8.5) so the majority would say their version in public, while the minority would insist on muttering theirs privately. The Tosefta records the earlier rulings, when the Shammaites said their blessing publicly, and the Talmud records the reversed rulings.

The reasons given for these rulings occur only in the later version but they may date back to the earlier version because the minority House would certainly force a debate on the issue, and the Tosefta frequently omits such reasons.

Analysis:

1a & 1b. The Houses state their rulings.

2a. "King" is a Symbol for God so Prov.14.28 teaches that God is glorified when blessed by a crowd rather than by an individual. The identification of King = God was so common that it would have been regarded as Peshat.

2b. Beth Shammai are given a valid reason by referring to Gamaliel I who was respected by Shammaites (mOrl.2.12 cf. mBetz.2.6).

I.4.20. *bBetz.16a:* (Mekh.Sim.p148)

It was taught:	תניא

1a

They said about Shammai the Elder:	אמרו עליו על שמאי הזקן
Every day he would eat	כל ימיו היה אוכל
to honour the Sabbath.	לכבוד שבת
[If] he found a comely animal	מצא בהמה נאה
he would say: This is for Sabbath.	אומר זו לשבת
[If] he later found a more comely [one]	מצא אחרת נאה הימנה
he laid aside the second	מניח את השניה
and he would eat the first.	ואוכל את הראשונה

1bi

But Hillel the Elder	אבל הלל הזקן
[had] another characteristic:	מדה אחרת
It used to be for him that all his works	היתה לו שכל מעשיו
[were] for the sake of heaven.	לשם שמים

1bii

As is written: [Ps.68.19(20)]	שנאמר
Blessed be YHWH day [by] day.	ברוך ה׳ יום יום

It is taught similarly thus:	תניא נמי הכי

2a

Beth Shammai say:	בית שמאי אומרים
From the start of the week	מחד שביך
[prepare] for the Sabbath.	לשבתיך

2b

And Beth Hillel say:	ובית הלל אומרים
Blessed be YHWH day [by] day.	ברוך ה׳ יום יום

Note:
Neusner (1971 I:324f.) concludes that 1ab preserves genuine traditions about Shammai, but Hillel's exegesis is likely to be a product of Beth Hillel. The second tradition (2ab) differs only in the Shammaite argument.

Analysis:
1a & 2a. The Shammaite position is established by means of a biographical detail and a rhyming mnemonic.

1bi. Hillel did not honour the Sabbath less, but honoured God every day.

1bii & 2b. A Peshat reading is used of the text as it is quoted, but the punctuation of Ps.68.20(19) is not certain. It may also be "Blessed be the Lord; day by day he bears burdens for us" (cf. Targum and Rashi). However the LXX gives witness to both punctuations: "Blessed be the Lord God; blessed be the Lord daily..." (67.19). The punctuation used by Beth Hillel was therefore not unknown and their exegesis can be said to be based on a Peshat reading of the text.

I.4.21. *bBetz.20b:* (yBetz.2.4)

It was taught: תניא

1b

Beth Hillel said to Beth Shammai:	אמרו להם בית הלל לבית שמאי
And if where it is forbidden to laymen	ומה במקום שאסור להדיוט
it is permitted to the Most High	מותר לגבוה
[then] where it is permitted for laymen	מקום שמותר להדיוט
is it not logical	אינו דין
that it is permitted for the Most High?	שמותר לגבוה

2a

Beth Shammai said to them:	אמרו להם בית שמאי
Vows and Freewill-offerings prove it	נדרים ונדבות יוכיחו
for they are permitted to laymen	שמותר להדיוט
and forbidden to the Most High.	ואסור לגבוה

2b

Beth Hillel said to them:	אמרו להם בית הלל
As for Vows and Freewill-offerings	מה לנדרים ונדבות
they have no fixed time.	שאין קבוע להם זמן
You have to say [the same]	תאמר
concerning a pilgrim burnt-offering	בעולת ראייה
which has a fixed time.	שקבוע לה זמן

3a

Beth Shammai said to them:	אמרו להם בית שמאי
Also this has no fixed time,	אף זו אין קבוע לה זמן
as we have learned: [mHag.1.6a]	דתנן
He who did not make-pilgrim-offering	מי שלא חג
on the first Good day of the feast	ביום טוב ראשון של חג
can make-a-pilgrim-offering	חוגג
throughout the whole feast,	והולך כל הרגל כולו
even on the last Good day of the feast.	ויום טוב האחרון של חג

3b

Beth Hillel said to them:	אמרו להם בית הלל
Also this has a fixed time.	אף זו קבוע לה זמן
As we have learned: [mHag.1.6b]	דתנן
[If] the festival passed and he did not	עבר הרגל ולא
make-pilgrim-offering,	חג
he is not liable for its omission.	אינו חייב באחריותו

4a

Beth Shammai said to them:	אמרו להם בית שמאי
But surely it is already said: [Ex.12.16]	והלא כבר נאמר
For you – and not for the Most High.	לכם ולא לגבוה

4b

Beth Hillel said to them:

And surely it is already said: [Ex.12.14]

For YHWH – everything which is for YHWH.

אמרו להם בית הלל
והלא כבר נאמר
לה׳ כל דלה׳

5a

If so, why does the text teach:

For you?

אם כן מה תלמוד לומר
לכם

5b

For you – and not for Samaritans.

For you – and not for dogs.

לכם ולא לכותים
לכם ולא לכלבים

Notes:

This dispute concerns whether or not one may present a Pilgrim offering on a Good day. A Good day was a first or last day of a feast and had restrictions similar to a Sabbath except that food could be prepared for personal consumption (Ex.12.16). The exact differences between Sabbath and Good day restrictions are vague in Scripture and were therefore the subject of endless debate.

This debate has no parallel in the Mishnah or Tosefta, but may have grown out of the lay/not-lay dispute (mBetz.2.4 – see S. Zeitlin 1966a) because it is immediately preceded by the story of a Hillelite who brought a private burnt offering to the Temple to lay hands on it during a festival. Beth Shammai forbade laying hands on an offering on Sabbaths and Good days.

The Shammaite exegesis is most forceful, and the Hillelite reply is not too convincing. It is possible that the final Hillelite reply was added later to an originally even-handed dispute.

Analysis:

1a. The background to the debate acts as the initial argument which is not actually stated in the debate. The Shammaites said that a pilgrim's burnt offering could not be brought on a Good day, presumably because by laying his hands on it he would be doing work. The Hillelites did not regard it as breaking Good day regulations.

1b. The Hillelites argue Qal vaHomer. If something is permitted to the Highest when it is forbidden to the lowest (הדיוט from ἰδιώτης) then surely it is permitted to the Highest when it is permitted to the lowest.

The thing forbidden or permitted is the slaughtering of an animal for food or sacrifice. On a Sabbath one cannot slaughter food for oneself, but the continual sacrifices are still slaughtered for God. On a Good day one can slaughter food for oneself, so surely one can bring a Pilgrim offering to be slaughtered for God.

2a. The Shammaites make a comparison between the Pilgrim's offering and a Peace offering (a vow or freewill offering).

The Peace offering is very similar to slaughtering an animal merely for food, except that the fat is burnt on the altar, and a portion goes to the priest, but the majority is eaten by the offerer and his friends or family. Therefore both are ways of slaughtering an animal but the Peace offering is shared with God.

The Shammaites point out that Peace offerings are not allowed on Good days, but the same animal could be slaughtered as food with none going to the temple. Therefore this is an example of something forbidden to God but allowed to laymen on a Good day.

Just as men were permitted to slaughter food for themselves but forbidden to bring a Peace offering on a Good day, so they were forbidden to bring a Pilgrim offering on a Good day.

2b. Beth Hillel dispute the comparison between a Pilgrim offering and Peace offering by pointing out a difference which was significant to this comparison. A Peace offering could be brought at any time, and so there was no need to bring it on a Sabbath, but a Pilgrim offering should be brought as soon as one reaches Jerusalem.

3a. Beth Shammai dispute this by quoting an established halakah recorded at mHag.1.6, which said that a Pilgrim offering could be brought on any day of the feast.

3b. Beth Hillel point out that there is still a fixed time limit because an offering forgotten throughout the feast could not be brought later.

They are probably also indicating that this provision is only for someone who has neglected to bring their offering on the first day. The pejorative tone of the rest of the halakah makes this plain: if someone forgets during the whole feast he is not permitted to make up his loss.

4a. Beth Shammai reply with the scripture which establishes that one may prepare food for personal consumption on a Good day, unlike on a Sabbath. Beth Shammai read this Nomologically to infer that food 'for yourself' excludes food 'for God', such as a burnt offering.

4b. The Hillelites reply with "a feast to YHWH", the Peshat meaning of which is that the whole Feast is "for" God. Beth Hillel infer Nomologically from this that anything "for" God is therefore allowed, including a Pilgrim offering.

5a. Beth Shammai point out that the Hillelite interpretation makes the phrase "for you" Redundant.

5b. Beth Hillel argue that "for you" means that food may not be prepared for 'non-you', i.e. Gentiles (לכותים and לכלבים may be intended as puns on לכם).

I.4.22. *bHag.12a:* (yHag.2.1; LevR.36.1; GenR.1.1;12.14)

Our Rabbis taught:	ת״ר

1a

Beth Shammai say:	ב״ש אומרים
The heavens were created first	שמים נבראו תחלה
and after that the earth was created,	ואח״כ נבראת הארץ
as it is said: [Gen.1.1]	שנאמר
In the beginning God created	בראשית ברא אלהים
the heavens and the earth.	את השמים ואת הארץ

1b

And Beth Hillel say:	וב״ה אומרים
The earth was created first	ארץ נבראת תחלה
and then the heavens,	ואח״כ שמים
as it is said: [Gen.2.4]	שנאמר
In the day YHWH God made	ביום עשות ה׳ אלהים
earth and heavens.	ארץ ושמים

2a

Beth Hillel said to Beth Shammai:	אמר להם ב״ה לב״ש
According to your words	לדבריכם
a man builds the upper-chamber	אדם בונה עלייה
and after that he builds the house,	ואח״כ בונה בית

as it is said: [Amos.9.6]   שנאמר
He who builds in the heavens his steps   הבונה בשמים מעלותיו
and founded his firmament over the earth.   ואגודתו על ארץ יסדה

2b

Beth Shammai said to Beth Hillel: אמר להם ב״ש לב״ה
According to your words   לדבריכם
a man makes a footstool   אדם עושה שרפרף
and after that makes a throne,   ואח״כ עושה כסא
as it is said: [Is.66.1]   שנאמר
Thus says YHWH: Heaven [is] my throne   כה אמר ה׳ השמים כסאי
and earth the stool of my feet.   והארץ הדום רגלי

3a

And the Sages say: וחכ״א
Both were created together,   זה וזה כאחת נבראו
as it is said: [Is.48.13]   שנאמר
Also my hand founded the earth   אף ידי יסדה ארץ
and my right hand stretched the heavens.   וימיני טפחה שמים
I called to them,   קורא אני אליהם
they stood together.   יעמדו יחדו

3b

And another [interpretation]:   ואידך
What does *Together* [mean]?   מאי יחדו
That they cannot be loosed from each other.   דלא משתלפי מהדדי

Notes

The opinion of the Sages is addressed by neither House and appears to be a later compromise, but its refutation indicates that the discussion did not stop there.

The absence of this tradition from Mishnah and Tosefta is probably because it has no halakic value. Neusner (1971 II:189f.) suggests that the exegeses were added later but the arguments are dependent on the texts quoted (with the possible exception of 2a).

The arguments 1a-2a can therefore probably be dated before 70 CE, but the rest were perhaps added later.

Analysis:

1a & 1b. Both Houses use a Nomological argument based on the Order of words.

2. Both Houses use a Mashal to suggest their opponents' order is illogical, and find a text to support it.

2a. Beth Shammai's text fits perfectly, which suggests that the Mashal was derived from it. Although the images of the earth as God's footstool and of the heavens as his throne occur elsewhere, they are together only in Is.66.

2b. However Beth Hillel' text is not well suited because it only forms a link with one element (עליה = מעלה, 'upperchamber' = 'stairs'). If the Mashal had come from the text it would presumably have referred to the 'foundations' rather than the 'house'. The text was therefore probably added later to balance out Beth Shammai's text.

3a. The Sages propose a compromise based on the Peshat understanding of "together" as 'at the same time'.

3b. Another Peshat meaning of "together" is 'inseparable', in which case this verse says nothing about the time at which they were created.

I.4.23. *bKet.16b-17a:*

Our Rabbis taught:	תנו רבנן
How does one sing before the bride?	כיצד מרקדין לפני הכלה
1a	
Beth Shammai say:	בית שמאי אומרים
Whatever the bride is like.	כלה כמות שהיא
1b	
And Beth Hillel say:	ובית הלל אומרים
A beautiful and graceful bride.	כלה נאה וחסודה
2a	
Beth Shammai say to Beth Hillel:	אמרו להן ב״ש לב״ה
In the case where she is	הרי שהיתה
lame or blind	חיגרת או סומא
do you say to her:	אומרי׳ לה
A beautiful and graceful bride?	כלה נאה וחסודה
for the Torah says: [Ex.23.7]	והתורה אמרה
Keep from a false word.	מדבר שקר תרחק
2b	
Beth Hillel say to Beth Shammai:	אמרו להם ב״ה לב״ש
According to your words,	לדבריכם
if someone purchases a bad purchase	מי שלקח מקח רע
from the market,	מן השוק
shall one praise it in his eyes	ישבחנו בעיניו
or denigrate it in his eyes?	או יגננו בעיניו
One must admit that	הוי אומר
one should praise it in his eyes.	ישבחנו בעיניו

Notes:
The debate concerns the social necessities of how to compliment a bride.

Neusner (1971:211f.) sees this as a late homily to illustrate the common theme of the kindly Hillel contrasted with the petulant Shammai. However the founders are not referred to in this House dispute, and it has none of the narrative qualities found in stories contrasting them.

Beth Shammai have the stronger argument, which suggests that this is an authentic debate, even though it is only recorded in the Babylonian Talmud.

Analysis:
1a & 1b. Beth Shammai is characteristically more severe.

2a. Beth Shammai say that one should only tell the strict truth. Ex.23 refers to lies which pervert justice, but Beth Shammai read it Nomologically so that, while not denying the context, they regard this precept as a separate and complete article of law.

1b. Beth Hillel replies with common sense, illustrated by a Mashal which is not based on Scripture.

I.4.24. *bTem.30b:* (bBQ.65b, 93b-94a)

1

Our Rabbis taught: [re. Deut.23.19(18)]	תנו רבנן
[If] he gave her [a harlot] wheat	נתן לה חיטין
and she made it into flour,	ועשאתן סולת
olives and she made them into oil,	זיתים ועשאתן שמן
grapes and she made them into wine:	ענבים ועשאתן יין
One [baraita] taught:	תני חדא
They are forbidden [for the altar].	אסורים
And another [baraita] taught:	ותניא אידך
They are permitted [for the altar].	מותרין
R. Yoseph said:	אמר רב יוסף
Gurion from Asporak taught:	תני גוריון דמן אספורק
Beth Shammai forbid,	בית שמאי אוסרין
and Beth Hillel permit.	ובית הלל מתירין

2a

Beth Hillel reasoned:	בית הלל סברי
Them but not their offspring,	הם ולא ולדותיהן
them but not their produce.	הם ולא שינוייהן

2b

Beth Shammai reasoned:	בית שמאי סברי
Them but not their offspring,	הם ולא ולדותיהן
also to include their produce.	גם לרבות שינוייהן

Notes:

Deut.23.19(18) forbids a sacrifice in fulfilment of a vow from the "hire of a harlot or the price of a dog [a sodomite] ... for [they are] an abomination to YHWH, even both of them [גם שניהם]". If the price of this hire is an animal, does the prohibition extend to its offspring, and if it is foodstuff, does it extend to its products?

The Mishnah makes clear that offspring are not prohibited (mTem.6.3) but evidently there were two contradictory traditions concerning products. Either one of these traditions was false (which called into question the validity of remembered traditions) or they represented contrary opinions of former scholars. Fortunately R. Yoseph (a 4th century Babylonian) remembered a tanna who taught these two opinions as a House dispute.

Neusner (1971 II:251) suggests that these contrary baraitot inspired the debate, rather than vice versa as Yoseph suggests. This is confirmed by Beth Shammai's use of an Aqivan exegetical technique, and the dependence of this dispute on the anonymous exegesis in Mishnah (see the analysis below). Although this text was probably discussed before 70 CE (cf. the exegesis of Yeshu b.Pantere, i.e. Jesus of Nazareth in bAZ.16b-17a, tHull.2.24 – see J. Klausner 1925:37f.), there is no reason to suppose that these exegeses were part of an original House debate.

Analysis:

The discussion in mTem.6.3 is based on an exegesis of the phrase "even both of them" [גם שניהם] in Deut.23.19(18). This appears to be superfluous so, according to the rule of No Redundancy, its presence must be explained. The Mishnah deals first with "even both" and then with "them". The 'House' debate is a continuation of the latter exegesis.

1i. Mishnah explains "Both" in mTem.6.3:

"The 'hire of a dog' and the 'price of a harlot' are permitted, for it is written: *Even both these* but not four."

That is, the 'price of a dog' and 'hire of a harlot' are the two referred to, but the two extra possibilities (the 'hire of a dog' and 'price of a harlot') are not forbidden. This is a Nomological reading which assumes that the divine legislator purposely demonstrated this limitation by using an apparently superfluous phrase.

1ii. Mishnah then explains the presence of "them" in a similar way:

"Their young are permitted for it is written *Them* – but not their young"

That is, the prohibition extends only to the hire itself, and not to any offspring. This is also a Nomological reading, assuming that if the divine legislator had meant "them and their offspring", He would have said so.

Unlike the previous exegesis, this had a more pragmatic value. It meant that one could offer an animal for sacrifice without having to present an endless pedigree to prove that it was not descended from a harlot's hire.

According to Yoseph's tanna, this exegesis is carried on by the Houses with regard to 'produce' rather than 'offspring'.

2a. Beth Hillel take the less strict view and permit both produce and offspring, using the Nomological exegesis of 1ii.

2b. Beth Shammai carry the exegesis further by explaining the significance of "Even" גם, using the Aqivan method of Extension (רבוי). According to this rule, the particle גם implies an extension to the ruling, so Beth Shammai assume that 'produce' is included. This is a Derash exegetical method because it supplies something which is not present in the text.

I.4.25. *bHull.88b:* (bSot.16a)

Our Rabbis taught:	תנו רבנן
1a	
One may not cover [blood] except with dust	אין מכסין אלא בעפר
– the words of Beth Shammai.	דברי בית שמאי
1b	
And Beth Hillel say:	ובית הלל אומרים
We find ash called "dust",	מצינו אפר שקרוי עפר
as it is written: [Num.19.17]	שנאמר
And for the unclean they shall take	ולקחו לטמא
of the dust of burning.	מעפר שריפת
2a	
And Beth Shammai:	ובית שמאי
It is called "dust of burning"	עפר שריפה איקרי
[but] it is not called "dust".	עפר סתמא לא איקרי

Notes:
Neusner (1971 II:169) points out that this does not follow the normal House dispute form, because one would expect the Hillelite reply to be "Also ashes". He suggests that this version has developed from the House dispute form, but (as usual) does not consider that it might be antecedent to the Yavnean collection and simplification of the disputes.

There are some indications that this is an ancient version of the debate: the Shammaites have the last word and appear to win the debate, and the subject matter appears to predate the ruling of the Mishnah. The Mishnah gives a list of substances which may be regarded as "dust", and Rn.Simeon b.Gamaliel II simplifies this list with the rule that "dust" is anything in which a plant can be grown (mHull.6.7). This list is clearly later than the ruling of the Hillelites, because their exegesis would be meaningless if they also taught that a host of other substances could be counted as "dust" – they would need an exegesis for each of them. The later acceptance of this list of substances would make Beth Hillel's ruling redundant, and this may be why it was not preserved in the Mishnah or Tosefta.

Analysis:
The debate concerns the definition of the "dust" with which the blood of a slaughtered animal must be covered (Lev.17.13).

1a. Beth Shammai accept the Peshat reading of Lev.17.13.

1b. Beth Hillel do not challenge this reading but point out that the word "dust" is also used when Scripture speaks about ashes. They use Gezerah Shavah (I) to define the word by means of its use in another text.

2a. Beth Shammai reply that the word "dust" refers to ashes because it occurs in the phrase "dust of burning". This annuls the Hillelite Gezerah Shavah by highlighting a difference between the use of the word in the two texts.

Beth Shammai appear to go beyond the normal Gezerah Shavah, which seeks an extended definition in only one other text, because they are making an implicit statement about the use of עפר throughout Scripture. They imply that עפר never refers to ashes except in the phrase עפר שרפת. Rosenblatt (1935: 8ff.) sees this kind of philological research behind almost every Gezerah Shavah in the Mishnah.

However, it is unlikely that Beth Shammai have intended to make a comment on the use of עפר throughout Scripture because neither they nor Beth Hillel mention 2K.23.4 where עפר is used to refer to ashes, and where although the word שרף also occurs in the same verse, it is not used to describe this dust.

I.4.26. *Pes.Rab.16 (84a)*: (Pes.Rab.48; Pes.Kah.6.61b)
1a

Lambs [Num.28.3]	כבשים
Beth Shammai say:	בית שמאי אומרים
that it is: "those supressing"	שהן כובשים
– the iniquities of Israel,	עונותיהם של ישראל
according as it is said: [Mic.7.19]	כד"א
He will turn, he will be merciful to us,	ישוב ירחמנו
he will supress our iniquities etc.	יכבוש עונותינו וגו'

1bi

And Beth Hillel say:	וב"ה אומרים
Everything which is suppressed	כל דבר שהיא נכבש

must finally surface.	סופו לצוף
But	אלא
1bii	
Lambs a year old	כבשים בני שנה
that this is: "those cleansing"	שהם מכבסים
– the iniquities of Israel,	עוונתיהם של ישראל
according as it is said: [Is.1.18]	כד"א
Though your sins	אם יהיו חטאיכם
are as scarlet. etc.	כשנים וגו'

Notes:

This tradition does not appear in any earlier text and should therefore be omitted from this study. It has been included because it is the only possible example of the Al Tiqré technique in pre-70 traditions. However it is argued below that this is neither pre-70 nor Al Tiqré.

Beth Hillel's reply 1bi ("Everything...But") appears to be added later, as the parallels also suggest.

Although there was probably much interest in the significance of the daily offerings before 70 CE, and TgJon regards them as atonements for the preceding night and day, there is no evidence that these exegeses can be dated that early. The lack of parallels in earlier texts suggest that they did not originate with the Houses.

Analysis:

The reason for this close examination of "lambs" is probably because Ex.29.38 says almost exactly the same thing, so this verse appears to be Redundant (W.G. Braude 1968). Therefore the text must have some extra significance, which is discovered here by Wordplay.

1a. Beth Shammai use Wordplay, changing כבשים to כובשים. This would probably not have been regarded as a change to the Torah text, because vowels are frequently added for plene spelling, and there was no differentiation between the letters Sin and Shin in unpointed texts.

1bi. Beth Hillel argue that supressing sins is inadequate, because they will only be uncovered again later.

1bii. Beth Hillel similarly change כבשים to כבסים by Wordplay but this involves changing the consonantal text.

They are able to explain more of the redundant verse than Beth Shammai because their quotation also includes "a year" [שנה] which is linked with "scarlet" [שנים] in Isaiah. R. Isaac (early 3rd C) uses a similar reading: "though your sins be like the years [כשנים]... from creation to now, they shall be white as snow" (bShab.89b).

This text had a special significance on the Day of Atonement because of the tradition of the scarlet thread tied to the goat which turns white (see I.2.47).

Both exegeses use a Derash reading which ignores the immediate context (although taking note of the general context of burnt offerings). They do not use Al Tiqré (emending the text in order to create a different reading) because they do not propose any different meaning for the text. The Wordplay is used to form a link with another text by Gezerah Shavah.

I.5. Techniques in Scribal Exegesis

I.5.1

Appendix 2 summarises the analyses of the 93 traditions surveyed in this study. These traditions yielded 195 separate arguments which are either exegetical or use a technique associated with exegesis. Of these, 168 arguments were exegetical, but only 120 are likely to have originated before 70 CE. The following results refer only to these 120, although some comparisons will be drawn with the Sadducean non-exegetical arguments.

No distinction is made between halakic and haggadic exegeses (roughly 75% and 25% respectively) because in the early Tannaitic period "there was no formal distinction in the methods of Halakic and Haggadic exposition" (W. Bacher 1892:419).

The following tables list the number of times different groups of exegetes used the various exegetical modes and techniques. These data are then used to compare the different groups to discover whether or not the exegeses collected in this study form a homogeneous corpus which can be collectively termed 'Scribal' exegesis.

The groups of exegetes examined are:
Early named authorities (up to Hillel)
Later named authorities (after Hillel)
Pharisees (including those answering on behalf of Pharisees)
Sadducees (including Boethusians)
Hillelites
Shammaites

The first table totals the number of times each exegetical mode was used by these groups:

Mode of Exegesis	Early	Later	Phar.	Sadd.	Hillel	Shammai	Totals
Peshat	10	9	10	8	9	10	56
Nomological	14	16	2	2	13	13	60
Ultra-Lit.		1			1	2	
Derash		1			1		2
Totals	24	26	12	10	24	24	120

The second table totals the number of times different exegetical techniques were used. Such techniques have been identified in 80 of these 120 arguments, while the rest interpret the text without using any special technique. A single argument frequently involves more than one technique, so the totals cannot be directly compared with the first table. Some examples of these techniques in non-exegetical contexts were also analysed, mainly in the Sadducean traditions, and these are recorded in brackets.

Technique of Exegesis	Early	Later	Phar.	Sadd.	Hillel	Sham-mai	Totals
HILLEL'S 7:							
1 Qal vaHomer	1	– (1)	– (2)	1 (2)	1	1	4 (5)
2 Gezerah Sh.	2	5	–	–	3	2	12
7 Context	4	3	1	–	1	–	9
ISHMAEL'S 13:							
13 Contradiction with 3rd text	–	2	1	–	–	–	3
ELIEZER'S 32:							
11 Punctuation	–	–	1	–	1	–	2
16 Unusual	–	2	–	–	1	1	4
26 Mashal	– (1)	–	–	– (2)	– (1)	1	1 (4)
28 Hint	–	1	–	–	2	– (1)	3 (1)
OTHERS:							
No Redundancy	3	5	–	1	5	3	17
Reductio ad Absurdum	–	–	– (4)	– (4)	–	2	2 (8)
Contradiction – no 3rd text	2	1	1	–	1	1	6
Order	1	–	2	–	1	2	6
Wordplay	–	–	–	–	2	–	2
Plural	3	–	1	–	1	1	6
Precedent	2	–	–	–	1	2	5
Symbol	1	1	–	–	1	1	4
Pragmatism	1	–	–	– (3)	– (1)	1	2 (4)
Illogicality	–	–	– (2)	– (2)	–	–	– (4)
Fulfilment	–	2	–	–	–	1	3
Heqesh	1	1	–	–	–	–	2
Sarcasm	–	–	1	–	–	–	1
Amalgamation	–	1	–	–	–	–	1
Totals	21(1)	24(1)	8 (8)	2(13)	21(2)	19(1)	95(26)

In general, the Peshat and Nomological modes were by far the most frequent, with hardly any use of Ultra-literal or Derash modes.

The techniques used in exegesis came more from the middoth of Hillel (25 examples) than the additional middoth in the lists of Ishmael or Eliezer (3 and 10 examples respectively), but most of the techniques employed were not found in any of these lists (57 examples).

This confirms the suggestion of previous scholars that the lists of middoth were later authorisations of a limited number of acceptable exegetical techniques, rather than a list of techniques which were in use (see 3.4).

I.5.2 *The exegeses in the different groups will now be compared* in order to discover whether or not this study has isolated a homogeneous body of 'Scribal' exegesis. Although the sample sizes are too small for detailed com-

parisons, some general conclusions can be made. It will be found that while
the Sadducees can be isolated as a group which restricted itself almost entirely to the Peshat mode, the other groups show considerable similarities and
their exegeses can be regarded as forming a single body of 'Scribal' exegesis.

The relative use of the Peshat and Nomological modes is approximately
2:3 in all the groups except the Sadducees and Pharisees which almost
always use Peshat.

This difference between the 'Pharisees' and the other groups (who probably overlapped to a great degree) is perhaps due to the fact that one's mode
of exegesis is largely determined by what is acceptable to one's opponents. If
the Sadducees understood Scripture only according to its plain meaning (as
suggested by I.3.11) they would not accept arguments based on a Nomological reading.

The relative uses of exegetical techniques show similar differences. The
Sadducees almost never use these techniques for exegesis and although the
Pharisees use them more frequently than the Sadducees, they use them far
less than the named authorities and the Houses.

The Sadducees were not ignorant of these techniques, but they used them
almost exclusively in non-exegetical arguments. When these are taken into
account, there is no difference in the frequency of these techniques in Pharisaic and Saducean arguments. The Sadducees tended to use the techniques
which were more applicable to non-exegetical debate, such as Qal vaHomer,
Reductio ad Absurdum, and Illogicality, but this is presumably due to their
preference for non-exegetical arguments.

The Sadducees normally introduce the use of these techniques into the
debates. On two occasions the Sadducees lead with a Qal vaHomer argument and the Pharisees respond with a Qal vaHomer refutation (I.3.4,6).
Similarly the Reductio ad absurdum by the Sadducees in I.3.2 prompts a
reply using the same technique. This suggests that the Sadducees were the
prime movers in these debates (contrary to how rabbinic literature tends to
present the situation) and that the types of argument used by the Pharisees
were determined to some extent by those used by their disputants.

I.5.3 *Some conclusions can be drawn from these results,* but they are necessarily generalised because of the small sample sizes of some groups.

The Sadducees stand out from the other groups by the almost total
absence of Nomological readings and special techniques in their exegeses,
although they regularly used these techniques in non-exegetical arguments.
This appears to have influenced the exegeses used by their opponents, the
Pharisees, who rarely responded with Nomological arguments, but who did
use the special techniques in their exegeses.

The other groups use the exegetical modes and techniques with very similar relative frequencies to each other. However rabbinic exegesis after 70 CE
is significantly different, using many exegetical methods which either never

occur in this survey, (such as Limitations, Extensions, Binyan Ab, General & Particular, Gematria, and Notariqon), or which occur rarely (such as Unusual form, Hint, Mashal, Order, Pun, and Atomisation), and they make more frequent use of the Ultra-literal and Derash modes (see I.7.1).

Therefore the named authorities, the Houses and the Pharisees can probably be regarded as a single group of exegetes, who differ significantly from the Sadducees and later rabbis.

The fact that the Sadducees often introduced exegetical techniques into the debates and that the Pharisees appear to follow their lead, may be an indication that these techniques originated with the Sadducees, and that the Pharisees were the first to apply them to exegesis.

This concurs with D. Daube's proposal (1961 : 249) that the Sadducees learned the exegetical techniques from the Hellenists but that the Pharisees used them to create new halakot from Scripture. This is similar to Lauterbach's thesis (1913) that the Sadducees based their authority on the plain sense of Scripture, and that they were the first to formulate the principle that "the words of Torah are according to the language of men" (which is normally attributed to R. Ishmael), while the Pharisees were the first to apply exegetical techniques to the Scriptures and thereby to treat the Scriptures as though they were written in higher than human language, saying "Let not our Torah be like your idle chatter" (which is normally attributed to Yohanan b.Zakkai, e.g. I.3.6, I.3.12, I.3.13).

Rabbinic literature presents a conflicting picture of the Sadducees, as both capable and incapable of exegesis. B.Z. Wacholder (1983 : 160ff.) has taken up G.R. Driver's suggestion (1965 : 260ff.) that rabbinic literature failed to distinguish between Sadducees and Zadokites (i.e. Qumran sectarians) and that those passages which demonstrate that the Sadducees had a knowledge of exegetical techniques are actually referring to Zadokites, while passages which show the Sadducees to be idiots, untrained in Torah, *are* speaking about the Sadducees. He cites J.M. Baumgarten (1980) for evidence of similarities between the halakah of Qumran and that attributed to the Sadducees. H.W. Basser (1984) rightly criticised Wacholder's cavalier use of rabbinic sources, and it must be noted that while there are very many parallels between the halakah and theology of Qumran and the Pharisees (e.g. Baumgarten 1977, L. Ginzberg 1970) there is no need to suggest that these groups have been confused with each other.

Josephus may have been more accurate when he said that the Sadducees "reckon it a virtue to dispute with [their] teachers" (Ant.18.16(1.4)). L.H. Feldman (1965) notes that Josephus calls their conduct in disputes "boorish" and "rude" (War.2.166(8.14)), suggesting that they were known for arguing with eachother rather than for scholarly discussion. However this may be due to Josephus' anti-Sadducean bias and, as D. Daube (1949 : 5) suggested, it may indicate that they followed the Greek tradition of rhetoric and free argument.

In conclusion, the exegeses collected in this study form a homogeneous body of exegetical arguments, with the probable exception of the Sadducean material. From now on, this body of material will be termed the 'Scribal' exegeses.

The results may also indicate that the Sadducees introduced the use of the special techniques, but that the Pharisees were the first to apply them to exegesis.

I.6 Assumptions in Scribal Exegesis

The 'Scribal' traditions have yielded a a homogeneous set of over a hundred exegetical arguments. The exegetical techniques used in these arguments will now be examined with regard to their underlying assumptions concerning Scripture.

Other studies have attempted to list the assumptions underlying rabbinic exegesis (e.g. G. Aicher 1906, I.L. Seeligman 1953, F. Maass 1955, A.T. Hanson 1983 : 25 f.) but these have not isolated the pre-70 CE material from the following centuries of rabbinic exegesis.

Other studies have also attempted to isolate an internally homogeneous body of rabbinic exegeses. Some of these have succeeded (e.g. J. Neusner 1970 re. Yohanan b.Zakkai, G. Porton 1976- re R. Ishmael, J.N. Lightstone 1979,1980 re. R. Yose) while some have been inconclusive due to lack of data (e.g. J. Neusner 1973b re. Eliezer b.Hyrcanus, T. Zahavy 1977 re. Eleazar b.Azariah, J. Gereboff 1979 re. R. Tarfon, S. Kanter 1980 re. Rn.Gamaliel II). These studies have produced some valuable results, but they all concern rabbinic exegesis after 70 CE.

I.6.1 *The term 'Nomological approach'* sums up the assumptions which have been inferred from the exegeses of pre-70 scribes. The Nomological approach regards Scripture as a legal document written by God.

Although the scribes nowhere stated that they used this approach to Scripture, it is implied by many of their exegeses and it underlies their whole thinking about Scripture.

This is illustrated by the following story about Hillel, which is based on the assumption that Scripture is interpreted like the very best legal document. Here Hillel is seen to interpret the legal documents of the common people with the rigour which some reserved only for Scripture.

Hillel the Elder expounded	דרש הילל הזקן
non-scriptural documents.	לשון הדיוט
The Alexandrians	כשהיו בני אלכסנדריא
used to betrothe women	מקדשין נשים
and [sometimes] another came from the market	ואחר בא מן השוק

and abducted her.	וחוטפה
The incident came to the Sages' notice,	ובא מעשה לפני חכמ׳
And they sought to declare	וביקשו לעשות
their sons Bastards.	בניהם ממזרים
[Hillel] said to them:	אמ׳ להם
Produce for me	הוציאו לי
the marriage contract of your mothers.	כתובת אימותיכם
They brought [it] to him	הוציאו לו
and there was written in it:	וכתוב בה
When you enter my house	כשתיכנם לביתי
you will be my wife.	תהא לי לאיתתו
according to the law of Moses and Israel.	כדת משה ויישר׳

(tKet.4.9, cf. yYeb.15.3, yKet.4.8, bBM.104a. Italics mark the use of Aramaic.)

The problem brought to the Sages concerned the legitimacy of children of women who had been abducted by one person after they had been betrothed to another. Betrothal was considered as the beginning of a marriage, so that these women were adulteresses and their children were illegitimate. Hillel seeks to solve the problem by finding out the definition of marriage in their culture, which he does by examining the marriage contract. He deduces that marriage commences when the woman enters the *huppah* at the marriage service. This means that the betrothed women were not married when they were abducted, so that their marriage to their abductors was legal.

The introduction to this baraita suggests that "Hillel would interpret the language of the documents of ordinary folk as carefully as the language of the Torah or of the Sages" (Neusner 1971 I:236). The story is used to address the question of whether the Aramaic legal documents of the common people should be interpreted with the same rigour as 'proper' Hebrew legal documents, because they may not have been written with the same precision and forethought. Hillel's example is cited to show that he interpreted Aramaic legal documents with the same rigour which he applied to Scripture. Underlying this is the assumption that Scripture is a legal document of the highest standard.

Although this tradition is difficult to date, it illustrates the underlying assumption that Scripture is a legal document. This assumption was so universally understood that it did not need to be stated even though it was essential to the meaning of this tradition.

The term 'Nomological' has been chosen to reflect the fact that Scripture was regarded as a legal document, but not in a legalistic way. C.H. Dodd (1936:25–34) highlighted the differences between 'Torah' (which implies teaching, instruction and revelation) and the LXX's translation νομος (a political or cosmic law). Although he emphasised that the LXX does not imply a legalistic meaning, it is not clear why this term was chosen, especially as it was so prone to this misinterpretation (even by Paul, according to Dodd

1936:34f.). N. De Lange has suggested to me that the choice of νομος may reflect the Nomological approach of the LXX translators.

The 'Nomological approach to Scripture' is not the same as the 'Nomological mode of exegesis'. The Nomological approach is an attitude or set of assumptions which regard Scripture as a legal document, which must therefore be interpreted with the intellectual rigour and honesty which would be applied to a document drawn up by the best legal mind imaginable.

The Nomological mode of exegesis is related to this, in that it reads the text as though it were a legal document, but it is not the only mode of exegesis which is used in the Nomological approach to Scripture. The Peshat mode, which reads the plain meaning of the text, is also used because a legal document is made up largely of normal prose, and only occasionally requires the type of analysis reserved for legal texts. Even the Ultra-literal and Derash modes are occasionally acceptable, with the proviso that they do not ignore the context (see I.6.2.3 below).

I.6.2 The precise attitude of the scribes towards Scripture is best determined by the techniques they used to interpret it. The scribes nowhere actually state their assumptions about Scripture, but there is evidence in the scribal exegeses for the following:
1. Scripture is totally self-consistent.
2. Every detail in Scripture is significant.
3. Scripture is understood according to its context.
4. Scripture does not have any secondary meaning.
5. There is only one valid text form of Scripture.

I.6.2.1 *Scripture is totally self-consistent:* The Nomological approach assumes that Scripture was written by a perfect divine legislator, so contradictions are unthinkable. This assumption is illustrated especially by some of the exegetical techniques employed by the scribes.

Underlying the rule of Contradiction is the assumption that Scripture never contradicts itself, so when a seeming contradiction does occur, it can even be used to infer further truths. An example of this is the contradiction concerning the number of days of Unleavened bread, being six in one text and seven in another, from which Hillel infers that for six days one must eat new unleavened bread and for seven one must eat old unleavened bread (I.2.13)

A related assumption lies behind the rules of Qal vaHomer and Gezerah Shavah II, namely that every part of Scripture can be compared with any other, and conclusions can be drawn from that comparison. An example is Hillel's argument that the Passover is more important than the Daily offering in terms of punishment for neglect (I.2.18). If the Daily offerings are more important than the Sabbath and override it, then surely the Passover is also allowed to override the Sabbath. This argument assumes that the three separate sets of laws concerning Daily offering, Passover and the Sabbath are all related in a self-consistent way, even though this relationship is never explored in Scripture.

Another related assumption lies behind Gezerah Shavah I: that Scripture is totally self-consistent in the terms and phrases which it uses. This means that if the same term or phrase is used in two texts, then a definition of the term in one text can be used to define that term in another. An example of this is Beth Hillel's interpretation of "from time to time" (lit: "from days to days") as meaning "from year to year" because the phrase "year of days" occurs in Lev.25.29 (I.4.1).

Incidents which occur in the Prophets and the Writings are assumed to illustrate the Law or even to add to it as though they were Precedents in legal history. Therefore when the Houses debated the minimum number of children which would excuse them from the obligation to procreate (I.4.15), Beth Shammai cited 1Chron.23.15 which names Moses's two sons, as an example of someone who separated from his wife (they were re-united in Ex.18). In a another debate (I.4.16) Beth Shammai prove that procreation is a duty from the example of God in Is.45.18 who formed the earth "to be inhabited". Moses and God are not being presented as good examples to follow but rather as precedents, because their examples do not become recommendations but legal rulings.

I.6.2.2 *Every detail in Scripture is significant:* A legislator strives to make every word in a legal text unambiguous and to remove every unnecessary word or phrase, so the divine legislator was assumed to have created a perfect Law in which every word and letter was significant. Therefore many details which would have little or no significance in a normal legal document are used as the basis for further deduction in scribal exegesis.

The presence of a singular or a plural is important even when the context would suggest that it is irrelevant. The Sadducees point out that a singular "you" is the one who offers the Daily offering in Num.28.4, from which they conclude that the Daily offering can be paid for by a single individual (I.3.12 – the only example of a Nomological use of Scripture by the Sadducees). Although the dual form of nouns occurs in biblical and mishnaic Hebrew, a simple plural is always regarded as 'two or more' (cf. I.2.11; I.4.9).

The rule which has been termed No Redundancy is based on the assumption that a seemingly superfluous phrase must have some other meaning which is not otherwise present in Scripture. This became so axiomatic that Ben Hé Hé seemed to be genuinely shocked when he discovered some poetic parallelism in Mal.3.18: "the righteous and the wicked, he who serves God and he who does not", but Hillel was able to show him that the passage is speaking about four different categories of people (I.2.25 cf. also I.2.24). G.B. Gray (1972:10–31) notes that although poetic parallelism is found as late as Baruch and 4 Esdras, the rabbis consistently failed to understand it.

Perhaps they recognised the poetic form, but read it Nomologically when it was found in Scripture, which they regarded as a legal document, not poetry.

Even the presence of a pronoun when it is not strictly necessary is deemed to be significant, as seen in the argument by Beth Hillel that the Sabbath commandment refers only to work which "you" do, and not to work which carries on without your intervention, such as the soaking of cloth or laying of an egg (I.4.4).

A similar understanding of Scripture underlies the method of Wordplay, which derives new insights by finding a word which is similar in some way to a word used by Scripture. A striking example is the exegesis concerning who was liable to go up to Jerusalem on the three main feasts, the result of which became such an established understanding of the text that it became part of the mishnah dealing with the subject (I.4.14). Beth Hillel argued from the word "times" (רגלים) that all those who could walk "on feet" (ברגליו) were liable to attend.

This assumption is taken even further by the rule of Unusual form, which finds special significance behind the unusual use or spelling of a word. This is based on the assumption that God would not have made a mistake in spelling or grammar, so any unusual forms which have been left in Scripture indicate that there is a hidden meaning to be discovered. Therefore, when Judah b.Bathyra discovered that the excess letters in the 'mis-spelled' words in the commands concerning Tabernacles (Num.29) made up the word for "water" [מים], he concluded that this was a vindication of the Water libation ceremony which was carried out during that feast (I.2.43).

I.6.2.3 *Scripture is understood according to its context:* Every single scribal exegesis examined could be quoted as an example to show that Scripture was interpreted according to its context. This is true from the plainest Peshat to the most ingenious Ultra-literal or Derash interpretation.

In the introduction, the Ultra-literal mode was distinguished from the Nomological mode because it ignored the idiomatic meaning of the words in their context (I.1.4c), and the Derash exegesis was defined as one which found a secondary meaning which was completely independent of the context or a supplementary meaning which added details not actually present in the text.

The Nomological approach to Scripture would normally rule out the use of these modes because of their disregard of the context and of the primary meaning of the text. If the Scriptures are a well written legal document, one would expect everything to occur in the correct context, and one would not expect to find hidden meanings.

However, on the rare occasions that these modes occur in Scribal exegeses, they take careful regard of the context, and do not abandon the plain meaning of the text.

The Ultra-literal mode occurs only twice. In the House debate concerning one's attitude when reciting the Shema (I.4.12), both Houses give Ultra-literal interpretations of Deut.6.7: "when you sit in your house, when you walk in the way, when you lie down and when you stand up". Ignoring the contextual meaning, which could be paraphrased as 'anywhere, any time', Beth Shammai argue that one should literally lie down or stand up while reciting, and Beth Hillel say that one should stay the "way" one finds oneself (i.e. remain standing if one is standing, lying if one is lying – the word דרך having the same double meaning as the English "way").

Although the Houses have ignored the plain contextual meaning, they have not ignored the context itself which *is* concerned with reciting the Shema. In fact these interpretations are so fundamental to subsequent hala-kah, and seem so 'natural' that they are often regarded by contemporary Jews as Peshat.

Derash also occurs twice, when Judah b.Bathyra constructed the word "water" from mis-spelled words (I.2.43) and when Beth Hillel read רגלים as "feet" although the context demanded "times" (I.4.14). However they both used texts within a passage dealing with the subject in hand, and their exegesis did not involve negating any aspect of the plain meaning of that text. In effect, they were looking for hints left by the divine legislator con-cerning matters which did not appear to be dealt with. This is equivalent to reading the intentions behind the small print in a legal document.

One other possible example of Derash interpretation occurs in a House debate which *may* involve a Limitation argument (I.4.7). Most of the instances of Limitation and Extension found in the scribal exegeses are due to later redaction (I.4.2,5,6), and one is clearly a late invention (I.4.24). The only possible exception is I.4.7 where אך is used either as a Limitation particle or as an Unusual word in the context.

Most Extension and Limitation exegeses are Derash interpretations, be-cause they find a secondary meaning unrelated to the plain sense or context. However, in I.4.7, the exegesis searches for a deeper aspect of the primary meaning in the context. In a situation where 'also' might be expected, אך ('except' i.e. 'howbeit') is found, so a search is made for something related to the context which was being excluded. This is similar to the actions of a lawyer who teases significance out of the smallest word.

One exegetical technique which is based on the assumption that the con-text is relevant is the rule of Order, which assumes that the order of words or phrases is significant. For example Beth Shammai argued that the negative command not to mix cotton and wool overrules the positive command to put woollen tassels on a cotton garment because it occurs immediately before it (I.4.18). A more extreme example is the House dispute concerning whether the heavens were created before the earth or vice versa, because of the different order of words in Gen.1.1 and Gen.2.4b respectively (I.4.22). Eliezer's rule 31, which says that the order may be ignored, is never used in scribal exegeses.

Hillel's seventh middah, "Meaning is learned from the Context", virtually states this exegetical assumption. Although this rule is rarely specifically mentioned, it is frequently implied. Many exegeses cannot be understood at all without reference to the context of the text which is quoted. When Beth Hillel argue that God's mercy saves the evenly balanced person from Sheol they quote Ps.116.1: "I love the Lord for he hears my voice and supplication" (I.4.17), but the relevance of this text only becomes plain when the whole Psalm is read, which is a thanksgiving for salvation from Sheol. Several other exegeses cannot be properly understood without regard to the context of the text quoted (I.2.2; I.2.11; I.2.30; I.2.33; I.2.35, I.2.37; I.2.41; I.3.8; I.3.13; I.4.15), although the relevant context has occasionally been obscured by the inaccurate identification of the text by previous scholars (e.g. I.2.13, I.2.16).

This phenomenon of seemingly obscure quotations which are only understood when the context is explored has also been highlighted by J. Mann (1940–) in his analysis of the homilies based on the sedarim (daily readings from the Torah) of the Palestinian triennial lectionary cycle. I. Sonne, who completed this work when Mann died, commented that the argument of the homilies often depends on the context of verses quoted from the haftorah (the section of the Prophets read with the seder), and sometimes even depend on texts outside the haftorah itself but still within the same general context (1940- II:xxxvii). Although these homilies themselves may be late, their form is likely to be early.

I.6.2.4 *Scripture does not have a secondary meaning:* Legal documents are written as unambiguously as possible, so a hidden secondary meaning would not be expected, although minute details may reveal further information about the primary meaning. Consequently, in none of the scribal exegeses is the primary meaning of the text ever supplanted or even accompanied by a secondary meaning. They always attempted to discover the primary or plain sense of the text, although what the scribes regarded as the primary sense may be very different from what a modern exegete would accept as the original intention of the authors of Scripture.

The only possible exception to this is Hananiah's interpretation of Cant. 1.6 (I.2.37), which appears to refer to an incident in 41 CE seen in the light of the destruction of Jerusalem. If this attribution is correct, it is likely that this marks the emergence of allegory among the rabbis, at a time when Canticles was still sung as a love song (mTaan.4.8). Hananiah's career spans across 70 CE, and his saying is roughly contemporary with the allegorical use of Cant.1.8 by Yohanan b.Zakkai (Mekh.Ish.Bah.1), who also popularised the allegorical Homer exegesis. However it is quite possible that Hananiah, like Aqiva, did not regard Canticles as a love song at all (tSanh.12.10; cf. bSanh.101a) and was therefore attempting to expound its 'plain' meaning – i.e. that which was for him of primary importance.

When Mashal or Symbolic interpretation is used by the scribes, it is always an attempt to derive the plain or primary meaning of the text, and not to find another secondary meaning hidden beneath it. Beth Shammai interpreted Is.66.1 according to Mashal (I.4.22), but this passage is already speaking metaphorically and they interpret the symbols in the way that the author intended (throne = heaven, footstool = earth).

When Scripture is interpreted symbolically the symbols are commonly accepted or self-evident, unlike the multitude of convoluted and varied symbolic values identified by Philo. These symbolic interpretations would therefore have been regarded as the 'plain' meaning of these scriptures at that time. The scribal exegeses use the following symbols and interpretations: father = God (I.2.2), ox = man (I.3.4), Lebanon = Temple (I.2.47), fire = Gehennah (I.4.17), and king = God (I.4.19). The symbolism of Lebanon = Temple does not seem self-evident to us, but G. Vermes has shown that this was an extremely common identification in early Jewish exegesis (1961), and although ox = man does not occur so often, it was clearly a widely accepted identification because it is accepted by both Pharisees and Sadducees, and it occurs in other rabbinic and NT traditions (bSanh.9ab; bYeb.4a; mBQ.1.4,6 etc; ICor.9.9; 1Tim.5.18).

The Ultra-literal and Derash interpretations discussed above (I.6.2.3) also attempt to derive the primary meaning, because they are striving to unpack the full meaning of the text. They regard the choice of an idiom or a word by the divine legislator to be significant in itself, so that in order to understand the full implications of the plain meaning of the context, all possible meanings of the idiom or word have to be explored thoroughly.

I.6.2.5 *There is only one valid text form of Scripture* A valid legal document can obviously only exist in one form, so the Scribes were reluctant to propose any emendations to the Scripture even when there appeared to be a mistake. In no scribal exegesis examined is any attempt made to 'correct' the Scriptures by proposing an emendation of the text or even by proposing a different oral reading (a קְרִי), and S. Rosenblatt (1935, 1974) has shown the same to be true for the whole of the Mishnah and Tosefta.

It is unlikely that the scribes believed that they had a perfect copy of the Scriptures, because it was inevitable that errors would be made. Although Readers were employed to check manuscripts (bKet.106a), variant readings existed even in the standard scrolls stored in the Temple (Sof.4.4 and parallels – see J.Z. Lauterbach 1917, M.H. Segal 1953, S. Talmon 1962b, S. Zeitlin 1966b), and the Severus Scroll, which shares some variants with 1QIs.a (S. Loewinger in the prologue of V. Aptowitzer 1970; J.P. Siegal 1975), probably came from Jerusalem before 70 CE.

In spite of this, the pre-70 rabbis avoided emendations even when the most obvious solution to a problem was that an error had occurred. Ben Hé Hé pointed out that in Qoh.1.15 the word "restored" [לְהִימָּנוֹת] is not really appropriate and that "filled" [להמלאות] would fit the context better. However he went out of his way to avoid this small emendation (I.2.24).

J. Bonsirven (1939:123) has suggested that the House dispute concerning the meaning of "lamb" in Num.28.3 (I.4.26) employs Al Tiqré to change vocalisation. However this is likely to be a late tradition (it is recorded only in the Pesiqtas) and the changes are proposed merely to provide a link with another text, and not to suggest a different interpretation, so the method is therefore more akin to Wordplay or Gezerah Shavah than Al Tiqré.

There are two possible examples of emended punctuation in Scribal exegeses. One is Beth Hillel's exegesis of Ps.68.20 (I.4.20) which depends on a clause division which is different from the MT, but this is attested to by the LXX and may have occurred in some MSS of the time. The other (I.3.13) is a hypothesised reply to a missing argument, for which the evidence is obviously weak.

This was one of the oldest exegetical devices ever used, and can be traced back as far as the Homeric commentator Sosibius (early 3rd C. BCE – S. Lieberman 1950), and was later institutionalised as one of Eliezer's middoth (no.11). However the the Scribes may have regarded the traditional punctuation as part of the unalterable text, so arguments based on changes in punctuation would be unacceptable.

This belief in a single valid text also meant that they did not approve of written targumim, as suggested by the story of Gamaliel II (late 1st C.) who recommended that a Targum should be "put away" (גנז) as though it were a defective copy of Scripture which had to be taken out of circulation (bShab.115a), and there were dire warnings for those who wrote translations of the Scriptures (bQid.49a). Oral translations however were allowed and appear to have been normal synagogue practice from an early date (M. McNamara 1972:48–52, P.S. Alexander 1976,1985, M.L. Klein 1988).

I.6.3 These five assumptions constitute a Nomological approach to Scripture. If Scripture is a legal document drawn up by God, a perfect legislator, then one would expect it to be totally internally consistent, without any superfluous phrases, words or even letters. Similarly one expects any legal document to be drawn up in a well-ordered fashion, so ignoring the context would suggest that it had been put together in a sloppy manner. One also expects a legal document to be unambiguous, without any secondary meanings, although this does not mean that there are no details which have to be teased out and expounded by lawyers. Finally one expects there to be only one valid version of a legal document, without later emendations or even 'corrections' unless they were authorised by both parties (which in this case would include God).

When the scribal exegeses are regarded in the light of these Nomological assumptions, based on the idea that Scripture is God's Law, their exegetical arguments are logically understandable and coherent.

I.7 Comparison of Scribal and Rabbinic Exegesis

The Peshat and Nomological modes continued to be important in later rabbinic exegesis, but the Ultra-literal and the Derash modes became equally popular especially in Haggadah (some examples in L.I. Rabinowitz 1967, J. Frankel 1978). This eventually necessitated a clearer distinction between the Peshat and Derash modes by later rabbis (R. Loewe 1964, B.J. Gelles 1981).

Of the five assumptions concerning Scripture identified in the scribal exegeses, the first two are found in almost all rabbinic literature, but the last three are unexpected. It is generally thought that the ancient rabbis used any text which helped their argument, irrespective of its context, that they regularly found several levels of meaning in one verse, and that they changed the reading of the text to suit their interpretation.

I.7.1 It was certainly the case that the rabbis used texts out of context. M. Kadushin (1952:288ff.) suggests that doctrines really did grow out of the seemingly irrelevant verses to which they are attached, but that because they did not develop from the plain sense of the text, they are often only linked "organismically" with the scriptures. Many non-contextual interpretations may possibly be explained in this way, but there remain a vast number of exegeses based on phrases plucked out of context and made to serve as proof texts. Even an apologist such as Z.H. Chajes (1952:160f.) admits this, and suggests that these texts may have acted merely as mnemonic devices by which to remember doctrines, even if the tradition appears to use the text to substantiate the doctrine. The middah of Context (Hillel's 7th and Ishmael's 12th), which teach that the meaning may be learned from the context, also suggest that this was not the normal way of interpreting the text.

I.7.2 The rabbis also used one verse as the source of many meanings. Conflicting interpretations are listed for the same verse in the Midrashim without any apparent embarrassment, each introduced simply as "Another interpretation" and each is treated with equal authority (Kadushin 1952:72–4). Even R. Ishmael, who is credited with the defence of the plain meaning of Scripture, recognised that one text could have many meanings (bSanh.34a).

Multiple interpretations were later organised into four different levels of meaning, summarised by the mnemonic
פרדס, 'paradise' (M. Fishbane 1982):
פשט – the plain or primary meaning
רמז – a "hint" in the text which points to a hidden meaning
דרש – a secondary or allegorical meaning
סוד – a mystical meaning hidden in the letters.

Prophecy in particular could have several layers of meaning, being re-applied to the present even though it had already been fulfilled. Perhaps the first example of this is Yohanan's use of Hos.4.14 to suggest that Jerusalem was destroyed because of the increase in adultery (I.2.46).

Allegory was used increasingly after about 70 CE, as demonstrated by Bonsirven's survey (1933). It was about this time that Canticles was transformed from a love song (eg mTaan.4.8) to an allegory (Hananiah, I.2.37; Yohanan b.Zakkai, Mekh.Ish.1) before it was totally allegorised by Aqiva (tSanh.12.10; bSanh.101a). This was also the time that Yohanan b.Zakkai popularised the allegorical 'Homer' exegesis of the Dorshe Hamurot (I.1.1).

Although the rabbis never went to the extremes of Philo, who could apparently find an allegorical or spiritual meaning for any text, there is evidence that there existed a continuous commentary on the text of the Amelek story, by Joshua b.Hananiah and Eleazar of Modim, the former giving the literal interpretation and the latter the allegorical (W. Bacher 1884:I.203–219; R. Kasher 1988:553f.).

I.7.3 The rabbis did accept that there was only one valid text of Scripture, but this did not prevent them from expounding variants which were not present in this text. This was done especially by the methods of Al Tiqré, introduced by ...**אלא**...**אל תקרי** ('do not read...but...' e.g. bBer.5a). This technique is extremely common among the Amoraim, and Bonsirven (1939:120–128) finds many examples in Tannaitic exegesis, but none before 70 CE.

Maimonides argued that Al Tiqré was merely a poetical exposition and not a suggested emendation – see Moreh Nebukhim 2.ch.43, also Chajes 1952:159f.,188–194 contra M. Güdemann 1892:348–50), and it is generally accepted that they did not try to change the written text itself (bibliography in S. Lowy 1969:n62), but this does not alter the fact that they were introducing a temporary emendation in order to introduce a meaning not otherwise present in the text.

This type of exegesis may have been used to preserve variants, because it is frequently used where there is no difficulty with the present text (R. Kasher 1988:572) and there are a few examples where they concur with variants preserved in other sources (examples in S. Talmon 1964). The Rabbis were certainly not ignorant of variant manuscripts and may even have used them, because some of the so-called citation errors in the Talmud are similar to the LXX (V. Aptowitzer 1970, I. Abrahams 1909). The variants collected by R. Meir were also used exegetically (e.g. GenR.20.12), and B. Albrektson (1978:54) suggests that the rule concerning four sections of the phylacteries may originally have been derived from a variant text.

The Ketiv and Qere (the written text and its oral substitution introduced by "It is written ...but we read...", ...**וקרינן**...**כתיב**, e.g. bNed.37b) can similarly be claimed not to represent actual changes to the text but merely oral substitutions. These are much more likely to preserve actual variants because they frequently resemble scribal errors such as confusion of similar letters, displacement of letters, haplography, dittography and wrong divisions of words (J. Weingreen 1951:177). Like the Al Tiqré, these variants became the basis for exegesis, and the exegeses of both the written and oral versions were given equal weight (e.g. bSanh.20a; R. Kasher 1988:573).

There was of course opposition to these trends in exegesis. There was some opposition to Derash exegesis (B.L. Visotzky 1988:263f.), and the disregard of context which led to the atomistic exegesis of Aqiva led the school of Ishmael to argue that "Scripture speaks the language of men" (bBer.31b; bNed.3a). The Al Tiqré method itself can be seen as a way of accepting the existence of a standard text while preserving variants in the form of exegeses. Opponents of allegory are called 'Scribes' by Gamaliel III (bSot.15a), perhaps because of the similarity of their position to that of the scribes before 70 CE.

Rabbinic exegesis was not totally transformed by these innovations, and Nomological principles can be found in much Amoraic exegesis (I. Frankel 1956). However, these new concepts of non-contextual exegesis, several layers of meaning and the interpretation of real or imagined variants also flourished, eventually necessitating in post-Amoraic times the distinction between Peshat and Derash exegesis.

Part II

Exegesis in Non-Scribal Traditions

II.1 Introduction to Non-Scribal Exegesis

The exegetical techniques and assumptions of the scribes will now be compared with those of their predecessors and contemporaries. The exegesis of their predecessors can only be identified tentatively as that preserved in the ancient texts and translations, such as the MT, LXX and Targumim, and the conclusions drawn from these are necessarily vague. The exegeses of their contemporaries however are abundantly preserved, especially that from Alexandria and Qumran, as well as Josephus and the Dorshe Reshumot/Hamurot.

These exegeses are examined by collating previous studies, so the amount of space given to each group is reflecting more the amount of relevant research published in that area than the relative importance of that group.

Works such as Pseudo Philo, I. Enoch, Jubilees, the Genesis Apocryphon, Gnostic literature etc. have received little attention as yet with regard to their exegesis, except for the listing of OT citations and some very general analysis (see G.W.E. Nickelsburg 1981, D. Patte 1975, J.W. Aageson 1983, J.H. Charlesworth 1987, D. Dimant 1988, A.N. Chester 1988, B.A. Pearson 1988).

The Samaritan literature provides useful parallels with rabbinic exegesis (J. Bowman 1950, I.R.M. Bóid 1988a), but is generally very late, the earliest dating from the fourth century. Even though their copyists and exegetes were extremely conservative (S. Lowy 1977: 58ff., 123ff., 220ff.), the language of their Targum is similar to Targum Aramaic (A. Tal 1988: 192), and their exegesis can be traced back to Roman times (R. Bóid 1988b:608–617), it is still virtually impossible to isolate early from late elements.

Comparisons with New Testament exegesis is omitted for the opposite reason that there is not sufficient room to deal with the wealth of material. Although it is difficult to make a selection, probably the most important work in this area has been done by J.W. Doeve (1954), E.E. Ellis (1957,1978), A.T. Hanson (1974, 1980, 1983), and R.N. Longenecker (1975, 1987). A useful collection of recent work is found in B. Lindars 1988.

Apart from some general comments concerning their exegetical assumptions, these bodies of literature have been regretfully omitted from this study.

II.2 Exegesis in Ancient Texts and Translations

The ancient texts and translations presumably preserve the emendations and glosses of the earliest exegetes, but dissecting these from the work of later redactors is usually impossible, and discerning the exegetical reasons behind such changes can now only be guesswork. Nevertheless, these sources do give an insight into the way in which the text was approached and an indication of the kinds of assumptions about Scripture which these oldest exegetes held.

II.2.1 *The Masoretic Text* may preserve the most ancient text. From the earliest reports to the most recent conclusions, the MT has stood out from among the mass of other texts at Qumran as a separate and ancient tradition (H.M. Orlinsky 1959, P.W. Skehan 1959 to E. Tov 1988).

The rabbis have always insisted that their exegetical techniques originate in the OT and this is certainly true for Qal vaHomer (GenR.92.7 finds several examples) and a few other techniques such as Pun (e.g. Is.54.13; Jer.1.11f.), and perhaps even Gematria (e.g. Gen.14.14; 15.2 – the numerical value of "Eliezer" is 318 – other examples in C. Levias 1903). Fishbane finds other techniques working within the text, such as Conjunction (i.e. Context, 1985:229f., 393ff.) and Athbash (reversal of alphabets, using ת for א, שׁ for ב etc, e.g. Jer. 25.26,51.41 where the meaningless שׁשׁך becomes בבל, Babylon).

The lists of "scribal emendations" and the Qere (verbal substitutions) in rabbinic traditions (e.g. bNed.37b; bMeg.25b) are presumably incomplete, and evidence of many glosses can been found in synonymous readings (S. Talmon 1960). J. Weingreen (1976:12,16) has found examples of Al Tiqré type changes where the original has been preserved within a parallel passage and instances where exegetical comments have become part of the text (1963), and Fishbane (1985) has uncovered evidence of many more.

Although one can theorise about the reasons for these changes, the rabbinic lists themselves suggest that they were made in order to change the meaning of the text rather than to clear up scribal errors, and Talmon (1962a) finds evidence in DSIs.a that such changes were made for exegetical reasons. The widespread use of such exegetical emendations is illustrated by the text "An Aramean was my father" (Deut.26.5: ארמי אבד אבי) which was offensive to many Jews. The LXX translated it "my father forsook (יאבד) Aram" while the Passover Haggadah (which includes traditions going back to 2nd C BCE – L. Finkelstein 1938b, D. Daube 1959, contra S. Stein 1957) reads "the Aramean would have destroyed (איבד) my father".

II.2.2 *The Targumic and Septuagintal literature* are also valuable indicators of ancient exegesis, but they are both difficult to date. Although they are based on extremely old material and both have been shown to employ methods similar to the Rabbinic middoth (see Z. Frankel 1841:163–172, L. Prijs 1948, D.W. Gooding 1976:18–29,37–40, J. Koenig 1982:47ff. and R.le Déaut 1984 re the LXX; see Vermes 1963b,1970,1975 and G.J. Brooke 1985:25–36 re the Targumim), it is almost impossible to say how old individual elements are. Even those portions of the LXX which have been transmitted 'unanimously' show signs of Christian editing (I.L. Seeligman 1948:25–31), and although much work has been done in trying to discover the early elements in the Targumim (especially P. Churgin 1928:126–145, G. Vermes 1961) it is still virtually impossible to isolate them from later influences.

The Targumim undoubtedly contain early traditions. Parallel traditions have been found in Qumran literature (N. Wieder 1953, W.H. Brownlee 1956, 1978:187f., M.R. Lehmann 1958, 1962, G. Vermes 1969a, contra R.P. Gordon 1974), in the LXX (Z. Frankel 1851, P. Churgin 1933, L.H. Brockington 1954, D.W. Gooding 1974, R. Le Déaut 1984), in Josephus (S. Rappaport 1930, R. Marcus 1934–), in other rabbinic aggadah (L. Ginzberg 1911-, P. Churgin 1928:93–110, G. Vermes 1961, J.W. Bowker 1969, M. Aberbach & B. Grossfeld 1982), and in the NT (M. McNamara 1966, 1972). There is evidence of pre-Tannaitic halakah (J. Heinemann 1974), non-Rabbinic theology such as the fallen angels of Gen.6.4 (E. Cashdan 1967; P.S. Alexander 1972) and anti-Sadducean polemic (S. Isenberg 1970), but there are also very late elements such as the names of Mohammed's wives (E. Cashdan 1967). Targums were transmitted orally, but followed traditional forms (A. Shinan 1983). These traditions were traced back to Ezra (bMeg.3a re Neh.8.8) and although no scholars would go as far as that, some advocate a fixed oral tradition in pre-Christian times (e.g. P. Kahle and M. McNamara). The earliest evidence for written targumim comes from Qumran where two fragments of what may be the same Targum on Job have been recovered, together with a possible fragment of a targum on Leviticus (J.A. Fitzmyer 1974). This adds support to the tradition that Rn.Gamaliel II came across a written targum of Job (bShab.115a), although this tradition shows that such a Targum was still officially disapproved of at that time.

However the early elements of the targumim cannot be isolated with any confidence from later additions and revisions. Although M. McNamara believes that "the Palestinian targumim to the Pentateuch transmit substantially the paraphrase of the Pentateuch formed in pre-Christian times" (1972:85), and G. Vermes has done much to substantiate R. Bloch's (1955) theory that the Palestinian targumim are the source for much rabbinic and non-rabbinic aggadah, there is always the possibility that individual traditions have been added or changed by later editors. Targum Onkelos (TgOnk) is likely to be a revision of the Palestinian Targumim, perhaps of Targum Pseudo-Jonathan (TgJon) in particular, towards a more literal rendering of the MT, but still retaining some haggadic elements (G. Vermes 1961,1963a,

J.W. Bowker 1967a, E. Levine 1974, M. Havazelet 1976, A. Shinan 1977).
P. Churgin (1933) showed that aggadah in TgJon but not in TgOnk was
often found also in the LXX, suggesting that TgJon may preserve earlier
traditions which have been removed from TgOnk during later revisions.
However he also notes that there are numerous later additions to TgJon
(1928), and although TgJon has not been revised as thoroughly as TgOnk, its
halakah is consistently Aqivan and its theology is largely in line with the later
rabbis (L. Smolar & M. Aberbach 1983). A. Chester (1986:253–9) warns
against any attempts to relate one targum tradition to another, because a
meturgeman would produce a targum with plenty of aggadah (like the Palestinian targumim) for the synagogue context while the same meturgeman
would produce a translation with little exegesis (like TgOnk) for the school-
room.

II.2.3 The situation with the LXX is much more hopeful. The texts which
have survived appear to be Jewish translations without much Christian influence (E. Tov 1988b:163f.). Pre-Christian manuscripts have now been found
which tend to confirm this (S.P. Brock 1986). P.de Lagarde's argument as
against P. Kahle's (1947) that a single Old Greek text lies behind the multitude of LXX versions, has been confirmed by the Qumran Minor prophet
scroll (D. Barthélemy 1953, 1963; R.A. Kraft 1965; cf. Jellicoe 1968 : 59–63,
M. Saebø 1978, E. Tov 1986 : 224f.). This Old Greek is now becoming acces-
sible in the text and apparatus of J.W. Wevers' *Septuaginta*. Much of the
work done on exegetical techniques in the LXX will have to be re-evaluated
in the light of this tool and a start has been made in this direction (e.g.
E. Tov 1978, P.E. Dion 1984).

However the fundamental characteristics of this Old Greek text is still
debated. Some regard it as a literal word for word translation, possibly by
professional dragomen without any theological background (E. Bickerman
1959, C. Rabin 1968), without any of the interpretive embellishments which
accumulated subsequently (H.M. Orlinsky 1975, E. Tov 1981:155–158,
S.P. Brock 1988), while others think that they were well versed in Jewish
exegesis and that their interpretations were among the elements which subsequent revisions attempted to remove (R. Marcus 1945, D.W. Gooding 1969,
1976:115f., H. Heater 1982:131f., P.E. Dion 1984).

In conclusion, many exegetical techniques are found in the ancient texts
and translations, including some which are not used by the scribes, such as
Athbash and Al Tiqré or emendation. However the problems of isolating
and dating early exegeses makes it impossible to form firm conclusions from
individual texts.

One exegetical technique is common to the LXX, targumim, Samaritan
Pentateuch and 1QIs.a, and is variously called 'amplification' (Z. Frankel
1841), 'complementation' (Churgin 1928), 'harmonisation' (P.W. Skehan
1957) 'haggadic retelling' (S. Sandmel 1961) 'expansionism' (Skehan 1965),

'analogy' (J. Koenig 1982 – cf. comments in E. Tov 1984b:121) and 'anaphoric translation' (H. Heater 1982). This technique copies a portion of scripture from one location into another where a similar vocabulary or subject matter provides a link, and therefore appears to be related to the later method of Gezerah Shavah. Skehan (1965:277) is probably correct in seeing behind this method a high regard for the sacred text which means that scripture can only be interpreted by utilising other scripture.

The mode of exegesis is almost always Peshat, in the Targumim and the LXX, with the additional interpretation of metaphors, filling of poetic gaps and removal of ambiguities and anthropomorphisms (P. Churgin 1928:93–110, R. Le Déaut 1971, 1984, D.H. Gard 1952). The LXX is a very literal translation containing little exegesis compared with the Targumim, but as Churgin (1928:79) points out, even the Targumim attempt only to explain the primary meaning of the text, and a secondary meaning is never sought out. P.S. Alexander (1985:16, 1988:236) also notes that the Targumim only offer one interpretation of each text, and that despite one's first impressions, the interpretation is based on an exact exegesis of the text.

These characteristics underlying the ancient texts and translations may suggest that the earliest attempts to interpret scripture were based on the assumptions that scripture has only one meaning and that the only means by which scripture may be understood is by comparing it with other scripture, utilising common words and subjects to establish a common context. These assumptions are similar to the Nomological assumptions that there is only one level of meaning and only one valid text.

However these conclusions can be given little weight. The common practice of amplifying Scripture suggests that the final form of the text was still being developed, and multiple interpretations may be absent simply because they would be out of place in a translation (cf. J. Barr 1979).

II.3 Exegesis of the Dorshe Reshumot and Dorshe Hamurot

The Dorshe Reshumot (דורשי רשומות) and the Dorshe Hamurot (דורשי חמורות) are two groups attributed with allegorical exegeses and which may have been in Palestine before 70 CE.

The etymology of these titles has been variously explained (W. Bacher 1905, B.Z. Lauterbach 1910-:292ff., 503ff.) but the simplest explanations are probably "Interpreters of Signs/Symbols" and "Interpreters of Difficulties" respectively. Most scholars have followed Rashi (re bBer.24a) in the assumption that these are two names for the same group, but there have been attempts to distinguish between them (I.Lévi 1910, B.Z. Lauterbach 1910-). However the frequent substitution of one title by the other in variant manuscripts or parallel texts means that any serious attempt to separate them into two schools is now impossible.

Dating these groups is very difficult because of the paucity of data. I. Sonne (1950) pointed out that their allegorical type of exegesis has many parallels with the 2nd C. Gnostics and suggested that it grew up during debates with Christians. However L. Ginzberg (1901a:405) said that their exegesis was "already archaic in the year 70", and Lauterbach (1910–) suggested that the relative absence of their exegeses from Talmudic literature indicates that the later rabbis tried to suppress them. I.Lévi (1910) placed their *terminus ad quem* at the beginning of the 2nd C because their exegesis was debated by Eleazar de Modin, R. Joshua and R. Eliezer b.Hyrcanos, and it may even be earlier because R. Yohanan b.Zakkai is attributed with exegeses 'after the manner of Homer' (tBQ.7.6; Mekh.Ish.76a; bQid.22b; bSot.15a). It seems likely that these groups existed before 70 CE, but they are not to be identified with the scribes or later rabbis. Although R. Yohanan b.Zakkai used their methods ("he interpreted according to the manner of Homer [חמר]" – tBQ.7.3–7 and many parallels, summarised in Neusner 1970:257–261), he does so in a rather uncharacteristic way (employing parables and metaphors rather than allegory), and the fact that he does so is carefully noted, which indicates that it was considered unusual. Lauterbach suggests that another title given to them was 'The Others' (1910–:328f.) and points out that the early Tannaim treated their exegeses with caution because of the danger that the literal meaning of the law might be neglected.

Although it is possible that they were yet another lost Palestinian sect, it is also likely that they are rabbinic titles given to groups which we know from other sources. They have been identified both with the Qumran exegetes (I. Sonne 1950, C. Roth 1960a, II.5.3d) and with Alexandrian allegorists such as Philo (Lauterbach concluded that the Dorshe Hamurot were Alexandrian Jews, and that Dorshe Reshumot were Palestinian Jews who inspired Philo). However they may also be generic terms for a type of exegesis which was associated with more than one group, which was characterised by 'difficult/deep' and 'symbolic' methods.

Lauterbach (1910–) collected together all their exegeses and attempted to show that the Dorshe Reshumot interpreted mainly by using Symbols, and the Dorshe Hamurot searched for deeper meanings in the text. His conclusions are perhaps too generalised to take into account the variety of methods used by these groups, but he has highlighted their main form of exegesis, i.e. the use of secondary or hidden meanings.

A couple of examples illustrate this, one from each group:

And they went 3 days in the wilderness	וילכו שלשת ימים במדבר
and they found no water. [Ex.15.22]	ולא מצאו מים
The Dorshe Reshumot say:	דורשי רשומות אמרו
They did not find the words of Torah,	לא מצאו דברי תורה
which are compared to water.	שנמשלו למים
As it is said:	שנאמר
Ho everyone that thirsts,	הוי כל צמא

come to the waters. [Is.55.1]   לכו למים

(text according to Lauterbach 1910-:310, from Mekh.Ish., Mekh.Sim., and bBQ82a with slight variations; cf. TgJon).

The Dorshe Reshumot use Mashal to interpret 'water' as the Torah, and supply a text to show this same Symbol being used elsewhere in Scripture. There is no reason to think that the Dorshe Reshumot regarded the Wilderness wanderings as mythological (as Lauterbach suggests, 1910-:330) so they are finding a secondary or hidden meaning behind the plain meaning of the text.

The Dorshe Hamurot interpreted in a similar way, as seen in the following exegesis based on Anah finding the mules in the wilderness (Gen.36.24), found only in bPes.54a:

The Dorshe Hamurot say: דורשי המורות אמרו
Anah was a bastard   ענה פסול היה
therefore he brought   לפיכך הביא
bastards into the world.   פסולין לעולם

This exegesis appears to be based on the common misunderstanding of Yohanan b.Zakkai's exegesis of Gen.36 (see I.3.6). They accepted Yohanan's apparent conclusion that Anah was a bastard, and saw a confirmation of this in Anah's discovery of (or even production of) the bastard species of mules, which are the product of a horse and an ass. This too is a hidden or secondary meaning which is independent of the plain meaning of the text.

In conclusion, the Dorshe Reshumot and Hamurot may have existed before 70 CE, and they may have been related to other groups such as Alexandrian allegorists or Qumran exegetes. However the rabbis regarded them as different from themselves, and were perhaps reticent to record their exegeses, although some became standard interpretations (e.g. 'water' = Torah). The few exegeses which have survived suggest that they were generally characterised by allegorical secondary meanings with little or no regard for context.

II.4 Exegesis in Josephus

Josephus covers the whole of OT history in his Antiquities, often adding exegetical embellishments not present in the text. However it is no simple task to discover the exegetical techniques or assumptions which he used because most of these embellishments have clearly been received from other sources.

II.4.1 *The Greek Bible was his main source.* He praised the LXX in the prologue to the Antiquities (1.10–12), followed its textual tradition and its form of proper names (A. Mez 1895), and used books such as Esdras and Maccabees which are not found in the Hebrew canon. The exact form of his

Greek Bible is not certain because although he mostly follows the Alexandrian text, he also frequently appears to use the Lucianic Kaige (G. Howard 1973b, H.W. Attridge 1984:212–4). L.H. Feldman (1988:457,465) suggested that he avoided citing the LXX because of its inferior style, except Esther which is more polished.

He also used the Hebrew (R.J.H. Shutt 1971) and probably a written Aramaic Targum (S. Rappaport 1930). Rappaport collected together the non-biblical traditions which Josephus added to his account of Jewish history and attempted to find the sources of these in contemporary literature. He found parallels in almost every instance, especially in the LXX, the targumim, Philo, Pseudo-Philo and Jubilees, and he found many other parallels with traditions recorded in later rabbinic works, and concluded that there was no need to propose oral tradition as one of his sources (xvf). Other parallels between Josephus and rabbinic traditions have been collected by L. Ginzberg (1911–) and R. Marcus's footnotes (1934–). The use of Aramaic targumim had also been proposed by H. St.J. Thackeray (1929), although H.W. Attridge (1976:32f.) is unconvinced, pointing out that there are no literary parallels and that the common traditions would have been part of oral tradition. A. Schalit (1965) has suggested that an Aramaic source may be behind some of Josephus' non-biblical history, although he concludes that this source had already been translated into Greek before Josephus saw it.

II.4.2 *Josephus' background and theological affiliations* are also important for understanding the influences on his exegesis. According to his own account he studied with the Pharisees, Sadducees and Essenes, then spent three years with a hermit and finally decided to join the Pharisees (Life 10–12). His Pharisaic affiliations have often been questioned (reviewed by Attridge 1976:6–15) because of the lack of references to their distinctive doctrines, such as oral law or resurrection. However Thackeray (1929 p97) has found several indications of belief in resurrection, and although Josephus does not give support for other Pharisaic beliefs, neither does he deny them.

The Essenes also appear to have had much influence on him, as seen especially in the *Wars* which was written soon after his three years of asceticism. The Sadducees may also have had some influence as seen in his emphasis on punishment and reward in this life (which is the 'message' of the *Antiquities* – 1.14), especially with regard to the *lex talionis* (Attridge 1976:147), and his emphasis on his own priestly descent and role (Attridge 1976:16f.). The only one of his 'four philosophies' to which he does not seem to owe any influence is the Zealots for whom he has only criticism, and whom F.F. Bruce (1965:153) suggests Josephus regarded as the Desolating Abomination of Daniel.

The influence of Greek traditions is even stronger than any of the above. Although his history concentrates unashamedly on Palestine with the virtual exclusion of the whole world, including the diaspora, he depends heavily on a vast array of Greek authors. He follows Greek forms and styles so exactly that Thackeray (1929:100–124) suggested that he had relied on several assistants, each of which imitated their favourite classical author, but this has subsequently been rejected (Attridge 1976:39).

In the final analysis however, Josephus must be seen as a highly independent historian who used a multitude of Jewish and Greek sources. He is quite capable of original exegesis, such as the novel vocalisation of חלב in Gen.4.4 to read "milk" (Ant.1.54), and uses different translations to find the exegesis which seems correct to him and which suits his own ends.

II.4.3 *Josephus' attitude to Scripture* can be seen in his aims, and in his claims about his use of Scripture.

His aims have been summarised by Attridge (1976 ch.4) as 'Moralising', using the history of Israel to illustrate that God rewards the righteous and punishes the wicked, as Josephus himself says in the preface to the Antiquities (1.14). Franxman (1979) has identified another aim: to show Israel in a good light. This general apologetic aim is obvious in the *Wars* (although the apology is often more in favour of himself than his people), but in the *Antiquities* it is seen more in omissions than additions, such as the omissions of Gen.35.22 and the whole of Gen.38, and any mention of the golden calf, as well as countless other small omissions. Franxman (1979:26) regards these omissions as far more important than the small amount of additional material for showing Josephus to be master of his text and his message.

Josephus claimed to record the contents of Scripture "without adding anything nor omitting anything" (Ant.1.17, cf. 4.197; 8.56; 10.218). Attridge (1976:59) suggests that this may have been influenced by Dionysius who records a similar treatment of old records by preceding historians, but he says this by way of criticising their naivety, so it seems more likely that Josephus was thinking of the warning in Deut.4.2 or 12.32. Considering Josephus' many additions and omissions (usefully summarised in P. Villalba I Varneda 1986:268–271), Franxman calls this claim "a bit of hyperbole" (1979:288 cf. Feldman 1988:466–470). However this does not take into account the high regard which Josephus had for Scripture for which, he claims, any Jew would cheerfully die (C. Ap.42). It is therefore likely that Josephus considered himself capable of inspired exegesis, so that he was capable of discerning the portions of Scripture which contained the message of God to his readership, and the exegetical embellishments and traditions which were required to convey this message. Such inspiration would allow him to omit and add portions of the text in order to convey rather than alter the divine message.

II.4.4 *The methods of exegesis* which can almost certainly be attributed to Josephus show not only his high regard for the letter of the text but also his belief in his own inspiration. These methods are etymology, allegory and typology.

II.4.4a Etymologies in Josephus have been studied in detail (Edersheim 1882:452, S. Rappaport 1930:xxxi-xxxiii, Thackeray 1929:77f., R.J.H. Shutt 1971, T.W. Franxman 1979) and although Rappaport and Edersheim find a few parallels with Philo, Rappaport concludes that they mostly originate with Josephus. Franxman (1979:11) points out that the Scriptures themselves are the model for Josephus' practice and method of etymology. He uses etymology especially where Scripture also follows this practice (e.g. in Genesis), and he uses the same methods of literal translation and word-play as found in Scripture. Although his etymologies are different from those suggested by Scripture, and even completely erroneous at times, they do demonstrate his belief in the inspiration of the individual words. Shutt pointed out that the etymologies are based on both the Hebrew and Greek text, though some appear to be independent of either, which suggests that he considers both texts to be inspired.

II.4.4b Allegory is used when Josephus wishes to show that the Laws of Moses conform to "nature" (e.g. Ant.4.226,228), but although he says that Moses spoke in allegory (Ant.1.24) he does not spend much time on allegorical interpretations. He uses it extensively when dealing with the Tabernacle and the priestly vestments (Ant.3.123, 179–187; Wars 5.217f.) where he demonstrates considerable parallels with Philo (Mos.2.88, 102f., 117–123 shares with Josephus: Holy of Holies = heaven, lampstand = planets, shewbread = months, veil = Elements, vestments = earth, oceans and heaven, sardonyxes = sun and moon, breastplate = zodiac). However he is also capable of independent thought, such as when Philo says that the 4 ingredients of incense are the 4 elements (Her.197) but Josephus, knowing that the priests actually prepared incense from 13 ingredients, said that they represented all things from the habitable and unhabitable places (Wars 5.218 and notes in Loeb ad loc.).

Allegory was far more important to Josephus than its minor role in the Antiquities suggests. Attridge (1976:140–142) points out that these few examples represent a limited expression of Josephus' stated plan to show in Antiquities that the Law of Moses conforms to Nature (Ant.1.24). Even in the prologue Josephus realised that he would have little room to pursue this theme and postponed it to another work which either he did not write or which has not survived (Ant.1.25).

II.4.4c Typology in Josephus has been recognised recently especially by D. Daube (1980b) and S. Niditch (1980). They have highlighted several examples where Josephus has used typology to apply past history to later situations, the most important of which is Josephus' own self-identification with Jeremiah. He not only compares himself with Jeremiah, almost taking on his mantle, but even says that when Jeremiah prophesied the siege of Jerusalem by Nebuchadnezzar he was also prophesying about the Romans (Ant.10.79). Daube (1980 : 23) suggests that the rationale behind this type of exegesis lies in a legal view of the OT, because when God deals with his people in a particular manner, this is seen as setting a precedent so that He will respond in a similar way in the future.

Josephus regarded himself as a priest and prophet (reviewed by J. Blenkinsopp 1974). He was well aware of his priestly descent, and used this to substantiate his claim to interpret dreams (Wars 3.351–4 cf. Life 208f.), to prophesy (Wars 4.622–9) and to interpret Scripture (War 3.353: "inspired to read their [sacred prophesies] meanings"). It is this self-understanding which explains the independence with which he utilises exegetical traditions, the confidence with which he adds his own etymologies, allegories and typologies, and the seemingly cavalier way in which he omits details and even whole chapters while still maintaining that he is transmitting a reliable account of God's dealings with the Jews.

In conclusion, Josephus used a very wide variety of sources, both Jewish and Gentile, Semitic and Greek, but he was master rather than servant of what he received, willing to change or ignore the traditions. Similarly he regarded himself as master of the text, omitting and adding details to the biblical account while maintaining that he did neither. This apparent contradiction may be explained by his self-image as priest and prophet, which he felt enabled him to interpret prophecy and may have entitled him to alter the contents of Scripture in order to better bring out its message.

II.5 Exegesis at Qumran

After an introduction on the relevance of the Qumran evidence, the exegetical techniques which have been found in Qumran literature will be outlined, and their possible origins will be explored. The underlying assumptions of Qumran exegetes will then be inferred from these techniques and from the way they transmitted the OT text.

II.5.1 The pre-70 CE date of all the documents found at Qumran can now be assumed to be established, in spite of the efforts of S. Zeitlin (1949,1950) and a few others (e.g. P.R. Weis 1950, J. Reider 1950) who doubted their antiquity. J. Murphy-O'Connor (1986 : 122), in his review of the evidence, gives due space to Zeitlin's arguments but finally dismisses them as "a lesson of the dangers of haste and obstinacy in scholarship". The relative dating of the different documents is, however, far less certain, and especially so with regard to the Pesharim which contain the bulk of Qumran exegesis.

The surviving texts of the Pesharim are all relatively late and there is only one copy of each text. The dates of the original works have therefore been deduced mainly from the contents, and especially from the identities proposed for the Wicked Priest and the Kittim, but the various proposals span from the 3rd C BCE (Simon and the Greeks) to the 1st C CE (Eleazar and the Romans). Most scholars have accepted the dating of the Wicked Priest in the Hasmonean period (see reviews by J. H. Charlesworth 1980 and R. Beckwith 1982; cf. Vermes in Schürer 1973- IIIa:431–4) although the case for a late date has been presented strongly by C. Roth (1958, 1960b) and G. R. Driver (1965).

A recent study by B. Z. Wacholder (1983) dates the Pesharim at the earliest possible date, in the early 2nd C BCE. He argues that pHab was written by the Teacher of Righteousness himself, because this is the only Qumran document which mentions his imperfections. He was therefore the inventor of the Pesher method which was imitated by his followers in the subsequent Pesharim.

P. R. Davies (1987) has also re-examined the evidence for the dating of the Pesharim and has concluded that very little can be concluded, but he tends to favour a very late date. He rejects the notion that the Wicked Priest or the Kittim had specific historical identities, and also warns that although the inhabitants of Qumran may be related to the Essenes there are also specific differences between them. He especially criticises the notion that the Pesharim can be read as exclusively referring to events in the 2nd or 3rd C BCE, because "the distance between the documents and some of the events they supposedly allude to [is] uncomfortably large" (p26). If the Qumran community was interested in contemporising biblical prophecy, why was it still copying out commentaries which related to events hundreds of years previous?

Strong links with NT and early rabbinic literature have been established. Many studies have related the Qumran discoveries to the NT (several seminal papers are collected in K. Stendahl 1954), and P. Benoit (1960) has pointed out that Qumran influences are stronger in Paul and second generation believers than in John or Jesus. O. Cullmann's thesis (1955) that the 'Hellenists' of Acts were Essenes related to Qumran has generally been rejected (M. Black 1961:75ff.). More specifically in the areas of exegesis, J. Schmitt (1978) has collected parallels between the exegesis in the two bodies of literature in terms of subject matter and the texts used, while J. A. Fitzmyer has compared the use of testimonia (1957) and introductory formulae (1961).

N. N. Glatzer (1958) has attempted to discover similar theological links between Qumran and the early rabbis, especially Hillel, but has generally failed, probably due to the types of material available for comparison. Studies in halakah have been much more fruitful in finding links with the Pharisees (L. Ginzberg 1922, ET 1970, C. Rabin 1957, J. M. Baumgarten 1977) and the Sadducees (G. R. Driver 1965: 531ff., J. M. Baumgarten 1980,

R. Eisenman 1983). The search for parallels in the exegesis of Qumran and the rabbis has also been very fruitful, as outlined below.

Wherever the debate ends, the documents will be dated within the period of our study and must be considered as a witness to Jewish exegesis before 70 CE.

II.5.2 *Exegetical techniques* used at Qumran were first enumerated by W.H. Brownlee (1951), and although there has been much subsequent criticism of this early study it has remained the starting point of most discussions of the subject. He found 13 'Hermeneutic Principles' at work in pHab:

II.5.2a

1. Everything the ancient prophet wrote has a *veiled, eschatological meaning*.

2. Since the ancient prophet wrote cryptically, his meaning is often to be ascertained through a *forced, or abnormal construction of the biblical text*.

3. The prophet's meaning may be detected through the study of the *textual or orthographic peculiarities* in the transmitted text. Thus the interpretation frequently turns upon the special readings of the text cited.

4. A *textual variant*, i.e. a different reading from the one cited, may also assist interpretation.

5. The application of the features of a verse may be determined by *analogous circumstances*, or by

6. *Allegorical propriety*.

7. For the full meaning of the prophet, more than one meaning may be attached to his words.

8. In some cases the original prophet so completely veiled his meaning that he can be understood only by an *equation of synonyms*, attaching to the original word a secondary meaning of one of its synonyms.

9. Sometimes the prophet veiled his message by writing one word instead of another, the interpreter being able to recover the prophet's meaning by a *rearrangement of the letters in a word*, or by

10. *The substitution of similar letters* for one or more of the letters in the word of the biblical text.

11. Sometimes the prophet's meaning is to be derived by *the division of one word into two or more parts*, and by expounding the parts.

12. At times the original prophet concealed his message beneath abbreviations, so that the cryptic meaning of a word is to be evolved through *interpretation of words, or parts of words, as abbreviations*. [Brownlee later rejected this principle – 1956:179].

13. *Other passages of scripture* may illumine the meaning of the original prophet.

Brownlee found many parallels between these principles and those used in the Midrashim. G.J. Brooke has attempted to restate this list using purely midrashic terminology (1985: 283ff.) and has largely succeeded. He pointed out that most of these 'principles' were directly equivalent to specific midrashic techniques such as al tiqré (nos.3,4,10), 'asmakta (no.5), paronomasia (nos.7,8), hilluf (no.9) and notariqon (nos.11,12), but that some of them were actually assumptions (no.1), summaries (no.2) or methods which involved multiple midrashic techniques (nos.2,6,13).

K. Elliger reviewed Brownlee's work in his own study of the exegesis of Qumran (1953: 159ff.) and criticised him for the complexity of some of his explanations, especially when the exegesis depended on many stages of interpretation. For example he examined Brownlee's suggestion as to how the word למכמרתו, "to his net" in Hab.1.16 (pHab.5.14) was interpreted: first it was divided into the two words למך מרתו then the first word למך was rearranged as כלם which was regarded as both an abbreviation of כלמה, "shame", indicating 'idolatry', and as an acrostic or abbreviation of המה כלי מלחמותם , "their war utensils which", and then the second word מרתו was changed to the visually similar מרה, "to rebel", which was read as the phonetically similar participle מרא so as to agree with the rest of the sentence.

Elliger argued that such complexities were unlikely to be appreciated by the original readers, and that they probably resulted from too enthusiastic an attempt to read later rabbinic middoth into the relatively undisciplined and 'inspired' exegesis of Qumran. The Teacher of Righteousness did not need to limit himself to a list of hermeneutic principles because he was an inspired exegete more in line with the tradition of Daniel than Hillel.

However, many other examples of these midrashic techniques have been found in the Qumran documents (e.g. P. Wernberg-Møller 1955, F.F. Bruce 1959, A. Finkel 1963, G.R. Driver 1965:335ff., E. Slomovic 1969, S. Talmon 1975, M. Fishbane 1977, 1988: 369–71,374f., D.J. Moo 1983: 36ff., G. Brooke 1980, 1981:496f., 1985, A.N. Chester 1988) and although the examples cited are not always convincing, it is clear that there was a considerable overlap in the techniques used at Qumran and by the rabbis.

II.5.2b The following example from a foundation document of the sect, (the Well Midrash of CD.6.3ff.) demonstrates these techniques as well as the difficulties of discovering the precise techniques used.

The Well which the princes dug,	באר חפרוה שרים
[which] the nobles of the people delved	כרוה נדיבי העם
in the decrees/with the Lawmaker/with a staff.	במחוקק
[Num.21.18]	
The *Well:* it is the Torah.	הבאר היא התורה
And *the diggers:*	וחופריה
they are the (re)turned of Israel	הם שבי ישראל
who went out from the land of Judah	היוצאים מארץ יהודה

and sojourned in the land of Damascus,	ויגורו בארץ דמשק
all of whom God called *Princes*	אשר קרא אל את כולם שרים
for they sought him	כי דרשוהו
and their glory was not rejected	ולא הושבה פארתם
by the mouth of [any]one.	בפי אחד

And the *Lawmaker:*	והמחוקק
it is the Searcher/Interpreter of the Law	הוא דורש התורה
[of] whom Isaiah speaks: [Is.54.16]	אשר אמר ישעיה
Bringing forth a vessel/tool for his work.	מוציא כלי למעשיהו

And *the nobles of the people:*	ונדיבי העם
they are those coming	הם הבאים
to delve the Well	לכרות את הבאר
with staffs/enactments	במחוקקות
which the Lawmaker decreed.	אשר חקק המחוקק

The date of the Well Midrash is difficult to ascertain because CD has been preserved in two text traditions (A and B) and although it is certain that it was part of A, it is not certain whether it was in B. J. Murphy-O'Connor (1971b) argued that the midrash was a secondary addition whose function was to link two originally separate documents, the Missionary Document (CD.2.14−6.1) and the Memorandum (CD.6.11b−8.3). He similarly argued (1971a) that the Amos-Numbers midrash was a later addition, but this has been disputed by Brooke (1980, 1985).

The interpretation follows the form found in the Pesharim of citing a text and then interpreting individual words or phrases, though without the characteristic פשר, 'the interpretation is'.

The digging of the Well is interpreted as searching the Scriptures, but the connection between them is not obvious. W.H. Brownlee (1951:56) suggested that Gezerah Shavah connects "well" with Deut.1.5: "Moses began to explain [באר] the Torah". F.F. Bruce (1959:31f.) simply regarded water as a natural allegory for Torah, but pointed out the word-play on מחקק as both "staff" and "law-giver", although C. Rabin (1954:22) objected that the latter meaning cannot be found before the 14th C. J.A. Fitzmyer (1961:39f.) supported the second meaning of מחקק from Gen.49.10 but concluded that the exegesis is "completely allegorical" because each text "is used with complete disregard of its original context" (cf. also M.A. Knibb 1987:48−50).

However the exegesis only falls into place when the context *is* considered, especially that of Is.54−55 which may have been an accompanying Haftarah reading (cf.Is.55.1: "Ho everyone who thirsts, come to the waters"). The word-play on במחקק is three-fold:
1) "in the decrees" – as in Prov.31.5

2) "with the Lawmaker" – Gen.49.10; Deut.33.21; Ps.60.7(9); 108.8(9); Is.33.22.

3) "with a staff" – as the context explains, מְשֻׁעֲנֹת, "staff" These three meanings are used in the three main interpretive comments, which also each refer to Is.54–55.

The first interpretation (Well = Torah) was traditional (L. Ginzberg 1911-VI:116, G. Vermes 1969a) and needed no support, but governs the whole midrash.

The Diggers = Returned is a product of reading "they dug...in the decrees" (Num.21.18, i.e. in the Torah). "Dig" can mean "seek" (cf. Josh.2.2f.) and is interpreted as "they searched/interpreted it". "They sought him", as in Is.55.6f.: "seek [דרש] YHWH while he may be found...and return [שוב]". This study of Scripture resulted in their princely "glory" (פאר in v5) which "was not rejected [הושבה] by the mouth of anyone" (cf. v11: "My word goes out of my mouth and does not return [ישוב] to me void"). Their "return" is explained by their history of leaving Judah, when they "sojourned" in Damascus (cf. גור three times in Is.54.15).

The Lawmaker = Searcher is less obvious in Is.54–55 so an explicit citation is given, which is interpreted as 'God forms a vessel for his use', using the common interpretation of Vessel = God's servant (C. Rabin 1954:22). "Bringing-forth" is the same root as *"went out* from the land", indicating that God brought the Interpreter out to Damascus. The immediate context (a smith forging a vessel/tool) appears to have been ignored, but if the smith is regarded as an agent of God, and if the "vessel" of v17 is a rival exegete, then the interpretation is contextual: "Every vessel formed against you... and every tongue that shall rise against you... you shall condemn."

The novel interpretation of מחקק as a staff is helped by the previous ambiguity of "vessel/tool", but especially by the explanatory gloss in Num.21.18. The "coming" ones are presumably those who flock to Israel in Is.54.15; 55.1,3,5,6 whom the sect would interpret as those joining themselves, the true Israel, in order to discover the correct principles for interpretation (the staffs).

A concluding sentence summarises the three meanings of מחקק: The staffs (3) are those which the Lawmaker (2) decrees (1).

II.5.3 *The origins of these exegetical techniques* have been searched for in many different areas such as Apocalyptic literature, Ancient Near Eastern (ANE) texts, Alexandrian exegesis in Philo and scribal traditions preserved in the Targumim and early rabbinic literature.

II.5.3a Apocalyptic links were first suggested by K. Elliger (1953) who pointed especially to Daniel. E. Osswald (1956) demonstrated parallels in the methods of exegesis, and F.F. Bruce (1959) pointed out that the key exegetical terms פשר, "interpretation" and רז, "mystery", were used with exactly the same nuance in Daniel and the Pesherim. O. Betz (1960) suggested that the contemporising of the prophetic message is carried out similarly in Apocalyptic and Qumran literature, although Scripture was interpreted more rigorously at Qumran. Such comparisons are now generally accepted (M.P. Horgan 1986: 250–3) but J.C. Trever's suggestion (1987) that the Teacher of Righteousness was himself the pseudonymous compiler of Daniel takes the evidence too far.

The term פשר is used particularly with regard to dream interpretation in Daniel. A. Finkel (1963) pointed out that the root פתר, which is related to פשר, is also linked with dream interpretation in mishnaic Hebrew (cf. Jastrow and W. Bacher 1905), and the rabbinic formula רבנן פתרין קרא ב... ('the rabbis explain this concerning...', e.g. GenR.38.1) is usually used for interpretations which include word-play. I. Rabinowitz (1973) made a careful study of פתר in Scripture, especially in the dream interpretations by Joseph, and compared this with the use of פשר at Qumran. Although he succeeded in demonstrating a uniform concept of interpretation in both sources, in his attempt to find a uniform English translation for every example of these words he fastened on the phrase "to be presaged", which may make the translation of Gen.40.5 more intelligible but obscures the meaning of most other texts. L.H. Silberman (1961) and J.H. Tigay (1983) pointed out that dream interpretation techniques in Apocalyptic, ANE and rabbinic literature have considerable parallels with the exegetical techniques at Qumran, especially those involving symbolism, atomization and wordplay. A. Finkel (1963) found more examples of rabbis using these dream interpretation techniques, including R. Ishmael (bBer.56b; yMS.55b) and the 24 interpreters of dreams in Jerusalem (bBer.55b).

Ancient Near Eastern texts also use similar techniques especially in dream interpretation. M. Fishbane (1977) has found examples of atomization, multiple interpretations, paronomasia, symbolism, notariqon and gematria. He has linked these directly with Daniel and פשר exegesis at Qumran by the Mesopotamian dream and astrology reports which often open with: *kî annî pišîršu*, "This is the interpretation of the word" (cf. Dan 5.26). C. Rabin (1955b:148–50) has even suggested literary dependence of the Pesharim on Egyptian Demotic Chronicles.

II.5.3b The Targumim have often been cited as providing parallels for specific interpretations found in Qumran literature. N. Wieder (1953) was the first to put an example in print, but Brownlee (1956) was quick to respond that he had already thought of it, and gave several more examples. Although they both attempted to prove that the Targum came first, there are too many unknown factors for their arguments to be convincing. The discovery of 11QTg.Job and 4QTg.Job prove that written targumim existed in the 1st C CE, and J.A. Fitzmyer (1974) has suggested that their language indicates an origin at least a century earlier, but the differences in style and the lack of any continuity between these fragments and the later rabbinic Targum of Job (Fitzmyer 1974, Ringgren 1978) makes it unlikely that they reached their final form at this date.

However the multitude of parallels discovered by other scholars (e.g. M.R. Lehmann 1962, G. Vermes 1961, 1969a, 1969b, though R.P. Gordon 1974 disagrees) have established at least that Qumran literature and the Targumim were drawing on the same pool of exegetical tradition. Non-sectarian literature at Qumran, such as the Genesis Apocryphon, also appears to draw on this same pool of traditions (Lehmann 1958).

II.5.3c The Philonic literature has distinct parallels with Qumran especially in its use of commentary form and allegory.

Philo and the Qumran exegetes are the only examples of systematic verse by verse commentary before 70 CE. Although translations and rewritings of Scripture (such as the Targumim, LXX, Genesis Apocryphon, Jubilees or the Temple Scroll) contain exegesis, this is added to the text as though it were an extension of it. Philo and the Qumran exegetes separated text and comment, and attempt to show that the comment is inferred from the text. Even the 4QFlorilegium, which appears at first to be a Testimonia, should be regarded as a commentary on II Samuel (W.R. Lane 1959, G.J. Brooke 1985).

The commentary form may also be seen as lying dormant in the rabbinic use of introductory formulae (IF) for Scripture quotations because these separated text from comment. J.A. Fitzmyer (1961) and D.J. Moo (1983:18f.) made independent collections of the IF at Qumran: both produced a list very similar to Metzger's (1968b) survey of IF in the NT and Mishnah, and F.L. Horton (1971) has proposed a historical development of the IF at Qumran which has parallels with the Mishnah. However rabbinic comments were not collected together till later, and there are few examples of verse by verse commentary. W. Bacher (1884- I:203–219) suggested that the rabbinic commentary form may be traced back as early as R. Eleazar de Modin and R. Joshua b.Hanania (early 2nd C CE) from whom a series of comments forming two parallel commentaries on Exodus ch.15–18, are preserved in the Mekhilta, and L. Finkelstein (1941:223) regards this haggadic material as the oldest in the Mekhilta. The apparent neglect of the commentary form by the rabbis may be due to their emphasis on the practice of the Law rather than on the fulfilment of prophecy, so that teaching was organised according to subject matter rather than according to Scripture.

The allegorical method used by Philo also has some parallels at Qumran, as proposed by Brownlee (principle no.6) and explored extensively by subsequent scholars (e.g. G.R. Driver 1965:531ff.).

E. Osswald (1956:246f.) and B.D. Chilton (1988:125f.) have cautioned against the use of the term 'allegory' to characterise Qumran exegesis, suggesting that 'typology' is more suitable. Osswald argues this because the exegesis is almost always based on a re-application of a concrete historical event to the present, rather than on the search for a hidden secondary meaning. Chilton prefers not to use 'allegory' because pesher exegesis is based on the text (though II.6.1c argues that Philonic allegory is also based on the text). Betz (1960) and J.A. Fitzmyer (1961:21f.) both agree that Qumran exegesis is a contemporising of a historical situation, but disagree that 'typology' is a suitable term to describe it.

The term 'typology' has been used in different ways concerning the Qumran use of Scripture. D. Patte (1975:263ff.) employed the term to describe some of the uses of Scripture in the Hodayoth, although J. Carmignac (1960) and S. Holm-Nielsen (1960) regarded this as a re-use of biblical terms rather than a re-application of the texts. Brownlee (1978:185ff.) used 'typology' to describe the re-working of Scripture in the Genesis Apocryphon, comparing it to the re-working of Samuel and Kings by the Chronicler, but the Apocryphon is a re-statement of Scripture rather than a re-application. J.A. Sanders (1959) has emphasised the similarity of typology at Qumran to the NT 'historical typology' which finds in Scripture a similar historical situation to the present and proceeds on the assumption that the old is a pattern for the new (cf. also H. Gabrion 1979:813–5).

Whatever term is used, it is clear that the method used by Qumran to contemporise the message of the OT has some marked similarities to that used by Philo. However, there are also differences between Qumran and Philonic allegory, especially in the application. Philo uses allegory primarily to discover philosophical truths in Scripture, while Qumran used it to illustrate present day events. However this may be due to differences in their reasons for exegesis rather than in their techniques.

II.5.3d Connections with the scribes are suggested by the similarity of their exegetical techniques. Such connections have been variously traced to a common origin (R.T. Beckwith 1982), to an influx of Pharisees into the community during the persecutions by John Hyrcanus (J.H. Charlesworth 1980:223f.) or to the merging of the remnants of the Qumran sect with mainstream Judaism after 70 CE (J.C. Trever 1958; N. Wieder 1957, 1962; J.H. Charlesworth 1980:232ff.). This latter theory is based mainly on the re-emergence of Qumran teachings in the later Karaite movement, and seems a more likely explanation than Zeitlin's theory of the Karaite origin of the Qumran documents or H.H. Rowley's (1952) theory that the Karaites discovered some Qumran documents in a cave.

It is likely that there was a general contact between the two groups as well as any or all of the above incidents. Although the rabbis appear to be silent concerning Qumran, there are many apparent references to the Pharisees in the sect's literature. The Pharisees are the most likely bearers of the title דורשי החלקות "the seekers/interpreters of smooth/easy things" (CD.1.18; 4QpIs.c.23.2.10; 4QpNah.1–2.2.7 [lacuna, suggested by M.P. Horgan 1979:170]; 3–4.1.2,7; 3–4.2.2,4; 3–4.3.3,7; Hod.2.15,32 cf. 4.10) because they are described as living in Jerusalem, having a 'council' and a 'congregation', and inviting Demetrius to Jerusalem. Brownlee (1951 : 60) suggested that the title was based on a pun with הלכות because the Qumran community tended to call their own legal decisions משפטים. Even P.R. Davies (1987), who generally dismisses all allusions to historic personages in the Qumran literature (including the Wicked Priest!) accepts that this phrase refers to the Pharisees in the Pesharim, but possibly not in the Hodayoth.

These "interpreters of easy things" are attacked in CD.1.16ff. because they "abolished the ways of righteousness and removed the boundary with which the forefathers had marked out their inheritance". L. Ginzberg suggested (1922, ET 1970 : 125) that this is likely to refer to the 'fence' which the Pharisees built around the law, but which the Qumran community felt was not rigorous enough. He also (1970 : 307f.) linked the apparently opposite phrase "builders of the wall" (CD 4.19; 8.12) with the Pharisees because the passage accused them of not making the wall strong enough. The Oral Law of the Pharisees may also be referred to in 4QpNah.3–4.2.8 where תלמוד (cf. 'Talmud', but here in the sense of 'teaching' – see B.Z. Wacholder 1966) is used in the general context of the interpreters of smooth things.

These references to the Pharisees in the Qumran literature have spurred the search for references to the Qumran community in the rabbinic literature, with little success. G.R. Driver (1965 : 531ff.) suggested that some of the rabbinic references to the Sadducees may in fact refer to the Qumran community because the Early Church Fathers and possibly the Amoraim occasionally confused the two groups. B.Z. Wacholder has used Driver's argument to explain why the Sadducees are sometimes portrayed as proficient in scripture exegesis (i.e. when they were confused with Qumran) and sometimes as babbling fools (i.e. an accurate description!). R. Eisenman (1983) has taken the idea even further by arguing that the Qumran community *were* Sadducees, and that their many differences with other Sadducees (such as belief in resurrection and angels) showed that they were a splinter group.

One interesting theory which does possibly find a reference to the Qumran sect in rabbinic literature is that postulated by C. Roth (1960a). He pointed out that the opposite of דורשי החלקות, "interpreters of smooth/light things" is found in the rabbinic title דורשי חמורות, "interpreters of heavy/difficult things" which may have been a retaliatory nickname for the Qumran exegetes.

II.5.4 *The assumptions underlying Qumran exegesis* can be summed up as a belief in inspiration not only of the Scriptures but also of its exegetes. In this respect they were very similar to the Essenes (Jos.War.1.78–80; 2.159) to whom the community may be related.

II.5.4a All of scripture was regarded as prophecy, including the Law and Psalms because Moses and David were prophets (CD.7.9ff.; 11QPs.a.27.11;

D. Dimant 1984:507f.). The Qumran community used the Prophets and Psalms far more than the rabbis, even for the establishment of commandments (L.H. Schiffman 1980), and used the Law as well as the Prophets to find eschatological messages.

The Teacher of Righteousness was an inspired exegete. God revealed to him the true meaning of the Habakkuk prophesies, which were not known even to Habakkuk (pHab.4.17ff.) so that his words came "from the mouth of God" (pHab.2.2). However, the Teacher of Righteousness was not the only individual capable of inspired pesher exegesis. Wacholder (1983:188ff.) has suggested that the Teacher of Righteousness invented the Pesher method and wrote the first example (pHab) and that his disciples wrote the other commentaries, as suggested by the references to the Teacher of Righteousness in the past or as highly honoured (cf. 4QpPs.a.1–10.3.14ff.; 4QpIs.e.1–2.2f.).

Every member of the community was probably considered capable of inspired exegesis (M. Fishbane 1988:364–7). The community was set apart by the hidden laws which had been revealed to them out of Scripture (1QS.5.20ff.; 8.11f.) and new knowledge was constantly expected to be revealed to members of the community who would then share that knowledge with the others (1QS.6.9f.).

II.5.4b The Scriptures which were commented on encompassed a canon very similar to that of the rabbis. Texts from every OT book except Esther have been discovered at Qumran and although many other texts have also been found, they are never cited for exegesis. However Qumran exegetes, unlike the rabbis, do not appear to have had any authoritative text, and there does not even appear to have been a preference for any particular text tradition.

The biblical texts discovered at Qumran are extremely varied. Although they have been classified into three traditions (Hebrew forerunners of the MT, LXX and Samaritan Pentateuch – see M.H. Gottstein 1953, F.M. Cross 1955, 1964, 1966, 1972, S. Talmon 1970), E. Tov (1982) has pointed out that this is an over-simplification, and that apart from the MT they should not be classified into any text traditions. There were no attempts to discover the 'true' text or even to comment on a single text tradition. There were not even a limited number of acceptable text traditons – which C. Rabin (1955a:180f.) contrasts with the 7 (or 10, or 14) accepted variant texts of the Koran. The exegetes used whatever reading best suited their interpretation, even when this reading was different from the text which they quoted in the commentary. Brownlee listed this method (no.4) and gave examples, and many others have been found by subsequent scholars (K. Elliger 1953, K. Stendahl 1954, F.F. Bruce 1959:12,70, Brownlee 1978:188).

More recently there has been an emphasis on what Brownlee also hinted at, that variants were being *invented* at Qumran. This was similar to the rabbinic method of al tiqré but unlike the rabbis, the Qumran exegetes appear to treat the new variant in the same way as scripture itself, without giving any indication that they are departing from the text (examples in G. Vermes 1969b, H. Ringgren 1978, D.J. Moo 1983:42ff., G.J. Brooke 1987). It may of course be that they were quoting a variant which has not survived, but Brooke has been particularly careful to show that the vast number of these occurrences without any surviving textual tradition argues forcibly against this possibility.

Some have seen this invention of variants as a deliberate twisting of the text in order to extract the required theology. B.J. Roberts (1968) compares this 'forced exegesis' to that which occurs in the NT and rejects them both, while J.C. Trever (1958) and W. Sanford (1987) blame this exegesis for producing the 'wrong eschatology' which resulted in the massacre of the community by the Romans.

However this view that the Qumran exegetes twisted Scripture to fit their own interpretation fails to take into account the high regard that they had for Scripture. N. Wieder (1962:215ff.) has argued persuasively that the 'Book of Hagu' which is mentioned with such reverence at Qumran is a title for the Scriptures. The true Israel are those who 'dig the Law' to find hidden truth (CD 8.3ff.; 1QS.7.12f.), and the community attempted to meditate on the Law day and night, by dividing the night into shifts and taking it in turns to expound Scripture (1QS.6.6).

The best way to understand this creation of new variants is probably as an honest attempt to discover the message of the inspired text, in the knowledge that many text traditions existed and that there was no way of deciding which one (if any) had the correct readings. Instead of using modern methods of textual criticism they used imagination and inspiration in the knowledge that as members of the true Israel they had the capability for inspired exegesis.

II.5.5 In conclusion, the Qumran exegetical techniques show possible influences from a number of sources but their use of the commentary form and allegory has more in common with Philonic than scribal traditions. The one concept which sums up the Qumran approach to Scripture is inspiration. They regarded the whole of the Law, Prophets and Psalms as inspired prophecy which was to be interpreted by inspired exegetes and even copied with some inspired creativity.

II.6 Exegesis in Philo

II.6.1. Philo lived and wrote at the start of the Christian era. Most of his prodigious output was exposition of Scripture which, as V. Nikiprowetzky (1973, 1977) has convincingly shown, can be seen as an attempt to construct a systematic exposition of the Pentateuch, probably based on the model of synagogue homilies (G.M. Newlands 1978:20ff.). The exegetical techniques used by Philo should therefore be representative of those known to the Jews of Alexandria.

The exegetical techniques found in Philo will be examined first, including the 'rules' and characteristics of allegory, and an example to illustrate them. The origins of Philo's exegesis will then be explored, both in terms of Jewish and Hellenistic influences and of possible sources. The assumptions underlying this exegesis will be inferred from his use of Scripture and his apparent acceptance of some Hellenistic concepts of inspiration.

II.6.1a *Philo's 'rules' of allegory* were listed in two early studies by Z. Frankel (1854) and C. Siegfried (1875, 1905) who both concluded that the middoth of Hillel and later rabbis are already evident in Philo who took the letter of the text seriously and based conclusions on the minutest points of grammar or spelling. Both lists are similar, but Siegfried's is more comprehensive, finding 23 different situations which indicated an allegorical meaning:

1. doubling of a word or phrase (e.g. the Infinitive Absolute)
2. superfluous words or phrases which do not add to the sense
3. superfluous facts which are unnecessary or previously stated
4. a pair of synonymous phrases, one of which is therefore superfluous
5. possible changes in punctuation which change the sense
6. synonymous words – the change in vocabulary must be significant
7. word-play, such as seeking puns, may open up a deeper meaning
8. the presence of particles, adverbs, prepositions etc.
9. independent parts of a word such as inseparable prepositions
10. other spheres of meaning of a word
11. small alterations in a word which make a new sense (al tiqré)
12. unusual or strange words or spellings
13. the number and tense of a verb
14. the gender of a word
15. the presence or absence of the article
16. a combination of words also used elsewhere
17. the context of the verse
18. an unusual combination of verses
19. the absence or exclusion of an expected phrase
20. unusual or unexpected statements
21. numbers, which can be interpreted symbolically
22. objects, which can be interpreted symbolically
23. names, which can be interpreted etymologically

Other examples of the middoth or their predecessors in Philo include the discovery of Gezerah Shavah (R.G. Hamerton-Kelly 1976), reversal of text order (R.D. Hecht 1980:131f.) and notariqon (Stein 1929:58; S. Belkin 1967:83ff.; A.T. Hanson 1967:136 – all discussing 'Abraham'). J. Cazeaux (1979, 1984:212) has identified a 'Teleological' method in Philo, which consists of basing the interpretation of a preceding verse or phrase on an as-yet unmentioned verse or phrase which is to follow, and is therefore similar to rabbinic rules of Context. S. Sowers (1965:24) has pointed out that Philo used the rule of a 'trifling matter' (Somn.I.92ff.) which is found also in the Letter of Aristeas (144) and perhaps in Paul (1Cor. 9.9 – A.T. Hanson 1974:163ff.).

E. Stein (1929) regarded these lists not as 'rules' but as the terminology for giving reasoned explanations to allegorical interpretations. Most scholars have followed Stein, but J.Pépin (1966) explored Siegfried's idea (e.g. 1905:11) that the role of these 'rules' was not to dictate *how* to interpret allegorically, but *when*. He reviewed the various attempts to explain why Philo sometimes applied allegorical interpretations and sometimes did not, and concluded that Philo regarded unusual, difficult or superfluous phrases as indicating that the text should be interpreted allegorically.

II.6.1b *Philonic allegory* is characterised by an attempt to find philosophic truth behind the Scriptures. Philo describes allegorists as those who look beyond the literal sense to find hidden meanings (V. Con.78; Mutat.65; Confus.190; Somn.I.164) or spiritual meanings (Abr.217), which are found in symbols (Spec.III.178) and in subtle nuances of the text (Opif.77; Mutat.138,140; Spec.I.8; Q. Gen.4.243). Philo, unlike the extreme allegorists (Migr.89ff.), never denies the validity of the Law, although he sometimes regards narrative as questionable (e.g. Plant.32ff.; Ebr.144; Somn.1. 94).

Although his motive was probably apologetic (R.D. Hecht 1984), he should not be compared with Stoic Homeric commentators or Aristobulus who wanted to remove contradictions and anthropomorphisms from Homer and the OT respectively. Y. Amir (1970) has argued that Philo's allegories are more akin to the very earliest Greek philosophers who, as J. Tate (1929-, 1934) pointed out, used allegory not to defend Homer but in the sincere belief that Homer was trying to teach philosophic truths (R. Loewe 1964:143f.).

The subject matter of these allegories has been classified by D.M. Hay (1980) as Cosmological, Mathematical, Sacred History, Ethical, Metaphysical and Psychological. All except for Sacred History are Greek philosophical concerns, and even when Philo deals with biblical Sacred History he does so like a Greek philosopher, seeing for example Paradise and Sodom as symbols of immortal virtue and the destruction of evil (Q. Gen.4.51). The form of these allegories has been classified by B.L. Mack (1975) and P. Borgen et al. (1976).

II.6.1c Philo's exposition of Gen.14 in Abr.232–244 illustrates some of these methods:
"He collected his servants,... made a roll-call... and distributed them into cen-

turies and advanced with three battalions... His nephew he brought back...
with all the horses of the cavalry..."

This is what we find in the scriptures read literally; but those who can contemplate facts stripped of the body and naked in reality, those who live with the soul rather than with the body, will say that of these nine kings, four are the power exercised within us by the four passions, pleasure, desire, fear and grief, and that the five are the five senses, sight, hearing, taste, smell and touch. For these nine are in a sense invested with sovereignty and are our kings and rulers but not all in the same way. For the five are subject to the four... Griefs and pleasures and fears and desires arise out of what we see or hear or smell or taste or touch...

There is much philosophic truth in saying that of the five kings two fell into the wells and three took to flight [v10]. For touch and taste descend to the lowest recesses of the body and transmit to its inward parts what may properly be dealt with by them; but eyes and ears and smell for the most part pass outside and escape enslavement by the body..." (F.H. Colson 1929–).

Philo gives a literal and then an allegorical interpretation, following the text carefully. The LXX is behind his "roll-call" (v14 ἠριθμησε, "numbered" – F.H. Colson ad loc.) and "cavalry" (v11,16 ἱππον "horses" – S. Sandmel 1971 : 134). His "centuries" are presumably inspired by the 318 servants and "battalions" (ταξεσιν from τασσω) may be a wordplay on v15 "he smote (ἐπαταξεν from πατασσω), or (as R. Loewe suggested to me) it may have been prompted by תניך, "trained men". The LXX nowhere says that Abraham"distributed" his men, but this detail may be Philo's interpretation of the difficult Hebrew of v15:

"And he divided the night against them" ויחלק עליהם לילה

or "And he divided against them. [By] night they struck..."

Philo, like Josephus, used the latter reading (S. Sandmel 1971 : 64) unlike the rabbis who said that God divided this night (which was Passover) into two halves, to conquer the nine kings and then Egypt (L. Ginzberg 1911-I:231, V:224; cf. Rashi, A.M. Silberman 1929 : 57). This may mean that Philo read Hebrew, but the rabbinic sources suggest that there was considerable discussion of this difficult "divided", with which Philo and Josephus might have been familiar.

This careful attention to the text continues in the allegorical interpretation. The numbers four and five are interpreted with seeming arbitrary symbolism, but this is tied in with textual details such as their kingship, the defeat of the five by four and the two falling into pits while three climb mountains.

II.6.2 *The origin of Philo's exegetical techniques and allegory* will be approached in two directions, first by exploring Greek and Jewish influences on Philo, and then by a search for specific sources which he may have used.

In spite of S. Sandmel's warnings (1962, 1971) that parallels do not necessarily indicate dependence, it is generally accepted that Philo has been influenced by Greek and/or Jewish exegesis. Disagreement is especially evident with regard to the exegetical techniques which H.A. Wolfson (1947) and others assumed were learnt from Palestinian Judaism but which D. Daube (1936, 1949, 1953, 1961, 1980a) and S. Lieberman (1950) demonstrated in Hellenistic sources such as the Homeric commentators. More Hellenistic parallels have since been found by others, including J. Cazeaux (1984:160ff.) who regarded Philo's minute examination of the text as characteristic of the Greek grammarians and I. Christiansen (1969) who saw Diairesis as the underlying logic to Philo's allegorical method. H.R. Moering (1979) has also pointed out that Philo's 'Arithmology' (interpretation of numbers) follows neo-Pythagorean methods, and that he never used Gematria (which some regard as originally a Jewish method, e.g. C. Levias 1903, and some as a Greek method, e.g. S. Sambursky 1978).

II.6.2a The question as to whether Philo was more influenced by his Graeco-Roman environment or by his Jewish background is not yet resolved because it involves a number of other unresolved questions such as whether or not Philo was acquainted with Hebrew and with Palestinian halakah and aggadah.

II.6.2ai Did Philo know any Hebrew? Siegfried assumed that he did, because his exegeses often depended on minor points of the Hebrew text. H.A. Wolfson (1947 I:88ff.) also felt that Philo knew enough Hebrew to check his Greek translation, but Wolfson generally attributed Philo with an intellect as imposing and broad as his own, and assumed, for example, that Philo had nowhere erred or contradicted himself.

Stein (1929:20f.) pointed out that most of the exegeses in Philo which seem to presuppose a knowledge of Hebrew involve etymology, and that although some etymologies showed a very good knowledge of Hebrew, others showed a poor grasp of the language. He concluded that the etymologies did not originate with Philo but that they came from two independent sources, and that Philo himself knew no Hebrew at all. A.T. Hanson (1967:132ff.) divided the etymologies into three groups: those which depended on a very good knowledge of Hebrew, those which showed a mediocre knowledge, and a third group which demonstrated elementary mistakes suggesting an extremely poor knowledge of Hebrew which he assumed originated with Philo himself.

N. De Lange (1976:117–121) pointed out that strange and ungrammatical etymologies were also used by the rabbis, and do not necessarily imply a poor grasp of Hebrew. Nikiprowetzky (1977:63ff.) and Sandmel (1978) reviewed all the arguments and concluded that Philo had no useful knowledge of Hebrew, but the debate continues.

II.6.2aii Did Philo know any Palestinian halakic traditions? E.R. Goodenough (1929) suggested that Alexandrian Jewish courts had built up their own halakah which was similar but slightly different in many respects to the Palestinian halakah. I. Heinemann (1932:142ff.) concluded that Philo's knowledge of the Festivals was based on an Alexandrian written source because his discussions of them contained a consistent use of Cynic categories. S. Belkin (1940) however, argued that Philo was well acquainted with the halakah of the rabbis in Palestine (D. Daube 1948 differs), although he followed the Alexandrian practice and did not always agree with the majority view in Palestine. These studies tended to assume that the halakah was a fixed entity, but G. Alon (1977:89ff.), who studied several of these apparent disagreements, concluded in each case that the received halakah had changed since the end of the second temple era, and that Philo had correctly followed the Palestinian halakah of his time.

II.6.2aiii Did Philo know any Palestinian Aggadah? Despite the many parallels which L. Ginzberg (1911–) discovered between Philo and the rabbinic traditions, and Stein's (1931) suggestion that Philo's allegorical aggadah was a development of Palestinian 'historical' aggadah, Sandmel (1962, 1971) is correct in concluding that there is little real evidence of common haggadic traditions, because most of the parallels can be explained as a result of common Scriptural sources. However J. Bamberger (1977) has collected 41 examples of common haggadic traditions which do not depend on Scripture or on Hellenistic traditions and other examples have also been demonstrated (J. Coppens 1948, P. Borgen 1965:122ff., 1984b:262ff., S. Belkin 1967).

Philo also records some haggadic traditions which are not represented in rabbinic literature, some of which are also found in Josephus or Jubilees but most of which are found only in Philo (Bamberger 1977). M. Petit (1976) has pointed out that Philo, Josephus, Artapanus and others sometimes appear to contradict Scripture (such as when Philo says that Israel never developed factions during their time in the Wilderness – Hypoth.6.2) and she assumes that this is another evidence for oral haggadic traditions which have not survived in any other form.

Philo's use of these traditions is much more free than in rabbinic sources which often preserve almost identical parallel versions. He even interprets the traditions differently, as Sandmel (1971:26f.) illustrated with the tradition that Abraham was expert in astrology, which the rabbis report without censure (except that God warns Abraham to trust Him, not astrology), and which Josephus says led Abraham to discover God, but which Philo says Abraham abandoned in contempt and discovered God by an inward study of his own soul. However he is also capable of giving a faithful rendition of a tradition, such as the story of the 70 translators of the LXX (Mos.II.25ff. cf Letter of Aristeas) or the tradition about why Adam was created last (Opif.77ff. which, as Borgen (1984a:135) points out, has remarkable parallels with tSanh.8.7ff.).

The paucity of rabbinic aggadah or of Hellenistic midrash (such as that found in Josephus by S. Rappaport 1930 and others) is probably not due to Philo's ignorance but, as Bamberger suggests, to Philo's dislike for aggadah. Much of Philo's allegorical exegesis is devoted to removing mythological elements from the biblical text, so he would not be expected to be enamoured of much of the aggadah preserved in rabbinic and hellenistic Jewish literature.

II.6.2b Philo's familiarity with hellenistic learning does not need to be supported with so many arguments. He had a classical Greek education of which he was proud (which he describes in Congr.74–76) and his writings are full of allusions to concepts from Pythagoras, Middle Platonism and Stoicism. His paragraphs are constructed with Greek forms such as Chreia (B.L. Mack 1984b), Diairesis (R.G. Hamerton-Kelly 1976:52ff.), and Genus-Species distinctions (R.D. Hecht 1980:129ff.) and whole works are constructed according to other Greek forms such as Bibliography (P. Borgen 1984b:235) or the complex patterns of the rhetorical forms (J. Cazeaux 1984). D.T. Runia (1986:409) has even demonstrated that he refers to the *Timaeus* in the process of interpreting almost every major unit of the Pentateuch. He concludes that it "exercises a direct influence on the way that Philo, as philosophising exegete reads the Pentateuchal text", although S. Sandmel (1984a:34) balances this by noting that "it is Genesis that he expounds by means of the *Timaeus,* not the *Timaeus* by means of Genesis".

Although only one example of a true literary dependence on a Greek source has been demonstrated (the 10 Tropes' of Aenesidemus – see B.L. Mack 1984a:232), there are innumerable allusions to other Greek traditions. Apart from his constant reference to philosophic concerns of the Stoic, Middle Platonist and Pythagorean schools, he also finds references in the Scriptures to incidents in Greek mythology (summarised in J. Dillon 1979). One of the most startling, and the most fully explored examples is his allegory of Abraham's relationship with Hagar, which he says is like the man who cannot yet attain to Wisdom (i.e. Jewish learning) so he consorts with Preliminary Studies (i.e. classical Greek education). S. Sandmel (1971:153ff.) and others have shown the parallels with a traditional allegorical interpretation, recorded by Plutarch, of the story of Penelope and her unsuccessful suitors who woo her maids instead. Borgen (1984b:237) has highlighted a further parallel in Philo's interpretation of Abraham, Isaac and Jacob as representing the acquisition of Wisdom by Study, Nature and Practice respectively (On Joseph 1; Mos.1.76) while Plutarch associates the same triad with Pythagoras, Socrates and Plato (De liberis educandis 2A-C).

The question of Philo's primary influence, Palestinian Judaism or Hèllenism, still divides scholars so that, as Nikiprowetzky (1977) suggests, Philo could almost be considered to have two names: Philo of Alexandria and Philo Judaeus.

II.6.2c *The sources used by Philo* provide a second approach to the question of the origin of Philo's exegetical methods. Philo undoubtedly used several sources because he frequently refers to them, and the multiplicity of his sources is also indicated by the contradictory interpretations which he gives for the same texts (see S. Sowers 1965: 32; Pépin 1966: 62).

II.6.2c.i The Therapeutae and the Essenes are two groups of allegorists with which Philo deals at length. Although the Essenes have oral traditions of allegorical interpretation (Prob.82) and the Therapeutae have written traditions (V. Con.29), Philo did not attribute any specific interpretations to them. M. Reinhold (1968: 320) has concluded that the exegetical methods of these two groups was essentially identical to Philo's and to the Pesher method of Qumran. Although this may over-state the similarity of these methods and of their influence on Philo, it is clear that he held them in high regard, and it is likely that many of his allegorical interpretations come from them.

II.6.2c.ii Aristobulus and Aristeas influenced Philo, directly or indirectly. Borgen (1984b:274ff.) traced a development in allegory from the Targumim and Septuagint to Aristobulus and then to Philo. The Septuagint and Targumim demonstrate undeveloped allegory based on anti-anthropomorphic grounds, and Aristobulus introduced the use of Greek philosophy and quotations. Borgen outlined the many similarities with Philo which can be found even in the small number of fragments of Aristobulus which have survived, but suggests that Philo developed his allegories far further than Aristobulus would have done, and that this created the distinction between literal and allegorical interpretations. The degree of similarity which Borgen has demonstrated between Philo and Aristobulus and which R.D. Hecht (1980: 112ff.) has demonstrated between Philo and Aristeas is impressive, but it should not be concluded that there was literary dependence.

The sources which Philo himself refers to are his fellow exegetes. He was clearly well aware of the work of his contemporaries, and he counsels other allegorists to learn from their fellows (Cher.48 cf Spec.I.214). There appears to have been a thriving community of allegorists in Alexandria, and presumably they shared ideas and regarded allegorical interpretations as common property.

II.6.2c.iii *Philo classifies exegetes as allegorists and literalists.* D.M. Hay, who collected all of Philo's references to allegorists (1980) and to literalists (forthcoming), suggested that this two-fold classification may have been widely accepted because he nowhere defends it. Some studies have subdivided these two groups into the faithful and the apostate (e.g. S. Sowers 1965:21; P. Borgen 1984b:259ff.) although Hay (1980:47ff.) pointed out that Philo only refers to apostate allegorists in one passage (Migr.89–93) where they are represented as a minority group of extreme allegorists. These extremists are those "who, regarding laws in their literal sense in the light of symbols of matters belonging to the intellect, are over-punctilious about the latter while treating the former with easy-going neglect", so that they were in danger of neglecting the literal observance of the Sabbath and circumcision.

The literalists are sometimes sub-divided by scholars into literalists who accepted both allegory and literal interpretations, and extreme literalists who totally rejected allegory (S. Belkin 1940:27f.; S. Sowers 1965:21f.; Wolfson I:65ff.). This division provides a neat parallel with the allegorists and the extreme allegorists but has little basis in Philonic texts. None of Philo's "literalists" are portrayed as accepting allegory, and if they did, there would be little to distinguish them from Philo and other allegorists. He himself often gives literal interpretations alongside allegorical ones, and in his *Questions and Answers on Genesis and Exodus* he deliberately presents both types of interpretation side by side, giving equal weight to each, but he never calls himself a 'literalist'.

The literalists are criticised by Philo, not for treating the text literally, but for rejecting allegorical interpretations. He calls them narrow-minded "citizens of a petty state" (Somn.I.39), "uninitiated into allegory" (Fug.179). He does not "blame such persons, for perhaps the truth is with them also" but he exhorts them "not to halt there but to proceed onward to figurative interpretations" (Confus.190).

There does appear to be a group of literalists whom Philo does not treat so courteously. However these individuals did not reject allegory any more vehemently, but they used the literal sense of Scripture to ridicule it and thereby to reject it (Confus.2,6–8; Agric.157; Ebr.65; Mutat.61f.). J. Shroyer (1936) rejects the notion that these were Gentiles because the examples in Philo of the objections which they raised presuppose a good knowledge of the Bible, so they were more likely to be apostate Jews, like Philo's nephew Tiberius Julius Alexander.

Some scholars have tried to identify the literalists with the Palestinian rabbis, and with the Pharisees in particular (Wolfson I:59ff.; Belkin 1940:27f.) while others have entertained the idea that Philo supported the Sadducean camp (E.R. Goodenough 1940:104; R. Marcus 1948 reporting the views of the 16th C scholar Azariah dei Rossi), but these efforts have been generally abandoned.

The literalists have generally been identified with conservative Jews in Alexandria and J. Shroyer (1936) has suggested that *Questions and Answers* may have been written for them because these works do not contain any criticisms of their opinions. The popular nature of this work and the elitism which Philo displays with regard to allegorical interpretation suggests that the literalists represented the majority but that the allegorists enjoyed increasing influence and respect.

It is tempting to find in these literalists the source of Philo's techniques for the minute analysis of the text which have been compared to the later rabbinic middoth. They would then form the link by which Philo learned these techniques from Jewish sources, perhaps originating in Palestine. However these literalists are portrayed as being less concerned with the minor details of the text than Philo, who criticises them for not seeking the reason behind the use of four different words meaning "farmer" in Scripture (Agric.20f.,26ff.,42f.,57), while they criticise the allegorists for "petty quibbling" (γλισχρολογια) about words (Somn. II.301). Philo uses this same term himself to describe the activities of another group which he does not identify: "those who are afflicted with the incurable disease of conceit, with petty quibbling about expressions and words, and with juggling tricks of manners, and who measure holiness and piety by no other standard" (Cher.42). This, as Wolfson (1947 I:63) suggests, may well refer to the Pharisees, but it does not lead us to think that Philo regarded them as his tutors in exegesis.

II.6.2c.iv *The etymological source* postulated by Stein (1929) has been confirmed to a large extent by discoveries of examples of onomastica similar to those which Stein assumed to be Philo's sources (e.g. D.A. Rokeah 1968). These typically consist of a lists of Hebrew names transcribed into Greek letters with the meaning alongside in Greek. This is very similar to the form which Stein (1929:21) presupposed in his explanation of Philo's mistaken interpretation of 'Shashai' (Ezra 10.40) as "outside me" (ἐκτος μου) which he suggested was a misreading by Philo of an entry in his source which read something like:

שְׁשַׁי = ἐκτος [i.e. reading it as שִׁשִּׁי, 'sixth'].

Philo needed a subject for "outside" so he took the final yod as a pronoun. A.T. Hanson (1967) used this example, among others, to argue that Philo did know a little Hebrew, and that some of the etymologies may have originated with him.

The origin of this etymological source is important because the etymologies often rely on a minute examination of the text and on plays with words which are similar to the methods outlined in the middoth. One example is the interpretation of Abraham as πατηρ ἐκλεκτος ἠχους ('an elect father of sound' – Mutat.66ff.; Cher.4; Gig.62ff.; Q. Gen.III.43) which appears to be based on Notariqon, where each letter is the abbreviation of a word. Stein (1929 p58) suggested that it was based on a partial Notariqon, interpreting אברהם as אב בר רהם, where רהם is a variant of רעם, 'thunder'. A.T. Hanson (1967:136) suggested the more straight-forward אב בר הום. S. Belkin (1967:83ff.) related this exegesis to a true Notariqon in bShab.105a where אב המון, "father of many" (used of Abraham in Gen.17.4) is understood to refer to the father (אב) who is chosen (בחור), king (מלך), distinguished (ותיק) and faithful (נאמן) among the nations. He suggested that Philo could not have referred to Abraham as King of the nations without giving ammunition to the anti-Semites of Alexandria, so he used only 'father' and 'chosen' and presumably finished the name off with הום. Whichever of these explanations is correct, the exegesis of 'Abraham' does appear to be based on Notariqon or something similar. Although it is impossible to date this etymological source, it may well be very early, because the onomastic form is found in the Greek world from the 3rd C BCE (P.B.R. Forbes et al 1970).

II.6.2c.v Source critical studies which have identified other possible sources used by Philo have been reviewed by R.G. Hamerton-Kelly (1972), who proposed that a concerted effort should be made to verify these studies and to find other traditions within Philo. This proposal was revised by B.L. Mack (1978) and was accepted as an on-going project by the Philo Institute which published the journal Studia Philonica, and later became the basis of the Claremont Philo Project. The aim of the project is to map the development of exegesis in Alexandria by identifying the various strata of traditions used by Philo but, as D.T. Runia (1986:15ff.) points out, it is based on the circular method of identifying the exegetical forms outlined by Mack, searching for them, and then redefining the forms according to what is discovered during the search. There is, as yet, no way of tying these forms to any dates or groups of exegetes so it is unlikely that this project will help to establish the origins of Philo's exegetical techniques.

II.6.3 *The main assumption underlying Philo's exegeses* is that the whole of Scripture is inspired prophecy, and that its interpretation and translation must be equally inspired.

II.6.3a Philo regarded the whole Bible as prophecy, including the Law. Philo frequently calls Moses 'the prophet' and speaks of him as possessing the Spirit which was also given to the prophesying elders (Gig.24). He is regarded as "the chief of the prophets, ... the Lawgiver who speaks in oracles...who speaks prophet-like the holy laws... truly God-inspired" (Mutat.125–128, cf. Mos.2.187–292, Decal.175). Y. Amir (1988: 429–428) has pointed out that Philo uses the hieratic terminology of the Delphic Oracle to describe the inspiration of Scripture, so although he is able to speak of Moses as an independent author (e.g. Sacrif.94: "Why did [Moses]... represent God as ...?"), his words are inspired because the hierophant is considered as a human representative of his god.

S.G. Sowers (1965:40ff.) and others (H. Chadwick 1967:151, G.W.H. Lampe 1977:53ff., Y. Amir 1973). have suggested that Philo had an Hellenised view of inspiration. He regarded the OT writers to have been inspired in the same ecstatic way as a Greek poet, who "knowing not what he does is filled with inspiration as the reason withdraws and surrenders the citadel of the soul to a new visitor and tenant, the divine spirit, which plays upon the vocal organism and dictates words" (Spec.IV.49, cf. Her.265). This view is found in the *Timaeus* which, as D.T. Runia (1986) demonstrated, had a profound influence on Philo: "No man achieves true and inspired divination when in his rational mind" (71E).

Philo also considered exegetes to be inspired like the original prophets, so that exegesis comes directly from God and not via rules or methods. He describes his own experience of receiving an exegesis in Cher.27: "But there is a higher thought than these. I heard it from a voice in my own soul, which often times is God-possessed, and then divines where it does not know. This thought I will record in words if I can.". Other times he has been "filled with a corybantic frenzy and been unconscious of anything, place, persons present myself, words spoken, lines written" (Migr.35 cf. also Mos.2.265, Somn.2.252 and H. Burkhardt 1988: 156–171). The fact that the prophets' reason had been divinely supplanted meant that irrationality accompanied their message, so that the message itself may best be derived by a third party who interprets the oracle, himself acting as a messenger of God (Timaeus 72A – G.W.H. Lampe 1977: 54).

R.M. Grant (1957: 34ff.) has pointed out that the Hellenistic model of inspiration also explains the Philonic 'rules' of allegory. Prophetic inspiration is marked by irrationality, and therefore requires inspired allegorical exegesis in order to understand it fully. Irrational prophetic messages in the pagan world could be recognised by mistakes in grammar, superfluous words and contradictions (H. Krämer 1968 VI:789) and therefore Philo may have used the 'rules' to highlight similar elements in the Scriptures. Whenever unacceptable nonsense such as mythological elements, anthropomorphisms, contradictions, grammatical difficulties such as spelling errors, strange sentence constructions or even poor style such as needless repetition occurred in Scripture, they indicated to Philo that prophetic irrationality was involved at this point and therefore that allegory had to be used in order to extract the inspired but obscured message.

Philo certainly felt himself to be the channel of inspired exegesis at times, and from the high regard he showed for the exegesis of fellow allegorists, it may be assumed that he regarded them as equally inspired.

II.6.3b Philo also regarded the translators of the Septuagint to be inspired. He consistently used the LXX, although there is some debate concerning exactly which version (H.E. Ryle 1894, R. Marcus 1950, P. Katz 1950, G.E. Howard 1973a)

He interprets individual words and phrases of the Greek text even when they differ from the Hebrew (e.g. Mos.I.158 re Ex.20.21, Moses *entered* the darkness; Her.243 re Gen.15.11, Abraham *sat among* the birds; Abr.234 re Gen.14.21, the spoils are *horses*). Such elementary errors would not have been tolerated by Philo's Jewish readership unless they believed the Greek translation to be inspired in its own right, as Philo did. Philo's belief in the inspiration of the Greek translation is evident from his simple acceptance of the story of the 70 translators employed by Ptolemy and his own comments that these scholars were enthused with divine inspiration like prophets and were prompted by God (Mos.II.25ff.). C. Perrot (1988:155) suggests that the Greek was actually read instead of the Hebrew in the synagogues, because the Alexandrian Jews "regard them [both versions] with admiration and respect like two sisters, or rather, as one and the same work" (Mos.2.40).

Philo may even have regarded himself as sufficiently inspired to make small changes in the reading of the text, because he frequently diverges from every known variant. P. Katz (1950) concluded that the few 'aberrant' readings were later emendations because they tend to agree with the later Aquila text and because where these readings occur, the commentary is still based on the LXX. G.E. Howard (1973a) pointed out that the opposite is often the case, with the commentary based on the 'aberrant' readings, and suggested that these readings may have been part of Philo's text because they show similarities with the pre-Aquila καίγε text identified by Barthélemy (1953, 1963) in the Qumran Minor Prophets. However Borgen (1984a:123) has pointed out that Philo is so free in his quotations that he cannot be used as a source for text criticism.

Philo's canon appears to be similar to the later Septuagint, except that he used the Pentateuch almost exclusively, unlike the rabbis who employed the whole Bible to illustrate their comments on the Pentateuch. *Biblia Patristica* (J. Allenbach 1975- Suppl.) takes 65 pages to list Philo's references and allusions to the OT, but less than two of these are concerned with non-Pentateuchal texts. To explain this lack of non-Pentateuchal texts W.L. Knox (1940) argued that the rest of the OT had not yet been translated into Greek, F.H. Colson (1940) replied that Philo 'specialised' in the Pentateuch, and Y. Amir (1973) suggested that there were no Haftarah readings in Alexandrian synagogues. Perhaps this phenomenon is more easily explained by the assumption underlying much of Greek literature that 'the oldest is best' (B. Winter 1988:ch.11). The greater antiquity of the Pentateuch than Plato not only means that Moses can be said to be a source for the Greek philosophers (as Aristobulus (2.4; 3.1) and Josephus (C. Ap.2.281) also argued) but it also means that Moses was very highly regarded, being called "the all wise" (πανσοφος – Deter.126; Poster.28,169; Agric.20,43; Plant.27 etc). However it may be that Philo, like the rabbis merely regarded the Pentateuch as more authoritative than the Prophets and Writings, though not as more inspired because he does use the rest of Scripture, and because not even the Sadducees rejected the inspiration of the Prophets and Writings (R.T. Beckwith 1988:73–75).

II.6.4 *In conclusion*, Philo appears to have had eclectic tastes, collecting interpretations from a number of different sources. He was familiar with the work of the allegorists and literalists, Jews and Greeks, the written Torah and probably the oral halakah and aggadah. His stated intention was to bring together the life and teachings of Moses "both from the sacred books... and from some of the elders of the nation; for I always interwove the narrated things with the things read" (Mos.I.4).

It is difficult to know whether Philo added much of his own original material to his collection of traditions and interpretations. One cannot assume that interpretations which are not attributed to other allegorists or literalists are his own, because, as Hay's careful survey has revealed (1980:44f.), many interpretations which he attributes to another exegete in one place are repeated elsewhere without any such attribution. It seems likely that Philo's own contribution amounts to very little because the obvious delight with which he does record an original interpretation suggests that such originality is rare (e.g. Cher.27).

Similarly the exegetical methods which he used are unlikely to be original. Many of these methods have been shown to have Greek origins and others can be found in the Jewish etymological source. It is perhaps meaningless to try to draw distinct dividing lines between Greek and Jewish exegetical methods in Alexandria. Even though Philo clearly regards Jewish learning (as symbolised by Sarah) to be superior to the Egyptian learning (symbolised by Hagar), he does not hesitate to use Greek philosophy to understand Scripture or to discover philosophical teaching within Scripture. He never defends this mixture of Jewish and Greek traditions, and presumably it was normal practice among his contemporaries.

Philo's methods of minute examination of the text, which are similar to the later middoth, may have been learnt from the literalists, from the Etymological sources, or from Jewish oral traditions. All these three sources are so closely related that distinctions are meaningless. However it cannot be concluded that Philo learned them from Greek sources because, although D. Daube (1936, 1949, 1953, 1961, 1980a) and S. Lieberman (1950) have put a strong case showing that similar methods had been known among the Greeks for more than a hundred years, Philo himself used them in conjunction with Jewish traditions such as the Etymologies. P. Borgen (1984a:135) highlighted a comment made by Philo which suggests that he recognised his indebtedness to traditional Jewish learning for these exegetical methods: following an exposition of Gen.2.10–14 which has striking parallels with tSanh.8.7–9, he says that the exposition is based on a tradition received from "those who have studied more deeply than others the laws of Moses and who examine their contents with all possible minuteness" (Opif.77f.).

Philo therefore knew many exegetical techniques which were similar to those outlined in the later lists of middoth, as well as others which were not. However we cannot conclude that these techniques were brought to Palestine from Alexandria or vice versa because, as S. Sandmel (1962) has rightly cautioned, parallels do not necessarily indicate dependence. Perhaps we should take note of the third option which Sandmel favoured (1971:10), that both Palestine and Alexandria learned from each other. This is certainly what Philo would have advocated.

However Philo's exegeses appear to have made very little impact on rabbinic literature and he is unmentioned until the 16th C when Azariah dei Rossi surveyed his literature and found much that was useful but said that "this man is indeed suspect in my eyes of not being wholly orthodox" and concluded that he was probably a Boethusian (R. Marcus 1948).

Therefore it seems likely that Philo's allegory came from the Greeks and his methods of minute examination of the text from the Jews and possibly also the Greeks. The Palestinian scribes did not consciously learn from him or from his Alexandrian contemporaries, although they must have been aware of these kinds of methods because they gradually made them their own.

His assumptions about Scriptures are 'Inspirational' because he regards the whole of Scripture as inspired prophecy, and regards allegorical exegetes and the translators of the Septuagint to be equally inspired.

II.7 Exegetical Techniques and Assumptions in Non-Scribal Traditions

The term 'non-scribal' encompasses many different groups, only some of which have been studied in any depth with regard to their exegesis. However those groups contemporary to the scribes which have been studied share similarities in their attitude towards Scripture, which may be broadly described as 'Inspirational'.

II.7.1 The Inspirational attitude can be characterised by a set of five assumptions, the first two of which are shared by the Nomological approach, while the other three negate the remaining Nomological assumptions:

1. Scripture is totally self-consistent.
2. Every detail in Scripture is significant.
3. Scripture may be interpreted contrary to or without regard to context.
4. Scripture has secondary meaning(s) independent of its plain meaning.
5. Variant texts and translations are valid forms of Scripture.

The Inspirational approach interprets the whole of Scripture as though it were prophecy. This implies the same belief in the self-consistency and significance of every detail of the text which characterises the Nomological approach to scripture.

However the Inspirational approach differs from the Nomological approach in that it frequently disregards the context in its search for secondary meanings, and interprets variant text forms and translations. Hidden or secondary meanings are found both through allegories and through Ultra-literal and non-contextual interpretations of words and phrases, by the inspiration (it is held) of the same spirit which inspired the prophecy. Exegeses based on variant texts and translations are regarded as equally authoritative because the copyists and translators were assumed to be inspired by the same spirit.

This Inspirational approach can be seen especially in the Qumran texts and Philo, but also appears in Josephus and the Dorshe Reshumot/ Hamurot. There is some evidence for this approach in Apocalyptic and Wisdom literature, but the Samaritan literature, and the ancient texts and translations tend more towards the Nomological approach.

II.7.1.1&2 *Scripture is totally self-consistent and every detail is significant.*

These assumptions are seen most clearly in the minute examination of the text by means of the special exegetical techniques. The exegetical techniques used at Qumran and Alexandria are similar both to each other and to those found in the LXX, Targumim, and in what M. Fishbane calls the 'mantological' interpretations throughout the Ancient Near East. They are also related to the later middoth but there is no evidence that Qumran exegetes or Philo restricted themselves to any defined set of exegetical techniques.

Although the exegesis is inspired, it is based on the minute examination of the text. This is far more evident in Qumran literature than in Philo, but probably only because more detailed analysis is still awaited for much Philonic exegesis. The etymologies in Philo, which have received a relatively large amount of attention, have been found to be based on the same minute examination of the text as found at Qumran, and Philo's boast that allegorists take far more note of small details in the text than do the literalists (Agric.27f.; Somn.2.301) should perhaps be taken more seriously (cf. II.6.1c).

II.7.1.3 *Scripture may be interpreted contrary to or without regard to context.*

Neither Philo nor Qumran exegetes show any concern for the context of the texts they interpret, in spite of the fact that both commonly use the commentary form and seek to interpret whole books of scripture.

Philo is quite happy to discuss a historic person or event as though it represented a philosophic truth or metaphysical reality which is completely unrelated to the historic or textual context found in scripture. This does not mean that he ignores the surrounding text, because he often draws in elements from before or after his text to illustrate a point, but the overall interpretation is completely different from the subject of the context.

Qumran exegetes are seemingly impervious to the general flow of a passage, finding so much detail in their atomistic analysis of the text that they ignore the overall context. The original meaning of the "Chaldeans" and the history behind Habakkuk's prophecy is never discussed in pHab and the context of the digging of the well in Num.21.18 is completely disregarded (cf. II.5.2b).

II.7.1.4 *Scripture has secondary meaning(s) independent of its plain meaning.*

Philo and the Qumran exegetes make extensive use of secondary meanings of the text, and although they often regard these as representing the most important interpretation of the text, they do not invalidate the plain or primary meaning. However, although they never reject the plain meaning, they often attached little importance to it. Philo often regarded the plain meaning as being trivial in the first place, especially with regard to mythological or even historical elements (e.g. Plant.32ff.; Ebr.144) and even certain elements of the Law (Somn.1.94). The Qumran exegetes seem to have completely disregarded the idea that the primary meaning of Habakkuk and other prophets might have referred to some other part of history than their own, and even if they had acknowledged this possibility they would probably have regarded *that* interpretation as a secondary meaning. Therefore one might say that both the Qumran exegetes and Philo were searching for what was, in their eyes, the primary meaning of the text, while regarding the author's original intentions as being of secondary importance.

Inspiration was the key to interpretation for both the allegorists of Alexandria and the Qumran exegetes. Philo regarded himself as an inspired exegete, and the Teacher of Righteousness was given his interpretation from God, probably based on the pattern of Daniel (cf. II.5.3a). However Philo evidently felt that his fellow allegorists were equally inspired and quotes their interpretations very extensively. Similarly at Qumran, although the sect held the Teacher of Righteousness in high regard, they also expected new hidden truths to be revealed to any member of the community.

II.7.1.5 *Variant manuscripts and translations are valid forms of Scripture.*

Inspiration guaranteed both the text of Scripture and its translation. Philo regarded the seventy translators of the LXX to be as inspired as the original authors of Scripture, and was happy to base his interpretation on the Greek text. The Qumran sect preserved many different families of OT text, including those of the MT and LXX, using whichever variant best fitted the interpretation which they felt had been revealed to them. There was no need for a textus receptus because each text was inspired and valuable.

II.7.2 Similar conclusions can be made concerning the exegeses of the Dorshe Reshumot/Hamurot (Dorshe R/H) and of Josephus but with less certainty, because very few exegeses of the former have survived and few of the latter appear to be original. The Dorshe R/H seemed to revel in secondary interpretations and took no regard of the context, and the same tendency is seen to a lesser extent in Josephus, especially in his allegorical expositions. He regarded the whole OT as prophetic, including Moses, to whom he ascribed "a book preserved in the temple, containing a prediction of future events in accordance with all that has come and is coming to pass" (Ant.4.303), and the historians, whom he regarded as inspired prophets (C. Ap.1.37). Josephus used more than one text tradition and presumably regarded them as equally inspired, and he appears to have relied on prophetic inspiration for exegesis and recognised prophetic exegesis in others (e.g. the Essenes –

War.2.159), although he usually used μαντις rather than προφητης for non-canonical prophets (D.E. Aune 1982 has found two exceptions).

II.7.3 The Apocalyptic writings fit into the Inspirational model better than the Nomological, because they have a concept of continuing inspiration by dreams, visions, and angels which help to interpret the OT text (D.S. Russell 1964:158–69). Wisdom literature also appears to fit into this mould because Wisdom herself inspires the exegete and "pours out teaching as prophecy" (Sira.24.33 cf. 39.6–8; Wisd.8.8). Fishbane (1985:539f.) traces the concept of inspired exegesis back into the OT text itself.

II.7.4 The Samaritans appear to follow the Nomological approach, although evidence from their literature is late and cannot be given much weight, however conservative their exegetes were. They too used the method of amplification found in ancient texts and translations, but the claims that they emended their text to suit doctrinal differences may be false, as suggested by support for their text found at Qumran (S. Lowy 1977:123ff.). Their exegetes were always very careful to cite the text exactly (Lowy 1977:100) and they never used Al Tiqré or Qeré (Lowy 1977:302f.,512). They very rarely used allegory (Lowy finds only one example, 1977:68ff.) or non-Peshat exegesis (Lowy 1977:108–20, 318f.). They followed R. Ishmael's principle that Scripture speaks with human language, while using middoth which were similar to his (R. Bóid 1988a:623f.), as well as Nomological principles such as No Redundancy (Lowy 1977:105f., 334f.).

II.7.5 The ancient texts and translations may lean towards the Nomological approach, but problems of dating and translation technique make any conclusions difficult.

II.7.6 In conclusion, while the scribes had a Nomological approach to scripture, which may have been shared by Samaritan exegetes, their contemporaries had a rather different approach which may be termed 'Inspirational', because it relies on prophetic inspiration for exegesis, assumes the prophetic inspiration of copyists and translators, and interprets the whole of Scripture as though it were prophecy.

II.8 Comparison of Non-Scribal with Scribal Exegesis

In Part 1 scribal exegesis was found to be characterised by a Nomological approach which regards all Scripture as law, and in this second Part the exegesis of their contemporaries has been found to be characterised by an

Inspirational approach which regards all Scripture as prophecy. Although this is undoubtedly in some regards an over-simplification, these two approaches to scripture appear to have co-existed in Judaism before 70CE.

The Nomological approach can be characterised by a set of five exegetical assumptions:

1. Scripture is totally self-consistent.
2. Every detail in Scripture is significant.
3. Scripture is understood according to its context.
4. Scripture does not have any secondary meaning.
5. There is only one valid text form of Scripture.

The Inspirational approach can be characterised by a similar set of assumptions, which differ only with regard to the last three:

3. Scripture may be interpreted contrary to or without regard to context.
4. Scripture has secondary meaning(s) independent of its plain meaning.
5. Variant manuscripts and translations are valid forms of Scripture.

II.8.1 *Why did the scribes restrict their exegesis* to the context, to the primary sense and to a single text form of Scripture? Without these restrictions it would have been far simpler to refute their opponents' arguments and to find exegetical bases for their halakic and theological doctrines. Two possible reasons for this restriction will be explored: the literalistic stance of their opponents, and their ignorance of 'Inspirational' exegesis. Both of these will be rejected in favour of an underlying understanding of the Scriptures as law rather than prophecy. The exegetical assumptions of both the scribes and their contemporaries were coherent and understandable, so they could understand each others' methods without feeling constrained to adopt them.

II.8.1.1 The scribes' opponents may have forced the scribes to restrict themselves by refusing to accept any types of exegesis which they considered to be invalid. This may help to explain why their reticence to use such methods disappeared when the main opposing groups within Judaism, the Sadducees and Pharisees, and the Houses, resolved their differences or disappeared into obscurity after 70 CE.

However, even if the Shammaites and/or Sadducees demanded Peshat interpretations which took note of the context and used only the standard text, why should this create restrictions on the named authorities who were not in debate with either group? In a similar situation in later years, when the rabbis rediscovered contextual exegesis in response to Karaite opposition, this did not result in the complete disappearance of Derash interpretations.

II.8.1.2 Alternatively, the scribes may have been ignorant of 'Inspirational' exegesis which may have been more in tune with Hellenistic ideas, such as the exegetical techniques used by Homeric commentators, or the inspired exegesis of Delphic priests.

II.8.1.2a *The scribes were not ignorant of Inspirational exegesis.* There was a constant traffic of people and ideas between Palestine and Alexandria. Although the overwhelming evidence from M. Hengel (1974,1980, cf. M. Smith 1956) may have to be tempered by the fact that the two communities tended to ignore each other (L.H. Feldman 1986), they cannot have been ignorant of each other's ideas. However, even if the rabbis were completely deaf to Alexandrian allegorists they could not have ignored the ideas of the Palestinians such as the Qumran sect and the Dorshe Reshumot/Hamurot.

It is even possible that Hillel and/or his teachers came from Alexandria. Daube (1949 : 3) suggested that Hillel's teachers Shemaiah and Abtalion may have come from Egypt because they used Egyptian measurements and were said to be proselytes (mEd.1.3; bYom.71b). Hillel spent some time in Alexandria (bBM.104a; tKet.4.9) and A. Kaminka (1926) even thinks that Hillel was Egyptian. A. Guttmann (1950:470) pointed out that Hillel's middoth are "a middle road between the literal interpretation of the Bible applied by the Sadducees and the allegorical interpretations applied later by Philo" and therefore suggests that he emphasised them in order to counter the Alexandrian methods.

Neither could the scribes have been ignorant of the different versions and translations of Scripture. The Alexandrians were proud of their Greek translation, and inaugurated an annual feast in its honour (Mos.2.41), while the presence of LXX fragments at Qumran and its almost universal use by Christians suggests that it was widely known in Palestine and throughout the diaspora. Although the Rabbinic discussions of the LXX variants appear only in Amoraic sources (e.g. bMeg.9a – cf. E. Tov 1984a) they include variants which no longer exist in any extant LXX versions, so they are likely to be based on very old traditions.

Nor could the scribes have been ignorant of the possibility of copyist's errors. In the days before printing, errors were a fact of life, so that some sages allowed a copyist up to three errors per page (M. Bar-Ilan 1988:30). Even the standard texts in the Temple were known to contain variants (yTaan.4.2; ARNb.46; Sifré Deut.356). To act like Ben Hé Hé, who avoided emending the text when a scribal error was probably the cause of the problem (bHag.9b) shows heroic faith.

II.8.1.2b The scribes also understood the concept of Scripture as prophecy. They regarded Moses as a prophet, mainly on the basis of Deut.34.10, Hos.12.13 and especially Deut.18.15ff. (H.M. Teeple 1957), and included the historians among the Former and Latter Prophets, because their function was to interpret the Books of Moses. However prophecy ended with Malachi and the Great Assembly, and the Holy Spirit departed from Israel (tSot.13.2–4; bSanh.11a), leaving the Torah to be interpreted by mere men. Therefore they treated Scripture as a fixed and finished legal document and not as living prophecy, to be interpreted primarily by means of reason, and not by inspiration. Nevertheless later rabbis could consider the rabbinic body to be inspired (cf. bBB.12a), and the sources indicate that even before 70 CE they were familiar with related topics such as prophetic utterance and the Holy Spirit.

The scribes were not ignorant or unpractised in prophetic utterance or in the interpretation of dreams and signs. The later rabbis were suspicious of mysticism and suppressed many of the visionary and Inspirational influences but there is evidence that this flourished even in early Tannaitic times (G. Scholem 1960; C.A. Newsom 1987). Josephus records that Pharisees had visions of the future (Ant.14.172–176; 15.3f.; 17.41–45) and that Scribes interpreted portents (War.6.5.3(291)), and the Talmud has an ancient tradition that "there were 24 interpreters of dreams in Jerusalem" (bBer.55b). However these prophecies and dreams were not used to interpret Scripture or vice versa, unlike the prophecies of the Essenes (War.2.159) and the dream interpretations of the rabbis (bBer.56a–58a – A. Finkel 1963:359f.).

The Holy Spirit was an important entity for the rabbis, although it is difficult to know exactly what their attitude towards it was before 70 CE. Their successors in Yavneh were in dispute concerning the relevance of the Bath Qol (the heavenly echo of the voice of the Holy Spirit) and of prophetic revelations to their exegesis and halakah. R. Eliezer b.Hyrcanus did not discount further prophetic revelations, even if they contained the injunction to temporarily ignore commands of the Torah (Sifré Deut.175) but R. Joshua (whose opinion was followed by later rabbis) said: "The Torah is not in heaven and we do not hearken to the Bath Qol" (references and comment in E.E. Urbach 1975 I:301f.). Although the Bath Qol was important in finally resolving the problem of the two Houses (bErub.13b), it was later emphasised that the Bath Qol was an unnecessary part of this decision (bBer.51b–52a; bErub.6b–7a; bYeb.14a; bPes.114a), and although the Bath Qol was occasionally listened to with regard to exegesis or halakah (e.g. bMeg.29a) on other occasions it was flatly rejected (bBM.59b).

It is very difficult to say whether or not the scribes accepted that the Holy Spirit provided any contemporary inspiration. Perhaps the clearest indication that they did is the saying of Hillel that "The Holy Spirit is upon them; if they are not prophets, they are sons of prophets" (tPis.4.13). The context is the occurrence of Passover on a Sabbath when Hillel, having shown that the Passover overrides the Sabbath, is asked what should be done about the common people who may not know about this ruling. Hillel answers that they will know what to do because they have the Holy Spirit. This is confirmed when the people all turn up with their animals and their sacrificial knives, which they kept hidden in case the temple authorities (who presumably are not similarly inspired) turned them away. However the Holy Spirit is here merely confirming what Hillel has already painstakingly proved by scriptural exegesis and tradition. Even though Hillel was himself "worthy that the shechinah should rest on him" (bSanh.11a; tSot.13.3) he was remembered not for his inspired exegesis but for his rationalistic exegetical techniques. These techniques were used by the scholars, but the common people had to rely on the Holy Spirit.

Therefore the scribes were aware of the different aspects of the Inspirational approach and yet rejected it. Their Nomological approach to Scripture was a conscious and consistent viewpoint which was regarded as superior to the Inspirational approach because the age of inspired prophecy and prophetic exegesis were past, and the Torah now resided with men, to be interpreted by men. They accepted some limited activity of the Holy Spirit, which inspired dreams, visions and their interpretations, and which may even have inspired the ignorant when they did not know correct halakah. However they rejected any appeal to the activity of the Holy Spirit in deciding halakic rulings or in the interpretation of Scripture.

II.8.2 *Similarly the contemporaries of the scribes were not ignorant of Nomological exegesis,* and they did not unthinkingly accept a concept of inspiration which flaunted all common sense and intellectual investigation. They regarded the Inspirational approach as intellectually and spiritually superior to the Nomological approach to Scripture.

Philo often referred to the literalists who interpreted only the plain sense of Scripture and who did not "proceed onwards to figurative interpretations" (Confus.190). He regarded them not so much wrong as "narrow-minded" (Somn.1.39) and "uninitiated" (Fug.179). The Qumran exegetes however did regard themselves in opposition to the scribes, and their reference to them as "interpreters of smooth/easy things" may be in conscious contrast to the allegorical Dorshe Hamurot or "interpreters of heavy/difficult things" (C. Roth 1960a).

The belief that copyists and translators were inspired did not result in a blind rejection of scholarship and textual criticism (such as it was at the time). It is likely that at Qumran there was some understanding that variants can originate from scribal errors, because the texts contain corrections and marginal emendations, and perhaps some of their variants were attempts to recover the original text. Even Aristeas, who is attempting to defend the divine origin of the LXX, says that the translators "reached agreement among themselves by comparing versions" (302) and Josephus says that they "set to work as ambitiously and painstakingly as possible to make the translation accurate" (Ant.12.104).

Neither did the concept of inspired exegesis result in unthinking acceptance of any and every interpretation. Philo normally backed up his allegories with many reasons, and the constant addition of further parallels with the text are not always in order to develop the allegory but to demonstrate that it is founded on Scripture itself, even if it was discovered by the aid of inspiration. The Qumran exegeses have been found to be based on minute analyses of the text, and Philo even criticises the literalists for not taking the wording of the text seriously enough.

Therefore the Inspirational approach was a conscious and consistent application of the principle that Scripture is to be regarded as inspired prophecy. This was regarded not as a replacement but a transcendence of the Nomological approach, because although the literal interpretation was still accepted and actively sought, the meaning revealed by inspired atomistic or allegoristic exegesis was perceived as having far greater value.

II.8.3 *The Nomological and Inspirational views are both coherent* and self-sufficient. Although it was probably true that the Nomological approach to Scripture was suited to an atmosphere of constant debate, and that the Inspirational approach was suited to a Hellenistic environment, these Jewish exegetes were not simply accepting the assumptions of those they lived with. Both the Nomological and Inspirational approach to Scripture were founded on an underlying understanding about the nature of Scripture itself, as being law or prophecy respectively.

The Nomological approach is logically coherent and understandable if one regards the whole of Scripture as law, drawn up by the divine legislator. Such a law would be totally consistent, using no superfluous or ambiguous language, with everything set in its correct context, and would of course exist in only one valid form.

The Inspirational approach is also logically coherent and understandable if one regards the whole of Scripture as inspired prophecy. Such prophecy would be self-consistent and perfect in detail, but would not be restricted to only one level of meaning. New meanings would be revealed for every situation and every time, hidden in individual words or phrases isolated from their contexts, or in pictures and narratives which can be interpreted like inspired visions or dreams. The same inspiration would also ensure that any copyists or translators of the sacred text would be protected from error, and would even suggest new nuances and meanings, or encourage the insertion of explanatory words or stories, which would become further sources of inspired exegesis.

The scribes and their contemporaries were not ignorant of each others' approaches to Scripture, but they regarded their own as superior. The scribes understood the concept of inspired prophecy and exegesis, but regarded it as belonging to a past age, and their contemporaries understood the concept of a perfect law and its interpretation but regarded their exegesis as having transcended it.

II.8.4 Josephus in one sense marks the interface between the Nomological and the Inspirational approaches to Scripture. He has clearly been influenced by both camps, preserving Pharisaic halakah and theology (Thackeray 1930: xiii; 1929:97) together with Philonic allegory and etymologies, and his typologies may be seen as dependent upon both.

Typology differs from allegory in that allegory finds a secondary meaning in a text without regard to the original meaning or context, while typology treats the original as a historical verity which is both the basis and confirmation of the secondary application (see R.P.C. Hanson 1959:7). Although this definition goes back to the Antiochene school (J.N.D. Kelly 1958:69ff., W. Horbury 1988:766), it is not always so obvious in early Jewish or NT writings (J. Barr 1966:103–13).

D. Daube, in his examination of Josephus' typologies, asks why this method occurs only in certain Jewish literature (1980b:23):

"To the question what motivates this procedure, a relatively simple answer is: the idea that God leads his chosen to their goal by a recognisable route, progress and also disruption *(Heils- und Unheilsgeschichte)* being manifest in a consistent fashion. But we may then enquire further: why is it that this idea has such a hold, with no parallel in other cultures? The explanation seems to lie in its initial legal affiliation. The earliest deliverance drawn on as a precedent, both in its entirety and in respect of a good many details, is that from Egypt; and it always remains the most prominent model."

Daube may have over-emphasised the uniqueness of typology to Israel, but this does not affect his conclusion that Jewish typology is grounded in Nomological assumptions, as exemplified by the use made of Exile imagery. When history is seen as part of God's legal code, every event becomes a legal precedent which God can be expected to follow in the future, so history becomes an insight into the present and the future.

Typology dominates the New Testament and, if messianic movements are an indication of popular thought, it also dominated pre-70 CE Palestinian Judaism, when false prophets lead people back into the Wilderness (War 2.258f.; Ant.20.167f.,188; cf. Mt.24.26), claimed that the Jordan would divide (Ant.20.97f.), waited on the Mount of Olives (War 2.261–3), and claimed that Jerusalem's walls would fall down (Ant.20.169–172), and when baptising sects gathered in the Wilderness and used immersion in the Jordan as a sign of a new beginning.

II.8.5 In conclusion, these two approaches to Scripture, the Nomological and Inspirational, both represented coherent and understandable systems of exegesis which could co-exist without losing any of their distinctive features. They had no reason to fear each other because both had reasons for believing that they were superior to the other.

However the general population might not be expected to remain firmly in either camp, and at the interface of the Nomological and the Inspirational views typology prospered. This involved both the Nomological assumption that God's activity in the past sets a precedent by which He works in the future, and the Inspirational assumption that new exegeses will always make the Scripture contemporary to each generation.

As seen in the comparison of the scribes with the rabbis after 70 CE, the Inspirational and Nomological approaches met and merged in the academies, although there were always some who had misgivings about the non-Peshat methods.

III.1 Conclusion

This study has examined the exegetical techniques and assumptions used by the the scribes (a term used to indicate the predecessors of the rabbis before 70 CE), as revealed by their exegeses preserved in Tannaitic sources. These exegeses were found in the traditions of named individuals living before 70 CE, in the Pharisee-Sadducee disputes and in the House disputes. These have been compared with the exegeses of their successors (the rabbis), their predecessors (represented by the ancient texts and translations) and their contemporaries (particularly at Qumran and Alexandria but also the Dorshe Reshumot/Hamurot and Josephus).

The analysis in Part 1 of the scribal exegeses found five main assumptions which characterised their approach to Scripture as 'Nomological', i.e. they interpreted Scripture as though it were a fixed and perfect law. They therefore regarded every word of Scripture as consistent and equally important, to be interpreted according to its context and according to its primary meaning only, and recognised a single valid text form. These practices were found to contrast with those of later rabbis who frequently ignored the context, found secondary meanings hidden in the text and who proposed alternate readings of the text for the purpose of exegesis.

The analysis in Part 2 of the exegesis of Jewish contemporaries of these scribes found that they largely followed an 'Inspirational' approach to Scripture. They interpreted Scripture as though it were a living prophecy inspired by a Spirit which continued to inspire its exegetes, copyists and translators. The Inspirational approach could also be summarised by five assumptions similar to those of the Nomological approach, the first two of which were identical but the last three of which were opposed. The Inspirational approach allowed the inspired exegete to interpret with disregard to the context, to find several levels of meaning, and to interpret variant manuscripts and translations.

Although these different approaches may have developed in relative isolation, the scribes and their contemporaries were well aware of each other's methods and assumptions, and both had reasons to believe that their approach was superior to the other.

This summary of all Jewish exegesis before 70 CE into two approaches which can each be characterised by a set of five assumptions is of course a gross simplification and generalization of several immensely complex and diverse bodies of literature. However these two approaches are significantly represented in the exegeses of this period, and are sufficiently different to warrant clear differentiation.

These results are unexpected and conflict with the generally held assumption that the scribes, like the rabbis after 70 CE, frequently interpreted the OT without regard to context, found hidden secondary meanings by means of allegory or atomistic exegesis, and temporarily changed the reading of the text to suit their exegesis.

The absence of these types of exegesis has been demonstrated not only by their total absence from more than 100 examples of scribal exegetical argument, but also by demonstrating that the scribes had a coherent approach to Scripture which entails the rejection of such methods.

Although these results conflict with generally held assumptions, they do not conflict with previous research.

III.2 *Previous studies* have suggested that despite the similarities between the exegeses of Qumran exegetes, Philo, Samaritans and the scribes, there are also fundamental differences in their approach to exegesis and to the use of glosses and emendations in textual transmission. An independent comparison of fundamental approaches to exegesis in various Jewish societies of the first century was carried out by S. Lowy (1969) who suggested a three-fold distinction between the Peshat of the Pharisees, the allegory of some Alexandrians and the literalism of the Sadducees and Samaritans. He also proposed that Qumran used all three types of exegesis because they used all three families of OT text (MT, LXX and Samaritan). This present study does not provide enough data to defend the distinct characteristics of the Sadducees and Samaritans but it does confirm the distinctiveness of Pharisees from Alexandrian allegorists.

The existence of standard texts before 70 CE was defended by B. Albrektson (1978) against the prevailing theory that the crisis at 70 CE prompted the selection of a single text and the editing of all texts towards that standard (e.g. G.G. Porton 1979, written 1974). He pointed out that before 70 CE there were scribes employed to check the accuracy of texts (bKet.106a) and that the MT does not have the characteristics of a 'corrected' text because it is full of inconsistent spellings and obvious scribal errors. Even M.H. Segal's (1953) bold assertion that the isolation of MT dates back to Maccabean times finds support at Qumran (E. Tov 1982).

E. Tov (1982 cf. 1988a) has also demonstrated a fundamental difference between the copyist traditions of Qumran and of the pre-70 CE Jerusalem authorities, the former allowing the accumulation of variants and non-standard texts, while the latter preserved only the standard text. He criticised the common practice of classifying texts into the three text 'families' of the LXX,

Samaritan Pentateuch and MT, because there are many texts at Qumran with unique readings which do not fit into any family, and because texts which contain LXX variants are just as likely also to contain Samaritan variants. He concluded that the vast majority of texts cannot be placed in any family, but that the proto-Masoretic texts stand out as qualitatively different, being characterised by fewer variants and a different copyist tradition. Tov suggests that this is because they have been imported from Jerusalem, and that they reflect the far more conservative copyist tradition of the Temple scribes in contrast to the diaspora and Qumran where they were willing to add glosses and preserve new variants.

The co-existence of two conflicting approaches to Scripture within Palestine, is implied by D.A. Koch's conclusions (1986) that Paul used diaspora exegesis and by M. Hengel's suggestion (1983b:53f.) that he was a member of a hellenistic synagogue in Jerusalem where the Greek Scriptures were used. The acceptance of inspired exegesis in almost all pre-70 CE Jewish groups, inside and outside Palestine, and its rejection by the scribes, has recently been highlighted by M.N.A. Bockmuehl's survey of revelation theology throughout the Jewish world contemporary with the NT (1987, cf. R. Meyer 1968).

S.P. Brock (1988 based on J. Barr 1979) has outlined two types of translation technique in the ancient world, the literal and the free, which mirror the two approaches to Scripture found in this study. He also suggests that two approaches to Scripture could have originated as separate answers to the problem of differences between the LXX and the MT. Main-stream Judaism on the one hand revised the LXX towards the MT (the Nomological approach) while Aristeas and Philo declared that the LXX had equal value to the MT because the translators were prophets (the Inspirational approach).

III.3 Therefore implications of the present study, such as the Peshat nature of scribal exegesis, the early isolation of the MT at Jerusalem due to the scribal insistence on a standard text, and the co-existence of two independent approaches to Scripture and exegesis, have been corroborated by independent studies.

Other, more far-reaching implications, have yet to be explored. These involve mainly the NT, which was presumably influenced by both Nomological and Inspirational approaches to Scripture, and the early rabbinic and Christian literatures which both demonstrate in some ways the tensions between these two approaches as they gradually merged.

For example, the relative absence of non-Peshat exegeses in scribal traditions necessitates a reassessment of the importance of 'midrashic' methods in the NT. B. Lindars has perhaps started this in his forthcoming *Theology of the Epistle to the Hebrews* which concludes that Hebrews uses no typology or allegory.

III.4 In conclusion, the differences between the exegesis of the scribes and their contemporaries can be summarised by their approach to Scripture. The scribes regarded scripture as fixed law while their contemporaries regarded it as living prophecy. This difference resulted in the scribes interpreting scripture according to its context, without looking for spiritual or secondary meanings, and accepting only one standard text as valid, while their contemporaries expected new secondary meanings to be revealed which might be completely independent of the original context and expected copyists and translators to be inspired so that all versions and text traditions were of equal value.

The distinctions between these two approaches to Scripture began to become blurred and disappear after 70 CE when the rabbis inherited both Nomological and Inspirational principles.

Ap.1 Appendix 1: The Lists of Middoth.

Ap.1.1 The Seven Middoth of Hillel

(ARNa.37.10 – cf I.2.18 for Sifra and tSanh.7.11 versions)

1   **קל וחומר**
Lightness and Heaviness.
i.e. Argument from major to minor and vice versa.

2   **גזרה שוה**
Equal decree. [cf. S. Lieberman 1950:58f.]
i.e. Analogy from similar words.

3   **בנין אב מכתוב אחד**
Building a family from one text.
i.e. What is stated in one text applies in all similar texts.

4   **בנין אב משני כתובים**
Building a family from two texts.
i.e. What is common between two texts applies to all similar texts.

5   **כלל ופרט**
(ופרט וכלל)
General and Particular
(and Particular and General)
i.e. A general term is restricted by a subsequent particular term (and a particular term is restricted by a subsequent general term).

6   **כיוצא בו במקום אחר**
As is similar with it in another text.
i.e. The meaning may be deduced from a similar text.

7   **דבר הלמד מענינו**
Meaning is learned from the context
i.e. The meaning may be deduced from nearby texts.

Notes:
Tosefta and Sifra divide the rules differently. Both string together rules 3 & 4 as one rule, but while Tosefta splits General/Particular (rule 5 in ARN) into two rules, Sifra appears to have only 6 rules.
Sifra's rule 3 reads **שני כתובים**, 'two texts'. Rabed regarded this as a rule similar to Ishmael's 13th and some modern scholars agree – cf. A. Schwarz 1913:193ff., J.W. Doeve 1954:68, R. Kasher 1988:584f.

Ap.1.2 The Thirteen Middoth of R. Ishmael

(Text and translation from the *Book of Prayer* ed. D. de Sola Pool, New York 1936:14f., cf. Sifra, J.H. Weiss 1862:1a-3a)

Inference from minor to major, or major to minor. **מקל וחמר** 1

Inference from similarity of phrases in texts. **מגזרה שוה** 2

מבנין אב וכתוב אחד מבנין אב ושני כתובים 3
A comprehensive principle derived from one text, or from two related texts.

A general proposition followed by a specifying particular. **מכלל ופרט** 4

A particular term followed by a specific proposition. **מפרט וכלל** 5

כלל ופרט וכלל אי אתה דן אלא כעין הפרט 6
A general law limited by a specific application and then treated again in general terms must be interpreted according to the tenor of the specific limitation.

מכלל שהוא צריך לפרט ומפרט שהוא צריך לכלל 7
A general proposition requiring a particular or specific term to explain it, and conversely, a particular term requiring a general one to complement it.

כל דבר שהיה בכלל ויצא מן הכלל ללמד לא ללמד על עצמו יצא אלא ללמד על הכלל כלו יצא 8
When a subject included in a general proposition is afterwards particularly excepted to give information concerning it, the exception is made not for that one instance only, but to apply to the general proposition as a whole.

כלדבר שהיה בכלל ויצא לטעון טעון אחר שהוא כעינו יצא להקל ולא להחמיר 9
Whenever anything is first included in a general proposition and is then excepted to prove another similar proposition, this specifying alleviates and does not aggravate the law's restriction.

כל דבר שהיה בכלל ויצא לטעון טעון אחר שלא כענינו יצא להקל ולהחמיר 10
But when anything is first included in a general proposition and is then excepted to state a case that is not a similar proposition, such specifying alleviates in some respects and in others aggravates the law's restriction.

כל דבר שהיה בכלל ויצא לדון בדבר חדש אי אתה יכול להחזירו לכללו עד שיחזירנו הכתוב לכללו בפרוש 11
Anything included in a general proposition and afterwards excepted to determine a new matter cannot be applied to the general proposition unless this be expressly done in the text.

דבר הלמד מעניגו ודבר הלמד מסופו 12

An interpretation may be deduced from the text or from subsequent terms of the text.

וכן שני כתובים המכחישים זה את זה עד שיבא 13
הכתוב השלישי ויכריע ביניהם

In like manner when two texts contradict each other, we follow the second, until a third text is found whcih reconciles the contradiction.

Notes:

Rules 1 & 2 are identical with Hillel's rules 1 & 2
Rule 3 is identical with Hillel's rules 3 + 4
Rules 4–11 are derived from Hillel's rule 5
Rule 12 is an extended form of Hillel's rule 7
Rule 13 appears to be totally new. J. W. Doeve (1954: 68) notes that this may be an interpretation of Hillel's rule 4.
Hillel's rule 6 is not present. It was probably deemed superfluous in the presence of rules 2 & 3

R. Kasher (1988: 586f.) counts 16 rules because numbers 3, 7 and 12 are, strictly speaking, two rules each.

Ap.1.3 The Thirty Two Middoth of Eliezer b.Jose HaGelili

The text is according to H.G. Enelow (1933) with significant differences from Midrash HaGadol (S. Schechter 1902) in brackets. Numbering conforms to the traditional 32 rules by means of a subdivision of no.29.

רבוי 1

Extension.
i.e. The extension particles כל את גם אף indicate inclusion or amplification.

מיעוט 2

Limitation.
i.e. The limitation particles מן רק אך indicate exclusion or diminution.

רבוי אחר רבוי 3

Extension after extension.
i.e. Two extension particles indicate limitation [or, occasionally, extension – cf. Stemberger 1982: 33].

מיעוט אחר מיעוט 4

Limitation after limitation.
i.e. Two limitation particles indicate extension.

קל וחומר מפורש 5

Light and heavy distinctly.
i.e. An argument from Major to Minor (or vice versa) which is explicit in the text.

קל וחומר סתום 6

Light and heavy concealed.
i.e. An argument from Major to Minor (or vice versa) which is not explicit in the text.

גזירה שווה 7

Equal decree.
i.e. Analogy from similar words.

8 בנין אב

Building a family
i.e. The meaning of one text can be applied to a class of similar text or texts.

9 דרך קצרה

Short path.
i.e. Abbreviated or elliptical phraseology in a text may necessitate the addition of missing words.

10 דבר שהוא שנוי

A matter which repeats.
i.e. Repetition indicates a second meaning.

11 סדור שנחלק

Arrangement which is divided.
i.e. Changing divisions of a sentence may reveal another meaning.

12 דבר שהוא בא ללמד
ונמצא למד

A matter which came to teach
and proves itself to be learning.
i.e. A passage used to help expound another may be expounded in the process.

13 כלל שאחריו מעשה
ואינו אלא פרטו
שלראשון

A General which [has] an instance following
is nothing but the Particular of
the former.
i.e. When a General is followed by an action, then that action is a Particular of the General.

14 דבר הנתלה בקטן ממנו
להשמיע את האוזן
כדרך שהיא שומעת
(מה שיכולה)

A matter hanging on a trivial thing
in order to make the ear hear
as it [is able to] hear.
(what it is able [to hear])
i.e. Something important is compared with something trivial which can be understood more easily.

15 שני כתובים המכחישין
זה את זה
עד שיבוא הכתיב השלישי
ויכריע ביניהן

Two texts which contradict
each other
till a third text comes
and balances between them.
i.e. Two contradictory texts which are harmonised by a third.

16 דבר המיוחד
במקומו

A matter [which is] significant/unusual
in its place.
i.e. An unusual word or phrase suggests a hidden meaning.

17 דבר שאינו מתפרש
במקומו
ומתפרש במקום אחר

A matter which is not clear
in its place
and is clear in another place.
i.e. A text whose meaning is not clear in its context may be clarified by another passage.

18 דבר שנאמר במקצת
ונוהג בכל

A matter which is said in some [cases]
but which is operative in all.

If so, why is it said in some [cases] only? אם כן מפני מה נאמר במקצת
Because of argument.   מפני ריב
(Because it is true in the majority)   (מפני שהוא רוב הנמצא)
i.e. A specific case is mentioned but this can imply all similar cases.

A matter which is said [with reference] to that   19 דבר שנאמר לזה
and it applies equally to its companion.   והוא הדין לחבירו
i.e. A statement made with reference to one case is also true for other similar cases.

A matter which speaks to this   20 דבר שנאמר לזה
and it is not relevant to it   ואינו ענין לו
but it is relevant to its companion: אבל הוא ענין לחבירו
you shall find it relevant to it   ואתה נותן לו ענין
and relevant to its companion   וענין לחבירו
(finding relevance to its companion).   (תניהו ענין לחבירו)
Whatever is needed by it   מי שצריך לו אינו ענין לו
[is not stated as being] relevant to it
(to that which needs it)   (שהוא צריך לו)
i.e. A statement which does not go well with the passage in which it occurs,
but contributes to the sense of another passage, may be applied to the other
passage.

A matter which is subjected to 2 middoth,   21 דבר שהוקש לשתי מדות
you shall apply to   ואתה נותן לו
that which is valid for them both.   כח היפה שבשתיהן
i.e. When something is interpreted by two exegetical rules, only that relevant
to both is interpreted.

A matter for which a matter   22 דבר שדבר
(A matter whose companion)   (דבר שחבירו)
is evidence to it.   מוכיח עליו
i.e. A proposition which requires to be supplemented from a parallel proposition.

A matter which is evidence   23 דבר שהוא מוכיח
for its companion.   על חבירו
i.e. A proposition which supplements a parallel proposition.

A matter which is included in a General [case]   24 דבר שהיה בכלל
and is excluded from the General [case]   ויצא מן הכלל
to teach [only] about itself.   ללמד על עצמו
i.e. Details concerning a Particular case which is made an exception from the
General case, refer only to that case.

A matter which is included in a General [case]   25 דבר שהיה בכלל
and is excluded from the General [case]   ויצא מן הכלל
to teach [also] about its companion.   ללמד על חבירו

i.e. Details concerning a Particular case which is made an exception from the General case, refer also to all similar cases.

Mashal.	משל	26

i.e. A parable, metaphor or simile.

Correspondence/opposite	כנגד	27

i.e. A number corresponds with a number elsewhere, or Typology.

Hint	רמז	28
(Harvest – some MSS)	(מעל)	

i.e. Paronomasia – derivation from the same root.

Language calculations	לשון גמטריא	29

(transliterated from γραμματεια)
i.e. Gematria: Computation of the numeric value of letters, or numerology.

Resemblance of letters.	לדמות האותיות	29b
(Exchange of letters.)	(חילוף האותיות)	

i.e. Secret alphabets or substitution of letters.

Abbreviation.	נוטריקון	30

(transliterated from voταρικόν)
i.e. Notariqon: Breaking up a word into
a) two or more words
b) single letters which each stand for an individual word

The Preceding and the Following	מוקדם ומאוחר	31
which are related.	שהוא בענין	

i.e. Latter and former phrases may be read reversed.

The Preceding and the Following	מוקדם ומאוחר	32
which are pericopes.	שהוא בפרשיות	

i.e. Latter and former events may have occurred in reverse.

Notes:
Rules 5 & 6 are subdivisions of Hillel/Ishmael's rule 1
Rule 7 is Hillel/Ishmael's rule 2
Rule 8 is Hillel/Ishmael's rule 3
Rule 15 is Ishmael's rule 13
Rule 25 is a modification of Ishmael's rule 8

The following tables include all the individual arguments used in the exegeses analysed. The Modes of interpretation are abbreviated as P(eshat), N(omological), U(ltra-literal) and D(erash). An asterisk indicates that the exegesis is likely to have originated after 70 CE.

Tradition:		References:		Exegesis:	
I.2.1	**Nazarites**	**tNaz.4.7**			
	Simeon the Just	Num.6.2	P		
I.2.2	**Honi the Circler**	**mTaan.3.8**			
	Simeon b.Shetah	Prov.23.25	P	Context	
I.2.3	**Single false witness**	**Mekh.Ish.-**			
		Kas.3.31–35			
	Simeon b.Shetah	Deut.17.6	N	G. Shavah	
				(II), Plural	
	or Judah b.Tabai				
I.2.4	**Single witness**	**Mekh.Ish.-**			
		Kas.3.35–41			
	Simeon b.Shetah	Deut.17.6	P	Plural	
	or Judah b.Tabai	or Deut.19.15			
I.2.5	**King Yannai's feast**	**yBer.7.2; bBer.48b**			
1b	*Simeon b.Shetah	Qoh.7.12a	P		
2bi	* " "	Is.26.20	P		
2bii	* " "	Qoh.7.12b	P		
3b	* " "	Ben Sira 11.1	P		
3b	* " "	Prov.4.8	P		
I.2.6	**King Yannai's trial**	**bSanh.19ab**			
1ai	Simeon b.Shetah	Ex.21.29	P	Symbol	
1aii	* " "	Deut.19.17	P		
I.2.7	**For who's sake?**	**Mekh.Ish.Besh.4.58–61**			
1a	Shemaiah	Gen.15.16	P		
1b	Abtalion	Ex.4.31	P		

I.2.8	**Hagigah on Sabbath**	**bPes.70b**		
1i	*Judah b.Durtai	Deut.16.2; Ex.12.5	N	Contradiction (no 3rd)
1ii	" "	Deut.16.2	P	Context
I.2.9	**Sender is guilty**	**bQid.43a**		
	Shammai	2Sam.12.9	N	Precedent
I.2.10	**Remember/Keep Sabbath**	**Mekh.Sim.p148**		
	Shammai	Ex.20.8; Deut.5.12	N	No Redundancy
I.2.11	**Sue for peace 3 days**	**Sifré Deut.203**		
1a	Anon	Deut.20.19	N	Plural
1b	Shammai	2Sam.1.1	N	Precedent
I.2.12	**Besieging on Sabbath**	**tErub.3.7**		
	Shammai	Deut.20.20	P	
I.2.13	**For three things …**	**yPes.6.1**		
1ab	Hillel	Lev.13.37	N	No Redundancy, Order
2ab	"	Deut.16.2; Ex.12.5	N	Contradiction (no 3rd)
3ab	"	Deut.16.8; Ex.12.15	N	Contradiction (no 3rd)
I.2.14	**Itch within baldness**	**Sifra Taz.Per.9.16**		
	Hillel	Lev.13.37	P	Context
I.2.15	**Prozbul**	**Sifré Deut.113**		
	Hillel	Deut.15.3	N	& Pragmatism
I.2.16	**Corpse in water**	**Sifra Shem.Par.9.5**		
	*Anon	–	–	Qal vaHomer
	Hillel	Lev.11.36	P	Context
I.2.17	**When they do, you do**	**tBer.2.21; 6.24**		
3	*Hillel	Qoh.3.4f.	P	
5	* "	Prov.11.24	P	
6	* "	Ps.119.126	P	Context
I.2.18	**Passover on Sabbath**	**tPis.4.13f.; yPes.6.1; b Pes.66b**		
1a	Hillel	–	N	Heqesh
Y1b	*Anon		N	Heqesh refutation
2a	Hillel	Num.28.2	N	Gezerah Shavah (I)

B2b	*Anon	Num.28.10	N	No Redundancy
3a	Hillel	–	N	Qal vaHomer
Y3b	*Anon		N	Qal vaHomer refutation
B3b	*Anon	–	N	Qal vaHomer refutation

I.2.19	**Feet lead to Temple**	**tSukk.4.3**		
	*Hillel	Ex.20.24	P	

I.2.20	**If we are here**	**ySukk.5.4**		
1	*Hillel	Dan.7.10	P	
2	* "	2Sam.23.1	P	
2	* "	Ps.22.4(3)	P	

I.2.21	**A cry from afar**	**yBer.9.5**		
	*Hillel	Ps.112.7	P	Wordplay?

I.2.22	**Self abasement exalts**	**LevR.1.5**		
	*Hillel	Ps.113.5f.	P	

I.2.23	**Disciple Yohanan**	**yNed.5.7**		
	*Hillel	Prov.8.21	P	Context, Symbol

I.2.24	**Forgotten offering**	**bHag.9b**		
	Bar Hé Hé	Qoh.1.15	N	

I.2.25	**Righteous and wicked**	**bHag.9a**		
1a	Bar Hé Hé	Mal.3.18	N	No Redundancy
1b	Hillel		N	No Redundancy refuted
2b	Hillel	–	–	Mashal

I.2.26	**Second Tithe purchase**	**bErub.27b**		
	Ben Bag Bag	Deut.14.26	N	No Redundancy

I.2.27	**Tamid examined**	**bPes.96a**		
4 days		Num.28.2; Ex.12.6	N	Gezerah Shavah (II)
	Ben Bag Bag			

I.2.28	**Redeem only with lamb**	**bBekh.12a**		
	Ben Bag Bag	Ex.12.5; 13.13	N	Gezerah Shavah (II)

I.2.29	**Imprisoned by Herod**	**bBB.4a**		
2b	Baba b.Buta	Qoh.10.20a	P	
3b	* " "	Qoh.10.20b	P	
4a	" "	Ex.22.27(28)	P	
4b	*Herod		P	

6a	*Baba b.Buta	Qoh.10.20c	P
A7bi	* " "	Prov.6.23	P	Symbol
A7bii	* " "	Is.2.2	D	Wordplay
B7bi	* " "	Num.15.24	N
B7bii	* " "	Ezk.24.21	P

I.2.30 God is jealous Mekh.Sim.p147
1a *Agrippas Deut.4.39 P Context
    *Gamaliel I Jer.2.13 P

I.2.31 Do not destroy altars Sifré Deut.61
    Gamaliel I Deut.12.3f. P Context

I.2.32 Two Torahs Sifré Deut.351
    *Agenitos Deut.33.10 N
    *Gamaliel I N

I.2.33 Beautiful woman bAZ.20a
    Simeon b.Gam.I Ps.104.24 P Context

I.2.34 Peace to the House Sifré Num.42
    Hananiah, Priest Num.6.26; Ps.112.5? N Gezerah Shavah (II)

I.2.35 Peace is great Sifré Num.42
    Hananiah, Priest Is.45.7; Am.4.13? P (Amalgamation?)

I.2.36 Rewards of Torah ARNa.20
    Hananiah, Priest Ps.19.9(8) ;
                      Dt.28.46ff. P Gezerah Shavah II

I.2.37 Rulers cast off yoke ARNa.20
    *Hananiah, Priest Cant.1.6 D Allegory, Context

I.2.38 Diverse Ephahs Sifré Deut.294
    Eliezer b.Hananiah Ezk.46.11;
                        Num.29.3f. N Contradiction (no 3rd)

I.2.39 Remember the Mekh.Ish.Bah.7
    Sabbath Ex.20.8 N
    Eliezer b.Hananiah
I.2.40 Betrothed eat
    Temurah bQid.10b-11a
    Judah b.Bathyra – – Qal vaHomer

I.2.41 Undesignated gifts mArak.8.6
1a Judah b.Bathyra Lev.27.28 P
1b Sages Lev.27.21 N Gezerah Shavah

| 2a | Judah b.Bathyra | Lev.27.28 | N | No Redundancy |
| 2b | Sages | | N | No Redundancy refuted |

| **I.2.42** | **Handful in left hand** | **bZeb.63a** | | |
| | Judah b.Bathyra | Lev.2.2 | N | Unusual/No Redundancy |

| **I.2.43** | **Water Libation** | **bShab.103b** | | |
| | Judah b.Bathyra | Num.29.19, 31, 33 | D | Unusual/ Hint, Context |

| **I.2.44** | **Do not destroy altars** | **Mid.Tann.p58** | | |
| | Yohanan b.Zakkai | Deut.12.2 | | (assumes I.2.31) |

I.2.45	**Two Torahs**	**Mid.Tann.p215**		
2a	Agrippas	Deut 33.10	N	
2b	Yohanan b.Zakkai		N	

| **I.2.46** | **Bitter Waters ceased** | **mSot.9.9** | | |
| | *Yohanan b.Zakkai | Hos.4.14 | P | Pragmatism, Fulfilment |

| **I.2.47** | **Temple door opened** | **bYom.39b** | | |
| | Yohanan b.Zakkai | Zech.11.1 | P | Symbol, Fulfilment |

I.2.48	**Vespasian to be king**	**bGit.56ab**		
1a	Yohanan b.Zakkai	Is.10.34	P	Prophetic Fulfilment
1ai	* " "	Jer.30.21	P	Symbol/ Gezerah Shavah I
1aii	* " "	Deut.3.25	P	Symbol/ Gezerah Shavah I

| **I.2.49** | **Murdering ox stoned** | **ySanh.1.2** | | |
| 2b | Yohanan b.Zakkai | Ex.21.29 | N | Heqesh |

| **I.2.50** | **Total no. of Levites** | **ySanh.1.4; NumR.3.14** | | |
| 1b | Yohanan b.Zakkai | Num.3.13, 22ff., 39 | N | Contradiction (+ 3rd) |

| **I.2.51** | **Valuing half-shekels** | **ySanh.1.4** | | |
| | Yohanan b.Zakkai | Ex.38.25f., 29; Ezk.45.12 | N | Contradiction (+ 3rd) |

| **I.3.1** | **Eternal rewards** | **ARNa.5** | | |
| 1a | Boethus. & Sadd. | (Antigonus) | – | Logical Inconsistency |

I.3.2	**Unclean Scripture**	mYad.4.6		
1a	Sadducees	–	–	Logical Incon- sistency
1b	Yohanan b.Zakkai	–	–	Logical Incon- sistency
2aii	Sadducees	–	–	Reductio ad Absur- dum
	Unclean Scripture	tYad.1.19		
	Yohanan b.Zakkai	–	–	Reductio ad Absur- dum

I.3.3	**Unbroken stream**	mYad.4.7		
1b	Pharisees	–	–	Logical Incon- sistency

I.3.4	**Damage by slave or ox**	mYad.4.7		
1a	Sadducees	–	–	Qal vaHomer
1b	Pharisees	–	–	Qal vaHomer refutation Reductio ad Absur- dum

I.3.5	**Name of God & Ruler**	mYad.4.8		
1b	Pharisees	Ex.5.2	–	Reductio ad Absur- dum

I.3.6	**Granddaughter as heir**	bBB.115b-116a; tYad.2.20		
1b	Sadducees	–	–	Reductio ad Absur- dum
2b	Sadducees	–	–	Qal vaHomer
3a	Yohanan b.Zakkai	Gen.36.2, 14, 20, 24	P	Contradiction (+ 3rd)
4a	" "	–	–	Qal vaHomer refutation

I.3.7	**Name before bathing**	tYad.2.20		
1b	Pharisees	–	–	Reductio ad Absur- dum

I.3.8	**Atonement incense**	tKipp.1.8; Sifra AH. Per.3.11		
1ai	Sadducees	–	P	Qal vaHomer, Mashal
1aii	Boethusians	Lev.16.13b	P	
1b	Sages	Lev.16.13a	P	Order
2a	Sadducees	Lev.16.2	N	No Redundancy
2b	Sages	Lev.16.2; Is.6.4?	P	

I.3.9	**Cleansing the Lamp**	**tHag.3.35**		
	Sadducees	–	–	Reductio ad Absurdum
I.3.10	**False witnesses**	**mMakk.1.6**		
1a	Sadducees	Deut.19.21	P	
1b	Sages	Deut.19.19	P	
2aii	Sadducees	–	–	Pragmatism, R.ad Absurdum
	Sages	Deut.19.21	P	
I.3.11	**Oral/Written law**	**Meg.Taan.p331**		
1bii	Sages	Deut.17.11	N	U? Context?
2a	Boethusians	Lev.24.20	P	
3a	"	Deut.22.17	P	
3a	"	Deut.25.9	P	
4b	*Sages	Ex.24.12	U	Atomization
4b	* "	Deut.31.19	U	Atomization No Redundancy
I.3.12	**Date of Sukkot**	**bMen.65ab**		
2b	Boethusians (	Lev.23.7f.)	–	Pragmatism
3a	Yohanan b.Zakkai	Deut.1.2	P	
4a	Yohanan b.Zakkai	Lev.23.15f.	N	Contradiction (no 3rd)
I.3.13	**Eat Cereal with ox**	**Meg.Taan.p338**		
2bi	Sadducees	–	–	Pragmatism
2bii	Sadducees	–	–	Mashal
3a	Yohanan b.Zakkai	Ex.15.27	P	Context
(4a)	Sadducees?	Lev.23.20	P	
4a	Yohanan b.Zakkai	Lev.23.18	P	Order, Punctuation?
I.3.14	**Payment for Tamid**	**bMen.65a**		
1a	Sadducees	Num.28.4	N	
1b	Pharisees	Num.28.2	P	Plural
I.3.15	**Skins for Tefillin**	**bShab.108a**		
4a	Boethusians	Ex.13.9	P	
4b	*Yoshua haGarsi	–	–	Mashal
5b	*Yoshua haGarsi	Deut.14.21	P	
I.3.16	**Temple court cries**	**bPes.57a**		
	Anon.	Ps.24.7	P	Sarcasm
I.4.1	**Examine Phylacteries**	**Mekh.Ish.Pis.17.209–216**		
1a	Beth Hillel	Ex.13.10; Lev.25.29	N	Gezerah Shavah (I)
I.4.2	**Using entrusted goods**	**Mekh.Ish.Nez.15.49–55; mBM.3.12**		

A1a	(Beth Hillel)	Ex.22.7(8)	P	
A1b	(Beth Shammai)	Ex.22.8(9)	P	
A2a	Beth Shammai	Ex.22.8(9)	P	
A2b	Beth Hillel	Ex.22.7(8)	P	
I.4.3	**Between the evenings**	**Mekh.Sim.p12.4f.**		
	Beth Hillel	Ex.12.6		– Pragmatism
I.4.4	**Work on the Sabbath**	**Mekh.Sim.p149**		
1a	Beth Shammai	Ex.20.9	P	
1b	Beth Hillel		N	No Redundancy
I.4.5	**81st day abortion**	**Sifra Taz.Per.3.1f.**		
	Beth Hillel	Lev.12.6	N	No Redundancy
I.4.6	**4th year gleanings**	**Sifra Qed.Par.3.7**		
	Beth Hillel	Lev.19.24	P	
I.4.7	**Festival offering**	**Sifra Emor Per.15.5**		
1a	Beth Shammai	Lev.23.39	P	Unusual?
1b	Beth Hillel		P	Unusual?
I.4.8	**Guarded 7th year crop**	**Sifra Behar Per.1.5**		
	(Beth Shammai)	Lev.25.6	P	
I.4.9	**Fringes**	**Sifré Deut.234**		
1a	Beth Hillel	Num.15.38;		
		Deut.22.12	N	Contradiction (no 3rd) Plural
1b	Beth Shammai		N	Contradiction (no 3rd) Plural
I.4.10	**1st fleece of a flock**	**Sifré Deut.166**		
1a	Beth Shammai	Deut.18.4; Is.7.21	N	Gezerah Shavah (I)
1b	Beth Hillel	Deut.18.4; ISam.25.18	N	Gezerah Shavah (I)
1c	*Aqiva	Deut.18.4	D	Parsing, Plural
I.4.11	**Reasons for divorce**	**Sifré Deut.269**		
1a	Beth Shammai	Deut.24.1	P	
1b	Beth Hillel		P	
2a	Beth Shammai	Deut.24.1	N	No Redundancy
2b	Beth Hillel		N	No Redundancy refuted
2c	*Aqiva		P	
I.4.12	**Attitude for Shema**	**mBer.1.3**		
1a	Beth Shammai	Deut.6.7b	U	

1b	Beth Hillel	Deut.6.7a	U	
2a	Beth Shammai	Deut.6.7b	N	No Redundancy
2b	Beth Hillel	Deut.6.7b	N	No Redundancy re-futed
I.4.13	**Incorrect Heave off.**	**tTer.3.16**		
2a	Beth Hillel	Num.18.27	P	
2b	Beth Shammai	Lev.27.30	P	Reductio ad Absur-dum
I.4.14	**Going up to Jerusalem**	**mHag.1.1**		
1b	Beth Hillel	Ex.23.14	D	Wordplay
I.4.15	**Minimum children**	**tYeb.8.4**		
1a	Beth Shammai	1Chron.23.15; Ex.18.2f.?	N	Precedent
1b	Beth Hillel	Gen.5.2	N	Precedent
I.4.16	**Half bondservant**	**mGit.4.5**		
1b	Beth Shammai	Is.45.18; Gen.1.28?	N	Precedent, R. Ab-surdum
1b		–	–	Pragmatism
I.4.17	**Eternity of 3rd group**	**tSanh.13.3**		
1aii	Beth Shammai	Zech.13.9	P	Symbol, Fulfilment
1aiii	1Sam.2.6	P		
1b	Beth Hillel	Ps.116.1	P	Context
I.4.18	**Tassels on linen coat**	**Mid.Tann.p138f.**		
2b	Beth Shammai	Deut.22.11f.	N	Order
I.4.19	**Blessing for lights**	**bBer.53a**		
2a	Beth Hillel	Prov.14.28	P	Symbol
I.4.20	**Honour Sabbath**	**bBetz.16a**		
1b, 2b	Beth Hillel	Ps.68.19(20)	P	Punctuation?
I.4.21	**Festival offering**	**bBetz.20b**		
1b	Beth Hillel	–	N	Qal vaHomer
2a	Beth Shammai	–	N	Qal vaHomer refutation
4a	Beth Shammai	Ex.12.16	N	
4b	Beth Hillel	Ex.12.14	N	
5a	Beth Shammai	Ex.12.16	N	No Redundancy
5b	Beth Hillel	Ex.12.16	N	No Redundancy re-futed Wordplay
I.4.22	**Created Heaven, Earth**	**bHag.12a**		
1a	Beth Shammai	Gen.1.1	N	Order

1b	Beth Hillel	Gen.2.4	N	Order
2a	*Beth Hillel	Amos.9.6	P	Mashal
2b	Beth Shammai	Is.66.1	P	Mashal

I.4.23	**Complimenting a bride**	**bKet.16b-17a**		
2a	Beth Shammai	Ex.23.7	N	
2b	Beth Hillel	–	–	Mashal

I.4.24	**Harlot's offering**	**bTem.30b**		
1i	*Anon.	Deut.23.19(18)	N	No Redundancy
1ii	*Anon.		N	No Redundancy
2a	*Beth Hillel		N	
2b	*Beth Shammai		D	Extension

I.4.25	**"Dust" to cover blood**	**bHull.88b**		
1b	Beth Hillel	Num.19.17	N	Gezerah Shavah (I)
2a	Beth Shammai		N	Gezerah Shavah refuted

I.4.26	**"lamb" as sin**	**Pes.Rab.16**		
1a	*Beth Shammai	Num.28.3; Mic.7.19	D	No Redundancy, Gezerah Shavah I
	*Beth Hillel	Num.28.3; Is.1.18	D	No Redundancy, Gezerah Shavah I

Bibliography & Abbreviations:

Bib.1 Standard Texts Transcribed in this Study:

Mishnah	P. Blackman 1964
Tosefta (till tNaz.)	S. Lieberman 1955–
(after tNaz.)	M.S. Zuckermandel 1937
Babylonian Talmud	Romm, Vilna 1880–6
Jerusalem Talmud	Krotoschin 1866
Aboth d'R. Nathan	S. Schechter 1887
Megillat Taanit	H. Lichtenstein 1932
Mekhilta d'R. Ishmael	J.Z. Lauterbach 1933–
Sifra	J.H. Weiss 1862
Sifré Numbers	H.S. Horovitz 1917
Sifré Deuteronomy	L. Finkelstein 1969b
Leviticus Rabbah	M. Margulies 1953–
Midrash Tannaim	D. Hoffman 1908–
Mekhilta d'R. Simeon	J.N. Epstein & E.Z. Melamed 1955
Pesiqta Rabbati	M. Friedmann 1880

Bib.2 Abbreviations:

Rabbinic texts:

b	Babylonian Talmud
m	Mishnah
t	Tosefta
y	Yerushalmi, Jerusalem Talmud
(m)	only in Mishnah and Babylonian Talmud
(t)	only in Tosefta and Jerusalem Talmud

Tractates of Mishnah, Tosefta and Talmuds:

Ab	Aboth (m)
Arak	Arakhin
AZ	Abodah Zarah
BB	Baba Batra
BM	Baba Metzia
BQ	Baba Qamma
Bekh	Bekhorot
Ber	Berakhot

Betz	Betzah (= Yom Tob)
Bikk	Bikkurim
Dem	Demai
Ed	Eduyot
Erub	Erubin
Git	Gittin
Hag	Hagigah (= tRayyah)
Hall	Hallah
Hor	Horayot
Hull	Hullin
Kel	Kelim
Ker	Keritot
Ket	Ketuboth
Kil	Kilaim
Kipp	Kippurim (Tosefta, = Yoma K. elsewhere)
MQ	Moed Qatan
MS	Maaser Sheni
Maas	Maaserot (m), Maaser Rashin (t)
Makk	Makkot
Maksh	Makshirin
Meg.	Megillah
Meil	Meilah
Men	Menahot
Midd	Middoth (m)
Miq	Miqvaot
Naz	Nazir (m), Nazirut (t)
Ned	Nedarim
Neg	Negaim
Nidd	Niddah
Ohol	Oholot
Orl	Orlah (m)
Par	Parah
Peah	Peah
Pes/Pis	Pesahim (m), Pisahim (t)
Qid	Qiddushin
Qinn	Qinnim (m)
RH	Rosh haShanah
Sanh	Sanhedrin
Shab	Shabbat
Shebi	Shebiit
Shebu	Shebuot
Sheq	Sheqalim
Sof	Soferim
Sot	Sotah
Sukk	Sukkah
Taan	Taanit
Tam	Tamid (m)
Tem	Temurah
Ter	Terumot

Tiq	Tiqunim (t)
Toh	Tohorot
TY	Tebul Yom
Uqtz	Uqtzin
YT	Yom Tob (= Betzah)
Yad	Yadaim
Yeb	Yebamot
Yom	Yoma
Zab	Zabim
Zeb	Zebahim

Other Rabbinic texts:

ARNa/b	Aboth d'R. Nathan A & B
Meg.Taan	Megillat Taanit
Mekh.Ish	Mekhilta d'R. Ishmael
– Pis	– Pisha
– Besh	– Beshallah
– Shir	– Shirta
– Vay	– Vayassa
– Amal	– Amalek
– Bah	– Bahodesh
– Nez	– Nezikim
– Kas	– Kaspa
– Shab	– Shabbat
Mekh.Sim	Mekhilta d'R. Simeon b.Yohai
Mid.Gadd	Midrash haGaddol
Mid.Tann	Midrash Tannaim
MidR	Midrash Rabbah
– LevR etc	– Leviticus Rabbah
Pes.Rab	Pesiqta Rabbati
Pes.Kah	Pesiqta d'R. Kahana
Sifra	Sifra
– Vay	– Vayiqra
– Sav	– Sav
– Shem	– Shemini
– Taz	– Tazria
– Mes	– Metsora
– AM	– Ahare Mot
– Qed	– Qedoshim
– Em	– Emor
– Behar	– Behar
– Behu	– Behuqotai
– Par	– Parashah
– Per	– Pereq
Sifré Num	Sifré Numbers
Sifré Deut	Sifré Deuteronomy
TgJon	Targum Pseudo-Jonathan
TgOnk	Targum Onkelos

TgN Targum Neofiti

Josephus:
Life Life of Flavius Josephus
Ant Antiquities of the Jews
Wars Wars of the Jews
C. Ap Contra Apion

Qumran Texts:
CD Damascus Covenant / Zadokite Rule
1QS Manual of Discipline / Community Rule
1QM, 4QM War of the Sons of light . . . / War Rule
11QT Temple Scroll
Hod Hymns of Thanksgiving / Hodayoth
Gen.Ap Genesis Apocryphon
nQpX Pesher commentary on X from Qumran cave n
  eg: 1QpHab, 1QpNah
nQX.a 1st (a) OT text of X from Qumran cave n
  eg: 4QIs.a

Philonic Texts:
The Allegory of the Laws:

Leg I-III	Legum Allegoriae I-III	re Gen.2.1–3.19
Cher	De Cherubim	re Gen.3.24–4.1
Sacrif	De sacrifiic Abelis et Caini	re Gen.4.2–4
Deter	Quod deterius potiori insidiari solet	re Gen 4.8–15
Poster	De posteritate Caini	re Gen.4.16–25
Gig	De gigantibus	re Gen.6.1–4a
Immut	Quod Deus sit immutabilis	re Gen.6.4b-12
Agric	De agricultura	re Gen.9.20–21
Plant	De plantatione	re Gen.9.20–21
Ebr	De ebrietate	re Gen.9.20–21
Sobr	De sobrietate	re Gen.9.24–27
Confus	De confusione linguarum	re Gen.11.1–9
Migr	De migratione Abrahami	re Gen.12.1–6
Her	Quis rerum divinarum heres sit	re Gen.15.2–18
Congr	De congressu eruditionis gratia	re Gen.16.1–6
Fug	De fuga et inventione	re Gen.16.6b-14
Mutat	De mutatione nominum	re Gen.17.1–5, 16–22
Somn I-II	De Somniis I-III	re Gen.28.10–22; 31.10–13; 37.8–11; 40.9–11, 16f.; 41.17–24

The Exposition:
Opif De opificio Mundi
Abr De Abrahamo

Ios	De Iosepho
Mos	De vita Mosis
Decal	De Decalogo
Spec I-IV	De specialibus legibus I-IV
Virt	De virtutibus
Praem	De praemiis et poenis, de exsecrationibus

Questions and Answers:

| Q. Gen | Quaestiones et solutiones in Genesim |
| Q. Ex | Quaestiones et solutiones in Exodum |

Others:

V. Con	De vita contemplativa
Aet	De aeternitate mundi
Flacc	In Flaccum
Legat	De legatione ad Gaium
Prov	De Providentia
Anim	De animalibus
Hypoth	Hypothetica
Prob	Quod omnis probus liber sit
Apol	Apologia pro Iudaeis

Abbreviations used in the bibliography:

ed.	edition
Ed.	Editor
ET	English Translation
Hon.	in honour of
Mon	Monograph
NS	New Series
Sup	Supplement
Trans.	Translator
AJSL	American Journal of Semitic Languages and Literature
AJSR	Association for Jewish Studies Review
ALUOS	The Annual of Leeds University Oriental Society
ANRW	*Aufstieg und Niedergang der römischen Welt*
ASTI	Annual of the Swedish Theological Institute
BA	The Biblical Archaeologist
BASOR	Bulletin of the American Schools of Oriental Research
Bib	Biblica
BJRL	Bulletin of the John Rylands Library
BO	Bibliotheca Orientalis
BR	Biblical Research
BSOAS	Bulletin of the School of Oriental and African Studies
BZAW	Beihefte zur ZAW
CBQ	Catholic Biblical Quarterly
CJ	Conservative Judaism
CNCNRS	Colloques Nationaux du Centre National de la Recherche Scientifique
CQ	Classical Quarterly
CR	Classical Review
DBSup	*Dictionaire de la Bible, Supplément* (Ed. L. Pirot, Paris 1928–)
DCB	*Dictionary of Christian Biography* (Eds. W. Smith, H. Wace, London 1877–87)
DJD	*Discoveries in the Judean Desert* (Oxford 1955–)
EncJ	*Encyclopaedia Judaica* (1971)
ETL	Ephemerides Theologicae Lovanienses
ExpT	The Expository Times
FJB	Frankfurter jüdaistische Beiträge
HR	History of Religions
HTR	Harvard Theological Review
HUCA	Hebrew Union College Annual
IDB	*Interpreter's Dictionary of the Bible*

IEJ	Israel Exploration Journal
Imman	Immanuel
Interp	Interpretation
JBL	Journal of Biblical Literature
JBR	Journal of Bible and Religion
JE	*The Jewish Encyclopedia*
JJLP	Journal of Jewish Lore and Philosophy
JJS	Journal of Jewish Studies
JJSoc	Jewish Journal of Sociology
JPOS	Journal of the Palestine Oriental Society
JQR	Jewish Quarterly Review
JR	Journal of Religion
JSJ	Journal for the Study of Judaism in the Persian, Hellenistic & Roman Period
JSNT	Journal for the Study of the NT
JSocS	Jewish Social Studies
JSOT	Journal for the Study of the Old Testament
JSS	Journal of Semetic Studies
JTS	Journal of Theological Studies
JTVI	Journal of the Transactions of the Victoria Institute
Jud	Judaica
LCL	*Loeb Classical Library*
LQR	Law Quarterly Review
MGWJ	Monatsschrift für Geschichte und Wissenschaft des Judenthums
NovT	Novum Testamentum
NTCS	Newsletter for Targumic and Cognate Studies
NTS	New Testament Studies
OS	*Oudtestamentische Studiën* (Ed. P.A.H.de Boer)
PAAJR	Proceedings of the American Academy for Jewish Research
Per	Personalist
PT	Prooftexts
PWCJS	Proceedings of the World Congress of Jewish Studies
RB	Revue Biblique
REJ	Revue des Études Juives
RHPR	Revue d'histoire et de philosophie religieuses
RQ	Revue de Qumran
RSR	Recherches de Science Religieuse
SBL	Society of Biblical Literature
Sef	Sefarad
SH	*Scripta Hierosolymitana*
SP	Studia Philonica
ST	Studia Theologica
SVT	Supplements to Vetus Testamentum
TAPS	Transactions of the American Philosophical Society, Philadelphia.
Tar	Tarbiz
TDNT	*Theological Dictionary of the New Testament* (Eds. G. Kittel et al.)
Them	Themelios
VT	Vetus Testamentum
ZAW	Zeitschrift für die alttestamentliche Wissenschaft
ZNW	Zeitschrift für die neutestamentliche Wissenschaft
ZTK	Zeitschrift für Theologie und Kirche

Bib. 3 *Works Referred to in this Study:*

Texts and translations:

M & Grossfeld, B. 1983
  Targum Onkelos to Genesis: A Critical Analysis Together with an English Translation of the Text. New York 1982
Barthélemy, D. 1963
  Les dévanciers d'Aquila: Première publication intégrale du texte des fragments du 'Dodécaprophéton' trouvés dans le désert de Juda . . . SVT 10 Leiden 1963
Blackman, P. (Ed. & Trans.) 1964
  Mishnayoth: Pointed Hebrew text, English Translation, Introductions . . . 6 vols. New York 1964
Braude, W.G. (Trans.) 1959
  The Midrash on Psalms. 2 vols. New Haven, 1959
Braude, W.G. (Trans.) 1968
  Pesihta Rabbati. 2 vols. New Haven, 1968
Brownlee, W.H. 1979
  The Midrash Pesher of Habakkuk SBL Mon 24, Missoula, Montana, 1979
Burrows, M. (Ed. & Trans.) 1950
  The Dead Sea Scrolls of St. Mark's Monastery. 2 vols. New Haven 1950–51
Charles, R.H. (Trans.) 1913
  The Apocrypha & Pseudepigrapha of the Old Testament. 2 vols. Oxford 1913
Charlesworth, J.H. (Ed.) 1985
  The Old Testament Pseudepigrapha. 2 vols. London 1985
Colson, F.H. et al. (Eds. & Trans.) 1929–
  Philo with an English Translation. LCL, 12 vols. London 1929–61
Danby, H. (Trans.) 1933
  The Mishnah: Translated from the Hebrew with Introduction and Brief Explanatory Notes. London 1933
Elliger, K. et al. (Eds.) 1984
  Biblica Hebraica. Stuttgart 1984, 1st ed. 1969–76
Enelow, H.G. 1933
  The Mishna of Rabbi Eliezer: The Midrash of Thirty Two Hermeneutic Rules. New York 1933
Epstein, I. (Ed.) 1935–
  The Babylonian Talmud. ET London 1935–65
Epstein, J.N. & Melamed, E.Z. (Eds.) 1955
  Mekhilta D'Rabbi Simeon b. Jochai: Fragmenta in Geniza Cairensi reperta digessit apparatu critico, notis, praefatione instruxit. Jerusalem 1955
Epstein, I. (Ed.) 1969–
  Hebrew-English Edition of the Babylonian Talmud. London 1969–

Feldman, L.H. (Ed. & Trans.) 1965
Josephus: Jewish Antiquities, Books 18–20. in H. St. J. Thackeray 1926–
Finkelstein, L. (Ed.) 1956
Sifra or Torat Kohanim according to Codex Assemani LXVI with a Hebrew introduction. New York 1956
Finkelstein, L. (Ed.) 1969b
Siphre ad Deuteronomium . . . cum variis lectionibus et adnotationibus. New York 1969, 1st ed. 1939
Freedman, H & Simon, M (Trans.) 1939
Midrash Rabbah. 10 vols. London, 1939
Friedmann, M. (Ed.) 1864
Sifre debe Rab, der älteste halachische und hagadische Midrasch zu Numeri und Deuteronomium. Wien 1864
Friedmann, M. (Ed.) 1880
Pesikta Rabbati. Wien 1880
Goldschmidt, L. (Ed. & Trans.) 1897–
Der Babylonische Talmud. 11 vols. Haag 1897–1935
Halevi (Hallewy), E.E. (Ed.) 1956–
Midrash Rabbah 8 vols. Tel Aviv 1956–63
Hammer, R. (Trans.) 1986
Sifre: A Tannaitic Commentary on the Book of Deuteronomy. New Haven 1986
Hoffmann, D. (Ed.) 1905
Mechilta de-Rabbi Simon b. Jochai: ein halachischer und haggadischer Midrasch zu Exodus. Frankfurt 1905
Hoffmann, D. (Ed.) 1908–
Midrash Tannaim zum Deuteronomium. 2 vols. Berlin 1908–09
Hoffmann, D. (Ed.) 1913–
Midrash Hag-gadol zum Buche Exodus. Berlin 1913–
Holm-Nielsen, S. 1960
Hodayot: Psalms from Qumran. Aarhus 1960
Horgan, Maurya P. 1979
Pesharim: Qumran Interpretations of Biblical Books. CBQMon 8 1979
Horovitz, H.S. (Ed.) 1917
Siphre D'Be Rab I: Sifre ad Numeros adjecto Siphre zutta cum variis lectionibus et adnotationibus. Lipsiae 1917
Horovitz, H.S. & Rabin, I.A. (Eds.) 1960
Mechilta D'Rabbi Ishmael cum variis lectionibus et adnotationibus. Jerusalem 1960, 1st ed. 1931
Koleditzky, S. (Ed.) 1948
Sifre on Numbers and Deuteronomy. Jerusalem 1948
Koleditzky, S. (Ed.) 1969
Sifra d'be Rab Torat Kohamim. 2 vols. Jerusalem 1969
Larsson, G. 1980
Der Toseftatraktat Jom hak-Kippurim: Text, Übersetzung, Kommentar. Lund 1980
Lauterbach, J.Z. (Ed. & Trans.) 1933–
Mekilta de Rabbi Ishmael: A critical edition on the basis of the manuscripts and early editions with an English translation introduction and notes. 3 vols. Philadelphia 1933–35
Levertoff, P.P. (Trans.) 1926
Midrash Sifre on Numbers: Selections from Early Rabbinic Interpretation. London 1926

Lichtenstein, H. (Ed.) 1932
"Megillath Ta'anith: Die Fastenrolle: eine Untersuchung zur Jüdisch Helleni-stischen Geschichte *HUCA* 8–9 (1931–32) 257–351

Lieberman, S. (Ed.) 1955–
The Tosephta According to Codex Vienna, with variants from Codex Erfurt Genizah MSS and Editio Princeps, with references to parallel passages and a brief commentary. 10 vols. up to tNaz. New York 1955–67

Macho, A.D. et al. (Ed. & Trans.) 1968–
Neofiti: Targum Palestinense MS de la Bibliotheca Vaticana. 6 vols. Madrid 1968–79

Marcus, R. (Ed. & Trans.) 1934–
Josephus with an English Translation: Antiquities Bks. 6–17. in H. St. J. Thackeray 1926–

Margulies, M. (Ed.) 1953–
Midrash Wayyikra Rabbah. A Critical Edition based on MSS... and on Genizah fragments with variants and notes. 5 vols. Jerusalem 1953–60

McNamara, M. (Ed.) 1987–
The Aramaic Bible: A Modern Translation of the Targums. Edinburgh 1987–

Neusner, J. (Trans.) 1977–
The Tosefta. New York, 1977–86

Neusner, J. (Trans.) 1982–
The Talmud of the Land of Israel: a preliminary translation and explanation. Chicago, 1982–

Neusner, J. et al. (Trans.) 1984–
Talmud of Babylonia: an American Translation. Chico, 1984–

Neusner, J. (Trans.) 1986
Sifré to Numbers: An American Translation and Explanation. Atlanta 1986

Neusner, J. (Trans.) 1987
Pesiqta deRab Kahana: An Analytical Translation. 2 vols. Atlanta 1987

Neusner, J. (Trans.) 1988
The Mishnah. A New Translation. Yale 1988

Rabin, C. (Ed. & Trans.) 1954
The Zadokite Documents. Oxford 1954

Saldarini, A.J. (Trans.) 1975
The Fathers According to Rabbi Nathan – Abot de Rabbi Nathan – Version B; a translation and commentary. Leiden 1975

Schechter, S. (Ed.) 1887
Aboth de Rabbi Nathan. Vindobonae 1887

Schechter, S. (Ed.) 1902
The Midrash Hag-Gadol. Cambridge, 1902

Schechter, S. (Ed. & Trans.) 1910
Documents of Jewish Sectaries. 2 vols. Cambridge 1910

Schwab, M. (Trans.) 1960
Le Talmud de Jérusalem. 6 vols. Paris, 1960. 1st ed, 1871

Silbermann, A.M. & Rosenbaum, M. (Ed. & Trans.) 1929
Pentateuch with Rashi's Commentary translated into English. 5 vols. London 1929

Singer, S. (Ed.) 1962
The Authorised Daily Prayer Book. London 1962

Sperber, A. (Ed.) 1959–
The Bible in Aramaic: Based on Old Manuscripts and Printed Texts. 4 vols. Leiden 1959–68

Taylor, C. 1877
   Sayings of the Jewish Fathers: Comprising Pirqe Aboth and Pereq R. Meir in Hebrew and English with critical and illustrative notes . . . Cambridge 1877
Thackeray, H. St. J. (Trans.) 1904
   The Letter of Aristeas. London, 1904
Thackeray, H. St. J. et al. (Eds. & Trans.) 1926–
   Josephus with an English Translation LCL, 10 vols. London 1926–65
Vermes, G. (Trans.) 1987
   The Dead Sea Scrolls in English. London, 1987, 1st ed. 1962
Weiss, J. H. (Ed.) 1862
   Sifra d'be Rab, Torat Kohanim. Wien 1862
Wevers, J. W. 1982–
   Septuaginta. Gottingen 1982–
Yadin, Y. 1983
   The Temple Scroll. 3 vols. Jerusalem, 1983
Zuckermandel, M. S. (Ed.) 1880
   Tosephta nach dem Erfurter und Wiener Handscriften mit Parallelstellen und Varianten. Pasewalk 1880
Zuckermandel, M. S. (Ed.) 1937
   Tosephta based on the Erfurt and Vienna Codices with parallels and variants. with *Supplement to the Tosephta* by S. Liebermann Jerusalem 1937

Reference works not listed in the Abbreviations:
Albeck, C. 1971
   Einführung in die Mischna. GT Berlin & New York 1971
Allenbach, J. 1975–
   Biblia Patristica: Index des Citations et Allusions Bibliques dans la Littérature Patristique. 4 vols. + supplement, Paris 1975–
Bacher, W. 1905
   Die exegetische Terminologie der jüdischen Traditionsliteratur. 2 vols. in one, Leipzig, 1905. 1st ed, 1899, 1905
Brock, S. P. et al. 1973
   A Classified Bibliography of the Septuagint. Eds. S. P. Brock, C. T. Fritsch, S. Jellicoe Leiden 1973
Brown, F., Driver, S. R. & Briggs, C. A. 1959
   Hebrew and English Lexicon of the Old Testament. London, 1959. 1st ed. 1906
Feldman, L. H. 1963
   Scholarship on Philo and Josephus 1937–1962. Studies in Judaica, New York, 1963? – no publishing date. Reprinted from *Classical World* 54–55 (1960–62)
Fitzmyer, J. A. 1977
   The Dead Sea Scrolls. Major Publications and Tools for Study. Missoula, Montana, 1977. 1st ed. 1975
Ginzberg, L. 1911–
   Legends of the Jews. 7 vols. Philadelphia, 1911–38
Goodenough, E. R. & Goodhart, H. L. 1938
   General Bibliography of Philo. New Haven, 1938
Grossfeld, B. 1972–
   Bibliography of Targum Literature. 2 vols. New York, 1972–77
Haas, L. 1981
   "Bibliography on Midrash" in J. Neusner 1981b I: 93–103
Hilgert, E. 1972
   "A Bibliography of Philo Studies 1963–1970" *SP* 1 (1972) 57–71

Hilgert, E. 1984
   "Bibliographa Philonica 1935–1981" *ANRW* II 21. 1 (1984) 47–97
Jastrow, M. 1926
   A Dictionary of the Targumim, the Talmud Babli and Yerushalmi and the Midrashic Literature. New York 1926
Keil, C.F. & Delitzsch, F. 1978–
   Biblical Commentary on the Old Testament. Grand Rapids 1978–81, 1st ET. 1868
Kelly, J.N.D. 1958
   Early Christian Doctrines. London 1958
Montefiore, C.G. & Loewe, H. 1974
   A Rabbinic Anthology selected and arranged with comments and introductions. New York 1974, 1st ed. London 1938
Neusner, J. 1974–
   A History of the Mishnaic Law of Purities. 22 vols. Leiden 1974–77
Neusner, J. 1978–
   A History of the Mishnaic Law of Holy Things. 6 vols. Leiden 1978–80
Neusner, J. 1980b
   A History of the Mishnaic Law of Women. 5 vols. Leiden 1980
Neusner, J. 1981–
   A History of the Mishnaic Law of Appointed Times. 5 vols. Leiden 1981–83
Neusner, J. 1983–
   A History of the Mishnaic Law of Damages. Leiden 1983–85
Segal, M.H. 1927
   A Grammar of Mishnaic Hebrew. Oxford 1927
Stemberger, G., reviser of Strack, H.L. 1982
   Einleitung in Talmud und Midrasch. Munich 1982
Strack, H.L. 1931
   Introduction to the Talmud and Midrash. Philadelphia 1931, ET of 5th ed. revised. 1st German ed. 1887
Strack, H.L. 1976
   Einleitung in Talmud und Midrasch. 1st ed. 1920, 6th & 7th revised ed. München 1976, 1982

Other works referred to:

Aageson, J.W. 1983
   Paul's Use of Scripture: a comparative study of Biblical Interpretation in early Palistinian Judaism and the NT with special reference to Rm. 9–11. Unpublished D. Phil. dissertation, Oxford 1983
Abrahams, I. 1909
   "Rabbinic Aids to Exegesis" in H.B. Swete 1909: 159–192
Ackroyd, P.R. & Evans, C.F. (Eds.) 1970
   The Cambridge History of the Bible. vol. 1, Cambridge 1970
Aicher, G. 1906
   Das Alte Testament in der Mischna. Freiburg 1906
Albrektson, B. 1978
   "Reflections on the Emergence of a Standard Text of the Hebrew Bible" *SVT* 29 (1978) 49–65
Albright, W.F. 1955
   "New Light on Early Recensions of the Hebrew Bible" *BASOR* 140 (1955) 27–33 and in F.M. Cross et al. 1975: 140–146
Alexander, P.S. 1972

"The Targumim and Early Exegesis of 'Sons of God' in Genesis 6" *JJS* 23 (1972) 60–71

Alexander, P.S. 1976
"The Rabbinic Lists of Forbidden Targumim" *JJS* 27 (1976) 177–191

Alexander, P.S. 1983
"Rabbinic Judaism and the New Testament" *ZNW* 74 (1983) 237–246

Alexander, P.S. 1985
"The Targumim and the Rabbinic Rules for the Delivery of the Targum" *SVT* 36 (1985) 14–28

Alexander, P.S. 1988
"Jewish Aramaic Translations of Hebrew Scriptures" in M.J. Mulder 1988a: 217–253

Alon, G. 1977
Jews, Judaism and the Classical World. Jerusalem 1977

Amir, Y. 1970
"The Allegory of Philo Compared with Homeric Allegory" *Esh* 6 (1970) 35–45. English abstract in *SP* 1 (1972) 73–74

Amir, Y. 1973
"Philo and the Bible" *SP* 2 (1973) 1–8

Amir, Y. 1988
"Authority and Interpretation of Scripture in the Writings of Philo" in M.J. Mulder 1988a: 421–453

Aptowitzer, V. 1928
"Spuren des Matriarchats im Jüdischen Schrifttum (Schluss): Exkurse." *HUCA* 5 (1928) 261–298

Aptowitzer, V. 1970
Das Schriftwort in der Rabbinischen Literatur. New York 1970, 1st ed. 1906–08

Armstrong, A.H. (Ed.) 1967
The Cambridge History of Later Greek and Early Medieval Philosophy. Cambridge 1967

Attridge, H.W. 1976
The Interpretation of Biblical History in the Antiquitates Judaicae of Flavius Josephus. Missoula 1976

Attridge, H.W. 1984
"Josephus and his Works" in M.E. Stone 1984: 185–226

Aune, D.E. 1982
"The Use of προφήτης in Josephus" *JBL* 101 (1982) 419–421

Bacher, W. 1884–
Die Agada der Tannaiten. 2 vols. Strassburg 1884–90

Bacher, W. 1892
"The Origin of the Word Haggada (Agada)" *JQR* 4 (1891–2) 406–429

Bacher, W. 1902
"Bible Exegesis" *JE* 3 (1902) 162–174

Bacher, W. 1904
"Hillel" *JE* 6 (1904) 397–400

Bamberger, B.J. 1949
"The Dating of Aggadic Materials" *JBL* 68 (1949) 115–123

Bamberger, B.J. 1977
"Philo and the Aggadah" *HUCA* 48 (1977) 153–185

Bar-Ilan, M. 1988
"Writing in Ancient Israel and Early Judaism. Pt. 2: Scribes and Books in the Late Second Commonwealth and Rabbinic Period" in M.J. Mulder 1988a: 21–38

Barr, J. 1966
Old and New in Interpretation. London 1966
Barr, J. 1979
The Typology of Literalism in Ancient Biblical Translations. Göttingen 1979
Barthélemy, D. 1953
"Rédecouverte d'un chaînon manquant de l'histoire de la Septante" *RB* 60 (1953)
18–29 and in F.M. Cross et al. 1975: 127–139
Barton, J. 1986
Oracles of God: Perceptions of Ancient Prophecy in Israel after the Exile. London
1986
Basser, H.W. 1984
"The Rabbinic Citations in Wacholder's *The Dawn of Qumran*" *RQ* 11 (1982–84)
549–560
Baumgarten, J.M. 1958
"Qumran Studies" *JBL* 72 (1958) 249–257
Baumgarten, J.M. 1972
"The Unwritten Law – the Pre-Rabbinic Period" *JSJ* 3 (1972) 7–29
Baumgarten, J.M. 1974
"Form Criticism and the Oral Law" *JSJ* 5 (1974) 34–40
Baumgarten, J.M. 1977
Studies in Qumran Law. Leiden 1977
Baumgarten, J.M. 1980
"The Pharisaic-Sadducean Controversies about Purity and the Qumran Texts" *JJS*
31 (1980) 157–170
Beckwith, R.T. 1982
"The Pre-History and Relationships of the Pharisees, Sadducees and Essenes: A
Tentative Reconstruction." *RQ* 11 (1982–84) 3–46
Beckwith, R.T. 1988
"Formation of the Hebrew Bible" in M.J. Mulder 1988a: 39–86
Belkin, S. 1940
*Philo and the Oral Law: The Philonic Interpretation of Biblical Law in Relation to
the Palestinian Halakah.* Harvard Semetic Series vol. 11, Cambridge Mass., 1940
Belkin, S. 1967
"Some Obscure Traditions Mutually Clarified in Philo and Rabbinic Literature" in
A.A. Neuman et al. 1967: 79–103
Benoit, P. 1960
"Qumran and the New Testament" *NTS* 7 (1960–61) 276–96 and in J. Murphy-
O'Connor 1968: 1–30
Berliner, A. 1903
Festschrift zum 70 Geburtstage A. Berliner's. Frankfurt 1903
Bernstein, M.J. 1983
"Deut. 21. 23: A Study in Early Jewish Exegesis" *JQR* 74 (1983–84) 21–45
Betz, O. 1960
Offenbarung und Schriftforschung in der Qumransekte. Tübingen 1960
Bickerman, E. 1951
"The Maxim of Antigonus of Socho" *HTR* 44 (1951) 153–165 and in E. Bickerman
1976-, II: 270–289
Bickerman, E. 1959
"The Septuagint as a Translation" *PAAJR* 28 (1959) and in E. Bickerman 1976-
I: 167–200
Bickerman, E. 1976–
Studies in Jewish and Christian History. 3 vols. Leiden 1976–86

Black, M. 1961
The Scrolls and Christian Origins. London, New York 1961
Black, M. 1962
"Scribe" *IDB* 4 (1962) 246–248
Black, M. (Hon.) 1969
Neotestamentica et Semitica. Studies in Honour of Matthew Black. Edinburgh 1969
Blenkinsopp, J. 1974
"Prophecy and Priesthood in Josephus" *JJS* 25 (1974) 239–262
Bloch, Renée 1955
"Note méthodologique pour l'étude de la littérature rabbinique" *RSR* 43 (1955) 194–227. Trans. by W.S. Green and W.J. Sullivan in W.S. Green, 1978, I: 51–76
Bloch, Renée 1957
"Midrash" *DBSup* 5. 1263–1280. Trans. by M.H. Callaway in W.S. Green 1978 I: 29–50
Bockmuehl, M.N.A. 1987
Revelation and Mystery in Ancient Judaism and Pauline Christianity. unpublished Ph. D. thesis, Cambridge 1987
Bóid, I.R.M. (M.N. Saraf) 1988a
Principles of Samaritan Halachah. Leiden 1988
Bóid, I.R.M. (M.N. Saraf) 1988b
"Use, Authority and Exegesis of Mikra in the Samaritan Tradition" in M.J. Mulder 1988a: 595–633
Bonsirven, J. 1933
"Exégèse allégorique chez les rabbins tannaites" *RSR* 23 (1933) 510–541
Bonsirven, J. 1939
Exégèse rabbinique et exégèse paulinienne. Paris 1939
Borgen, P. 1965
Bread from Heaven : An exegetical study of the concept of Manna in the Gospel of John and the writings of Philo. Leiden 1965
Borgen, P. & Skarsten, R. 1976
"*Quaestiones et Solutiones:* Some Observations on the Form of Philo's exegesis" *SP* 4 (1976–77) 1–12
Borgen, P. 1984a
"Philo of Alexandria: A Critical and Synthetical Survey of Research since World War II" *ANRW* II 21. 1 (1984) 98–154
Borgen, P. 1984b
"Philo of Alexandria" in M.E. Stone 1984: 232–282
Bowker, J.W. 1967a
"Haggadah in Targum Onqelos" *JSS* 12 (1967) 51–65
Bowker, J.W. 1967b
"A Study in Proem and Yelammedenu Form" *NTS* 14 (1967–68) 96–111
Bowker, J.W. 1969
The Targums and Rabbinic Literature. Cambridge 1969
Bowker, J.W. 1973
Jesus and the Pharisees. Cambridge 1973
Bowman, J. 1950
"The Exegesis of the Pentateuch among the Samaritans and among the Rabbis" *OS* 8 (1950) 220–262
Bregman, M. 1979
"Review of J. Heinemann's *Aggadah and its Development,* 1970" *Imman* 9 (1979) 58–62

Brock, S.P. 1986
"Other Manuscript Discoveries" in R.A. Kraft 1986: 157–173
Brock, S.P. 1988
"Translating the Old Testament" in B. Lindars 1988: 87–98
Brockington, L.H. 1954
"Septuagint and Targum" *ZAW NF* 66 (1954) 80–87
Brodie, I. (Hon.) 1967
Essays presented to Chief Rabbi Israel Brodie on the occasion of his seventieth Birthday. Eds. Zimmels, H.J. et al. London 1967
Brooke, G.J. 1980
"The Amos-Numbers Midrash (CD 7. 13b–8. 1a) and Messianic Expectation" *ZAW NS* 51 (1980) 397–404
Brooke, G.J. 1981
"Qumran Pesher: Towards the Redefinition of a Genre" *RQ* 10 (1979–81) 483–503
Brooke, G.J. 1985
Exegesis at Qumran: 4QFlorilegium in its Jewish Context. JSOTSup 29, Shefield 1985
Brooke, G.J. 1987
"The Biblical Texts in the Qumran Commentaries: Scribal Errors or Exegetical Variants?" in W.H. Brownlee 1987: 85–100
Brownlee, W.H. 1951
"Biblical Interpretation among the Sectaries of the Dead Sea Scrolls" *BA* 14 (1951) 54–76
Brownlee, W.H. 1955
"John the Baptist in the New Light of Ancient Scrolls" *Interp.* 9 (1955) 71–90, revised in K. Stendahl 1958: 33–53
Brownlee, W.H. 1956
"The Habakkuk Midrash and the Targum of Jonathan" *JJS* 7 (1956) 169–186
Brownlee, W.H. 1964
The Meaning of the Qumran Scrolls for the Bible with Special Attention to the Book of Isaiah. New York 1964
Brownlee, W.H. 1978
"The Background of Biblical Interpretation at Qumran" in M. Delcor 1978: 183–193
Brownlee, W.H. 1987
Early Jewish and Christian Exegesis: Studies in Memory of William Hugh Brownlee. Eds. C.A. Evans & W.F. Stinespring, Atlanta, Georgia 1987
Bruce, F.F. 1959
Biblical Exegesis in the Qumran Texts. London 1959
Bruce, F.F. 1965
"Josephus and Daniel" *ASTI* 4 (1965) 148–162
Bruce, F.F. 1987
"Biblical Exposition at Qumran" in R.T. France et al. 1983
Burkhardt, H. 1988
Die Inspiration heiliger Schriften bei Philo von Alexandrien. Basel 1988
Büchler, A. 1928
Studies in Sin and Atonement in the Rabbinic Literature of the First Century. London 1928
Carmignac, J. 1960
"Les citations de l'Ancien Testament, et spécialement des poèmes du Serviteur, dans les hymnes de Qumran." *RQ* 2 (1959–60) 357–394

Cashdan, E. 1967
"Names and Interpretation of Names in Pseudo-Jonathan Targum to the Book of Genesis" in Brodie 1967: 31–40

Cazeaux, J. 1979
"Système implicite dans l'exégèse de Philon: Un example: le *De praemiis*" *SP* 6 (1979–80) 3–36

Cazeaux, J. 1984
"Philon d'Alexandrie, exégète." *ANRW* II 21. 1 (1984) 156–226

Chadwick, H. 1967
"Philo and the Beginnings of Christian Thought" in A.H. Armstrong 1967: 137–192

Chajes, Z.H. 1952
The Student's Guide through the Talmud. Trans. & Ed. J. Shachter, London 1952. 1st ed. *Introduction to the Talmud,* in Hebrew, Zolkiev 1845

Charlesworth, J.H. 1980
"The Origin and Subsequent History of the Authors of the Dead Sea Scrolls: Four Transitional Phases among the Qumran Essenes" *RQ* 10 (1979–81) 213–233

Charlesworth, J.H. 1987
"The Pseudepigrapha as Biblical Exegesis" in W.H. Brownlee 1987: 139–152

Chernick, M. 1980
"The Use of Ribbuyim and Mi'utim in the Halakic Midrash of R. Ishmael" *JQR NS* 70 (1980) 96–116

Chester, A.N. 1986
Divine Revelation and Divine Titles in the Pentateuchal Targumim. Tübingen 1986

Chester, A.N. 1988
"Citing the Old Testament" in B. Lindars 1988: 141–169

Childs, B.S. 1972
"Midrash and the Old Testament" in M.S. Enslin 1972: 45–59

Chilton, B.D. 1988
"Commenting on the Old Testament" in B. Lindars 1988: 122–140

Christiansen, Irmgard 1969
Die Technik der allegorischen Auslegungswissenschaft bei Philon von Alexandrien. Beiträge zur Geschichte der biblischen Hermeneutik 7, Tübingen 1969

Churgin, P. 1928
Targum Jonathan to the Prophets. New Haven 1928, reprinted with L. Smolar et al. 1983

Churgin, P. 1933
"The Targum and the Septuagint" *AJSL* 50 (1933–34) 41–65

Colson, F.H. 1940
"Philo's Quotations from the Old Testament" *JTS* 41 (1940) 237–251

Coppens, J. 1948
"Philon et l'exégèse targumique" *ETL* 24 (1948) 430–31

Corré, A. (Ed.) 1975
Understanding the Talmud. New York 1975

Cross, F.M. 1955
"The Oldest Manuscripts from Qumran" *JBL* 74 (1955) 147–172 and in F.M. Cross et al. 1975: 147–176

Cross, F.M. 1964
"History of the Biblical Text in the Light of Discoveries in the Judean Desert" *HTR* 57 (1964) 281–299 and in F.M. Cross et al. 1975: 177–195

Cross, F.M. 1966
"The Contribution of the Qumran Discoveries to the Study of the Biblical Text"
IEJ 16 (1966) 81–95 and in F.M. Cross et al. 1975: 278–292
Cross, F.M. 1972
"The Evolution of a Theory of Local Texts" Septuagint and Cognate Studies 2,
Missoula, MT 1972: 108–126 and in F.M. Cross et al. 1975: 306–321
Cross, F.M. & Talmon, S. 1975
Qumran and the History of the Biblical Text. Cambridge, Mass. 1975
Cullmann, O. 1955
"The Significance of the Qumran Texts for Research into the Beginnings of
Christianity" *JBL* 74 (1955) 213–226 and in K. Stendahl 1958: 18–32
Daube, D. 1936
"On the Third Chapter of the Lex Aquila" *LQR* 52 (1936) 253–268
Daube, D. 1948
"Review of Samuel Belkin's *Philo and the Oral Law*" *BO* 5 (1948) 64–65
Daube, D. 1949
"Rabbinic Methods of Interpretation and Hellenistic Rhetoric" *HUCA* 22 (1949)
239–263 and in A. Corré 1975: 275–289
Daube, D. 1953
"Alexandrian Methods of Interpretation and the Rabbis" in Lewald, H. 1953:
27–44 and in H.A. Fischel 1977: 165–182
Daube, D. 1956
The New Testament and Rabbinic Judaism. London 1956
Daube, D. 1959
"The Earliest Structure of the Gospels" *NTS* 5 (1958–59) 174–187
Daube, D. 1961
"Texts and Interpretation in Jewish and Roman Law" *JJSoc* 3 (1961) 3–28 and in
H.A. Fischel 1977: 165–182
Daube, D. 1980a
"Jewish Law in the Hellenistic World" in Jackson, B.S. 1980
Daube, D. 1980b
"Typology in Josephus" *JJS* 31 (1980) 18–36
Davies, P.R. 1987
Behind the Essenes: History and Ideology in the Dead Sea Scrolls. Atlanta 1987
Davies, W.D. (Hon.) 1976
*Jews, Greeks and Christians: Religious Cultures in Late Antiquity. Essays in Honour
of William David Davies*. Eds. R.G. Hamerton-Kelly & R. Scroggs, Leiden 1976
Davis, M. (Ed.) 1956
Israel, its Role in Civilization. New York 1956
De Lange, N.M. R. 1976
*Origen and the Jews: Studies in Jewish-Christian Relations in Third Century
Palestine*. Cambridge 1976
Delcor, M. (Ed.) 1978
Qumrân: Sa pieté, sa théologie et son milieu. Paris 1978
Dillon, J. 1979
"Ganymede as the Logos: Traces of a Forgotten Allegorization in Philo" *SP* 6
(1979–80) 37–40
Dimant, D. 1984
"Qumran Sectarian Literature" in M.E. Stone 1984: 483–550
Dimant, D. 1988
"Use and Interpretation of Mikra in the Apocrypha and Pseudepigrapha" in M.J.

Mulder 1988a: 379–419

Dion, P. 1984
"The Greek Version of Deut. 21. 1–9 and its Variants: A Record of Early Exegesis" in J.W. Wevers 1984: 151–160

Dodd, C.H. 1935
The Bible and the Greeks. London 1935

Doeve, J.W. 1954
Jewish Hermeneutics in the Synoptic Gospels and Acts. Assen 1954

Dörrie, H. 1974
"Zur Methodik antiker Exegese" *ZNW* 65 (1974) 121–38

Driver, G.R. 1960
"Abbreviations in the Massoretic Text" *Textus* 1 (1960) 112–131

Driver, G.R. 1965
The Judean Scrolls: The Problem and a Solution. Oxford 1965

Edersheim, A. 1882
"Josephus" *DCB* 3: 441–460

Edersheim, A. 1926
The Temple: Its Ministry and Services as they were at the time of Jesus Christ. London 1926. Ist ed. 1901

Eisenman, R. 1983
Maccabees, Zadokites, Christians and Qumran: A new hypothesis of Qumran origins. Leiden 1983

Elliger, K. 1953
Studien zum Habakuk-Kommentar vom Totem Meer. Tübingen 1953

Ellis, E.E. 1957
Paul's Use of the Old Testament. Edinburgh 1957

Ellis, E.E. 1969
"Midrash, Targum and the New Testament Quotations" in M. Black 1969: 61–69 and in E.E. Ellis 1978: 188–91

Ellis, E.E. 1978
Prophecy and Hermeneutic in Early Christianity. Wissenschaftliche Untersuchungen zum Neuen Testament 18, Tübingen 1978

Enelow, H.G. 1932–
"The Midrash of 32 Rules of Interpretation" *JQR NS* 23 (1932–33) 357–67

Enslin, M.S. (Hon.) 1972
Understanding the Sacred Text: Essays in Honour of Morton S. Enslin on the Hebrew Bible and Christian Beginnings. Valley Forge, Pa 1972

Feldman, L.H. 1986
"How Much Hellenism in Jewish Palestine?" *HUCA* 57 (1986) 83–111

Feldman, L.H. 1988
"Use, Authority and Exegesis of Mikra in the Writings of Josephus" in M.J. Mulder 1988a: 455–518

Finkel, A. 1963
"The Pesher of Dreams and Scriptures" *RQ* 4 (1963–64) 357–370

Finkelstein, L. 1923
"The Book of Jubilees and the Rabbinic Halaka" *HTR* 16 (1928) 39–61

Finkelstein, L. 1938a
"Introduction to Pirke Abot" *JBL* 57 (1938) 13–50 & in L. Finkelstein 1972

Finkelstein, L. 1938b
"The Oldest Midrash: Pre-Rabbinic Ideals and Teachings in the Passover Haggadah" *HTR* 31 (1938) 291–317 and in L. Finkelstein 1972

Finkelstein, L. 1941a
"The Transmission of Tannaitic Midrashim" *HUCA* 16 (1941) 115–135
Finkelstein, L. 1941b
"The Sources of Tannaitic Midrashim" *JQR NS* 31 (1940–41) 211–243
Finkelstein, L. 1962
The Pharisees: The Sociological Background of their Faith. 2 vols. Philadelphia, 3rd ed. 1962 with Supplement; 1st & 2nd ed. 1938 1940
Finkelstein, L. 1969a
"The Origin of the Pharisees" *CJ* 33 (1969) 25–36 and in L. Finkelstein 1972: 175–186
Finkelstein, L. 1972
Pharisaism in the Making. New York 1972
Finkelstein, J.J. 1981
The Ox that Gored. TAPS 71. 2, Philadelphia 1981
Fischel, H.A. 1973
Rabbinic Literature and Greco-Roman Philosophy: A study of Epicurea and Rhetorica in Early Midrashic Writings. Leiden 1973
Fischel, H.A. (Ed.) 1977
Essays in Greco-Roman and Related Rabbinic Literature. New York 1977
Fishbane, M. 1977
"The Qumran Pesher and Traits of Ancient Hermeneutics" *PWCJS* 6 (1977) I: 97–114
Fishbane, M. 1982
"Jewish Biblical Exegesis: Presuppositions and Principles" in F.E. Greenspahn 1982: 92–110
Fishbane, M. 1985
Biblical Interpretation in Ancient Israel. Oxford 1985
Fishbane, M. 1988
"Use, Authority and Interpretation of Mikra at Qumran" in M.J. Mulder 1988a: 339–377
Fitzmyer, J.A. 1957
"4Q Testimonia and the NT" *JS* 18 (1957) 513–37 & in S.J. Fitzmyer 1971
Fitzmyer, J.A. 1961
"The Use of Explicit OT Quotations in Qumran Literature and in the NT" *NTS* 7 (1960–61) 297–333 and in S.J. Fitzmyer 1971
Fitzmyer, J.A. 1971
Essays on the Semetic Background of the New Testament. London 1971
Fitzmyer, J.A. 1974
"The First Century Targum of Job from Qumran Cave XI" *CBQ* 36 (1974) 503–524 and in J.A. Fitzmyer 1979: 161–182
Fitzmyer, J.A. 1979
A Wandering Aramean: Collected Aramaic Essays. SBL Mon 25, Missoula, Montanna 1979
Forbes, P.B.R. & Browning, R. 1970
"Glossa, Glossary (Greek)" Oxford Classical Dictionary 1970: 468f.
Fraenkel, J. 1978
"Paranomasia in Aggadic Narratives" *SH* 27 (1978) 27–51
France, R.T. & Wenham, D. (Eds.) 1983
Gospel Perspectives III: Studies in Midrash and Historiography. Sheffield 1983
Frankel, I. 1956
Peshat (Plain Exegesis) in Talmudic and Midrashic Literature. Toronto 1956

Frankel, Z. 1841
Vorstudien zu der Septuaginta. Leipzig 1841
Frankel, Z. 1851
Ueber den Einfluss der palästinischen Exegese auf die alexandrinische Hermeneutik.
Leipzig 1851
Frankel, Z. 1854
Ueber palästinische und alexandrinische Schriftforschung. Breslau 1854
Franxman, T.W. 1979
Genesis and the 'Jewish Antiquities' of Flavius Josephus. Rome 1979
Gabrion, H. 1979
"L'interprétation de l'Ecriture dans la littérature de Qumran" *ANRW* II 19. 1
(1979) 779–848
Gard, D.H. 1952
The Exegetical Method of the Greek Translator of the Book of Job. JBL Mon. 8,
Philadelphia 1952
Geiger, A. 1857
*Urschrift und Uebersetzungen der Bibel in ihrer Abhängigkeit von der innern Entwick-
elung des Judenthums.* Breslau 1857
Gelles, B.J. 1981
Peshat and Derash in the Exegesis of Rashi. Leiden 1981
Gereboff, J. 1979
Rabbi Tarfon: The Tradition, the Man and early Rabbinic Judaism. Missoula, Mon-
tana 1979
Gerhardsson, I. -B. 1961
*Memory and Manuscript: Oral Tradition and Written Transmission in Rabbinic
Judaism and Early Christianity.* Trans. E.J. Sharp, Copenhagen & Lund 1961
Gertner, M. 1962
"Terms of Scriptural Interpretations: A Study in Hebrew Semantics" *BSOAS* 25
(1962) 1–27
Ginzberg, L. 1901a
"Allegorical Interpretation" *JE* 1 (1901) 403–411 and in L. Ginzberg 1981:
127–152
Ginzberg, L. 1901b
"Antoninus in the Talmud" *JE* 1 (1901) 656–657
Ginzberg, L. 1902
"Boethusians" *JE* 3 (1902) 284–285
Ginzberg, L. (Hon.) 1945
Louis Ginzberg Jubilee Volume. Eds. A. Marx et al. New York 1945
Ginzberg, L. 1970
An Unknown Jewish Sect. New York 1970, incl. trans. of *Eine unbekannte jüdische
Sekte,* 1922
Ginzberg, L. 1981
On Jewish Law and Lore. New York 1981, 1st ed. 1955
Glatzer, N.N. 1958
"Hillel the Elder in the Light of the Dead Sea Scrolls" in K. Stendahl 1958:
232–244
Goldberg, A. 1985
"Form-Analysis of Midrashic Literature as a Method of Description" *JJS* 36
(1985) 159–174
Goldberg, A. 1987a
"The Mishna – a Study Book of Halakha" in S. Safrai 1987a: 211–251

Goldberg, A. 1987b
"The Tosefta – Companion to the Mishna" in S. Safrai 1987a: 283–301
Goldberg, A. 1987c
"The Palestinian Talmud" in S. Safrai 1987a: 303–319
Goldberg, A. 1987d
"The Babylonian Talmud" in Safrai 1987a: 323–345
Goldenberg, R. 1982
"Early Rabbinic Explanations of the Destruction of Jerusalem" *JJS* 33 (1982) 517–525
Goodenough, E.R. 1929
The Jurisprudence of the Jewish Courts in Egypt: legal administration by the Jews under the early Roman Empire as described by Philo Judaeus. New Haven 1929
Goodenough, E.R. 1940
An Introduction to Philo Judaeus. New Haven 1940; Oxford 1962
Gooding, D.W. 1969
"Problems of Text and Midrash in the Third Book of Reigns" *Tex* 7 (1969) 1–29
Gooding, D.W. 1974
"On the Use of the LXX for Dating Midrashic Elements in the Targums" *JTS NS* 25 (1974) 1–11
Gooding, D.W. 1976
Relics of Ancient Exegesis: A Study of the Miscellanies in 3 Reigns 2. Cambridge 1976
Gordon, R.P. 1974
"The Targum to the Minor Prophets and the Dead Sea Texts: Textual and Exegetical Notes." *RQ* 8 (1972–75) 425–29
Gottlieb, I.B. 1979
"Formula Comparison in Midrash Research" *JQR NS* (1979–80) 28–40
Gottstein, M.H. 1953
"Bible Quotations in the Sectarian Dead Sea Scrolls" *VT* 3 (1953) 79–82
Goulder, M.D. 1976
Review of *Biblical Exegesis in the Apostolic Period.* by R. Longenecker. *JTS NS* 27 (1976) 204–206
Grabbe, L.L. 1982
"Aquila's Translation and Rabbinic Exegesis" *JJS* 33 (1982) 527–536
Grant, R.M. 1957
The Letter and the Spirit. London 1957
Gray, G.B. 1972
The Forms of Hebrew Poetry: Considered with special reference to the criticism and interpretation of the Old Testament. New Jersey, 1972, 1st ed. London 1915
Gräz, H. 1851
"Hillel und seine sieben Interpretationsregeln" *MGWJ* 1 (1851–2) 156–162
Green, W.S. (Ed.) 1978–
Approaches to Ancient Judaism: Theory and Practice. 2 vols. Missoula, Montana 1978, 1980
Greenspahn, F.E. (Ed.) 1982
Scripture in the Jewish and Christian Tradition: Authority, Interpretation, Relevance. Nashville, TN 1982
Greenstone, J.H. 1905
"Prosbul" *JE* 10 (1905) 219–220
Güdemann, M. 1892
"Spirit and Letter in Judaism and Christianity" *JQR* 4 (1891–2) 345–56

Guttmann, A. 1950
"Foundations of Rabbinic Judaism" *HUCA* 23. 1 (1950–51) 453–473
Guttmann, A. 1962
"Pharisaism in Transition"in S.B. Freehof 1964 and in A. Guttmann 1976
Guttmann, A. 1970
Rabbinic Judaism in the Making: The Halakhah from Ezra to Judah I. Detroit 1970
Guttmann, A. 1976
Studies in Rabbinic Judaism. New York 1976
Halevi (Hallewy), E.E. 1959
"The Writers of the Aggada and the Greek Grammarians" [Heb. with English summary] *Tar* 29 (1959) 45–55 and in H.A. Fishchel 1977: 230–239
Halevi (Hallewy), E.E. 1961
"Midrash ha-aggadah u-midrash Homeros" [with English summary] *Tar* 31 (1961–62) 157–169, 264–280
Hamerton-Kelly, R.G. 1972
"Sources and Traditions in Philo Judaeus: Prolegomana to an Analysis of his Writings" *SP* 1 (1972) 3–26
Hamerton-Kelly, R.G. 1976
"Some Techniques of Composition in Philo's Allegorical Commentary with Special Reference to *De Agricultura – a Study in the Hellenistic Midrash.* in W.D. Davies 1976: 45–56
Hanson, A.T. 1967
"Philo's Etymologies" *JTS NS* 18 (1967) 128–139
Hanson, A.T. 1974
Studies in Paul's Technique and Theology. London 1974
Hanson, A.T. 1980
The New Testament Interpretation of Scripture. London 1980
Hanson, A.T. 1983
The Living Utterances of God: The New Testament Exegesis of the Old. London 1983
Hanson, R.P. C. 1959
Allegory and Event. London 1959
Harris, I. 1888
"The Rise and Development of the Massorah" *JQR* 1 (1888–9) 128–142, 223–257
Havazelet, M. 1976
"Parallel References to the Haggadah in the Targum Jonathan ben 'Uziel and Neofiti: Genesis, Exodus and Leviticus"
Hay, D.M. 1980
"Philo's References to Other Allegorists" *SP* 6 (1979–80) 41–75
Hay, D.M. –
"Literalists and Literal Interpretation in Philo's World" [promised as "forthcoming" in D.T. Runia 1986]
Heater, H. 1982
A Septuagint Translation Technique in the Book of Job. Washington 1982
Hecht, R.D. 1980
"Patterns of Exegesis in Philo's Interpretation of Leviticus" *SP* 6 (1979–80) 77–155
Hecht, R.D. 1984
"The Exegetical Contexts of Philo's Interpretation of Circumcision" in S. Sandmel 1984: 51–79
Heinemann, I. 1932
Philons griechische und jüdische Bildung: Kulturvergleichende Untersuchungen zu Philons Darstellung der jüdischen Gesetze. Breslau 1932

Heinemann, I. 1951
The Methods of the Agada. (Hebrew) Jerusalem 1949: review & summary, M. Kadushin, *JSocS* 13 (1951) 181–184

Heinemann, J. & Noy, D. (Eds.) 1971
Studies in Aggadah and Folk-literature SH 22 (1971)

Heinemann, J. 1974a
"Early Halakhah in the Palestinian Targumim" *JJS* 25 (1974) 114–122 and = chapter 10 of J. Heinemann 1974b

Heinemann, J. 1974b
Aggadah and its Development. Heb. Jerusalem 1974

Heinemann, J. 1975
The Liturature of the Synagogue. New York 1975

Hengel, M. 1974
Judaism and Hellenism: Studies in their Encounter in Palestine during the early Hellenistic Period. Trans. J. Bowden, 2 vols. 2nd ed. Philadelphia 1974

Hengel, M. 1980
Jews, Greeks and Barbarians. London 1980

Hengel, M. 1983a
Between Jesus and Paul: Studies in the Earliest History of Christianity. London 1983

Hengel, M. 1983b
"The Origins of the Christian Mission" in M. Hengel 1983a: 48–64, Transl. J. Bowden from "Die Ursprünge der Christlichen Mission", *NTS* 18 (1971) 15–38

Herford, R. Travers 1912
Pharisaism, Its Aim and its Method. London 1912

Herford, R. Travers 1924
The Pharisees. London 1924

Herr, M.D. 1971a
"The Historical Significance of the Dialogue Between Jewish Sages and Roman Dignitaries" in J. Heinemann 1971: 123–150

Herr, M.D. 1971b
"Aggadah" *EncJ* 2: 354–66

Herr, M.D. 1971c
"Mekhilta of R. Ishmael" *EncJ* 11: 1267–9

Herr, M.D. 1971d
"Mekhilta of R. Simeon Ben Yohai" *EncJ* 11: 1269–70

Herr, M.D. 1971e
"Midrash" *EncJ* 11: 1507–14, 1521–3

Herr, M.D. 1971f.
"Sifra" *EncJ* 14: 1517–19

Hirschfeld, H.S. 1840
Halachische Exegese: Ein Beitrag zur Geschichte der Exegese und zur Methodologie des Talmuds. Berlin 1840

Hirschfeld, H.S. 1847
Die haggadische Exegese: Ein Beitrag zur Geschichte der Exegese und zur Methodologie des Midrasch. Berlin 1847

Hoffmann, D. 1903
"Ein Midrasch über die dreizehn Middot" in A. Berliner 1903: 55–71 of Hebrew section

Hoffmann, D. 1977
The First Mishna and the Controversies of the Tannaim & The Highest Court in the City of the Sanctuary. Trans. P. Forchheimer, New York, 1977, 1st ed. 1882

Hooke, S.H. (Hon.) 1963
  Promise and Fulfilment: Essays Presented to S.H. Hooke. Ed. F.F. Bruce, Edinburgh 1963
Horbury, W. 1980
  "Keeping Up with Recent Studies. V. Rabbinics." *ExpT* 91 (1980) 233–40
Horbury, W. 1988
  "Old Testament Interpretation in the Writings of the Church Fathers" in M.J. Mulder 1988a: 727–787
Horgan, Maurya P. 1986
  "The Bible Explained" in R.A. Kraft 1986: 247–258
Horovitz, H.S. 1904
  "Midrash" *JE* 8 (1904) 548–550
Horton, F.L. 1971
  "Formulas of Introduction in the Qumran Literature" *RQ* 7 (1969–71) 505–514
Howard, G.E. 1973a
  "The 'Aberrant' Text of Philo's Quotations Reconsidered" *HUCA* 44 (1973) 197–209
Howard, G.E. 1973b
  "KaigeReadings in Josepus" *Tex* 8 (1973) 45–54
Isenberg, S.R. 1970
  "An Anti-Sadducee Polemic in the Palestinian Targum Tradition" *HTR* 63 (1970) 433–44
Jackson, B.S. (Ed.) 1980
  Jewish Law in Legal History and the Modern World. Leiden 1980
Jacobs, L. 1961
  Studies in Talmudic Logic and Methodology. London 1961
Jacobs, L. 1971a
  "Halakhah" *EncJ* 7: 1156–66
Jacobs, L. 1971b
  "Hermeneutics" *EncJ* 8: 366–372
Jacobs, L. 1971c
  "Are there Fictitious Baraitot in the Babylonian Talmud?" *HUCA* 42 (1971) 185–196
Jacobs, L. 1973
  Jewish Bible Exegesis. New York 1973
Jacobs, L. 1977
  "How much of the Babylonian Talmud is Pseudepigraphic?" *JJS* 28 (1977) 46–59
Jacobs, L. 1984
  The Talmudic Argument. Cambridge 1984
Jellicoe, S. 1961
  "Aristeas, Philo and the Septuagint Vorlage" *JTS NS* 12 (1961) 261–71
Jellicoe, S. 1968
  The Septuagint and Modern Study. Oxford 1968
Jeremias, J. 1964
  Γραμματεύς ET *TDNT* I: 740–742
Jeremias, J. 1969
  Jerusalem in the Time of Jesus. ET London 1969
Kadushin, M. 1951
  Review of I. Heinemann: *The Methods of the Agada. JSocS* 13 (1951) 181–184
Kadushin, M. 1952
  The Rabbinic Mind. New York 1952

Kahle, P. 1947
    The Cairo Geniza. London 1947. 2nd Ed. 1959
Kaminka, A. 1926
    "Hillel's Life and Work" *REJ* 82 (1926) 233–252 and in H.A. Fischel 1977: 78–93
Kanter, S. 1980
    Rabban Gamaliel II: The Legal Traditions. Chico, CA 1980
Kasher, R. 1988
    "The Interpretation of Scripture in Rabbinic Literature" in M.J. Mulder 1988a:
    547–594
Katz, P. 1950
    *Philo's Bible: The Aberrant Text of Bible Quotations in Some Philonic Writings and
    its Place in the Textual History of the Greek Bible*. Cambridge 1950
Klausner, J. 1925
    Jesus of Nazareth: His life, times, and teaching. Trans. H. Danby, London 1925
Klein, M.L. 1988
    "Not to be Translated in Public" *JJS* 39 (1988) 80–91
Knibb, M.A. 1987
    The Qumran Community. Cambridge 1987
Knox, W.L. 1940
    "A Note on Philo's Use of the Old Testament" *JTS* 41 (1940) 30–34
Koch, D.A. 1986
    *Die Schrift als Zeuge des Evangeliums: Untersuchungen zur Verwendung und zum
    Verständnis der Scrift bei Paulus*. Tübingen 1986
Koenig, J. 1982
    L'Herméneutique analogique du Judaïsme antique d'après les témoins textuels d'Isaïe.
    (SVT 33, Leiden 1982
Kohler, K. 1893
    "The Pre-Talmudic Haggadah" *JQR* 5 (1893) 399–419
Kohler, K. (Hon.) 1913
    Studies in Jewish Literature issued in honour of K. Kohler. Berlin, 1913
Kraft, R.A. 1965
    Review of D. Barthélemy's *Les devanciers d'Aquila*. (1963) *Gnomon* 37 (1965)
    474–483
Kraft, R.A. & Nickelsburg, G.W.E. (Eds) 1986
    Early Judaism and its Modern Interpreters. Philadelphia 1986
Krämer, H. 1968　　"Προφήτης, Προφῆτις, Προφητεύω, Προφητεία, Προφη-
    τικός, Ψευδοπροφήτης" ET *TDNT* 6: 781–796 Kuntzmann, R. et al. (Eds.) 1984
    Études sur le judaïsme hellénistique. Paris 1984
Lampe, G.W.H. 1977
    God as Spirit. Oxford 1977
Lane, W.R. 1959
    "A New Commentary Structure in 4Q Florilegium." *JBL* 78 (1959) 343–346
Lauterbach, J.Z. 1904a
    "Mekilta" *JE* 8 (1904) 444–447
Lauterbach, J.Z. 1904b
    "Middoth" *JE* 8 (1904) 545–546
Lauterbach, J.Z. 1905
    "Rules of Eliezer b. Yose ha-Gelili, the Thirty Two"; "Rules of Ishmael, the Thir-
    teen"; "Rules of Hillel, the Seven"; *JE* 10 (1905) 510–512
Lauterbach, J.Z. 1906a
    "Talmud Hermeneutics" *JE* 12 (1907) 30–33

Lauterbach, J.Z. 1906b
"Weights and Measures" *JE* 12 (1907) 483–490
Lauterbach, J.Z. 1910–
"Ancient Jewish Allegorists in Talmud and Midrash" *JQR NS* 1 (1910–11) 291–333, 503–531
Lauterbach, J.Z. 1913
"The Sadducees and Pharisees. A study of their respective attitudes towards the Law." in K. Kohler 1913: 176–198 and in J.Z. Lauterbach 1951: 23–50
Lauterbach, J.Z. 1914–
"Midrash and Mishnah. A study in the early history of the Halakah" *JQR NS* 5 (1914–15) 503–507; 6 (1915–16) 23–95, 303–323 and in J.Z. Lauterbach 1951: 163–258
Lauterbach, J.Z. 1917
"The Three Books Found in the Temple at Jerusalem" *JQR NS* 8 (1917–18) 385–423 and in S.Z. Leiman 1974: 416–454
Lauterbach, J.Z. 1927
"A Significant Controversy between the Sadducees and the Pharisees" *HUCA* 4 (1927) 173–205 and in J.Z. Lauterbach 1951: 51–83
Lauterbach, J.Z. 1929
"The Pharisees and their teachings" *HUCA* 6 (1929) 69–139 and in J.Z. Lauterbach 1951: 87–162
Lauterbach, J.Z. 1951
Rabbinic Essays. Cincinnati 1951
Le Déaut, R. 1971a
"A propos d'une définition du midrash" *Bib* 50 (1969) 395–413, Trans. M. Howard in *Interp* July 1971
Le Déaut, R. 1971b
"Un phénomène spontané de l'herméneutique juive ancienne: le targoumisme" *Bib* 32 (1971) 505–525
Le Déaut, R. 1984
"La Septante, Un Targum?" in R. Kuntzmann et al. 1984: 147–195
Le Moyne, J. 1972
Les Sadducéens. Paris 1972
Lehmann, M.R. 1958
"1Q Genesis Apocryphon in the light of the Targumim and Midrashim" *RQ* 1 (1958–59) 249–263
Lehmann, M.R. 1962
"Midrashic Parallels to Selected Qumran Texts" *RQ* 3 (1961–62) 545–51
Leiman, S.Z. 1974
The Canon and Masorah of the Hebrew Bible: An Introductory Reader. New York 1974
Levias, C. 1903
"Gematria" *JE* 5 (1903) 589–592
Levine, E. 1974
"Loca Parallela to the Midrashic Elements of Targum Neophyti Pt. 1: Genesis" *Sef* 34 (1974) 3–30
Lévi, I. 1910
"Les Dorshè Reschoumot" *REJ* 60 (1910) 24–31
Liagre Bohl, F.M. Th. de 1926
"Wortspiele im Alten Testament" *JPOS* 6 (1926) 196–216 and in F.M. Th. de Liagre Bohl 1953: 11–25

Liagre Bohl, F.M. Th. de 1953
Opera Minora. Groningen 1953
Lieberman, S. 1950
Hellenism in Jewish Palestine. New York 1950
Lightstone, J.N. 1979
Yose the Galilean: I. Traditions in Mishnah-Tosefta. Leiden 1979
Lightstone, J.N. 1980
"Yosé the Galilean in the Mishnah-Tosephta and the History of Early Rabbinic Judaism" *JJS* 31 (1980) 37–45
Lindars, B. 1961
New Testament Apologetic. London 1961
Lindars, B. (Hon.) 1988
It is Written: Scripture Citing Scripture. Essays in Honour of Barnabas Lindars, SSF Eds. D.A. Carson, H.G. M. Williamson, Cambridge 1988
Livingstone, Elizabeth, A. 1979
Studia Biblica: 6th International Congress on Biblical Studies, Oxford 3–7 April 1978, JSOT Sup 2, Sheffield 1979
Loewe, R. 1964
"The 'Plain' Meaning of Scripture in Early Jewish Exegesis" *PIJS* 1 (1964) 140–185
Logan, A.H. B. 1978
"The Jealousy of God: Exod. 20. 5 in Gnostic and Rabbinic Theology" in E.A. Livingstone 1978 I: 197–203
Longenecker, R.N. 1975
Biblical Exegesis in the Apostolic Age. Grand Rapids 1975
Longenecker, R.N. 1987
"Who is the Prophet Talking About? Some Reflections on the New Testament's use of the Old" *Them* 13 (1987) 4–8
Lowy, S. 1969
"Some Aspects of Normative and Sectarian Interpretation of the Scriptures" *ALUOS* 6 (1966–68), with "Dead Sea Scroll Studies" 1969, 98–163
Lowy, S. 1977
The Principles of Samaritan Bible Exegesis. Leiden 1977
Maass, F. 1955
"Von den Ursprüngen der rabbinischen Schriftauslegung" *ZTK* 52 (1955) 129–161
Mack, B.L. 1975
"Exegetical Tradition in Alexandrian Judaism" *SP* 3 (1974–75) 71–112
Mack, B.L. 1978
"Weisheit und Allegorie bei Philo von Alexandrien" *SP* 5 (1978) 57–105
Mack, B.L. 1984a
"Philo Judaeus and Exegetical Traditions in Alexandria" *ANRW* II 21. 1 (1984) 227–271
Mack, B.L. 1984b
"Decoding the Scripture: Philo and the Rules of Rhetoric" in S. Sandmel 1984b: 81–115
Mann, J. & Sonne, I. 1940–
The Bible as Read and Preached in the Old Synagogue. 2 vols. Cincinnati, Ohio 1940, 1966
Marcus, R. 1945
"Jewish and Greek Elements in the Septuagint" in L. Ginzburg 1945: 227–245
Marcus, R. 1948
"A 16th Century Hebrew Critique of Philo: Azariah dei Rossi's *Meor Eynayim*. Pt. I ch. 3–6." *HUCA* 21 (1948) 29–58

Marcus, R. 1950
"A Textual-exegetical note on Philo's Bible" *JBL* 69 (1950) 363–365
Marmorstein, A. 1929
"The Background of the Haggada" *HUCA* 6 (1929) 141–202, and in A. Marmorstein 1950
Marmorstein, A. (Hon.) 1950
The Arthur Marmorstein Memorial Volume. London 1950
McNamara, M. 1966
The New Testament and the Palestinian Targum to the Pentateuch. Rome 1966
McNamara, M. 1972
Targum and Testament: Aramaic Paraphrase of the Hebrew Bible: A light on the New Testament. Dublin 1972
Meeks, W.A. 1978
"Towards a Social Description of Pauline Christianity" in W.S. Green 1978, II: 27–42
Metzger, B.M. 1968a
Historical and Literary Studies: Pagan Jewish and Christian. New Testament Tools and Studies VIII, Leiden 1968
Metzger, B.M. 1968b
"The Formulas Introducing Quotations of Scripture in the New Testatment and in the Mishnah" in B.M. Metzger 1968
Meyer, R. 1968
"Prophecy and Prophets in the Judaism of the Hellenistic-Roman Period" ET *TDNT* 6 812–828
Mez, A. 1895
Die Bibel des Josephus untersucht für Bücher v-vii der Archäologie. Basle 1895
Mielziner, M 1968
Introduction to the Talmud. New York 4th ed. 1968. incl. bibiography by A. Guttmann. 1st ed. 1894
Miller, M.P. 1971
"Targum, Midrash, and the Use of the Old Testament in the New Testament" *JSJ* 2 (1971) 29–82
Mirkin, M.A. (Ed.) 1956–
Midrash Rabbah 11 vols. Tel Aviv 1956–67
Mirsky, S.K. 1967
"The Schools of Hillel, R. Ishmael and R. Akiva in Penteteuchal Interpretation" in I. Brodie 1967: 291–299
Moehring, H.R. 1979
"Moses and Pythagoras: Arithmology as an Exegetical Tool in Philo" in E.A. Livingstone 1979 I: 205–208
Moo, D.J. 1983
The Old Testament in the Gospel Passion Narratives. Sheffield 1983
Moore, G.F. 1927
Judaism in the First Centuries of the Christian Era: The Age of the Tannaim. 3 vols. Cambridge, Mass. 1927–30
Mulder, M.J. (Ed.) 1988a
Miqra: Text, Translation, Reading and Interpretation of the Hebrew Bible in Ancient Judaism and Early Christianity. Compendia Rerum Iudaicarum ad Novum Testamentum. II. 1, Philadelphia 1988
Mulder, M.J. 1988b
"The Transmission of the Biblical Text" in M.J. Mulder 1988a: 87–135

Murphy-O'Conner, J. 1968
Paul and Qumran: Studies in New Testament Exegesis. London 1968
Murphy-O'Connor, J. 1971a
"The Original Text of CD 7. 9–8. 2 = 19. 5–14" *HTR* 64 (1971) 379–386
Murphy-O'Connor, J. 1971b
"A Literary Analysis of Damascus Document VI. 2-VIII. 3" *RB* 78 (1971) 210–232
Murphy-O'Conor, J. 1986
"The Judean Desert" in R.A. Kraft et al. 1986: 119–156
Neuman, A.A. & S. Zeitlin, S. 1967
The Seventy-Fifth Anniversary Volume of the Jewish Quarterly Review. Philadelphia 1967
Neusner, J. 1962
A Life of Yohannan ben Zakkai. Leiden 1962
Neusner, J. 1965
A History of the Jews in Babylonia: The Parthian Period. Leiden 1965
Neusner, J. 1970
Development of a Legend. Leiden 1970
Neusner, J. 1971
The Rabbinic Traditions about the Pharisees before 70. 3 vols. Leiden, 1971
Neusner, J. 1973a
"The Written Tradition in the Pre-Rabbinic Period" *JSJ* 4 (1973) 56–65 and in J. Neusner 1975a: 90–99
Neusner, J. 1973b
Eliezer ben Hyrcanus: the Tradition and the Man. 2 vols. Leiden 1973
Neusner, J. 1973c
"Pharisaic 'Rabbinic' Judaism: A Clarification" *HR* 12 (1973) 250–270 and in J. Neusner 1975a: 50–70
Neusner, J. 1973d
From Politics to Piety: The Emergence of Pharisaic Judaism. New Jersey 1973
Neusner, J. 1974
"From Exegesis to Fable in Rabbinic Traditions about the Pharisees" *JJS* 25 (1974) 263–269
Neusner, J. 1975a
Early Rabbinic Judaism: Historical studies in religion, literature and art. Leiden 1975
Neusner, J. 1975b
"The Meaning of Oral Torah with Special Reference to Kelim and Ohalot" *AJSR* I (1976) 151–70 and in J. Neusner 1975a: 3–33
Neusner, J. 1980a
"Scripture and Tradition in Judaism" in W.S. Green 1978-, II: 173–193
Neusner, J. 1981a
Judaism: The Evidence of the Mishna. Chicago 1981
Neusner, J. (Ed.) 1981b
The Study of Ancient Judaism ... 2 vols. New York 1981
Neusner, J. 1983
Midrash in Context: Exegesis in Formative Judaism ... Philadelphia 1983
Neusner, J. 1984
From Scripture to Mishna: The Problem of the Unattributed Sayings with Special Reference to the Division of Purities. Chico, California, 1984
Newlands, G.M. 1978
Hilary of Poitiers: A Study in Theological Method. Bern 1978

Newsom, C.A. 1987
"Merkabah Exegesis in the Qumran Sabbath Shirot" *JJS* 38 (1987) 11–30
Nickelsburg, G.W. E. 1981
Jewish Literature Between the Bible and the Mishnah: A Historical and Literary Introduction. London 1981
Niditch, S. 1980
"Father-Son Folktale Patterns and Tyrant Typologies in Josephus' Ant. 12. 160–222" *JJS* 32 (1981) 47–55
Nikiprowetzky, V. 1973
"L'Exégèse de Philon d'Alexandrie" *RHPR* 53 (1973) 309–329
Nikiprowetzky, V. 1977
Le commentaire de l'écriture chez Philon d'Alexandrie: son caractère et sa portée. Observations philologiques... Leiden 1977
Orlinsky, H.M. 1959
"Qumran and the Present State of Old Testament Studies: The Septuagint Text" *JBL* 78 (1959) 26–33
Orlinski, H.M. 1975
"The Septuagint as Holy Writ and the Philosophy of the Translators" *HUCA* 46 (1975) 89–114
Osswald, E. 1956
"Zur Hermeneutik des Habakuk-Kommentars" *ZAW NS* 27 (1956) 242–256
Patte, D. 1975
Early Jewish Hermeneutic in Palestine. Missoula, Montana 1975
Pearson, B.A. 1988
"Use, Authority and Exegesis of Mikra in Gnostic Literature" in M.J. Mulder 1988a: 635–652
Perrot, C. 1988
"The Reading of the Bible in the Ancient Synagogue" in M.J. Mulder 1988a: 137–159
Petit, M. 1976
"A propos d'une traversée exemplaire du désert du Sinaï selon Philon *(Hypothetica* VI, 2–3. 3) : texte biblique et apologétique concernant Moïse chez quelques écrivains juifs." *Sem* 26 (1976) 137–142
Pépin, J. 1958
Mythe et Allégorie. Les origines grecque et les contestations judéochrétiennes. Paris 1958 1976
Pépin, J. 1966
"Remarques sur la théorie de l'exégèse allégorique chez Philon" *CNCNRS* 1966, Paris 1967: 131–168
Porton, G.G. 1976–
The Traditions of Rabbi Ishmael. 4 vols. Leiden 1976, 1977, 1979, 1982
Porton, G.G. 1979
"Midrash: Palestinian Jews and the Hebrew Bible in the Graeco-Roman World" *ANRW* II 19. 2 (1979) 103–138
Porton, G.G. 1981
"Defining Midrash" in J. Neusner 1981b I: 55–92
Porton, G.G. 1986
"Diversity in Postbiblical Judaism" in R.A. Kraft 1986: 57–80
Prijs, L. 1948
Beiträge zur Frage der Jüdische Tradition in der Septuaginta. Leiden, 1948
Rabin, C. 1955a
"The Dead Sea Scrolls and the History of the O.T. Text" *JTS NS* 6 (1955) 174–182

Rabin, C. 1955b
"Notes on the Habakkuk Scroll and the Damascus Document" *VT* 5 (1955) 168–177
Rabin, C. 1957
Qumran Studies. Scripta Judaica II, Oxford 1957; New York 1975
Rabin, C. 1968
"The Translation Process and the Character of the Septuagint" *Tex* 6 (1968) 1–26
Rabinowitz, L, I. 1967
"The Study of a Midrash" *JQR NS* 58 (1967) 143–
Rabinowitz, L.I. 1973
"'Pesher/Pittaron': Its Biblical Meaning and its Significance in the Qumran Literature" *RQ* 8 (1972–75) 219–232
Rappaport, S. 1930
Agada und Exegese bei Flavius Josephus. Vienna 1930
Reider, J. 1950
"The Dead Sea Scrolls" *JQR NS* 41 (1950–51) 59–70
Reinhold, M. 1968
"Geschichtserfahrung und Schriftauslegung. Zur Hermeneutik des frühen Judentums" in O. Loretz 1968: 290–355
Reiss, W. 1978
"Wortsubstitution als Mittel der Deutung: Bermerkungen zur Formel אלא... אין. *FJB* 6 (1978) 27–67
Ringgren, H. 1978
"Some Observations on the Qumran Targum of Job" *ASTI* 11 (1977–78) 119- 126
Rivkin, E. 1969
"Defining the Pharisees: The Tannaitic Sources" *HUCA* 40–41 (1969–70) 205–249
Rivkin, E. 1978
A Hidden Revolution. Nashville 1978
Robert, A. 1957
"Littéraires (Genres)" *BDSup* 4 c411–421
Roberts, B.J. 1968
"Bible Exegesis and Fulfillment in Qumran" in D.W. Thomas 1968: 195–207
Rokeah, D.A. 1968
"A New Onomasticon Fragment from Oxyrhynchus and Philo's Etymologies" *JTS NS* 19 (1968) 70–82
Rosenblatt, S. 1935
Interpretation of the Bible in the Mishnah. Baltimore 1935
Rosenblatt, S. 1974
The Interpretation of the Bible in the Tosefta. JQR Mon 4, Philadelphia 1974
Rosenthal, J.M. 1969
"Biblical Exegesis of 4QpIs" *JQR* 60 (1969) 27–36
Roth, C. 1958
The Historical Background of the Dead Sea Scrolls. Oxford 1958
Roth, C. 1960a
"A Talmudic Reference to the Qumran Sect?" *RQ* 2 (1959–60) 261–268
Roth, C. 1960b
"The Subject Matter of Qumran Exegesis" *VT* 10 (1960) 51–68
Rowley, H.H. 1952
The Zadokite Fragments and the Dead Sea Scrolls. Oxford 1952
Runia, D.T. 1986
Philo of Alexandria and the Timeaeus *of Plato.* Leiden 1986

Russell, D.S. 1964
The Method and Message of Jewish Apocalyptic. London 1964
Ryle, H.E. 1895
Philo and Holy Scripture or the Quotations of Philo from the Books of the Old Testament with an Introduction and Notes. London 1895
Saebø, M. 1978
"From Pluriformity to Uniformity: Some Remarks on the Emergence of the Massoretic Text, with Special Reference to its Theological Significance" *ASTI* 11 (1977–78) 127–137
Safrai, S. (Ed.) 1987a
The Literature of the Sages Pt 1: Oral Tora, Halakha, Mishna, Tosefta, Talmud, External Tractates. Compendia Rerum Iudiacarum ad Novum Testament. II. 3, Assen & Philadelphia 1987
Safrai, S. 1987b
"Oral Torah" in S. Safrai 1987a: 35–119
Safrai, S. 1987c
"Halakha" in S. Safrai 1987a: 121–209
Salderini, A.J. 1982
Scholastic Rabbinism: a literary study of the Fathers according to R. Nathan. Chico 1982
Saldarini, A.J. 1986
"Reconstruction of Rabbinic Judaism" in R.A. Kraft et al. 1986: 437–477
Sambursky, S. 1978
"On the Origin and Significance of the Term Gematria" *JJS* 29 (1978) 35–38
Sanders, J.A. 1959
"Habakkuk in Qumran, Paul and the Old Testament" *JR* 39 (1959) 232–44
Sandmel, S. 1961
"The Haggadah Within Scripture" *JBL* 80 (1961) 105–22
Sandmel, S. 1962
"Parallelomania" *JBL* 81 (1962) 1–13
Sandmel, S. 1971
Philo's Place in Judaism: A Study of Conceptions of Abraham in Jewish Literature. Cincinnati 1956; Augmented ed. New York 1971. First publ. in *HUCA* 25 (1954) 209–238; 26 (1955) 151–332
Sandmel, S. 1954
"Philo's Environment and Philo's Exegesis" *JBR* 22 (1954) 248–253
Sandmel, S. 1978
"Philo's Knowledge of Hebrew" *SP* 5 (1978) 107–112
Sandmel, S. 1984a
"Philo Judaeus: An Introduction to the Man, his Writings, and his Significance" *ANRW* II 12. 1 (1984) 3–46
Sandmel, S. (Hon.) 1984b
Nourished with Peace. Chico, California 1984
Sanford, W. 1987
"Interpretation and Infallibility: Lessons from the Dead Sea Scrolls" in W.H. Brownlee 1987: 123–137
Sarason, R.S. 1980
"Mishnah and Scriptures: Preliminary Observations on the Law of Tithing" in W.S. Green 1980, II: 81–96
Schalit, A. 1965
"Evidence of an Aramaic Source in Josephus' 'Antiquities of the Jews'" *ASTI* 4 (1965) 163–188

Schiffman, L.H. 1980
"The Temple Scroll in Literary and Philological Perspective" in W.S. Green 1980, II: 143–158
Schmitt, J. 1978
"Qumran et L'exégèse apostolique" *DBSup* 9 c1011–1014
Scholem, G, G. 1960
Jewish Gnosticism, Merkabah Mysticism and Talmudic Tradition. New York 1960
Schürer, E. 1973–
The History of the Jewish People in the Age of Jesus Christ: New English Version. 3 vols. 4 parts, Eds. G. Vermes, F. Millar, M. Goodman, P. Vermes, M. Black, Edinburgh 1973–87, 1st German ed. 1885
Schwarz, A. 1897
Die hermeneutische Analogie in der talmudischen Litteratur. Vienna 1897
Schwarz, A. 1901
Die hermeneutische Syllogismus in der talmudischen Litteratur. Vienna, 1901
Schwarz, A. 1909
Die hermeneutische Induktion in der talmudischen Litteratur. Ein Beitrag zur geshichte der Logik. Vienna 1909
Schwarz, A. 1912
"La Victoire des Pharisiens sur les Sadducéens en matière de droit successoral." *REJ* 63 (1912) 51–62
Schwarz, A. 1913
Die hermeneutische Antinomie in der talmudischen Litteratur. Vienna 1913
Schwarz, A. 1916
Die hermeneutische Quantitätsrelation in der talmudischen Litteratur. Vienna 1916
Seeligman, I.L. 1948
The Septuagint of Isaiah. A Discussion of its Problems. Leiden 1948
Seeligman, I.L. 1953
"Voraussetzungen der Midraschexegese" *SVT* 1 (1953) Congress Volume (Copenhagen) 150–181
Segal, M.H. 1953
"The Promulgation of the Authoritative Text of the Hebrew Bible" *JBL* 72 (1953) 35–47
Shinan, A. 1977
"Midrashic Parallels to Targumic Traditions" *JSJ* 8 (1977) 185–91
Shinan, A. 1983
"Live Translation: On the Nature of the Aramaic Targums to the Pentateuch" *PT* 3 (1983) 41–49
Shroyer, M. 1936
"Alexandrian Jewish Literalists" *JBL* 55 (1936) 261–284
Shutt, R.J.H. 1971
"Biblical Names and their Meanings in Josephus, Jewish Antiquities, Books I and II, 1–200" *JSJ* 2 (1971) 167–182
Siegel, J.P. 1975
The Severus Scroll and 1QIs.a. Missoula, Montana 1975
Siegfried, C. 1875
Philo von Alexandria als Ausleger des alten Testaments. Jena 1875
Siegfried, C. 1905
"Philo Judaeus" *JE* 10 (1905) 6–15
Silberman, L.H. 1961
"Unriddling the Riddle" *RQ* 3 (1961–62) 323–364

Skehan, P.W. 1957
"The Qumran Manuscripts and Textual Criticism" *SVT* 4 (1957) 148–160 and in
F.M. Cross et al. 1975: 212–225
Skehan, P.W. 1959
"Qumran and the Present State of Old Testament Studies: The Massoretic Text"
JBL 78 (1959) 21–25
Skehan, P.W. 1965
"The Biblical Scrolls from Qumran and the Text of the Old Testament" *BA* 28
(1965) 87–100 and in F.M. Cross et al. 1975: 264–278
Slomovic, E. 1969
"Towards an Understanding of the Exegesis in the Dead Sea Scrolls" *RQ* 7
(1969–71) 3–15
Slonimsky, H. 1956
"The Philosophy Implicit in the Midrash" *HUCA* 27 (1956) 235–290
Smith, M. 1956
"Palestinian Judaism in the First Century" in M. Davis 1956: 67–81 and in H.A.
Fischel 1977: 183–187
Smolar, L. & Aberbach, M. 1983
Studies in Targum Jonathan to the Prophets. New York & Baltimore 1983
Sonne, I. 1945
"The Schools of Shammai and Hillel Seen from Within" in L. Ginzberg 1945:
275–292 and in H.A. Fischel 1977: 94–110
Sonne, I. 1950
"A Hymn against Heretics in the Newly Discovered Scrolls" *HUCA* (1950- 51)
275–313
Sowers, S.G. 1965
*The Hermeneutics of Philo and Hebrews: A Comparison of the Interpretation of the
Old Testament in Philo Judaeus and the Epistle to the Hebrews*. Richmond Virg. &
Zurich 1965
Sparks, H.F.D. 1959
"The Symbolic Interpretation of Lebanon in the Fathers" *JTS NS* 10 (1959)
264–279
Stein, E. 1929
"Die allegorische Exegese des Philo aus Alexandreia" *ZAW* 51 (1929 1) 1–61
Stein, E. 1931
"Philo und der Midrasch: Philos Schilderung der Gestalten des Pentateuch vergli-
chen mit der des Midrasch" *ZAW* 57 (1931 1) 1–52
Stein, S. 1957
"The Influence of Symposia Literature on the Literary Form of the Pesah Hagga-
dah" *JJS* 8 (1957) 13–44
Stemberger, G. 1975
"La recherche rabbinique depuis Strack" *RHPR* 55 (1975) 543–574
Stendahl, K. 1954
The School of St. Matthew. Upsala 1954
Stendahl, K. (Ed.) 1958
The Scrolls and the New Testament. London 1958
Stone, M.E. (Ed.) 1984
*Jewish Writings of the Second Temple Period: Apocrypha, Pseudepigrapha, Qumran
Sectarian Writings, Philo, Josephus. Compendia Rerum Iudaicarum ad Novum Testa-
mentum*. II. 2, Philadelphia 1984

Stuhlmueller, Carroll 1958
"The Influence of Oral Tradition upon Exegesis and the Senses of Scripture" *CBQ* 20 (1958) 299–326

Suter, D.W. 1981
"Masal in the Similitudes of Enoch" *JBL* 100 (1981) 193–212

Swete, H.B. (Ed.) 1909
Essays on Some Biblical Questions of the Day: by Members of the University of Cambridge. London 1909

Tadmor, H. & Weinfeld, M. (Eds.) 1983
History, Hisoriography and Interpretation. Jerusalem 1983

Tal, A. 1988
"The Samaritan Targum of the Pentateuch" in M.J. Mulder 1988a: 189–216

Talmon, S. 1960
"Double Readings in the Massoretic Text" *Tex* 1 (1960) 144–184

Talmon, S. 1962a
"DSIa as a Witness to Ancient Exegesis of the Book of Isaiah" *ASTI* 1 (1962) 62–72 and in F.M. Cross et al. 1975: 116–127

Talmon, S. 1962b
"The Three Scrolls of the Law that were Found in the Temple Court" *Tex* 2 (1982) 14–27 and in S.Z. Leiman 1974: 455–467

Talmon, S. 1964
"Aspects of the Textual Transmission of the Bible in the Light of Qumran Manuscripts" *Tex* 4 (1964) 95–132 and in F.M. Cross et al. 1975: 226–263

Talmon, S. 1970
"The Old Testament Text" in P.R. Ackroyd et al. 1970, I: 159–199 and in F.M. Cross et al. 1975: 1–43

Talmon, S. 1975
"The Textual Study of the Bible – A New Outlook" in F.M. Cross et al. 1975: 321–400

Tate, J. 1927
"The Beginnings of Greek Allegory" *CR* 41 (1927) 214–215

Tate, J. 1929–
"Plato and Allegorical Interpretation" *CQ* 23 (1929) 142–154; 24 (1930) 1–10

Tate, J. 1934
"On the History of Allegorism" *CQ* 28 (1934) 105–114

Teeple, H.M. 1957
The Mosaic Eschatological Prophet JBL Mon 10, Philadelphia 1957

Thackeray, H. St. J. 1929
Josephus, the Man and the Historian. New York 1929

Theodor, J. 1904
"Midrash Haggadah" *JE* 8 (1904) 550–569

Thomas, D.W. (Hon.) 1968
Words and Meanings: Essays Presented to David Winton Thomas. Eds. P.R. Ackroyd & B. Lindars, Cambridge 1968

Tigay, J.H. 1983
"An Early Technique of Aggadic Exegesis" in H. Tadmor et al. 1983: 169–189

Tobin, T.H. 1983
The Creation of Man: Philo and the History of Interpretation. CBQ Mon 14 Washington 1983

Tov, E. 1978
Midrash-Type Exegesis in the LXX of Joshua" *RB* 85 (1978) 50–61

Tov, E. 1981
The Text-Critical Use of the Septuagint in Biblical Research. Jerusalem 1981
Tov, E. 1982
"A Modern Textual Outlook Based on the Qumran Scrolls" *HUCA* 53 (1982) 11–27
Tov, E. 1984a
"The Rabbinic Traditions Concerning the 'Alterations' inserted into the Greek Pentateuch and their relationship to the original text of the LXX" *JSJ* 15 (1984) 65–89
Tov, E. 1984b
"Review of J. Koenig's *L'herméneutique analogique du judaïsme antique . . .,* 1982" *Bib* 65 (1984) 118–121
Tov, E. 1986
"Jewish Greek Scriptures" in R.A. Kraft et al. 1986: 223–237
Tov, E. 1988a
"Hebrew Biblical Manuscripts from the Judean Desert: Their Contribution to Textual Criticism" *JSS* 39 (1988) 5–37
Tov, E. 1988b
"The Septuagint" in M.J. Mulder 1988a: 161–188
Towner, W.S. 1982
"Hermeneutical Systems of Hillel and the Tannaim: A Fresh Look" *HUCA* 53 (1982) 101–135
Trever, J.C. 1958
"The Qumran Covenanters and Their Use of Scripture" *Per* 39 (1958) 127–138
Trever, J.C. 1987
"The Qumran Teacher – Another Candidate?" in W.H. Brownlee 1987: 101–121
Urbach, E.E. 1957–
"The Derasha as a Basis of the Halakha and the Problem of the Sopherim" *Tar* 27 (1957) 166–182, Eng. Summ. vi-viii
Urbach, E.E. 1975
The Sages. 2 vols. ET Jerusalem 1975
Vermes, G. 1961
Scripture and Tradition in Judaism: Haggadic studies. Studia Postbiblica, 4, Leiden 1961
Vermes, G. 1963a
"The Targumic Versions of Genesis IV 3–16" *ALUOS* 3 (1963) 81–114 and in G. Vermes 1975: 92–126
Vermes, G. 1963b
"Haggadah in the Onkelos Targum" *JSS* 8 (1963) 159–169 and in G. Vermes 1975: 127–138
Vermes, G. 1969a
"He is the Bread – Targum Neofiti Exodus 16. 15" in M. Black 1969: 256–263 and G. Vermes 1975: 139–146
Vermes, G. 1969b
"The Qumran Interpretation of Scripture in its Historical Setting" *ALUOS* 6 (1969) *Dead Sea Scroll Studies* 85–97 and in G. Vermes 1975: 37–49
Vermes, G. 1970
"The Bible and Midrash: Early Old Testament Exegesis" in P.R. Ackroyd et al. 1970: 199–231, 532 and in G. Vermes 1975: 59–91
Vermes, G. 1975
Post-Biblical Jewish Studies. Leiden 1975

Vermes, G. 1976
"Interpretation (History of) at Qumran and in the Targums" *IDBSupp* (1976) 438–43
Vermes, G. 1983
Jesus and the World of Judaism. London 1983
Villalba I. Varneda, P. 1986
The Historical Method of Flavius Josephus. Leiden 1986
Visotzky, B.L. 1983
"Most Tender and Fairest of Women: A Study in the Transmission of Aggada" *HTR* 76 (1983) 403–418
Visotzky, B.L. 1988
"Jots and Tittles: On Scriptural Interpretation in Rabbinic and Patristic Literatures" *PT* 8 (1988) 257–269
Wacholder, B.Z. 1966
"A Qumran Attack on the Oral Exegesis? : The Phrase *'sr btlmwd sqrm* in 4Q Pesher Nahum" *RQ* 5 (1964–66) 575–578
Wacholder, B. Z 1968
"The Date of the Mekilta de-Rabbi Ishmael" *HUCA* 39 (1968) 117–144
Wacholder, B.Z. 1983
The Dawn of Qumran: The Sectarian Torah and the Teacher of Righteousness. Cincinnati 1983
Weingreen, J. 1951
"The Rabbinic Approach to the Study of the Old Testament" *BJRL* 34 (1951–52) 166–190
Weingreen, J. 1963
"Exposition in the Old Testament and in Rabbinical Literature" in S.H. Hooke 1963: 187–201
Weingreen, J. 1976
From Bible to Mishna: The Continuity of Tradition. Manchester 1976
Weis, P.R. 1950
"The Date of the Habakkuk Scroll" *JQR NS* 41 (1950–51) 125–154
Wernberg-Møller, P. 1955
"Some Reflections on the Biblical Material in the Manual of Discipline" *ST* 9 (1955) 40–66
Wevers, J.W. (Hon.) 1984
De Septuaginta: Studies in honour of John William Wevers on his sixtyfifth birthday. Eds. A. Pietersma & C. Cox, Mississauga 1984
Wieder, N. 1953
"The Habakkuk Scroll and the Targum" *JJS* 4 (1953) 14–18
Wieder, N. 1957
"Sanctuary as a Metaphor for Scripture" *JJS* 8 (1957) 165–175
Wieder, N. 1962
The Judean Scrolls and Karaism. London 1962
Winter, B. 1988
Philo and Paul among the Sophists: A Hellenistic Jewish and Christian Response. Unpublished PhD Dissertation, Macquarie University 1988
Wolfson, H.A. 1947
Philo: Foundations of Religious Philosophy in Judaism, Christianity and Islam. 2 Vols. Cambridge, Mass. 1947
Wright, A.G. 1966
"The Literary Genre Midrash" *CBQ* 28 (1966) 105–138, 417–457; New York 1967

York, A.D. 1974
"The Dating of Targumic Literature" *JSJ* 5 (1974) 49–62
Zahavy, T. 1977
The Traditions of Eleazar Ben Azariah. Missoula, Montanna 1977
Zeitlin, S. 1917
"The Semikah Controversy Between the Zugoth" *JQR NS* 7 (1917) 499–517 and in
S. Zeitlin 1973- IV: 92–110
Zeitlin, S. 1919
"Studies in Tannaitic Jurisprudence – Intention as a Legal Principle" *JJLP* 1919:
297–311 and in S. Zeitlin 1973- IV: 57–71
Zeitlin, S. 1922
*Megillat Tannit as a Source for Jewish Chronology and History in the Hellenistic and
Roman Periods.* Philadelphia 1922, and in *JQR NS* 9 (1918–19) 71–104; 10
(1919–20) 49–80, 237–290
Zeitlin, S. 1936
"The Sadducees and the Pharisees: A Chapter in the Development of the Halakah"
Horeb 62 (1936), Trans. in S. Zeitlin 1973- II: 259–291
Zeitlin, S. 1948
"The Halaka: Introduction to Tannaitic Jurisprudence" *JQR NS* 39 (1948–49)
1–40
Zeitlin, S. 1949
"'Commentary on the Book of Habakkuk'. Important Discovery or Hoax?" *JQR
NS* 39 (1948–49) 235–247
Zeitlin, S. 1950
"The Hebrew Scrolls: Once more and Finally" *JQR NS* 41 (1950–51) 1–58
Zeitlin, S. 1953
"Midrash: A Historical Study"
Zeitlin, S. 1961
"The Pharisees: A Historical Study" *JQR NS* 52 (1961–62) 97–129 and in S.
Zeitlin 1973- II: 226–258
Zeitlin, S. 1963
"Hillel and the Hermeneutic Rules" *JQR NS* 54 (1963–64) 161–73 and in S. Zeitlin
1973- I: 339–51
Zeitlin, S. 1966a
"The Semikah Controversy Between the School of Shammai and Hillel" *JQR NS*
56 (1965–66) and in S. Zeitlin 1973- IV: 111–115
Zeitlin, S. 1966b
"Were there Three Torah Scrolls in the Azerah?" *JQR NS* 56 (1965–66) 269–272
and in S.Z. Leiman 1974: 469–472
Zeitlin, S. 1973–
Studies in the Early History of Judaism. 4 vols. New York 1973–78
Zunz, L. 1892
Die gottesdienstlichen Vorträge der Juden, historisch entwickelt. Frankfurt 1892

Index

Index of Subjects

Index of Modern Authors

Index of References

- p338 111
- p342f 98
Mekh.Ish.1 173
- 76a 182
- Bah.1 169
- 7 33, 71
- Besh.4.58–61 31
- Kas.3.37–41 26
- 3.31–35 25
- Nez.6.45 109
- 13.17 109
- 15.49–55 120
- Pis.5.118–120 124, 125
- 17.209–216 118

Mekh.Sim.p12.4–5 124
- p147.22–148.3 63
- p148 33, 71, 149
- p149.15–21 125
- p218.28–29) 140

Mid.Tann.Deut.34.2 37
- p.58 75
- p138f 146
- p215 76

Pes.Kah.6.61b 157
- Rab.16 157
- Rab.48 157
Sifra Introduction 46
- AM.3.11 101
- Behar.1.5 132
- Em.15.5 131
- Qed.3.7 130
- Shem.9.5 38
- Taz.3.1–2 126
- 9.16 36
- Vay.13.13b 120
Sifre Num.22 23
- 42 67
- 115 134, 135
- 117 71, 72
Sifre Deut.34 138
- 61 64
- 113 37
- 143 140
- 166 135
- 175 218
- 190 104
- 203 15, 33, 35
- 234 134
- 237 109
- 269 136
- 294 70

- 351 65
- 356 217
Tg.Onk. Deut.23.18 144
Tg.Ps-Jon. Deut.17.17 90

Bible
Gen.1.1 145, 152, 168
- 1.27 143
- 1.28 142, 145
- 2.4 152, 168
- 2.10–14 211
- 2.15 133
- 3.24 133
- 4.4 185
- 5.2 142, 143
- 6.4 179
- 12.5 41
- 14 200
- 14.14 178
- 14.21 209
- 15.2 178
- 15.6 31
- 15.11 209
- 17.4 207
- 21.28 135
- 24.63 125
- 35.22 185
- 36 183
- 36.20 97
- 36.24 183
- 38 185
- 40.5 193
- 49.10 191, 192
Ex.4.31 31
- 9.27 96
- 12.5 59
- 12.6 124, 125
- 12.14 151
- 12.15 36
- 12.16 150
- 13.9 116, 117
- 13.10 118, 119
- 13.13 59
- 14.27 125
- 14.31 31
- 15–18 194
- 15.22 182
- 15.27 112
- 16.12 58, 125
- 18.2f 143
- 20.8 33
- 20.9 125
- 20.21 209
- 20.24 50